WARRIOR WISDOM

EDITED BY C. R. JAHN

ESSAYS BY C. R. JAHN

WARRIOR WISDOM

The most infamous, offensive, and subversive collection of quotations, maxims, and anecdotes on the Internet! BE WARNED: These words are dangerous, as they may forever change the way you view the world around you! Dare you open your mind???
— RWT website (defunct)

"Darkness, call me brother!
that I may not fear
which I seek."
— Anonymous

CONTENTS

INTRODUCTION

Hi. Permit me to introduce myself. I am C. R. Jahn, AKA Captain Hook, AKA tyr_shadowblade.

Many, many, many years ago, back when the interwebz was still new, myself and a few friends decided to form an online "Literary & Philosophical Society" we dubbed the "Righteous Warrior Temple." Within a few years we had nearly a hundred members and issued patches and handbooks and did other stupid things which brought us to the attention of the feds as a possible "subversive" organization. After a couple of somewhat alarming incidents, we decided to disband and destroy the membership list, but as the "Director" I paid out of my own pocket to keep the website up and running in order to preserve some of the data therein, chiefly this huge accumulation of quotes which were compiled over the course of about five years. The website had been online since 1999 and it is now 2012 . . . as nothing had been added to it in quite some time and I'm unable to edit it due to some odd computer glitch, it is time for that website to finally fade into the ether.

Anyhow, this Kindle edition contains nearly all of the original online quotes. If you read it in its entirety, I guarantee a few quotes will resonate with you, answer an unasked question, or even change the way you perceive the world or your place in it . . . and I think you'll benefit from this. A few other quotes you will surely disagree with, if not be shocked or angered by, and that's to be expected as well – in some cases these quotes come from individuals at the extreme edges of the human experience, and the rawness and even ugliness of their words does not invalidate them. As a bonus, I'm also including a few favorite essays: "The Protection Dog." "Martial Arts Mythology," "Ode to a Scattergun," and the classic "Gorilla Punch." Trust me, this eBook is well worth a dollar.

Best Regards,

C. R. Jahn

Fmr Director of Righteous Warrior Temple
Author of: *FTW Self Defense, Hardcore Self Defense, Underground,* Co-Author & Editor of
Arcane Lore

CATEGORIZED QUOTATIONS

WARRIORSHIP

"Wherever I go,
Everyone is a little bit safer,
Because I am there."
— Robert L. Humphrey

"New-Age America produces books and workshops on the 'New Warrior,' a man or woman who lives impeccably — austere, protecting the weak, willing, perhaps, to stand his or her ground and fight, but more important, calm and graceful — the warrior as metaphor. We imagine the warrior in bed, in the boardroom, in marriage, the warrior on the golf-course. But these writers seem to forget that the warrior's values, as admirable as they may be, are won at terrible cost. The warrior as metaphor often offends me, because the battlefield stinks of blood and shit, and sings of screams and flies. Certainly the values that writers such as Dan Millman extol are admirable, but I would hesitate to call anyone a warrior unless we are not talking about a fellow ubermenschen, but instead a deeply flawed and guilty human being, who strives at the risk of the loss of comfort, of home, of even his or her own soul to protect what must be protected, to maintain a moral sense in a place where no morality can conceivably exist."
— Ellis Amdur, *Dueling with O-sensei* (p. 121)

"Down these mean streets a man must go who is not himself mean, who is neither tarnished nor afraid. . . . He is the hero, he is everything. He must be a complete man and a common man and yet an unusual man. He must be, to use a rather weathered phrase, a man of honor, by instinct, by inevitability, without thought of it, and certainly without saying it. He must be the best man in his world and a good enough man for any world."
— Raymond Chandler, *The Second Chandler Omnibus* (pp. 14-15)

"Warriorship is a profession of courage, a calling to valor — not just on the battlefield, but in all of life's conflicts."
— Forrest E. Morgan

"The warrior preserves and protects but does not conquer, dominate, or subjugate. Only the enemy will have to fear a warrior's skills."
— Richard Heckler

"The warrior's role in society is to protect life and social order by placing himself between that which would endanger both."
— Greg Walker

"If there is any hope for the future, it surely must rest upon the ability to stare unflinchingly into the heart of darkness."
— unknown

"To practice Zen or the Martial Arts, you must live intensely, wholeheartedly, without reserve — as if you might die in the next instant."
— Taisen Deshimaru

"A complete warrior is one who can act appropriately. Such an individual can kill if that is necessary to preserve other's lives, or he can die for others. But such an individual also possesses the power to find a way through conflicts to a non-combative resolution. This power can create a real peace between people. Such a person's presence, rather than intimidating, calms and gives strength to others."
— Ellis Amdur, *Old School* (p. 37)

"A warrior's strategy is designed to bring his commitment into action, develop his being, and enhance his knowledge. Living strategically requires the warrior to eliminate impulsive, whimsical actions and cease being a slave to his likes and dislikes. Actions and decisions are to be based on the warrior's strategy and have a well-considered quality to them, even when undertaken with lightning speed. To abandon one's strategy is to abandon the path itself."
— Robert L. Spencer, *The Craft of the Warrior* (p. 33)

"The quest of a true martial artist, in any culture or society, is to preserve life — not destroy it."
— Dan Inosanto, *The Filipino Martial Arts* (p. 170)

"Only one who devotes himself to a cause with his whole body and soul can be a true master. For this reason, mastery demands all of a person."
— unknown

"Warriors use their intent and will to shape their lives. All of their actions are conscious, intentional, and complete."
— Kerr Cuhulain

"They don't join cliques — more times than not, they stand alone — but they recognize and gravitate towards one another. Only warriors understand other warriors."
— Forrest E. Morgan

"A kung fu man lives without being dependant on the opinions of others, and a master, unlike the beginner, holds himself in reserve. He is quiet and unassuming, with no desire to show off."
— Bruce Lee

"It has always been my ideal in war to eliminate all feelings of hatred and to treat my enemy as an enemy only in battle and to honour him as a man according to his courage."
— Ernst Junger

"Beholding them with pity there came an old soldier who asked me if there was any means of curing them. I told him no. At once he approached them and cut their throats gently and, seeing this great cruelty, I shouted at him that he was a villain. He answered me that he prayed to God that should he be in such a state he might find someone who would do the same for him, to the end that he might not languish miserably."
— Ambroise Pare', speaking of three badly-burnt soldiers, 1536

". . . he was placed in charge of a unit which had suffered extremely heavy casualties, during which time he felt compelled to shoot an American pilot who had been disemboweled in a crash. This act was necessary according to the code of the warrior (an honorable fighting man puts his comrades out of their misery) but resulted in his rejection by a primarily enlisted brotherhood who held a more 'civilian' concept of the warrior ethos."
— Joanna Bourke, *An Intimate History of Killing* (p. 38)

"People who really study the arts of war are almost without exception nonviolent individuals. The achievement of real skill requires considerable discipline and self control, two traits which eradicate violent behavior."
— Richard Ryan, *Master of the Blade* (p. 21)

"Every man is responsible for defending every woman and every child. When the male no longer takes this role, when he no longer has the courage or feels the moral responsibility, then that society will no longer be a society where honor and virtue are esteemed. Laws and government cannot replace this personal caring and commitment. In the absence of the Warrior protector, the only way that a government can protect a society is to remove the freedom of the people. And the sons and daughters of lions become sheep."
— James Williams

"Do every act of your life as if it were your last."
— Marcus Aurelis

"In ourselves our safety must be sought,
By our own right hand it must be wrought."
— William Wordsworth

"It is better to deserve honours and not have them, than to have them and not to deserve them."
— Mark Twain

"The strength of our beliefs and our loyalty to each other has transformed our ideals into the strongest of brotherhoods. We exist, we are the warrior in you, and our message is dangerous to the existing order."
— excerpted from the introduction of *Hell's Angels Forever*

"I tell you this. As war becomes dishonored and its nobility called into question those honorable men who recognize the sanctity of blood will become excluded from the dance, which is the warrior's right, and thereby will the dance become a false dance and the dancers false dancers."
— Cormac McCarthy, *Blood Meridian* (p. 331)

"Warriorship . . . does not refer to making war on others. Aggression is the source of our problems, not the solution. . . . Warriorship . . . is the tradition of human bravery, or the tradition of fearlessness."
— Chogyam Trungpa

"Assurance, superior judgement, the ability to impose discipline, the capacity to inspire fear: these are the qualities of an authority."
— Richard Sennett, *Authority* (pp. 17-18)

"The gentleman desires to be halting in speech but quick in action."
— Confucius

"The frightening nature of knowledge leaves one no alternative but to become a warrior."
— "don Juan," from Casteneda's *A Separate Reality* (p. 150)

". . .the development of a warrior rests upon stopping the internal dialogue. Unnecessary talking is related to other unnecessary physical movements and bodily tensions, twitches, fidgeting, finger drumming, foot tapping, grimacing, and so on, which serve to drain the daily ration of energy. . ."
— Kathleen Riordan Speeth, *The Gurdjieff Work* (p. 44)

"He who has great power should use it lightly."
— Seneca

"Adventure is just a romantic name for trouble. It sounds swell when you write about it, but it's hell when you meet it face-to-face in a dark and lonely place."
— Louis L'Amour

"If I had a formula for bypassing trouble, I would not pass it round. Trouble creates a capacity to handle it. I don't embrace trouble; that's as bad as treating it as an enemy. But I do say meet it as a friend, for you'll see a lot of it and had better be on speaking terms with it."
— Oliver Wendell Holmes

"Nothing to laugh at in the ugliness of crime, the grimness of poverty, the tragedy of death; not a smile's worth of fun in the weeping wives and the sad and sometimes savage face of humanity? No, it isn't funny; and that is why laughter has to break through, probably more than in other jobs."
— Keith Simpson, *Forty Years of Murder* (p. 10)

"The true spirit of the warrior is found in the desire to defend the weaker against the aggression of the stronger. In this way an essential balance is kept in the world. The warrior trains so that he will be prepared and will thus not fail in his role."
— Peyton Quinn, *A Bouncer's Guide to Barroom Brawling* (p. 147)

"Evil has no physical reality, but it is still a force. . . . We cannot destroy it, but we can learn to keep ourselves safe from it."
— Anderson Reed, *Shouting at the Wolf* (pp. 56-57)

"The warrior is not the master, he is not the sifu nor the sensei. These are just physical words that we put upon ourselves to make us seem important or better than those whom we guide. The warrior is a friend to his students, and so cannot be their master. He does not wish to gather students, as they will search him out. And those who need to have a master or a sensei will not stay; they will keep searching until they realize that what they seek is within them, and who they seek can only be their guide."
— Erle Montaigue

"With the conviction came a store of assurance. He felt a quiet manhood, non-assertive but of sturdy and strong blood. He knew that he would no more quail before his guides wherever they should point. He had been to touch the great death, and found that, after all, it was but the great death. He was a man."
— Stephen Crane, *The Red Badge of Courage* (p. 156)

"Act the way you'd like to be, and soon you'll be the way you act."
— Kerr Cuhulain, *Full Contact Magick* (p. 107)

"Excellence, then, is not an act, but a habit."
— Aristotle

"The White Knight uses his sword in innocence, unaware of the harm he causes. The Red Knight lifts his sword in outraged self-righteousness, uncaring about the damage he leaves in the trail behind him. The Black Knight wields his sword reluctantly and only when he has reached the sober realization that it is necessary."
— Robert Moore & Douglas Gillette, *The Warrior Within* (p. 165)

"When all peaceful means to resolve a crucial problem fail, it is justifiable to wield the sword."
— Guru Gobind Singh

"At a glance, every individual's own measure of dignity is manifested just as it is. There is dignity in personal appearance. There is dignity in a calm aspect. There is dignity in a paucity of words. There is dignity in flawlessness of manners. There is dignity in solemn behavior. And there is dignity in deep insight and a clear perspective. These are all reflected on the surface. But in the end, their foundation is simplicity of thought and tautness of spirit."
— Yamamoto Tsunetomo, *Hagakure* (Wilson translation)

"They all had dignity, a certain serenity and pride that was theirs completely. . . . They knew where they had been and what they had seen and done, and were content. Something was theirs,

something within themselves that neither time passing nor man nor hard times could take from them."
— Louis L'Amour, *Education of a Wandering Man* (p. 38)

"If there is one thing that always sticks in my mind about how Delta Force goes about a mission, it is the utterly businesslike attitude of the men. There is none of that Hollywood crap. No posturing, no sloganeering, no high fives, no posing, no bluster, and no bombast. Just a quiet determination to get on with the job."
— Eric L. Haney, *Inside Delta Force* (p. 191)

"In a critical situation, where even the slightest hesitation may prove fatal, the warrior counts on his readiness to improvise, survive, and win. The warrior shapes his own destiny. He defines the limits of his own possibilities. He creates his own luck."
— Col. John B. Alexander, Major Richard Groller, and Janet Morris, *The Warrior's Edge* (p. 106)

"It's not our weaknesses that frighten us. It's our strengths."
— Nelson Mandela

HONOR

"Only honor separates the warriors from the thugs."
— Forrest E. Morgan

"You must work out your own honor system for yourself. For the warrior it becomes a code, a way of life, unbending and unaltered, often without ant verbal guidelines. When all of your possessions are far from you, you will still have your honor, your core. A handshake or simply saying, 'I will do this,' is your bond, more concrete than any signature on paper should be. Your actions demonstrate your code. To abuse your knowledge, betray a comrade, lie, things such as that, you will have broken your pact with yourself and have lost your honor. If you act in accordance with your beliefs as well as you can, you will retain your honor always."
— Lenox Cramer, *War with Empty Hands*

"Once examined, fights for "honor" almost always turn out to be fights to save face . . . Face refers to one's reputation . . . it is, in essence, prestige . . . Face can be taken from you, so it's something you can fight to keep. On the other hand, honor depends solely on your commitment to meet your just obligations. Since only you can do that, no-one can take honor from you . . . You can have all the face in the world and still lose your honor. Conversely, you can remain honorable no matter what the world thinks of you. Forced to choose between these two conditions, the superior warrior will pick the latter."

— Forrest E. Morgan, *Living the Martial Way* (pp. 151-152)

"Do right, fear no man."
— unknown

"Most of all, warriors are honorable because to be otherwise is cowardly!"
— Forrest E. Morgan

"Honour is manly decency. The shame of being found wanting in it means everything to us. Is this, then, the indefinable, the sacred thing?"
— Alfred de Vigny

"Warriors are dangerous people. Therefore, they have a solemn obligation to restrain themselves from tyrannizing and assaulting weaker members of society."
— Forrest E. Morgan

"If you don't want somebody to know something, just don't speak to them about it. Never lie."
— Sylvester L. Liddy

"Men whose acts are at variance with their words command no respect, and what they say has but little weight."
— Samuel Smiles

"The Samurai were an aristocracy of warriors, mighty touchy about their honor, with a fanatical reverence for exactitude in the spoken word — that is the tradition, anyway. They had one answer to questions — yes or no. A Samurai was supposed to tell the truth, and be quick to lay his two-handed sword across anybody who said he didn't."
— Ralph Townsend

"All you got in life is your honor, man, your own self-image, your own self-respect. If you lose that, or if you give it away or if you sell it, then you ain't got it no more."
— Lemmy Kilmister

"One's dignity may be assaulted, vandalized and cruelly mocked, but cannot be taken away until it is surrendered."
— Michael J. Fox

"Killing instincts can be tempered with good sense! The more competent a fighter becomes, the less he has to prove and the less likely he is to misuse his abilities. . . . Once they become competent and gain self-respect, they no longer have a reason to be a bully."
— Robert K. Spear, *Survival on the Battlefield* (p. 153)

"Men who take up arms against one another in public war, do not cease on this account to be moral beings . . . Military necessity does not admit cruelty — that is the infliction of suffering for revenge."
— Francis Lieber (1863)

"Never compromise your integrity; always respect yourself."
— Robert J. Ringer

"A man is only as good as his word."
— Grandfather

"It is scarcely a matter for wonder that dueling was a commonplace of those days. There are certain sorts of attack which, even today, may make the mildest man feel for a moment or two that the only suitable reply is a pistol-shot or a sword-thrust."
— John McConaughy

"You show us respect, we show you respect. If you don't show the Angels respect, the Angels don't show you respect. And we're very good at disrespecting people."
— Butch Garcia, HAMC

"It's nice to be nice."
— the personal motto of the most dangerous man my father ever knew

"If a man remembers what is right at the sight of profit, is ready to lay down his life in the face of danger, and does not forget sentiments he has repeated all his life even when he has been in straitened circumstances for a long time, he may be said to be a complete man."
— Confucius

"(seppuku) was used as a privileged alternative to execution, to atone for a misdeed or an unworthy act, and to avoid capture in battle — seen as a contemptible end for any warrior and a safeguard against likely torture."
— Richard Cohen, *By the Sword* (p. 155)

"A Sikh is enjoined to raise the sword only when all other means of correcting an injustice have failed. Hence, when a weapon is lifted, it should be accompanied by a sense of righteousness. . . . if the true path is followed, then the whole combat will flow correctly, like a dance."
— Guru Gobind Singh Ji (paraphrased & revised)

"I advise you secondly, that you should never swear an oath,
Unless you will keep it,
Grim wyrd goes with oathbreaking,
Wretched is such a varg"
— from *Sigrdrifumal*, verse 23, Plowright translation

"Our deeds determine us, as much as we determine our deeds."
— George Eliot, *Adam Bede*

"Lying is done with words and also with silence."
— Adrienne Rich, *On Lies, Secrets, and Silence*

"Never esteem anything as of advantage to you that will make you break your word or lose your self-respect."

— Marcus Aurelius Antonius (c. 121-180 A.D.)

"They are never alone that are accompanied with noble thoughts."
— Sir Phillip Sidney, *Arcadia*

"If you stand straight, do not fear a crooked shadow."
— Chinese proverb

"Do what manhood bids thy do,
From none but self expect applause;
He noblest lives and noblest dies
Who makes and keeps his self-made laws."
— Sir Richard Francis Burton

LOYALTY

"A man does not extricate himself from difficulty at the expense of his associates."
— Sylvester L. Liddy

"It's kind of hard to put into words, but it's like having somebody that you love. If you served and you were willing to die, you wanted to have a person there you would not mind dying for or dying with. A lot of people don't understand that."
— Medal of Honor recipient Bob Howard

"It is important that group members openly and directly declare their willingness to protect one another. Psychologically, the act of swearing loyalty is of far greater value than the mere assumption of the same."
— Etta Place

"But there's another piece of me. The part that's with my family. The family I chose; the family that chose me. I feel everything that hurts them, or makes them sad. I wouldn't just kill for them; I'd die for them. They're all I have. They're everything I have. And what they give me is . . . that piece of myself that's clean."
— Burke, from *Pain Management* by Andrew Vachss

"Look at your brother standing next to you and ask yourself if you would give him half of what you have in your pocket. Or half of what you have to eat. If a citizen hits your Brother, will you be on him without asking why? There is no why. Your Brother isn't always right, but he is always your Brother!"
— from the creed of the Outlaws Motorcycle Club

"You haveta *be* a bro ta have a bro . . ."
— old biker aphorism

"Evildoers are generally a lot more fun to hang out with, but they have no concept of loyalty. Being self-centered egomaniacs, they are loyal to no-one but themselves. They are unreliable and are notorious for betraying their allies in the face of danger. At their core, they are nothing but selfish, immature cowards. Seeing them as they truly are made it easy for me to swear allegiance with the forces of Good. People who are unafraid to die for their principles at any moment can never be considered cowardly."
— Scribe 27 (RWT)

"Not much more than twenty-five members were in the Club at any given time. The Kid liked it that way, a tight, loyal group — only the guys he could absolutely count on; men who wouldn't run off when it came time to stand together."
— Richard "Gypsy" Anderson

VALOR

"Courage is resistance to fear, mastery of fear — not absence of fear."
— Mark Twain

"Courage, like fear, is contagious, and allows individuals to do the impossible."
— Col. John B. Alexander, Major Richard Groller, and Janet Morris, *The Warrior's Edge* (p. 68)

"He was insanely calm. He never showed fear. He was a professional soldier, an ideal leader of men in the field . . . He did not yearn for battle. But neither was he concerned about the prospect."
— Tim O' Brien (speaking of his platoon commander)

"*I* could never run away."
— unknown

"One of my biggest problems (although I used to think of it as one of my greatest strengths) is the fact that I am completely fearless. In short, I truly do not 'give a rat's ass' if I live or die, and will refuse to back down from any perceived threat, regardless of the odds against me."
— Scribe 27, *Arcane Lore* (p. 266)

"Moral courage is the fortitude it takes to do what is right, no matter what the personal cost."
— Forrest E. Morgan

"In situations where you lack confidence, you must fill the void with courage."
— Forrest E. Morgan

"I'm not afraid of knives. I've been cut on the job. Unless there's meat hanging out, I just tape the cuts up with duct tape. . ."
— Duncan

"My knowledge of pain, learned with the saber, taught me not to be afraid of fear. And just as in dueling you must fix your mind on striking at the enemy's head, so, too, in war. You cannot waste time feinting and sidestepping. You must decide on your target and go in."
— Col. Otto Skorzeny

"Having heart meant a willingness to fight, regardless of the odds, and to withstand death or a beating instead of backing down. Even enemies could respect each other for having heart; no one respected a punk."
— Eric C. Schneider

"Such a stupid act. Sometimes, heroics revolted him; they seemed like an insult to the soldier who weighed the risks of the situation and made calm, cunning decisions based on experience and imagination; the sort of unshowy soldiering that didn't win medals but wars."
— Iain M. Banks, *Use of Weapons* (p. 148)

"For a lot of the Latin gang kids I knew coming up, it wasn't whether you died that counted, it was how you died."
— Burke, from *Pain Management* by Andrew Vachss

"All True Warriors know that medals are bullshit. Heroism usually goes unrecognized. When a soldier distinguishes himself in battle and is recommended for a high decoration, invariably the medal awarded will be of much less significance (i.e., the Distinguished Service Cross is often reduced to a mere Bronze Star by government bureaucrats); yet if an officer with a West Point ring on his finger 'thinks he was shot at,' he can reasonably expect to be awarded the Silver Star with no questions asked! Unless an officer has a Ranger tab or a 'Budweiser' crest, his rows upon rows of colorful ribbons probably represent nothing except 'brownie points.'"
— C. R. Jahn

"Anne Boleyn, consort of the King, was ready to pay with her life for her involvement with royalty. She was calm to the last. Turning to a companion who was trembling violently, Anne said: 'Take courage. The executioner is an expert of many years' training — and my neck is very slender.'"
— Frank Edwards

"I am the best bodyguard, because I'll take a bullet, I'll take a stab wound, I'll take a hit upside the head; I'm like a kamikaze pilot."
— Mr. T

"You must do the thing you think you cannot do."
— Eleanor Roosevelt, *You Learn by Living*

"Life shrinks or expands in proportion to one's courage."
— Anais Nin

"Courage consists not in blindly overlooking danger, but in meeting it with the eyes open."
— Jean Paul Richter

"To be a hero, one must give an order to oneself."
— Simone Weil

"The Way of the Samurai is found in death. When it comes to either/or, there is only the quick choice of death. It is not particularly difficult. Be determined and advance. . . . (if) one is able to live as though his body were already dead, he gains freedom in the Way."
— Yamamoto Tsunetomo, *Hagakure* (Wilson translation)

WILLPOWER

"Focus on your one purpose."
— Japanese motto

"Nothing in the world is as fearsome as a bloody, battered opponent who will never surrender."
— Gerry Spence

"To face each of my fears and overcome them would require years of psychic and physical pain. But it had to be done. I had seen the fruits of fearlessness and the power of the will. I could no longer live without them."

— G. Gordon Liddy, *Will* (p. 24)

"You must have complete determination. The worst opponent you can come across is one whose aim has become an obsession. For instance, if a man has decided that he is going to bite your nose off no matter what happens to him in the process, the chances are that he will succeed in doing it. He may be severely beaten up but that will not stop him carrying out his original objective. That is the real fighter."
— Bruce Lee

". . . concentrating 100 percent of your mental and physical power on one objective is far more effective than splitting your concentration by trying different moves."
— Sanford Strong, *Strong on Defense* (p. 63)

"If you go into the fight resolved to destroy your opponent no matter what the cost — if you go into battle truly committed to die for the opportunity to kill your enemy — his spirit will read it in your eyes and he will be crushed."
— Forrest E. Morgan

"Ruthless determination will overshadow technique or choice of weapon every time. The will to win is more important than the skill to win . . . Determination is the only thing that will get you off the ground after being stabbed, shot, or punched."
— Don Pentecost

"Make sure you continue your attack so you can stop that man who shot you. If you are fortunate, your wound will not be serious. But if you stop, scream, moan, or cry, he might just finish you off because he won't want any witnesses."
— John M. La Tourrette

"Try? Try not. Do, or do not. There is no "try.""
— Yoda

"Where there's a will, there's a way."
— unknown

"Those who are patient in the trivial things in life and control themselves will one day have the same mastery in great and important things."
— Hapkido Master Bong Soo Han

"Control your emotion or it will control you."
— Chinese adage

"And the will lieth therein, which dieth not. Who knoweth the mysteries of the will with its vigour? For God is but a great will pervading all things by nature of its intentness. Man doth not yield himself to the Angels nor to death utterly, save only through the weakness of his feeble will."
— Joseph Glanvill (17 c.)

"'Old time' hypnotists knew that if you helped an individual to use their 'imaginins,' they could control, or eliminate pain."
— Heller & Steele, *Monsters and Magical Sticks* (p. 37)

"By the use of his Will, (the master) attains a degree of poise and mental firmness (nearly inconceivable to) those who allow themselves to be swung backward and forward by the mental pendulum of moods and feelings."
— *Kybalion*

"Pure 'guts' have won many a gunfight. The man who has determination is hard to down. You can keep on fighting even if you are hit. If you make up your mind that you are going to get your bullet into the other man, you will probably do it. And maybe that hit you took will turn out not so bad as you thought, particularly if you stop him and keep him from hitting you again."
— William H. Jordan, *No Second Place Winner* (pp. 111-112)

"Pursue one great decisive aim with force and determination."
— Karl von Clausewitz, *Principles of War*

"It has been conclusively proven that focused visualization can significantly increase body temperature. By visualizing one's hands being engulfed with flames, it is possible for an amateur to raise the surface temperature of his hands by approximately 3 degrees Fahrenheit (an adept can more than double this). Buddhists monks use a similar visualization technique to dry their wet robes during outdoor Winter meditations. With sufficient willpower, it is possible to completely transcend fear, hunger and pain."
— Scribe 27 (RWT)

"Initiates learn a complex set of breathing and meditational exercises and retire to a remote area to train. Each day they bathe in icy streams and sit naked in the snow thinking of internal fires. When the training is complete, a test is made on a windy winter night by wrapping the student in a sheet that has been dipped into the river through a hole in the ice and has to be completely dried just by

body heat at least three times during the night."
— Lyall Watson, on the Tibetan practice of tumo, in *Supernature* (p. 226)

"Men with chest wounds — open, sucking wounds — have stuffed them with handkerchiefs or torn shirts and kept going. Men have broken their backs when they bailed out or hit the ground. After regaining consciousness, they have rolled around for a stick or board, strapped it to them in a fashion and moved on. Men with severe wounds have amputated a limb, whittled a crutch, and kept going. Many things are possible to those with will and determination."
— Dr. Gene N. Lam

"I tried to lift it, and it wouldn't move; I tried to lift it again, and it wouldn't move; then I tried to lift it really hard — and my left bicep snapped and rolled up in a bunch. It had to be surgically reattached."
— Bob Franks

"Singlemindedness is all-powerful."
— Yamamoto Tsunetomo, *Hagakure* (Wilson translation)

"Don't eye the top of the ladder, eye the next rung."
— Gen. Colin Powell

"Success seems to be largely a matter of hanging on after others have let go."
— William Feather

"I saw a guy get hit in the thigh. . . . Five fucking minutes and the guy checks out. . . . and it wasn't even a serious wound. Wasn't even bleeding that bad. And then there was another guy that got hit in the guts, and for 72 hours, because we were in constant fire, he was literally at one point . . . stuffing his intestines back in his friggin body. All of us thought it was goodbye time. He kept saying, 'Don't fucking look at me like that, I'm not dying.' And the sonofabitch didn't die."
— Harley Swiftdeer

"An idea upon which attention is peculiarly concentrated is an idea which tends to realize itself."
— Charles Baudouin

"Proper visualization by the exercise of concentration and willpower enables us to materialize thoughts, not only as dreams or visions in the mental realm, but also as experiences in the material realm."
— Paramahansa Yogananda, *Man's Eternal Quest* (p. 238)

"Energy is not just what we do, but also what we think and feel. Intention is energy given direction. Desire is energy focused and magnified."
— Anderson Reed, *Shouting at the Wolf* (p. 61)

"Discard and forget, I beg you, the demons, dolls, and mumbo-jumbo. What you are actually doing is tearing out your own emotional guts at the same time you're trying to tear someone else's emotional guts to pieces. I have paid a heavy price for learning these things, and I shall never practice that sort of magic again, whether for good or evil."
— William Seabrook, *Witchcraft* (pp. 99-100)

"Mind is the wielder of muscles. The force of a hammer blow depends on the energy applied; the power expressed by a man's bodily instrument depends on his aggressive will and courage. The body is literally manufactured and sustained by mind. . . . Outward frailty has a mental origin; in a vicious circle, the habit-bound body thwarts the mind. . . . My earliest ambition was to fight tigers. My will was mighty, but my body was feeble. It was by indomitable persistency in thoughts of health and strength that I overcame my handicap. I have every reason to extol the compelling mental vigor which I found to be the real subduer of royal Bengals."
— Sohong, the "Tiger Swami," from *Autobiography of a Yogi* by Paramahansa Yogananda (p. 62)

"There is no weapon more deadly than the will."
— Bruce Lee

CHARACTER

"Iron is full of impurities that weaken it; through forging, it becomes steel and is transformed into a razor sharp sword. Human beings develop in the same fashion."
— Morihei Ueshiba, *The Art of Peace* (p. 56)

"Personal power leads the warrior to absolute dignity. A man who (lives his life as if he may) die tomorrow doesn't act like a clown; he doesn't make a fool of himself in public. He chooses his words carefully; he doesn't want some trivial nonsense to be remembered as his last utterance. When men and women of power speak, others listen. They can feel the power in their words and they know these people will stand behind what they say."

— Forrest E. Morgan, *Living the Martial Way* (p. 279)

"He gives but not to receive
He works but not for reward
He completes but not for results"
— Lao Tzu, *Tao Te Ching, The Definitive Edition* (Star translation), Verse 2

"Weakness of attitude becomes weakness of character."
— Albert Einstein

"Knowledge will give you power, but character will give you respect."
— unknown

"Sow an action and reap a habit; sow a habit and reap a character; sow a character and reap a destiny."
— Ralph Waldo Emerson

"Have character, but don't be a character."
— Richard Marcinko

"Don't say things. What you are stands over you the while, and thunders so I cannot hear what you say to the contrary."
— Emerson

"Personality is to man what perfume is to a flower."
— Charles M. Schwab, *Ten Commandments of Success*

"Men of character are the conscience of the society to which they belong."
— Ralph Waldo Emerson

"That which does not kill me makes me stronger."
— Friedrich Nietzsche

"You might've been right, but you weren't *righteous* . . ."
— old biker aphorism

"A man *is* what he does. . ."
— the weird little mutant from *Total Recall*

"To educate a person in mind and not in morals is to educate a menace to society."
— Theodore Roosevelt

"There is nothing noble in being superior to some other man. The true nobility is in being superior to your previous self."
— Hindustani proverb

"It's easier to fight for one's principles than to live up to them."
— Adlai Stevenson

"Use your wit as a shield, not as a dagger."
— American proverb

"Define yourself by what you do, by how you treat others, and how they see you."
— George F. Burns

"The best index to a person's character is (a) how he treats people who can't do him any good, and (b) how he treats people who can't fight back."
— Abigail Van Buren

"Parents can only give good advice or put them on the right paths, but the final forming of a person's character lies in their own hands."
— Anne Frank, *Diary of a Young Girl*

"The respect that is only bought with gold is not worth much."
— Frances Ellen Watkins Harper (1859)

"By men's words we know them."
— Marie de France (12th c.)

"A man's presence is dependent upon the promise of power which he embodies. If the promise is large and credible his presence is striking. If it is small or incredible, he is found to have little

presence. The promised power may be moral, physical, temperamental, economic, social, sexual — but its object is always exterior to the man. A man's presence suggests what he is capable of doing to you or for you. His presence may be fabricated, in the sense that he pretends to be capable of what he is not. But the pretense is always towards a power which he exercises on others."
— Peter Smith, *Ways of Seeing* (pp. 45-46)

"Most people have certain weaknesses of character which must be considered in your dealings with them. You must ask yourself what this individual can be trusted with. Common weaknesses include: drink, gambling, compulsive spending, sex, a favorite illicit drug, a weak ego, and simple stupidity. Once you know an individual's weakness, you can take precautions against inadvertently tempting him to neglect his responsibilities; or, adversely, you could choose to exploit this weakness for reasons of your own (perhaps to teach him an important lesson). If you have weaknesses of your own, you must be honest with yourself and take steps to overcome them."
— Scribe 27 (RWT)

"It is difficult to deny one's vices altogether, but it's easy to cut back — this is achieved through the use of willpower, and by raising one's standards. If there are certain lines that you refuse to cross under any circumstances, then you'll be able to easily deny many forms of temptation. For example, you could make it a rule that you will never drink cheap booze, smoke inferior bud, or fuck ugly women. Become a connoisseur and you'll allow yourself far fewer opportunities to slip up."
— anonymous (RWT)

"Having something to fight significantly helps a person when coping with strong Neg problems. Once the cause is realized . . . Neg controls are significantly weakened. It's for this reason that Negs make great efforts to hide their existence. . . . If you cannot beat Neg influences, you can learn to work around them. Some people may never rid themselves entirely of Neg influences, but they can learn to control them, and in controlling them you will grow steadily stronger while Negs grow weaker. . . . Knowing that Negs can alter moods and cause spontaneous impulses, and recognizing the possibility of this when they occur, greatly improves the chances of weathering and surviving them intact."
— Robert Bruce, *Practical Psychic Self-Defense* (p. 144, 162)

"From another's evil qualities a wise man corrects his own."
— Publicus Syrus

"You can't cheat an honest man."
— con man's saying

"Moderation in all things."

— Terence (Publius Terentius Afer, c. 190-159 B.C.)

"It is not our abilities that show what we truly are; it is our choices."
— "Aldus Dumbledore," from *Harry Potter and the Chamber of Secrets*, by J. K. Rowling

"We are what we think. All that we are arises with our thoughts. With our thoughts we make the world."
— Buddha

"He who conquers himself is the mightiest warrior."
— Confucius

ASSERTIVENESS

"Declining to hear 'no' is a signal that someone is either seeking control or refusing to relinquish

it. With strangers, even those with the best intentions, never, ever relent on the issue of 'no,' because it sets the stage for more efforts to control. If you let someone talk you out of the word 'no,' you might as well wear a sign that reads, 'You are in charge.'"
— Gavin de Becker, *The Gift of Fear*

"It is impossible to teach true self-defense to someone without them first overcoming fear and the critical voice. True self-defense is an awareness that can't be switched on instantaneously. It is automatic, in the sense that it is always switched on. Your spirit should automatically rise to defeat your opposition when it has been transgressed. You have your limits and your rights, and nobody has the right to be there unless you give them permission. You are the ruler of yourself, and right or wrong, these are the things that you hold sacred. You would rather die than see them defaced."
— Marc "Animal" MacYoung, *Cheap Shots, Ambushes, and Other Lessons* (p. 11)

"Every decision you make stems from what you think you are, and represents the value that you put upon yourself."
— anonymous

"Being assertive will avoid problems; being aggressive will bring them on. The danger of using verbal aggression is that, while it works under normal circumstances, it can lull you into assuming that it will work in all situations."
— Marc MacYoung and Chris Pfouts, *Safe in the City* (p. 281)

"The objective of the violent criminal is to control you, emotionally and physically. Everything he does — his threats and promises — is intended to terrify and control you. . . . For most crime victims, their temporary cooperation backfired into full control over them."
— Sanford Strong, *Strong on Defense* (p. 50)

"The only way a (parasitic individual) could return after being got rid of was through pity. The same is true of any type of evil. Feeling sorry for people who are engaged in wrong action does nobody any good."

— Anderson Reed, *Shouting at the Wolf* (p. 41)

"To an aggressor, assertiveness is indistinguishable from rudeness, yet tact and diplomacy (or worse yet — an apology) is a sure sign of weakness, and an aggressor will show no mercy to a weakling — indeed, he may even become violently enraged upon any show of resistance from those he considers his rightful prey."
— anonymous (RWT)

"I am not arguing with you — I am telling you."
— J. McN. Whistler

"What you gonna do now, tough guy?"
— a query oft heard directed at belligerent lightweights

"You need to leave now . . ."
— the last thing numerous dipshits have heard (and chose to ignore) before later waking up with multiple contusions

"I don't like your attitude, and I don't like *you*."
— said with conviction, even the dimmest moron will realize that he's worn out his welcome.

"In the Korean village in which I grew up, there was a woman who was often beaten by her husband. One day she tired of the mistreatment. She told her husband, 'If you ever lay a hand on me again, I will stay awake all night if necessary until you are asleep. Then, when you are defenseless, I will beat you with a stick.' He understood her meaning and humbly begged her forgiveness. He never mistreated her again."
— Master Bong Soo Han

"When, against one's will, one is high-pressured into making a hurried decision, the best answer is always 'No,' because 'No' is more easily changed to 'Yes' than 'Yes' is changed to 'No.'"
— Charles E. Nielsen

"Always go before our enemies with confidence, otherwise our apparent uneasiness inspires them with greater boldness."
— Napoleon I

"Attacks must be answered. An assertion unanswered is an assertion agreed to."
— Geoff Garin

"A bully is not reasonable — he is persuaded only by threats."
— Marie de France (12th c.)

"It is impossible to teach true self-defense to someone without them first overcoming fear and the critical voice. True self-defense is an awareness that can't be switched on instantaneously. It is

automatic, in the sense that it is always switched on. Your spirit should automatically rise to defeat your opposition when it has been transgressed. You have your limits and your rights, and nobody has the right to be there unless you give them permission. You are the ruler of yourself, and right or wrong, these are the things that you hold sacred. You would rather die than see them defaced."
— Marc "Animal" MacYoung, *Cheap Shots, Ambushes, and Other Lessons* (p. 11)

"Declining to hear 'no' is a signal that someone is either seeking control or refusing to relinquish it. With strangers, even those with the best intentions, never, ever relent on the issue of 'no,' because it sets the stage for more efforts to control. If you let someone talk you out of the word 'no,' you might as well wear a sign that reads, 'You are in charge.'"
— Gavin de Becker, *The Gift of Fear*

"We do not apologize for a damned thing."
— Ralph "Sonny" Barger, *Ridin' High, Livin' Free* (p. 184)

"The majority of the time, just prior to a mugging, stomping, or sexual assault, the perpetrator(s) will 'interview' the prospective victim. This may simply consist of bumming a cigarette or spare change, or it might be an inappropriately chummy street person suddenly trying to be your 'bestest pal.' Your reaction to this interview will let them know if you're a safe (soft and weak) target."
— Jake Bishop (RWT)

"If a person has his sword out all the time, he is habitually swinging a naked blade; people will not approach him and he will have no allies. If a sword is always sheathed, it will become rusty, the blade will dull, and people will think as much of its owner."
— Yamamoto Tsunetomo, *Hagakure* (Wilson translation)

"The direct, unwavering stare is a form of threat . . ."
— Flora Davis, *Inside Intuition* (p. 63)

"Silence gives consent."
— Oliver Goldsmith

"Self-defense is nature's eldest law."
— John Dryden, *Absalom and Achitophel*

"Better to be pissed off than pissed on."
— old hillbilly sayin'

WARFARE

"Junior Bush was a fighter pilot during the war in Vietnam, not in the United States Air Force, where one could get seriously hurt, but in the Texas air force, known as the Air Guard. Texas's toy army, an artefact of Civil War days, is a favorite club for warmongers a bit squeamish about actual combat. Membership excused these weekend warriors from the military draft and the real shoot 'em up in 'Nam. Young George W. tested at 25 out of 100, one point above 'too-dumb-to-fly' status, yet leaped ahead of hundreds of applicants to get the Guard slot."
— Greg Palast, *The Best Democracy Money Can Buy* (p. 147)

"I had other priorities."
— Dick Cheney, on why he refused to serve in the military during Vietnam

"The master-class has always made the wars, and the worker-class has always fought them."
— Eugene V. Debs

"The more lives the soldier succeeds in accounting for, the prouder he is likely to feel. To his people he is a genuine hero, and to himself, as well. For him, war is in no sense a game or a dirty mess. It is a mission, a holy cause, his chance to prove himself and gain a supreme purpose in living. His hatred of the enemy makes this soldier feel supremely real, and in combat his hatred finds its only appropriate appeasement."
— J. Glen Gray

"If I had time . . . to study war, I think I should concentrate almost entirely on the 'actualities of war'— the effects of tiredness, hunger, fear, lack of sleep, weather . . . The principles of strategy and tactics, and the logistics of war are really absurdly simple: it is the actualities that make war so complicated and so difficult, and are usually so neglected by historians."
— Field-Marshal Lord Wavell

"In the military, it is said that amateurs talk of battles and tactics while professionals talk of logistics."
— Col. John B. Alexander, Major Richard Groller, and Janet Morris, *The Warrior's Edge* (p. 169)

"The distance at which all shooting weapons take effect screens the killer against the stimulus sensation which would otherwise activate his killing inhibitions. The deep, emotional layers of our personality simply do not register the fact that the crooking of the finger to release a shot tears the entrails of another man."
— Konrad Lorenz

"Palliation is as common on the battlefield as ants in an anthill. It includes a wide variety of 'inter-psychic modes' affecting the individual's subconscious, such as denial, in which he simply denies that a threat exists, displacement, when he 'escapes' from the battlefield in spirit although not in body; ritualisation; humor, and so on. The process of palliation may be assisted by the use of drugs or alcohol, which, similarly, make the situation no safer — they may actually make it more dangerous — but help the soldier to deal with stress by making his plight seem less threatening.
— Richard Holmes (paraphrasing R.S. Lazarus)

"If a person enlisting in the military is a criminal, he may find dangerous situations highly exciting and have few qualms about killing. Such a person could be an asset in combat. However, during peacetime service, he may prove hard to get along with. Bored and disgruntled, such an individual may fail to comply with rules and regulations and may commit crimes."
— Stanton E. Samenow, *Straight Talk about Criminals* (p. 15)

"In military protocol, the warrior stands firm and speaks directly. When deployed in battle, the warrior focuses on his duty and acts accordingly. During battle, those wearing battle armor need not bow. Those in war chariots need not follow the rules of protocol. In times of war, one does not worry about seniority. One acts. The common patterns of human behavior, during times of war, are like inside and outside. The citizen and the warrior are like left and right, night and day."
— Su-ma Fu

"You get in the way of an M-14 or M-60 machine gun and there's no tellin' who's gonna get killed. And you get an angry 18-year-old kid behind the gun and he's just seen his buddy gettin' killed. And he's not gonna have no remorse for who's on the receiving end of that M-60 machine gun."
— Jack Hill, USMC

"Thousands of our men will be returning to you. They will have been gone a long time and done and felt things you cannot know. They will be changed. They will have to learn to adjust themselves to peace."
— Ernie Pyle

"There has seldom, if ever, been a shortage of eager young males prepared to kill and die to preserve the security, comfort, and prejudices of their elders."
— unknown

"They rode into the city of Chihuahua to a hero's welcome, driving the harlequin horses before them through the dust of the streets in a pandemonium of teeth and whited eyes. Small boys ran among the hooves and the victors in their gory rags smiled through the filth and the dust and the caked blood as they bore on poles the desiccated heads of the enemy through that fantasy of music

and flowers."
— Cormac McCarthy, *Blood Meridian* (p. 165)

"Here, old men dazed with blows watched the dying agonies of their murdered wives who clutched their children to their bleeding breasts; there, disemboweled girls who had been made to satisfy the natural appetites of heroes gasped their last sighs; others, half-burned, begged to be put to death. Brains were scattered on the ground among dismembered arms and legs."
— Voltaire, *Candide*

"The enemy is whoever wants to get you killed, whichever side they're on."
—— "Yossarian," from Joseph Heller's *Catch-22*

"You can't expect any kind of mercy,
On the battlefield. . ."
— Suzanne Vega, "When Heroes Go Down"

"If you are going to fight a war and you intend to be the victor, you must have a clearly stated and totally understood military objective."
— Carl von Clausewitz, *On War*

"Long have they pass'd,
Faces and trenches and fields,
Where through the carnage I moved with a callous composure,
Or away from the fallen,
Onward I sped at the time —
But now of their forms at night,
I dream, I dream, I dream."
— Walt Whitman, "Old War-Dreams"

"War's a brain-spattering, windpipe-slitting art,
Unless her cause by right be justified."
— Lord Byron, *Don Juan*

"It is forbidden to kill; therefore all murderers are punished unless they kill in large numbers and to the sound of trumpets."
— Voltaire

"If officers desire to have control over their commands, they must remain habitually with them,

industriously attend to their instruction and comfort, and in battle lead them well."
— General Thomas J. "Stonewall" Jackson

"I give orders only when they are necessary. I expect them to be executed at once and to the letter and that no unit under my command shall make changes, still less give orders to the contrary or delay execution through unnecessary red tape."
— Field Marshal Erwin Rommel

"The leader of men in warfare can show himself to his followers only through a mask, a mask that he must make for himself, but a mask made in such form as will mark him to men of his time and place as the leader they want and need."
— John Keegan

"There is required for the composition of a great commander not only massive common sense and reasoning power, not only imagination, but also an element of legerdemain, an original and sinister touch, which leaves the enemy puzzled as well as beaten."
— Winston Churchill

"In all forms of warfare the loser is beaten in spirit before he is beaten in fact."
— David J. Rogers

"I considered war to be an utter waste of my time and energy, since most wars involved people I did not know arguing about matters I did not care about in pursuit of goals that would not have any direct impact upon me."
— Peter David, *Sir Apropos of Nothing* (p. 2)

"The worst thing about war is that so many people enjoy it."
— Ellen Glasgow

"One third, or 654 of 2054 American tanks used during Desert Storm, were equipped with (depleted) uranium armor plating, providing them with a tactical advantage, because the conventional Iraqi weapons would have no chance of penetrating them. But by their use, the American tank crews were exposed to whole-body gamma radiation, similar to X-rays emanating from the uranium armor. . . . (Furthermore,) external gamma radiation emitted from (depleted) uranium shells can be as high as 200 millirads per hour . . ."
— Dr. Helen Caldicott, *The New Nuclear Danger* (pp. 151-152)

"Aerosol DU exposures to soldiers on the battlefield could be significant with potential radiological

and toxicological effects. Under combat conditions, the MEIs (most exposed individuals) are probably the ground troops that reenter a battlefield following the exchange of armor-piercing munitions, either on foot or motorized transport."
— an unnamed Army contractor in a report from July 1990

"Think of having your eyelid pierced with a pin or your sex organs split with a scalpel. Imagine the pain of having your teeth extracted — not by a dentist using an anesthetic, but by someone with a pocketknife and pliers. Now consider what your thoughts would be if you were exposed to those circumstances while you were unable to defend yourself; under supervision by enemy soldier."
— Dirk von Schrader, *Elementary Field Interrogation* (p. 24)

"Lots of young soldiers these days put in a lot of time in the gym. All well and good, but physical fitness on its own is not enough. It's time to sweep away the action-movie stuff; fantastic muscle tone and fancy gear is not going to save you in a firefight."
— Peter McAleese, *McAleese's Fighting Manual* (p. ix)

"A soldier's energies may be excited to the point of hysteria because he knows he may be killed at any moment. If he is killed, he may panic and enter the body of the first accommodating living person he can find. The most suitable being is usually a nearby soldier . . . this happens often. The living warrior goes home after the war and finds himself doing things not in keeping with his personality. Because he has been involved in a war, his loved ones and therapist attribute his changed behavior to stress. It is not stress. It is the daily influence of another person, living right alongside the warrior's body."
— Anderson Reed, *Shouting at the Wolf* (p. 117)

"That sense of power, of looking down the barrel of a rifle at somebody and saying, 'Wow, I can drill this guy.' Doing it is something else too. You don't necessarily feel bad; you feel proud, especially if it's one on one, he has a chance."
— James Hebron, USMC Scout/Sniper

"All you do is move that finger so imperceptibly, just a wish flashing across your mind like a shadow, not even a full brain synapse, and poof! In a blast of sound and energy and light a truck or a house or even people disappear, everything flying and settling back into dust."
— William Broyles

"Killing itself could be seen as an act of carnival: combat gear, painted faces, and the endless refrain that men turn into 'animals' were the martial equivalent of the carnival mask. They enabled men to invert the moral order while still remaining innocent and committed to that order. . . . Carnivalesque rites of killing did not demand rejection of the law, but a reassertion of men's commitment to rules against extreme violence. Transgression could be enjoyable because the law was well-respected. . . .

Carnivalesque rites and fantasies drawn from a wide range of combat literature and films enabled combatants to refashion themselves as heroic warriors."
— Joanna Bourke, *An Intimate History of Killing* (pp. 25, 30-31)

"Frighteningly, psychiatrists recognized that more men broke down in war because they were not allowed to kill than under the strain of killing."
— Joanna Bourke, *An Intimate History of Killing* (p. 237)

"It was morally right to shoot an unarmed Vietnamese who was running, but wrong to shoot one who was standing or walking; it was wrong to shoot an enemy prisoner at close range, but right for a sniper at long range to kill an enemy soldier who was no more able than a prisoner to defend himself; it was wrong for infantrymen to destroy a village with white-phosphorus grenades, but right for a fighter pilot to drop napalm on it."
— *A Rumor of War*, Phillip Caputo (pp. 229-230)

"The rules of war are like the rules of the road: any honest and realistic person will expect them to be broken, but some drivers will commit more frequent and more serious violations than others, and there may be other drivers who very rarely offend."
— Kenneth Maddock

"The best warrior
leads without haste
fights without anger
overcomes without confrontation
He puts himself below
and brings out the highest in his men"
— Lao Tzu, *Tao Te Ching, The Definitive Edition* (Star translation), Verse 68

"When I died they washed me out of the turret with a hose."
— Randall Jarrell, "The Death of the Ball Turret Gunner"

"May you die with your boots on!"
— olde riflemen's toast

MARTIAL-ARTS

"Martial arts are 80 percent baloney. That's right, when it comes to real fighting, when it comes to a knock-down, drag-out, bite-your-face-off, do-anything-to-survive encounter with a highly motivated attacker, most martial arts systems and techniques are predominately useless. Yet they prosper. Self defense is big business, and business is good."
— Richard Ryan, *Master of the Blade* (p. 11)

"There's nothing wrong with the martial arts except that as normally instructed, they're not the answer to surviving violence. . . . Parents ask me if their children should study martial arts. My answer is yes, but not for crime survival. Do it for pride in personal accomplishment, respect for others, ability to concentrate, unsurpassed balance, self-control, and development of self-discipline. It's also a great way for a youngster to experience some physical pain — to learn what it is like to be hit, knocked down and get back up, to not give up. But the martial arts, as customarily taught, are not intended and do not work as a crime survival technique."
— Sanford Strong, *Strong on Defense* (p. 11)

"Spirit first, technique second."
— Ginchin Funakoshi

"The experienced fighter, along with the beginner, must always remember that knife attacks represent an extreme threat to life, a threat against which the greatest unarmed combat skills will be poor at best."
— James Loriega, *Sevillian Steel* (p. 130)

"Why spend years training to fight experienced tournament fighters when that isn't what you're going to be running into in the real world?"
— Marc MacYoung, *A Professional's Guide to Ending Violence Quickly* (p. 138)

"Many people like to 'dress up' when they do their martial arts . . . The Chinese only wear uniforms

when they do tournaments. This is obviously so that each team can be recognized easily. Apart from that, they do their martial arts in their normal clothes on the way to work, or on the way home, etc. The Chinese of old used to do their martial arts in the normal clothes of the time."
— Erle Montaigue

"You'll never learn to fight until you know the feel of hitting and being hit."
— Forrest E. Morgan

"Ultimately, you must forget about technique. The further you progress, the fewer teachings there are. The Great Path is really NO PATH."
— Ueshiba Morihei

"Forget about yourself and follow the opponent's movement. Let your mind do the counter-movement without deliberation. Learn the art of detachment."
— Bruce Lee

"True kung fu is rooted in the feet. It develops in the legs, is directed by the waist, and functions through the fingers."
— Bruce Lee

"Moving is used as a means of defense, a means of deception, a means of securing proper distance for attack and a means of conserving energy. The essence of fighting is the art of moving.
— Bruce Lee

"As a child, both his thumbs had been broken deliberately by his father in two places, then tied back so that they grew into recurving hooks that were nearly useless for gripping but rigid as steel and able to tear out a throat or disembowel a man with a single backward stroke."
— G. Gordon Liddy, of a Mongolian he befriended whilst incarcerated

"There are people who believe that the practice of the martial arts only proves useful when the need for self-defense arises. True martial arts are to be practiced in such a manner that they are useful at all times and benefit all things."
— Miyamoto Musashi

"I'm gonna rip off yer arm and beat you with the wet end!"
— an anonymous former Ranger

"You kung-fu pretty goo . . ."
— innumerable translators of Chinese kung-fu movies (usually followed with *". . . but not goo enough!"* and an ineffectual counter-attack).

"Gentlemen don't mutilate or deform their own bodies."
— Hapkido Master Ji Han Jae, on hand conditioning

"A man who has attained mastery of an art reveals it in his every action."
— samurai maxim

"Make the opponent yours. Absorb and incorporate his thinking into your own. Become one with him so you know him perfectly and can be one step ahead of his every movement."
— Ueshiba Sensei

"If the enemy leaves a door open, you must rush in."
— Sun Tzu, *Art of War*

"Never renew an attack along the same line or in the same form once it has been beaten back."
— David J. Rogers

"No fighter ever won his fight by covering up — by merely fending off the other's blows. The winner hits and keeps on hitting even though he has to be able to take some stiff blows in order to be able to keep on hitting."
— Admiral Ernest J. King

"With such safety equipment and body armor, one could take all kinds of 'risks,' diving in to strike while allowing the edge of te opponent's 'weapon' to slide across the femoral artery or the back of the neck with no thought to the fatal injury one would suffer if dueling with real weapons. . . . Because there is no sense of danger or even a need to protect undesignated targets, many competitors do not move or respond in a natural way. Blows that would sever arms, disfigure, or even kill are ignored because they are not designated targets."
— Ellis Amdur, *Old School* (pp. 203, 217)

". . . I always stress that there is a difference between the mat and the alley. In a dojo, nobody is going to ambush you, bust a chair across your teeth, or knock a trash can into your footwork. You can also pretty much count out the chance of getting chain-whipped. However, I speak from experience when I say these things do happen in alleys and bars."
— Marc "Animal" MacYoung, *Pool Cues, Beer Bottles, & Baseball Bats* (pp. 2-3)

"The real problem with being on the ground with your opponent still standing is that, unlike in a dojo, your attacker isn't going to stop. Either he is going to start kicking you (possibly with the help of his friends) or he's likely to pick up a chair and try to swat you like a bug."
— Marc "Animal" MacYoung, *Floor Fighting* (p. 5)

"In swordsmanship, always train and discipline yourself, but don't show it — hide it, be modest about it."
— Yagyu Muneyoshi (1529-1606)

TRAINING

"You can't learn to shoot by reading a book. Physical skills that require hand-eye coordination must be tried, practiced, and experienced in a physical way in order to be learned. It's more a matter of developing good motor habits than of gaining mental knowledge."
— Bill Clede, *Police Handgun Manual* (p.11)

"At the range he worked on his stance, breath control, eye focus. The idea was to build almost a second self. Someone smarter and more detached. Do this perfectly and you've developed a new standard for times of danger and stress."
— unknown

"I wanted to be the best gunfighter in the world. That, I knew, would take years of effort. I was willing . . . Soon, the inside flesh of my trigger finger was worn off, and I was wiping my blood from the trigger when I cleaned my revolver at the end of the day."
— G. Gordon Liddy, *Will* (p. 88)

"Clear your mind with a black image . . . think black. That is the color of nothingness. If a man is just firing his handgun without thinking about it, he's just doing it. But the moment he thinks, "I might miss," he's lost his focus of concentration. He's listening to a little voice that's saying, 'Can I or can't I?' And the answer will be, 'I can't.'"
— Michael Echanis

"Every animal moves in a different way, (and) every man fights in a different way. Observe, but don't copy!"
— Master Bimba

"Musashi, who trained himself, became a master swordsman who was never defeated."

— Kerr Cuhulain

"Using the suction tipped darts against a full length mirror, where the student can see his own mistakes and aim at the reflection of his own body, will help a great deal. The darts will stick on the mirror at the point of impact, showing where the bullets would've hit if a gun had been used. Basic errors are much more easily corrected with training of this type."
—Rex Applegate, *Kill or Be Killed* (pp. 126-127)

"There is little to be gained by wasting time and resources maintaining a level of strength or fitness far beyond that which you may need. These levels can be adjusted to cope with increased needs as they arise. Excessive training can cause undue wear on joints which will be regretted later."
— Sweyn Plowright, *True Helm* (p. 25)

"If you intend to carry a blade for defensive (as well as utilitarian) purposes, it is imperative that you learn how to make proper cuts. The only way one can perfect their cuts is to occasionally practice with a suitable training target. By far, the best target medium would be a fresh side of beef — but if such an item is not practical for you, a discarded exercise mat or carpet (rolled, taped, and stood vertically against the wall) works almost as well. If your cutting techniques are untested, it will be impossible for you ever to reach your full potential. Imaginary opponents can only get you so far."
— anonymous (RWT)

"Weapons, such as knives, eliminate most grappling techniques. Try wrestling with an opponent wielding a Magic Marker and see how long you can avoid being turned into a piece of graffiti."
— John Perkins, Al Ridenhour, and Matt Kovsky, *Attack Proof* (p. 174)

"Another training technique is the puncturing of an orange. This may sound fairly simple, but pick up an orange and try sticking your finger into it. The flexibility of the orange gives it considerable strength. Now place two or three fingers closely together and, again, using psychokinesis or ki, project the fingers through the fruit. Strike very quickly, with the mind projecting force ahead of the strike."
— Col. John B. Alexander, Major Richard Groller, and Janet Morris, *The Warrior's Edge* (p. 195)

"A knight cannot shine in war if he is has not prepared for it in tournaments. He must have seen his own blood flow, have had his teeth crackle under the blows of his adversary, have been dashed to the earth with such force as to feel the weight of his foe, and disarmed twenty times; he must twenty times have retrieved his failures, more set than ever upon the combat. Then he will be able to confront actual war with the hope of being victorious."
— Roger de Hovenden

"The exercising of weapons putteth away aches, griefs, and diseases, it increaseth strength and sharpenth the wits, it giveth a perfect judgement, it expelleth melancholy, choleric, and evil conceits, it keepeth a man in breath, perfect health, and long life."
— George Silver, *Paradoxes of Defence* (1599)

"Wax on, wax off . . ."
— Mister Miyogi, from "The Karate Kid"

FIGHTING

"Fighting is not combat! A fight can be many things, and occasionally it can escalate into combat, but it isn't initially. Combat and fighting call for radically different mindsets. Often, a fight is used to settle disputes and to establish dominance. Combat has no rules. It is a fight to the death or the crippling of your opponent."
— Marc "Animal" MacYoung, *Cheap Shots, Ambushes, and Other Lessons* (p. 12)

"The right to self-defense is the right to life itself."
— from the Loompanics catalog

"Only a warrior chooses pacifism; others are condemned to it."
— unknown

"Even if it seems certain that you will lose, retaliate. Neither wisdom nor technique has a place in this. . . . (do) not think of victory or defeat."
— Yamamoto Tsunetomo, *Hagakire* (Wilson translation)

"I dislike death, however, there are some things I dislike more than death. Therefore, there are times when I will not avoid danger."
— Mencius

"I have a high art, I hurt with cruelty those who would damage me."
— Archirocus, 650 BC

"A man who has nothing for which he is willing to fight; nothing he cares about more than his own personal safety; is a miserable creature who has no chance of being free, unless made and kept so by the exertions of better men than himself."
— John Stuart Mill

When facing multiple opponents, you must attack first and keep attacking until the danger subdues."
— Miyomo Musashi, *The Book of Five Rings*

"You know, a lot of guys wearing black sashes and teaching fighting have never had a real fight in their lives. They may be good at fighting by rules, even be called champions by some people. But I know a few guys whose only training is lifting a glass of sour mash to their lips; who could see these "champions" off and not even raise a sweat."
— Cacoy Hernandez

"In Hollywood action movies, the fight scenes are full of exaggerated, flashy moves. Stunt people go bouncing off of springboards doing soaring kicks. Serious martial artists and police officers will tell you that, in real life, the best moves are the most subtle ones. The best moves are quick, hard to see, and devastatingly effective."
— Kerr Cuhulain, *Full Contact Magick* (p. 71)

"Do not underestimate your opponent. It is very possible that he is: more experienced at fighting, accustomed to being hit, highly motivated, physically strong, has knowledge of martial arts, incapable of backing down, or armed. Never assume he's just some wussy who'll fall down or run away."
— anonymous (RWT)

"In self-defense, there is one rule which you must obey: there are no rules! Always use a weapon as opposed to "fighting fair." Sometimes a deterrent is just as good, and don't threaten to do it — do it! If a guy calls you out, smack him down straight away and when he's down, make sure that he doesn't get up easily."
— Cacoy Hernandez

"I was small and anti-social, with a reputation for not winning, not quitting, and using a blade to avoid losing. I was tough-guy repellent. Bragging about pounding some bone-rack into the ground is not worth getting shanked over."
— James LaFond

"A small injustice can be drowned by a cup of wine; a great injustice can be drowned only by the sword."
— unknown

"Avoidance is the best possible defense. Avoid the criminal and you won't be obliged to risk your life to defend yourself."
— George Hunter

"WAKE THE FUCK UP, PAL! Avoiding the fight is a goddamn technique, and not just a self-defense technique, either. It is an absolutely essential survival technique."
— Peyton Quinn

"ANYTIME YOU STEP INTO THE ARENA A PHYSICAL VIOLENCE, YOU HAVE TO ACCEPT THAT IT MAY NOT END UNTIL EITHER YOU OR YOUR OPPONENT, MAYBE BOTH, ARE DEAD. I don't care if it's just a warning slap to someone — it can escalate! Anytime you are tempted to resort to violence, this is the bottom line: if you ain't ready to die for it or kill for it, don't do it."
— Marc MacYoung, *A Professional's Guide to Ending Violence Quickly* (p. 13)

"Do yourself a favor and don't bother hitting people in the mouth! The reason is two-fold. One, the mouth is backed up by bones. Bones are hard, and they hurt your hand. Second — and this is the real motive behind avoiding the mouth as a target — is that this is one of the dirtiest, most bacteria-riddled portions of the body. . . . If you hit someone in the mouth and cut your hand on his teeth, you can get seriously infected! I mean possibly hospital-time infected."
— Marc "Animal" MacYoung, *Fists, Wits, and a Wicked Right* (p. 75)

"All-or-none, black-or-white perceptions and responses are a major problem in human life, of course. Someone makes a slighting remark to you and your adrenaline begins flowing, your muscles tighten, your body prepares for fight or flight, and you feel very threatened, angry, or anxious. Yet it was only a small verbal slight; no bodily response was called for. We overreact or underreact too often, whereas we need to react in correct proportion to the reality of the situation."
— Charles T. Tart, *Waking Up* (p.28)

"Back when I was younger, if you got into a barfight the bartender would yell at you and say that you couldn't come back until you'd paid for the damages. Nowadays, you'd be arrested for felony assault and sent to prison — even if the guy you hurt refused to press charges! Things sure have changed a lot over the past 30 years."
— anonymous (RWT)

"Remember; if you harm someone, you will have to answer for it — and live with what you have done."
— Richard Chun

"Don't hit at all, if it is honorably possible to avoid hitting; but never hit soft."
— Theodore Roosevelt

"Never do an enemy a small injury."
— Machiavelli

"Violence should be exclusively reserved for use towards truly deserving individuals who possess the ability and means to adequately defend themselves."
— C. R. Jahn

"Approach the enemy with the attitude of defeating him without delay."
— Miyamoto Musashi

"Once (you) engage the opponent, emotion disappears. It is replaced by total concentration and dedication to a single ideal — victory."
— Hanho

"It is fundamental in all fighting that he who strikes first wins, unless his opponent is prepared."
— General John Ross Delafield

". . . never underestimate how fast someone can attack you. When motivated, people can explode on you in a fraction of a second. Never take your eyes off an attacker even for an instant. . . . A person standing within arms' reach of you (or closer) is in your kill zone. . . . At this distance, you have little or no time to react to an attack, especially if it is fast and non-telegraphic."
— Richard Ryan, *Master of the Blade* (p. 17, 74)

"You should always conserve your energy, save a little in reserve in case a supreme effort is suddenly needed. Two essential aspects are inner calmness and a degree of self-awareness. Experienced martial artists learn to use economical movements. Often an experienced fighter in his 30s or 40s can hold his own against much younger, stronger opponents because of this factor."
— Robert K. Spear, *Survival on the Battlefield* (p. 9)

"To generate great power you must first totally relax and gather your strength, and then concentrate your mind and all your strength on hitting your target."
— Bruce Lee

"Once going to the ground, never stop moving. Start rolling or try to get back on your feet as quickly as possible. If you can't get up and can't roll, pivot on your hips and shoulders so you can face your opponent and block with your feet any attempt to close with you."
—Rex Applegate, *Kill or Be Killed* (p. 15)

"When a man's fight begins within himself, he is worth something."
— Robert Browning

"Don't fight a battle if you don't gain anything by winning."
— General George S. Patton, Jr.

"Don't go looking for a fight — but if you're hit, deck the bastard."
— Roger Ailes

"Precision is of the utmost importance when engaged in any sort of conflict. A carefully aimed pistol shot is typically far more effective than emptying an entire magazine from the hip; an accurate strike with a properly formed hand weapon usually does far more damage than a flurry of undirected blows; and a short factual statement consisting of carefully chosen words delivered in an appropriate tone will most likely elicit the desired response, whereas a mere exchange of taunts delivered with a rapid high-pitched voice will often prove counter-productive."
— anonymous (RWT)

"When it looks like the shit is going to hit the fan, you don't want to be jacking your jaw. Keep your mouth shut and locked. Most broken jaws occur when the mouth is open."
— Marc "Animal" MacYoung, *Violence, Blunders, and Fractured Jaws* (p. 238)

"A fight is a sociological function, in which there are rules and limits. Combat is a free-for-all, where victory is awarded to the survivor. There are no rules; in combat, you do what you have to do to win. These things are as different as night and day. If you can't differentiate between them, you can land in a heap of trouble. . . . Most situations are not combat; they are fights, and therefore less intense. So relax about it."
— Marc "Animal" MacYoung, *Cheap Shots, Ambushes, and Other Lessons* (p. 6)

"Street fighters usually do not have any special stance or approach; they usually just come wading

in. . . . Most street fighters have one or two special techniques which they have found from practical experience to be effective. They usually attempt one of these favored moves at the start of a fight, hoping to end it quickly and flashily. . . . A street fighter will rarely give up. If he does, he will probably attack again the moment you relax your vigilance."
— Joe Hyams, *Playboy's Book of Practical Self-Defense* (p. 52)

"Don't be overconfident. There is always someone stronger or better than you, regardless of size or physical shape. . . . Some fat people have remarkably strong stomachs that can withstand the hardest blow you can throw. Some persons who appear frail are strong and supple as a willow. . . . It is foolhardy to think that because you are bigger and seem to be in better condition or have some fighting experience you can handle any situation or person. It is much wiser to assume that your opponent is more dangerous than you think. This is especially true when confronting a street fighter."
— Joe Hyams, *Playboy's Book of Practical Self-Defense* (p. 52-53)

"Reality is not a movie. You can't withstand a barrage of blows like Clint Eastwood in an old western barroom brawl and remain standing. When an elbow is slammed into your neck, your neck breaks. When a fist is buried deep into your kidneys, you land in the hospital. Tightening your neck muscles won't stop a chop to your throat, nor will closing your eyelids stop an eye gouge. It's simply a joke to think the ability to do 500 sit-ups will protect your midsection. What muscles protect your ribcage?
— John Perkins, Al Ridenhour, and Matt Kovsky, *Attack Proof* (p. 46)

"Getting hit with an elbow is like getting hit with a baseball bat."
— John Perkins, Al Ridenhour, and Matt Kovsky, *Attack Proof* (p. 141)

"Three men can have a hard time fighting against one. They must train together or their rhythm is off, they get in one another's way, they have to be careful not to attack a friend. The lone man has no such problems. Everyone is an enemy. The thought and the action are one."
— James D. Macdonald, *The Apocalypse Door* (p. 188)

"Back off as much as possible, and never square off as though you are planning to attack. You should take your opponent by surprise. If a fight is inevitable and he's within range, get off the first punch and make it effective."
— Bruce Lee

". . . as we know, the first rule of Unarmed Combat is to 'arm yourself' . . ."
— C. R. Jahn, *Hardcore Self-Defense* (p. 41)

"How people choose to defend themselves is as much a part of national character as literature, costumes or cooking."
— Richard F. Burton, *The Sentiment of the Sword* (1911)

"Violence never settles anything."
— Genghis Khan

STREETFIGHTING

"Commit yourself violently and totally. Attack to destroy. Never fight anybody on equal terms."
— Lt.Col. Anthony B. Herbert

"The folowing actions are effective: Pulling hair, tearing a lip, grasping and twisting (or tearing) the nose. A grip with the point of thumb and forefinger, or bite, on the thick muscles that extend from the neck to the shoulder; a thumb and forefinger grip, or bite, across the breast muscles to the arm; kicking or biting the Achilles tendon back of the heel — all are effective."
—Rex Applegate, *Kill or Be Killed* (p. 11)

"Rip using your hands to squeeze and tear at any soft tissue areas of the body. . . . Pull at the eyes, neck, throat, ears, groin, lips, hair, fingers, or any loose fold of skin, like around the underarms, waist, corners of the mouth, or the like."
— John Perkins, Al Ridenhour, and Matt Kovsky, *Attack Proof* (pp. 21-22)

"With his right hand he grabbed at the re-bar man's face. His huge thumb slid into the man's mouth between cheek and gum. He clenched his grip tightly and pulled viciously down. One side of the man's face was torn open in a jagged, bloody line from ear to jaw."
— Michael Detroit, *Chain of Evidence* (p. 230)

"Take a look at the way your ears are connected to the side of your head. They are glued on in an up and down direction. That's how you want to try to take them off. . . . Straight down or past his chest is the angle you want to go for."
— Marc "Animal" MacYoung, *Floor Fighting* (pp. 159-160)

"If you succeed in hooking two fingertips into your opponent's nostrils, it is possible to peel his nose off his face by suddenly jerking it upwards, shearing the moorings. If you pull someone's nose off, you'll be able to see his tonsils."
— C. R. Jahn, *Hardcore Self-Defense* (p. 62)

"(He) taught me several tricks of waterfront fighting that were often useful. One was the so-called Liverpool Kiss, where you catch a man behind his neck and jerk his face down to meet your upcoming skull. Done properly it can obliterate, for the time being, a man's features and make him less than anxious to pursue the argument."
— Louis L'Amour, *Education of a Wandering Man* (p. 23)

"Kneeing him in the groin is okay, nothing wrong with biting, but gouging the eyes works best. . . . they are the most sensitive body part, requiring the least force from you. You don't even have to touch someone's eyes to produce a reflective movement."
— Sanford Strong, *Strong on Defense* (p. 63)

"Bite a chunk out of his cheek, nose, or neck. I know these . . . pictures I am placing in your mind are ugly. Remember, you must be as uncivilized as he is for a few seconds in order to escape. . . . Pound for pound of square-inch power, nothing matches your jaw."
— Sanford Strong, *Strong on Defense* (p. 65)

"Your teeth are a most effective natural weapon. If, for example, you are immobilized by a bear-hug, bite into your opponent's shoulder. If a hand is over your mouth, bite it. If any portion of your opponent's body is touching your face, bite hard."
— Joe Hyams, *Playboy's Book of Practical Self-Defense* (p. 27)

"A friend of mine was telling me about a bad fight that happened at the club he was DJing. About a

half-dozen guys were cutting each other up with knives in the front of the room . . . real bad situation. Know how they broke it up? About fifty people started throwing forties (40 oz beer bottles) at them until they stopped! That's some fucked up shit."
— The Chinaman (RWT)

"End the fight as rapidly as possible — give no quarter; be totally ruthless; do not stop short of total victory."
— Anthony B. Herbert, *Military Manual of Self Defense* (p. 12)

"Put on your shitkickers and kick some shit!"
— House of Pain

KNIFEFIGHTING

"There is one unquestionable rule in knife fighting: never get into a knife fight. There are no winners in edged weapon contests — only losers to varying degrees."
— Fred Rexer, Jr.

"Haven't you ever wondered what it would be like? What would be the feeling of a real blade entering another man's body? That initial resistance — and that sudden giving? The surprise on another man's face!"
— "The Villainous Master" in *By the Sword* (1991)

"After massive bleeding (exsanguination) and infection, most deaths are caused by air in the

bloodstream (embolism), suffocation (asphyxia), or collapsed lung (pneumothorax). Even if major arteries are cut and severe loss of blood ensues, an adult can remain fully conscious from two to thirty seconds . . . Even mortally wounded duelists were sometimes able to continue fighting effectively long enough to take the lives of those who had taken theirs. A stricken man frequently does not feel the full effects of his wound and, blinded with rage, may simply throw himself on his opponent with renewed fury."
— Richard Cohen, *By the Sword* (pp. 286-287)

"After all, the weapon itself is designed for antagonistic combat. Its point can indeed be described only with the cliche' of 'needle-sharp.' It will snag veins, arteries, and muscles on its path through the body, tearing them as the blade progresses. The resulting damage is a function of organs hit and depth of penetration. Given the anatomical variants of the opponent's body, a deliberate attempt at an instant kill with a thrust into a 'vital point' could be compared with trying to impale an airborne fly hovering behind a curtain."
— Christopher Amberger, *Secret History of the Sword* (p. 103)

"The untrained or poorly skilled knife user will stab and slash at anything offered him in the hope of seeing success. Any idiot can pick up a knife and engage in a free-for-all cutting spree. The expert knife player studies human anatomy with the intensity of a surgeon. The right strike at the right point is his goal. A fight can be concluded with a single shallow cut if it is delivered properly."
— Greg Walker, *Modern Knife Combat* (p. 52)

"The key point of an effective slash is in the amount of contact made with the sharp edge of the blade. Conversely, the main point in thrusting is to have maximum power in the stabbing motion."
— Michael De Alba

"A slash (or cut) can be long and deep or short and shallow, depending upon the bladesman's skill and the flow of the confrontation. Contrary to popular thought, slashes can be every bit as lethal as a thrust depending upon the target area affected. In most cases, however, the slash is meant to soften up the opponent through mental shock from being cut and physical trauma brought on by bleeding. Filipino knife philosophy offers a thought process of 'three strikes and the man is down.' The slash may commonly be used as the opening strike in such a scenario, with a second slash followed by a thrust completing the equation, or with a thrust inserted between two slashes."
— Greg Walker, *Modern Knife Combat* (p. 20)

"Since the daga is very sharp and needle-pointed, the mere twisting of the wrist or the turning of the finger is all that is needed to inflict deep puncture wounds. . . . Fighting with the daga might as well be fighting with the empty hand. You will be well within punching, kicking, head-butting, and wrestling distance, so there is the great need for quick feet to vary distances abruptly."
— Amante Marinas, *Pananandata* (p. 50)

"When I pin that foot — as well as shoving a knife into his eyeball — he loses his balance. He goes down very quickly. . . . A quick jab is all you need. We're not trying to kill this adversary. We're trying to dissuade him from attacking us further. To say that this is a humanitarian act — to puncture someone's eye . . . is a little bit far-fetched. But compared to what you could do with a knife, yes — it is humanitarian. You are trying not to kill."
— James Keating, from the COMTECH video, *Reverse Grip Knifefighting* (0:34, 0:50)

"The knife, it must be remembered, is a universal phenomenon. It exists in some form or other in every culture of the world. When used for personal protection, the techniques for its deployment vary as much as one culture varies from another."
— James Loriega, *Sevillian Steel* (p. 2)

"Don't wait for him to attack! Pick up a light chair and rush him with it, lion-tamer fashion. Aim one foot of the chair at his throat and the opposite foot at his groin. The seat of the chair serves as a very reliable shield to protect you from the knife. Remember to thrust or charge with the legs of the chair. Don't make the TV mistake of swinging the chair like an axe or club."
— N. Mashiro, Ph.D., *Black Medicine III* (p. 118)

"Using a coat, leather jacket, smock, or a spare shirt to defend against a blade is certainly a practice as old as the blade itself. It would only be natural for the prehistoric hunter to armor himself with the skin of his prey."
— James LaFond

"More than mere technique, he taught the spirit of the use of cold steel as a weapon of preference of a man of honor and a gentleman."
— G. Gordon Liddy, speaking of Captain Stevens

"Hand to hand combat with edged weapons is the most demanding of human physical combat. It not only demands the most skill, both physical and mental, it develops in the adept abilities that separates him from others and elevates intuition, reflexes, and technique to the highest degree . . . the emotional tie is stronger than for other weapons, and the training for its use strengthens spirit."
— Lynn Thompson

"If you're considering training with weapons and are still deciding which one to master first, I'd recommend the butcher knife. The average butcher knife has a wicked 8" blade with a comfortable grip, good balance, and an integral hilt. Not only do they take a far better edge than most flea market fighting knives, but you can find one in virtually any home — just look in the kitchen. It's easy to learn how to use it effectively, it's legal to own, and it'll command a lot more respect than a

broomstick or a belt (as Charlie Manson once said, 'Everybody's afraid of gettin' cut!'). Once you believe that you've nearly mastered the use of the butcher knife as a weapon, start training with one in either hand."
— anonymous (RWT)

"A heavy knife is a club with a sharp edge. You chop with it. The feeling is like chopping at a piece of firewood with a hatchet. The heavy knife can cut or break bone where the light knife can only slice soft tissue."
— N. Mashiro, *Black Medicine, Vol. IV, Equalizers* (p. 49)

"In close quarters fighting there is no more deadly weapon than the knife. An entirely unarmed man has no certain defense against it, and, further, merely the sudden flashing of a knife is frequently enough to strike fear into your opponent, causing him to lose confidence . . . A quick draw (an essential in knife fighting) can not be accomplished unless the sheath is firmly secured to the clothing or equipment. Moreover, speed on the draw can be accomplished only by constant daily practice."
— W. E. Fairbairn, *Get Tough!* (p. 96)

"If you're relying upon a 3" 'tactical folder' or a 2" 'neck knife' for personal defense, be sure you're free of any grandiose delusions about your 'weapon's' capabilities."
— C. R. Jahn, *Hardcore Self-Defense* (p. 87)

"When utilizing a knife without a proper guard — such as the balisong and many boot knives — it is advised that one 'cap' the pommel with one's thumb if the knife is being grasped in the 'reverse' or 'icepick' grip. Although this may weaken the grip if the weapon is subjected to lateral pressure, it will effectively prevent one's fingers from being sliced if the hand slides up over the blade after impacting bone."

— C. R. Jahn

". . . the greatest advantage of the edged weapon is that it need only touch you to do damage. Contact usually means cutting. . . . The edged weapon requires very little speed and even less strength to do its job. . . . When steel meets human flesh, flesh loses and a slash can open up large wounds. This is because the skin is somewhat elastic and, when severed, the tissue separates around the wound. . . . What would happen if you took a pin and popped a hole in (a garden) hose? You would instantly get a violent spray of water. If you were to slash the hose, the water would surge forth at a rapid rate. So it is with arteries. . . . Cut anything you can. Cut the hands, arms, legs, feet, face, body, anything you can reach, and especially the hand with the (weapon) in it."
— Richard Ryan, *Master of the Blade* (p. 18, 45, 54, 100)

"When withdrawing the knife from a deep stab wound it is oftentimes difficult because the flesh of the body has a tendency to contract and grip the blade and suction adds to the problem and care should be taken not to snap the blade. If penetration was as deep as it should have been you may well require both hands to withdraw the knife. . . . Most experts say to leave the knife in but I don't advocate it because it can be traced . . ."
— John Minnery, *How to Kill, Vol. I* (p. 23)

"Be warned! The only way to know whether you are master of balisong is to fight with it — for real!"
— Master Bimba

"The blade must be your constant companion. . . . she should be at your side in whatever you do, always providing assistance, support, and confidence. Treat her well, keep her sharp, and she will be faithful to you to the end."
— Don Santiago Rivera

COMBAT

"Remember: once you have ascertained that you are dealing with hostile intruders, the staircase becomes a free-fire zone."
— Massad Ayoob

"If he is willing to kill, then he must be prepared to die. It is only right."
— C. W. Nicol

"Once you've accepted your own death, you can become really proficient at killing because it is no longer important if you die."
— Dave Nelson, USMC Scout/Sniper

"He found the best way to accept his predicament was to just assume that he was dead already. He was dead already. He just kept doing his job."
— Mark Bowden, *Blackhawk Down* (p. 255)

"Killing someone is a unique ability all by itself. Not everyone can lay a weapon's sights on a fellow human being and crank off a round. The Army has been keeping data on soldiers' killing abilities ever since WWII. The data supports the conclusion that out of an entire platoon of soldiers, you have perhaps two men who qualify as genuine killers. Men who actually see enemy troops, put the front sight blade on them, and blow them away . . . Genuine killers are not to be confused with guys who simply spray an area and happen to hit and kill someone . . . It takes a certain something not found in everybody."
— Medal of Honor recipient Franklin D. Miller

"My first reaction, rooted in the illusion that anyone trying to kill ne must have a personal motive, was: 'Why does he want to kill me? What did I ever do to him?' A moment later, I realized there was nothing personal about it. All he saw was a man in the wrong uniform. He was trying to kill me and he would try again because that was his job."
— Phillip Caputo

"Battle scenes in films often make people who have been in battles restless. On the screen there are particular conventions to be observed. Men blown up by high explosives in real war, for example, are often torn apart quite hideously; in films, there is a big bang and bodies, intact, fly through the air with the greatest of ease. If they are shot . . . they fall down like children in a game, to lie motionless. The most harrowing thing in real battles is that they usually don't lie still; only the lucky ones are killed outright."
— General Sir John Hackett

"When you made contact with the enemy, you went from the most horrible boredom to the most intense excitement I've ever known in my life. You couldn't remain detached. Someone was trying to kill you and you were trying to kill someone, and it was like every thrill hitting you all at once. . ."
— Mark Smith

"There is no hunting like the hunting of man, and those who have hunted armed men long enough and liked it, never care for anything else thereafter."
— Ernest Hemingway

"Many had died there, and others were in the last agonies as we passed. Their groans and cries were heart rending . . . The gory corpses lying all about us, in every imaginable attitude, and slain by an inconceivable variety of wounds, were shocking to behold."
— unknown Union soldier at Shiloh

"Attacking such a person or his family, or even posing to do so, is an express ticket to the morgue. In the morgue, your corpse will lie on a cold, stainless-steel tray."
— Peyton Quinn

"There is nothing more exhilarating than to be shot at without result."
— Winston Churchill

"*Yah ta hey! Hoka hey!*" ("It is a good day to fight! It is a good day to die!")
— Lakota Sioux war cry.

"Become the perfect dance partner. Before you engage, show the terrible joy of your true face. Put on the True Helm of Terror and lay waste to the psychic battleground with the realization that your enemy is self-defeated. This is one of the great secrets of victory."
— Sweyn Plowright, *True Helm*

"FINISH HIM!!!"
— from the Mortal Kombat videogame

CHAIRBORNE

"What I aspired to be, and was not, comforts me."

— R. Browning

"He who can, does. He who cannot, teaches."
— Bernard Shaw

"I hadn't trained myself for years to be a warrior, only to spend my life behind a typewriter writing and editing."
— G. Gordon Liddy, *Will* (p. 76)

"How I would've loved to vault over his desk and strangle the bastard, fat squeezing through my fingers. He was condemning me to spend the remainder of my time on this crummy little island in the middle of the East China Sea while my friends went to Vietnam and romped and stomped in the jungles, laughing at me when they came home, covered in honors and medals, while I sat pounding out tepid news release copy . . . It was my misfortune that I had the only journalism degree in the 1st Special Forces Group."
— Jim Morris, *War Story* (p. 140)

"They were all Special Forces guys, of course. Not a leg in the bunch. There were about thirty of us in all. The clerks were all guys who had volunteered for the army, volunteered for jump training, volunteered for the Forces, and volunteered for Nam. Then somebody had discovered that they could type or something . . ."
— Jim Morris, *War Story* (p. 266)

"Those guys would stay around because of the status involved. They were somebody because they were at the place where that dangerous job was done. But they didn't want to or couldn't do that job. The staff sections usually had people in them who had been in the woods once or twice. But that was it. They never went back in again."
— Medal of Honor recipient Franklin D. Miller

"Many men look back to the days of war with an intense longing. They miss a time in their lives when they felt on the edge, intensely alive, a time when life and love walked hand in hand with death and destruction."
— Robert Moore & Douglas Gillette, *The Warrior Within* (p. 54)

"The military is a profession that brands itself on the soul and causes you forever after to view the world and all human endeavor through a unique set of mental filters. . . . Close brutal combat puts a callous layer on each individual who undergoes the experience. With some men, their souls become trapped inside those accrued layers and they stay tightly bound up within themselves, unable or unwilling to reach outside that hard protective shell. For others, the effect is just the opposite. That

coating becomes like a looking glass, highlighting and magnifying the things that are really important in life. Every sensation becomes precious and delicious."
— Eric L. Haney, *Inside Delta Force* (pp. vi-vii)

"Many of the well-known difficulties faced by Vietnam vets upon their return home stemmed from a lack of respect for this necessary period of psychological adjustment. Instead of being mustered out over a period of weeks, as in other wars, somebody in the Pentagon decided the more humane approach would be to send the soldiers straight home. Many soldiers found themselves in their quiet hometowns less than seventy-two hours after leaving horrific combat situations. Add to this the indifference or active disrespect with which they were greeted, and their problems in adjusting are clear."
— Robert Moore & Douglas Gillette, *The Warrior Within* (pp. 67-69)

"You had a very weird energy; it was just a completely different energy after you did that thing. You weren't fit for normal people."
— Bill Murray (in reference to something completely different, but it works here too)

"We wise, who with a thought besmirch
Blood over all our soul,
How should we see our task
But through his blunt and lashless eyes?
Alive, he is not vital overmuch;
Dying, not mortal overmuch;
Nor sad, nor proud,
Nor curious at all.
He cannot tell
Old men's placidity from his."
— Wilfred Owen, "Insensibility," stanza V

"Our scars remind us that the past was real."
— Hannibal Lecter, from the screenplay for *Red Dragon*

WEAPONRY

"Your mind is your most powerful weapon."
— unofficial motto of the United States Special Forces

"In ancient times, tools and weapons meant survival. . . . To an extent, the same is true today. Weapons, or the threat of their deployment, are still used to wage war, to maintain law and order, and deter aggression. Above all else, weapons have kept us alive in a world in which we are physically inferior. Without them, we would have only been a footnote in the evolutionary chain."
— Richard Ryan, *Master of the Blade* (p. 2)

"I train my students first in the use of weapons. As the student becomes more skilled in weapons use, there is instilled in him a mental attitude that weapons training and empty-hands training are identical. Thus, they come to realize that the transition from weapons to empty-hand training is more of a change in mental attitude than a physical one."
— Amante Marinas, *Pananandata* (p. 137)

"The old Filipinos who made stick fighting an art preferred to hit the bone and preferred a stick to a blade. Instead of a clean cut, the stick left shattered bone. The business end of a stick can travel many times the speed of the empty hand. And it feels nothing, whether it hits hard bone or soft flesh."
— Dan Inosanto, *The Filipino Martial Arts* (p. 11)

"If you're going to carry a weapon, make damn sure that it is legal for you to do so! Many states require a permit to carry a concealed handgun, and if you don't have that official 'permission slip' on your person, you will go to jail. Most states will allow you to carry a knife — even a full-sized hunting knife — but if you're caught carrying a double-edged dagger with a spiked knucklebow, you will go to jail. Most states will allow you to carry pepperspray, a sword cane, a butterfly knife or an oversized 'tactical folder' — but if you instead choose to carry nunchaku, a blackjack, brass knuckles, a switchblade, or a springblade 'ballistic knife,' you will go to jail. Familiarize yourself with your jurisdiction's laws, and don't take the stupid and unnecessary risk of carrying contraband weaponry when a legal alternative will work nearly as well!"
— anonymous (RWT)

"When the World is at Peace, a gentleman keeps his sword by his side."
— Wu Tsu

"The use of one's bare hands to defend against attack or to launch an attack has always been a desperation move, a method of last resort, by any people at any time and anywhere on this squalid little planet. It has only been rather recently in mankind's history that the habitual carrying of weapons has become something less than the universal norm."
— Peyton Quinn

"Don't hit your friend with your soft little hand — use this stick, it's harder!"
— remembered line from an old *Cracked* comic

"If someone attacks me on the street, I don't wanna just make him cry and give him a runny nose —
I wanna *wound* the bastard!"
— anonymous female (when asked why she carries a knife instead of pepperspray)

"Do not hesitate to use your weapon when you and your loved ones face mortal danger."
— Eugene Sockut

"Weapons were named, surnamed, slang-named, christened, titled and dubbed. Protective devices.
Bearings of perfect performance. Reciting these names was the soldier's poetry, his counterjargon
to death."
— unknown

"An armed society is a polite society"
— Robert Heinlein

"Every tool is a weapon if you hold it right."
— Ani DiFranco

"For among other evils caused by being disarmed, it renders you contemptible."
— Machiavelli

"Armed individuals carry a weapon out of the primitive urge of the animal kingdom, self-
preservation of themselves, their family and their chosen territory; whether it be their car, their
house, or the bar stool they are sitting on."
— John M. La Tourrette

"It needs to be realized that fighting tactics come from techniques, and techniques are derived
primarily (though not exclusively) from the mechanics of the weapon itself."
— John Clements, *Renaissance Swordsmanship*

"A good weapon is an instrument of fear. All creatures have distaste for them."
— Lao Tzu

"The more weapons of violence, the more misery to mankind. The triumph of violence ends in a festival of mourning."
— Lao-tzu

"Speak softly and carry a big stick; you will go far."
Theodore Roosevelt (quoted as an African proverb)

"Give them enough food, give them enough arms, and the common people will have trust in you . . . . when there is no trust, the common people will have nothing to stand on."
— Confucius

"For psychological reasons, a man will have more confidence in a weapon of his own choosing; hence the weapon will have a direct bearing on his proficiency in practice and in combat."
— Rex Applegate, *Kill or Be Killed* (p. 123)

"A man without a weapon to defend himself, especially after long exposure, is very likely to give up in despair. It is remarkable what a difference it would make in his morale if he had a small stick or cane in his hand. Now, add to this the knowledge that he could, with ease, kill any opponent with a stick, and you will then see how easy it is to cultivate the offensive spirit which is so essential in present-day warfare."
— W. E. Fairbairn, *Get Tough!* (p. 74)

"One loves to possess arms, though they hope never to have occasion for them."
— Thomas Jefferson (to George Washington, 1796)

"One should never be far from one's weapons
When faring from home
You can never be certain when you will need
The use of your spear while out and about"
— *Havamal*, verse 38, Plowright translation

"When the gods made man, they made a weapon."
— Dr. Mark L. Mirabello, *The Odin Brotherhood*

"If you do not have a sword, sell your cloak and buy one."
— Luke 22:36, attributed to Jesus (although many theologians are in disagreement as to this book's

accuracy).

"If it looks like the shit is gonna go down, I reach into my pocket, smile, and whip a handful of pennies right in the fucker's face. Unlike Mace or aquarium gravel, a pocketful of change won't get a second glance if you happen to get frisked by the cops."
— anonymous (RWT)

"'I see two knives,' Mowery said calmly. 'Skinny guy in the middle, bald prick on the left.' Shifter laughed. 'Wait'll they see my sword." He smashed his cue stick violently on the edge of the pool table. When the stick snapped it broke along the grain, creating a long, very sharp point."
— Michael Detroit, *Chain of Evidence* (p. 228)

"A flail is a flexible weapon like a chain or an extremely lightweight stick like a metal curtain rod or automobile antenna. . . . The amount of pain inflicted can be large even when the weapon is very light and insubstantial. . . . One of the really nice things about the light flail is the sound it makes as you swing it through the air. It 'hums.' People who hear that sound usually back off. Make it sing for you."
— N. Mashiro, *Black Medicine, Vol. IV, Equalizers* (pp. 31-32)

"There was no way he could claim that he was just a tourist with a handgun in his pants. The same went for knives, garottes, and other aids to mayhem. Harsh language and a dangerous attitude would be all he had — that and a talent for turning household items to unintended purposes."
— James D. Macdonald, *The Apocalypse Door* (p. 40)

"All uncouth, unknown wights are terrifyed by nothing earthly so much as by cold iron."
— Robert Kirk (1691)

"Don't carry a weapon unless you're going to pull it. Don't pull it unless you're going to use it. Don't use it unless you're going to kill with it."
— Animal's 3rd Law of Weapons

"The right to buy weapons is the right to be free."
— A. E. Van Vogt, *The Weapon Shops of Isher*

GUNFIGHTING

"The man who wears a gun carries with it the power of life and death, and therefore the responsibility to deport himself with greater calm and wisdom than his unarmed counterpart, whose panic or misjudgement in crisis situations will have less serious consequences."
— Massad Ayoob

"A gun will not crawl out of a drawer to attack you; it will not change you into a hero or a villain; it will not drive you mad with power; and it will not make you capable of anything except expelling a lead projectile by means of expanding gases. Therefore, do not fear the handgun, and do not expect it to save you from your own weaknesses. It is only a tool."
— Fred Rexer, Jr.

"A lotta people belittle the diminutive .25 ACP pistol, but it has always been a favorite of mine. The Beretta Jetfire is lightweight and nearly invisible when you drop it in a vest pocket — you barely know it's there. It has almost no recoil, so one can easily rapidfire 9 rounds into a beer can-sized target 15 feet away in under 2 seconds. It may not be able to drop a man with a single shot, but it will always remain my carry weapon of choice."
— Jake Bishop

"If you have to shoot a man, keep shooting until he is either unconscious, dead, disarmed, or so torn apart that he can't function. A major fallacy is that the criminal will fall with the first bullet. He may take a clipload before he goes down, and if you wait for him to fall after the first hit, you may get shot yourself. Keep firing 'til he can't shoot back."
— Massad Ayoob, *The Gravest Extreme* (p. 113)

"Rapid fire comprises strings of shots usually fired at clearly definable targets at short range. Twenty aimed shots a minute is rapid fire . . . remember that your aim will suffer if you try to hold your breath and sight picture for more than seven or eight seconds. Rapid fire heats up rifles to an uncomfortable degree, so if you get a pause in the firing, lock back the action to allow air to circulate around the chamber. . . . Not only is fully automatic fire inaccurate, it eats up your ammo at an incredible rate."
— Peter McAleese, *McAleese's Fighting Manual* (pp. 169-170)

"With (a) 12-gauge shotgun, you've got buckshot that does the same thing as your pistol — times nine — each time you pull the trigger."
— Bill Clede, *Police Shotgun Manual* (p, 15)

"I'd rather not oil the gun at all than use too much oil. For that reason, I don't like spray cans. You can easily spray too much. Use a simple squeeze bottle, so you can put on just one drop of oil."
— Don Vivenzio, Smith & Wesson's Armorers School

"Over 90 percent of gunfights occur within 21 feet. More than half of these occur within 5 feet. Most people, when put to the test, can't even get their guns out in time to defend against a person rushing them from across a large room. You also must know hand-to-hand combat."
— John Perkins, Al Ridenhour, and Matt Kovsky, *Attack Proof* (p. 199)

"A prudent man will not rely upon hip shooting at distances greater than seven yards, the practical limit of fast gunmanship. Beyond this distance the pistol should be brought up toward eye level as the range increases until at the longer ranges it is fired by looking down the barrel or actually using the sights."
— William H. Jordan, *No Second Place Winner* (p. 62)

"You should neither see the sights nor be conscious of them. The weapon must be a natural extension of your arm; look at where you're going to shoot and think the bullet into the target."
— John Minnery, *How to Kill, Vol. I* (p. 51)

"These experts believed that shooting was 20 percent physical and 80 percent mental. . . . Each became one with the weapon. The gun was an extension of the shooter. They let the bullet go down range — they didn't fire it. . . . Surprisingly, these experts do not need to hold their weapons perfectly still to shoot accurately. Under observation, the shooters displayed a great deal of arm movement as they were firing. They mentally controlled the trigger squeeze, and would not allow the bullet to 'go down range' until their sights were on target. This mental control was an unconscious process that allowed trigger squeeze to occur only when the sights were aligned. The expert shooters call their technique 'controlling the smallest arc of movement.' They knew they would be moving and controlled the arc."
— Col. John B. Alexander, Major Richard Groller, and Janet Morris, *The Warrior's Edge* (pp. 78-79)

"Don't always assume that by having a gun you have all of life's answers — because you don't."
— James Keating, from the COMTECH video *Crossada: American Blade Concepts* (1:10)

"Bring a gun (more than one, if possible); bring all your friends who have guns — preferably long guns."
— adapted from "Rules for a Gunfight" (author unknown)

SURVIVAL

"The fundamental principal of surviving violence is mental. Not physical, not gadgetry, but mental preparation, mind-setting. It consists of visualizing a crime scene and mentally rehearsing your response. Mind-setting gives you this crucial advantage when violence strikes: 'This is not new to me, I've thought about this before. I know what to do.' Then your instincts trained for this moment will kick in."
— Sanford Strong, *Strong on Defense* (p. 35)

"Cops play what-if games in their minds, alone and with each other. Every time they read a newspaper account of something or investigate a crime, they reenact it, mentally transferring themselves into other crime situations, and plan a response. Stories, as gruesome as they may be, are an important part of survival planning. They motivate people to plan against that same crime happening against them."
— Capt. Mark Leap, LAPD

"Survival is the art of staying alive. Any equipment you have must be considered a bonus. You must know how to take everything possible from nature and use it to the full."
— John Wiseman

"The human body has an amazing ability to cope with arduous situations and testing environments. People who have come through, after enduring terrible hardship under seemingly impossible conditions, are a living proof of this."
— John Wiseman

"Lack of food constitutes the biggest single assault upon morale . . . Apart from its purely chemical effects upon the body, it has woeful effects upon the mind. One is in the dismal condition of having nothing to look forward to."
— Brigadier Bernard Fergusson

"The standard 'safe' shelf life of canned food is 2 years from the date of manufacture. But consider this: In the 1820s, Sir William Edward Parry carried a 4-pound tin of roasted veal on two expeditions to the Northwest Passage. The can was never opened, so it was kept as an artifact. In 1938, scientists analyzed the 100-year-old contents and found them to be intact both physically and

nutritionally. The veal was then fed to a cat, who had no complaints. According to the Canned Food Alliance, unless your can bulges, is dented, or squirts when opened, the contents are edible."
— David Joachim, *A Man, A Can, A Plan* (p. 16)

"The Russians, he found, could march incredible distances, sleep in wet rags, live on roots from the fields. They had stomachs that would digest anything; he saw prisoners tear raw chunks from a long-dead horse and march on, refreshed. Such insensibility is a high military asset. It meant that they could drink from marshes and shell holes . . . they could even exist without supply columns."
— Charles Foley, *Commando Extraordinary* (p. 21)

"On some day, in the not too distant future, Shit will Happen, and the streets will be filled with a conglomeration of sorry fucks looking to get out, get off, get paid, or get that last can of wax beans sitting way in the back of that empty supermarket shelf. The entire fucking city would turn into a gigantic parking lot as traffic stopped, and the cops would say 'fuck this' and disappear, leaving Joe Citizen to fend for himself."
— C. R. Jahn, *Underground* (p. 264)

"She had the loaded handbag of someone who camps out and seldom goes home, or one who imagines life must be full of emergencies."
— Mavis Gallant, *A Fairly Good Time*

"Animal food will give you the most food value per pound. Anything that creeps, crawls, swims or flies is a possible source of food."
— excerpted from S.A.S. *Combat Survival* course notes

"If you are captured, someone soon will bring you a bucket of slop and, after your stomach has flipped from the sight and smell of it, you say, 'I can't (or won't) eat that stuff.' You'd better eat it because that's all you'll get and it may get progressively fouler and skimpier. . . . You must eat everything you can get — issued rations, things you can steal, things you procure from the environment. . . . You will be revolted by the food given you as a POW, but if you miss one meal as a prisoner it will take you weeks to regain your lost strength. You can't afford to miss a single bite when you're on a bare subsistence diet."
— Dr. Gene N. Lam

". . . most recruits in Western armies have come from urban backgrounds and have little or no understanding of the countryside. Theses days, almost everyone buys their meat pre-cut in packs from the supermarket; families no longer keep chickens, rabbits and the odd pig to eat. So not only do few young soldiers have the skills to hunt animals for food, they won't have a clue how to skin and butcher them either."
— Peter McAleese, *McAlees's Fighting Manual* (p. 158)

"Are you willing to do everything necessary in order to live?"
— Shiguro Takada, *Contingency Cannibalism* (p. 4)

AWARENESS

"Be a calm beholder of what is happening around you."
— Bruce Lee

"Observe things as they are and don't pay attention to other people."
— Huang Po

"You always want to know what's going on around you. Always. When you're walking or driving, you're constantly scanning, right sidewalk to the left sidewalk, left sidewalk to the right sidewalk. You just look for something out of the ordinary. Something that doesn't look right. And the best way to do it is — if it catches your eye, if it makes you take a second look, look at it a third time. Satisfy your curiosity."
— anonymous, from *What Cops Know*, by Connie Fletcher (p. 20)

"Modern life so celebrates intellect that we ignore instinct, but when recon men "felt" something — danger, anticipation, anxiety, hackles rising on their neck — they thought it a subconscious warning. Some hints might be too oblique to be articulated but were to be considered real nonetheless. It could be the gut feeling that someone's watching you, or an overwhelming foreboding about climbing a hill. Recon men learned to trust their instincts."
— John L. Plaster

"If as a kid, they see a dragon, they get smacked for asking about it. Once they forget that these sort of questions exist, they are given a pair of sunglasses. These sunglasses are ultraviolet and dragon-blocking. Put them on and you don't see dragons . . . These sunglasses, in reality, are various operating systems. Take this operating system and you won't see dragons. Take this one and you won't see violence. Take this one and you won't see drug/alcohol abuse. This way people can wander around happily not seeing things."
— Marc "Animal" MacYoung

"The best way to avoid violence is to always be aware of what's going on in your surroundings, and to feel secure enough in your manhood that you cannot be made to fight over insignificant things."
— C.R. Jahn

"Nurture the ability to perceive the truth in all matters. Perceive that which cannot be seen with the eye."
— Miyamoto Musahi

"Observe what is with undivided awareness."
— Bruce Lee

"Keep your eyes open when entering,
Always wary, always watchful,
You may never know if an enemy,
May sit in hiding within the hall"
— *Havamal*, verse 1, Plowright translation

"There's really no such thing as an 'ex-cop' or a cop who's 'off-duty' or 'retired.' Once trained, once indoctrinated, a cop is always alert, assessing reality in terms of its potential for illegal acts."
— Sue Grafton, *"H" is for Homicide*

"Never ignore a gut feeling, but never believe that it's enough."
— Robert Heller

"When you're ridin' high on the open highway, senses heighten as you absorb the sights. Initially, there's an internal dialogue; you talk to yourself. After a while, everything settles down to a cerebral level; you become still. With a 360-degree panoramic view, everything seeps in and registers. The little voice that natters and chatters in your head eventually disappears. Many riders slip into a free form of meditation, except you're much more alert."
— Ralph "Sonny" Barger, *Ridin' High, Livin' Free* (p. 51)

"He experienced 360 degree vision while running away from a German machine-gun nest. Not only could he see ahead as he ran, but he could see the gunners trying to draw a bead on him from behind."
— Robert Sullivan, referring to a WWII veteran, from *Light* by Moody & Perry (p. 129)

"Your heart is still pounding from that burst of speed and energy, but your mind has to remain calm

and detached. It's like you have to observe yourself and the scene from outside your body — from a spot on the ceiling where you can take it all in with a fish-eye lens."
— Eric L. Haney, *Inside Delta Force* (p. 105)

"Your greatest weapons are your awareness and the reactions that become instinctive tools of your awareness."
— Marc "Animal" MacYoung, *Cheap Shots, Ambushes, and Other Lessons* (p. 5)

"One of the things that saved my ass in the bar was continually scanning everyone around me. You can and must learn to do this on a subconscious level in such a way that nobody even notices you're doing it. This is the 'see everything and see nothing' Zen concept. It means you never allow your full consciousness to settle on any one thing, but you are continually aware of everything."
— Peyton Quinn, *A Bouncer's Guide to Barroom Brawling* (p. 8)

"To stand silent and aware while the suspect is taunting, insulting, and otherwise trying to distract you gives you a distinct advantage. You can read the person's body language and sense his energy if you don't focus on the abusive and derogatory behavior. It doesn't distract you from what the suspect is actually doing. This allows you to respond quicker and use less force to control him should he become violent. Often it permits you to deal with the situation without resorting to physical means at all."
— Kerr Cuhulain, *Full Contact Magick* (p. 81)

"Pay attention to what they tell you to forget."
— Muriel Rukeyser

"WAKE UP!!!"
— G. I. Gurdjieff

FEAR

"DON'T PANIC!!!"
— from *The Hitchhiker's Guide to the Universe*, by Douglas Adams

"Without mind-setting, people freeze up; they have no way to cut through the overwhelming fear that boxes them in during a crisis."
— Sanford Strong, *Strong on Defense* (p. 19)

"If what you fear more than anything else is injury, you will not have the determination necessary to escape a criminal attack. Never. When frozen by fear of injury, you will believe all the criminal's promises, you'll be unable to concentrate on saving yourself, and you'll never notice any fleeting opportunities to escape. The criminal will use your fear to control everything you do."
— Sanford Strong, *Strong on Defense* (p. 26)

"Truly fearless people are extremely rare — they tend to be robotic psychopaths who, having no hope of future happiness, simply do not care what happens to them. Most foolhardy idiots who appear 'fearless' are either drunk or trying to impress others."
— C. R. Jahn, *Hardcore Self-Defense* (p. 7)

"To instil fear, you must appear to be without fear yourself."
— Harold S, Long

"I have no fear of an opponent in front of me."

— Bruce Lee

"It is within your power to transfigure your fear of death. If you learn not to be afraid of your death, then you realize that you do not need to fear anything else either. A glimpse at the face of your death can bring immense freedom to your life. It can make you aware of the urgency of the time you have here.
— John O'Donohue

"Man's greatest fear is death. But think of the power you have when you throw off any fear of dying."
— Forrest E. Morgan

"Die in your thoughts every morning and you will no longer fear death."
— *Hagakure*

"To learn to die is to be liberated from it."
— unknown

"Though warriors aspire to fearlessness, they shun bravado and taking unnecessary risks."
— Robert L. Spencer

"Fear is a good thing. It keeps you alert. It keeps you alive. You can do a lot of things when you're scared."
— Steve Hartman

"Overcoming fear? I don't look at it as fear. I look at it as an adrenaline rush."
— Dennis Chalker

"When you feel great fear, your body goes into a mild state of shock. The blood which normally flows freely throughout the body is pooled into the vital organs by the restriction of the capillaries in the extremities. . . . Adrenaline is dumped into the system. Adrenaline is super soldier serum. It's like tapping into a power generator. It supercharges your system, making you many times faster, more powerful, and more alert than you were a moment ago."
— Richard Ryan, *Master of the Blade* (p. 134)

"I'd be lying between my teeth if I said I never get scared. I wouldn't want to work with a police officer who said he's never scared. That macho act — can't nothing hurt me; can't nothing touch

me — that's all it is, an act."
— anonymous, from *Pure Cop* by Connie Fletcher (p. 253)

"My greater fear was not that I might be killed, but that I might be grievously wounded and left a victim of suffering on the field."
— Lieutenant Frederick Hitchcock

"'Fear of being a coward' was the most strongly felt sensation on the part of troops going into action for the first time. Other major fears — of being crippled, killed, captured and tortured, or painfully wounded — were markedly less common."
— John Dollard (paraphrased)

"There was great assurance in looking over, narrow-eyed and tense, your thumb easing the CAR-15 safety off, to see your partner's eyes just the same, both knowing that no matter the fury to be unleashed he would not run off and leave you, nor would you leave him. That's not cheap talk. When ten times as many NVA as anyone should reasonably fight suddenly appear, eons of evolution and every bit of common sense screams Run! Afraid? Beyond words. But you stay and fight."
— John L. Plaster

"The coward and the hero both feel the same feelings in the face of adversity. The hero controls these feelings; the coward doesn't."
— Geoff Thompson

"Scared to death, but I'd rather die than have my friends think I was chickenshit."
— Ken McMullin

"The truth is, when bullets are whacking against tree-trunks and solid shot are cracking skulls like egg-shells, the consuming passion in the breast of the average man is to get out of the way. Between the physical fear of going forward and the moral fear of turning back, there is a predicament of exceptional awkwardness."
— unknown Union veteran of Antietam

"A kung fu man who was really good was not proud at all. Pride emphasizes the superiority of one's status. There has to be fear and insecurity in pride, because when you aim at being highly esteemed and achieve such status, you automatically start to worry about losing status."
— Bruce Lee

"What else is there in life to be feared more than fear itself? Fear paralyzes the very being of a

person. Fear destroys the whole capacity for rebellion. Fear makes any change impossible. Fear binds one to the known, and the journey to the unknown is completely stopped — although whatever is worth knowing and achieving in life is all unknown."
— Osho

"As we are liberated from our own fear, our presence automatically liberates others."
— Nelson Mandela

"Do the thing we fear, and death of fear is certain."
— Ralph Waldo Emerson

"Fears are educated into us, and can, if we wish, be educated out."
— Karl A. Menniger

"Fear is only natural. Don't be ashamed of it. It has probably saved your life before and will do so again."
— Edward Lewis, from Hostile Ground (p. 2)

"A man may destroy everything within himself, love and hate and belief, and even doubt; but as long as he clings to life he cannot destroy fear; the fear, subtle, indestructible, and terrible, that pervades his being; that tinges his thoughts; that lurks in his heart; that watches on his lips the struggle of his last breath."
— Joseph Conrad, *An Outpost of Progress*

"If you are possessed of fear, do not waste time trying to 'kill out' fear, but instead cultivate the quality of courage and the fear will disappear."
— *Kybalion*

"Succeed in not fearing the lion, and the lion will fear you."
— Eliphas Levi

"When someone goes white (or just pales, depending on his pigment), it means that the blood is rushing away from the skin and into the muscles, readying him for action. People in this state can take blows that would ordinarily drop them and not even feel it — as in, 'keep coming at you.' Pain sensors get turned off. Adrenaline is pumped. The arms and legs go anaerobic. The pupils contract. Jaw and back muscles constrict. Trembling sometimes occurs. Basically, physiology aside, all hell breaks loose."
— Marc "Animal" MacYoung, *Cheap Shots, Ambushes, and Other Lessons* (p. 115)

"Unless you're a fool you're going to be scared. Your hands are going to sweat — dry them. Your knees are going to knock — brace them. Your stomach is going to be queasy — this is caused by your diaphragm falling on it, making you want to vomit and have butterflies. It can be controlled by thrusting both hands under your rib cage and lifting it off your stomach. Take a deep breath and still clutch the diaphragm and bend over. Straighten up and the diaphragm should be back in place and a lot of your fear will have left you. If it comes back, repeat. One of the biggest problems is holding your breath upon approaching the subject. You must make every effort to breathe deeply and naturally."
— John Minnery, *How to Kill, Vol. I* (p. 57)

"Fear is nothing but idleness of the will."
— Eliphas Levi

"Knowledge is the antidote to fear."

— Ralph Waldo Emerson, *Courage*

"We have won against the most dangerous of our foes. We have conquered fear."
— Franklin Delano Roosevelt

"Where there's fear, there's power."
— olde witchy sayin'

GLORY

"The nearest way to glory is to strive to be what you wish to be thought to be."
— Socrates

"The paths of glory lead but to the grave."
— Gray

"Glory is largely a theatrical concept. There is no striving for glory without a vivid awareness of an audience — the knowledge that our mighty deeds will come to the ears of our contemporaries or 'of those who are to be.'"
— Eric Hoffer, *The True Believer* (#47)

"At the end of the course, all students should go through a rites-of-passage ceremony to bond them to their unit and each other. They should be given something to wear as a symbol that they have paid their dues and are now one of the guys."

— Robert K. Spear, *Survival on the Battlefield* (p. 166)

"Glory was incompatible with retreat."
— Hershman & Lieb, *A Brotherhood of Tyrants* (p. 78)

"Our greatest glory is not in never failing, but in rising every time we fail."
— Confucius

"The greater the difficulty, the greater the glory."
— Cicero

"Surely a king who loves pleasure is less dangerous than one who loves glory."
— Nancy Mitford, *The Water Beetle*

". . . (his) training was psychological as well as physical, and he was drilled in a sort of camouflage calculated to conceal the miseries and terrors of war and to exaggerate its glory and glamour. The stoicism of the Spartan is proverbial — it was not in his code to admit that sorrow was sorrowful, that misfortune was misfortunate, or that life was preferable to death."
— Stanton A, Coblentz, *From Arrow to Atom Bomb* (p. 104)

"He had, of course, dreamed of battles all his life — of vague and bloody conflicts that had thrilled him with their sweep and fire. In visions he had seen himself in many struggles. He had imagined peoples secure in the shadow of his eagle-eyed prowess."
— Stephen Crane, *The Red Badge of Courage* (p. 3)

"At times he regarded the wounded soldiers in an envious way. He conceived persons with torn bodies to be particularly happy. He wished that he, too, had a wound, a red badge of courage."
— Stephen Crane, *The Red Badge of Courage* (p. 62)

"Their minds are full of romanticized, Hollywood versions of their future activity in combat, colored with vague ideas of being a hero and winning ribbons and decorations."
— Roy R. Grinker and John P. Spiegel, *Men Under Stress*

"Showing off is the fool's idea of glory."
— Bruce Lee

"Without showing himself, he shines forth
Without promoting himself, he is distinguished
Without claiming reward, he gains endless merit
Without seeking glory, his glory endures"
— Lao Tzu, *Tao Te Ching, The Definitive Edition* (Star translation), Verse 22

MURDER

"There is no excuse for taking a man's life for life is precious. Any man can take a life but no man can give back a life. Killing is then a matter between a man and his own personal conviction and conscience. It is a matter of your own personal belief of right or wrong."
— Dan Inosanto, *The Filipino Martial Arts* (p. 168)

"Self-defense is not murder!"
— from the script for "Enough"

"Murder weapons — they use whatever's handy. Murder is, in most cases, a spontaneous act, and whatever is the first thing they can pick up is what they're going to use. Bricks and rocks and bottles, electric fans, frying pans, gasoline, table legs. We get a lot of barbecue-fork murders in the summertime."
— anonymous, from Connie Fletcher's *What Cops Know* (p. 71)

"There are a lot of people in prison, and a lot more in graveyards, because a barroom brawl or streetfight got "out of hand." I don't think those people in prison wanted to go there, and I don't think those people in the graveyard wanted to die. They went to prison or were killed because they did not think beyond some machismo bullshit they were sold at some point in their lives."
— Peyton Quinn

"If somebody pointed a gun in here, sure these people would be nervous, but do they know what a gun could do? Only veterans of combat and cops know what high-velocity gunfire does to a body. You'll see heads completely exploded, limbs torn off. The people sitting here — if somebody pulled out a large hunting knife and went to attack someone else, nobody here knows what would happen. They haven't seen somebody's eye carved out of the head. Do these people in here know how much blood there is with a stabbing — that the heart keeps pumping and there'd be a geyser shooting to the ceiling with every pump? When you've seen this and somebody draws a knife on you, you know you've got just one chance."
— anonymous, from *Pure Cop* by Connie Fletcher (pp. 246-247)

"One thing that must be considered at this point is the issue of blood — there is a terrific amount gushed about in any throat cutting operation. It can squirt back into your mouth — keep it closed; into your eyes — try to avoid it because it will temporarily blind and disconcert you. . . . Be prepared for the bowels and bladder to let go while you're holding him. . . . blood will fall onto your pantleg and shoes. . . . An added precaution could be an overcoat or reversible jacket."
— John Minnery, *How to Kill, Vol. I* (p. 21)

"The straight razor is the weapon most likely to be used to inflict a pressure cut (slice). It is the blade preferred by black women . . . The aptly named screwdriver, the Darth Vader of shanks, is the preferred weapon of the impoverished male sociopath . . . The butcher knife is the weapon of choice of the white working-class woman."
— James LaFond, *The Logic of Steel* (p. 6)

"Murder? Let me tell you about murder . . .
It's fun . . .
It's easy . . .
And you're gonna learn all about it . . ."
— "Tin Tin," from *The Crow* screenplay

"Let us, then, be practical, let us call ourselves murderers as our enemies do, let us take the moral horror out of this great historical tool and just examine closely whether perchance our enemies may claim a special privilege in the matter of murder. If to kill is always a crime, then it is forbidden equally to all; if it is not crime, then it is permitted equally to all. Once one has overcome the

objection that murder per se is a crime, all that remains is to believe one is in the right against one's enemy and to possess the power to obliterate him."
— Karl Heinzen (1849)

"God, if people knew what murder is. So silly, so stupid, so — ugly."
— Ray Bradbury, "A Touch of Petulance"

"It is an awful thing to handle the still-warm body of a man you've just killed. It feels like God has you under a powerful microscope, and is minutely examining the wrinkles and hidden recesses of your soul. It is a moment that is sad, solemn, and utterly lonely."
— Eric L. Haney, *Inside Delta Force* (p. 313)

BAD MUTHAFUKAH

"Until a man is twenty-five, he still thinks, ever so often, that under the right circumstances he could be the baddest motherfucker in the world. If I moved to a martial arts monastery in China and studied real hard for ten years. If my family was wiped out by Columbian drug dealers and I swore myself to revenge. If I got a fatal disease, had one year to live, devoted it to wiping out street crime. If I just dropped out and devoted my life to being bad."
— Neal Stephenson, *Snow Crash* (p. 271)

"Rene' Alleau relates that in each of these schools, men, stripped to the waist and without any defensive weapons, were taught to become hard by such ordeals as fighting off for twelve minutes attack dogs that were unleashed and incited to kill. If the candidates took flight, they were shot. . . . Officer candidates were often told to pull a pin out of a grenade, balance it on their helmets, and

stand at attention until it exploded."
— Dusty Sklar, *Gods and Men* (p. 100)

"Here's to you, as good as you are,
And here's to me, as bad as I am;
But as good as you are, and as bad as I am,
I am as good as you are, as bad as I am."
— olde Scottish toast

"In Texas a cop asked me, 'Excuse me, partner, but . . . why do you and your friends carry those big knives?'
I told him, 'Because we're all felons and we can't carry a big gun like you.'"
— Ralph "Sonny" Barger, HAMC

"There is a story told of a karate master in Japan who was challenged to a fight by a belligerent sailor in a bar. The karate master reluctantly agreed to the contest, but first walked over to a nearby table and picked up a large bread knife. He dropped it on the floor and kicked it over to the astonished sailor. 'Pick it up,' said the martial artist quietly. 'You are going to need it.'"
— recounted by N. Mashiro in *Black Medicine IV, Equalizers* (p. 83)

"I shot two people in December, but neither died . . . Both I sprayed with buckshot. I liked to see the buckshot eat away their clothing, almost like piranha fish."
— Monster Kody Scott

"After I kill you, I'm gonna cut off yer head and take it home to my dog."
— an unknown biker, after being "threatened" by a punk with a set of nunchaku (he ran away when the Bowie knife came out).

"The way of revenge lies in simply forcing one's way into a place and being cut down. . . . No matter if the enemy has thousands of men, there is fulfillment in simply standing them off and being determined to cut them all down, starting from one end."
— Yamamoto Tsunetomo, *Hagakure* (Wilson translation)

"I showered and shaved, put on a chambray shirt with a plain black knit tie under a cream-colored leather jacket. Looked at myself in the mirror and realized it was all for nothing — dressing me up was like tying a red ribbon around the handle of an ice pick."
— Burke, from *Pain Management* by Andrew Vachss

"From what I understand and from how I've seen it used, Drano will cause internal bleeding. It used to be one of the oldest methods, a lot of the pimps would use it on their prostitutes. They would hold them down on the floor and then pour Drano down the person's throat. This would cause convulsions, and the person's insides start bleeding. It eats up the entire body. That is one method commonly used in the Agency."
— Robert J. Hunt

"I see a car following me — I got all kindsa enemies that wanna kill me — so I try to check it out. I sneak up behind it, see two bad-looking dudes. I bang hard on the car with the butt of my gun. They turn quick — it looks to me like they're reaching for guns. I empty my two guns, 26 fucking rounds, into their heads. Then I say, 'Gee, I'm sorry . . . I made a mistake.' Prove me a murderer!"
— an anonymous street narcotics agent, relating how he plotted to kill two inspectors who were dogging him day and night.

"I like to look them in the eyes. I want to see their eyes. At the moment of death — I mean the exact moment — you can see the eyes change, like the eyes of a fish. That's why I love the knife. It's personal. You know what I'm saying? You can feel it; you're part of it. You know what I mean?"
— Roberto Torrez, fmr CIA "asset"

"The guy was a seasoned pro, there's no doubt about that. His fast draw, lack of hesitation or nervousness, and choice of the kneecap as a target all indicate that I was just one more nick in a very notched grip. . . . Amateurs panic, and amateurs waste shots. My guy was cool and calm with his pistol, loose and relaxed. The two-bit street corner version of Al Pacino's Tony Montana in Scarface."
— Chris Pfouts, *Lead Poisoning* (p. 13)

"There have been incidences where people with tattoos — phoney Hell's Angels tattoos — have had them cut off their arms, had the whole tattoo just removed by knife. . . . A lot of people just more or less canned it and showed it around, showed it off. I know one guy, he kept one for a couple of years. It was considered quite a trophy."
— Addie Crouch, HAMC

"Dismemberment is probably the most efficient method of disposal. You'll have to detach yourself from what you're doing, or it could really screw you up emotionally — even some of the toughest criminals I've known would have difficulty cutting a warm human body into pieces. After several hours have passed, the blood will begin to thicken, and the task will be considerably less messy."
— C. R. Jahn, *Hardcore Self-Defense* (p. 161)

"What can I do? The man isn't being reasonable."
— "Don Corleone" from *The Godfather* (paraphrased).

"But — I never killed anyone who didn't *deserve* it!"
— Christopher Walken's character in *King of New York*

"Look carefully at what is in front of you, and listen. I am going to ask you questions, many questions. If you don't answer fully and truthfully, I will untape your left hand, lay it on the table, and hammer a spike through it. Then I'll take that knife and cut your fingers off — one by one. You won't bleed to death. That's an electric soldering-iron. I'll use it to cauterize the stubs."
— A. J. Quinnell, *Man on Fire* (p. 225)

"They have an air of coiled tenseness about them. Motion is something that is done deliberately and with great control, usually very slowly. Something about these people makes you just want to step out of their way when they approach. . . . When they look at you, it's like having a scope dropped on you; a little target is projected on you. . . . The average tough will look at you and try to guess if they could take you out or not. These people look at you and know how they would take you out if they had to."
— Marc "Animal" MacYoung, *Cheap Shots, Ambushes, and Other Lessons* (pp. 134-135)

"You want to avoid any physical hassles with these 'most dangerous' people. Recognize when you are molesting such an individual. If you force him to it and leave him no way out (or he's given reason to believe he is in, or directly headed for, such a situation), then you will die. Do not make the fatal mistake of confusing this with an expression of machismo. It is not. Machismo is a false thing; this is a very real thing. Attacking such a person or his family or even posing to do so is an express ticket to the morgue."
— Peyton Quinn, *A Bouncer's Guide to Barroom Brawling* (p. 18)

"The bad guys kill the bad guys. The bad guys kill the good guys. If you want to survive the bad guys, you have to have some bad in you — a lot actually. You have to know what they know."
— Henry Rollins, *The Portable Henry Rollins* (p. 230)

THE DEMON

"This is the aspect of the Warrior we fear so much within ourselves and others. Whether or not we act out the sociopathic rage that takes us over as the barrier is crossed, we are left afterward with a

feeling that we were not 'ourselves.' Indeed, we were not. This is the 'battle frenzy' and 'blood lust' celebrated by the epics of patriarchal societies and guarded against by its laws."
— Robert Moore & Douglas Gillette, *The Warrior Within* (pp. 133-134)

"Once they see you don't mind dying, they're in serious trouble and know it."
— Marc "Animal" MacYoung

"There was no soul in the eyes, no emotion — They were just eyes."
— Captain Bill O'Rourke

"He had this way of looking at you with his eyes half open. If he looked at me like that, I'd just about freeze."
— Frank Burkhart

"Aiki is the art of defeating your opponent with a single glance."
— Forrest E. Morgan

"Thugs are greatly unsettled by confident opponents. The mugger threatens you and you don't look scared. In fact, you start to grin and circle closer to him. He decides he has made a mistake. Sometimes this will end the situation with no further action."
— N. Mashiro, Ph.D., *Black Medicine IV* (p. 84)

"My temper represented a grave threat to me; it signified a loss of control by the reason and will and a surrender to ungovernable emotion. I felt as if there were a terrible creature within me whom I must never let escape or he'd destroy blindly — friend, foe, and innocent bystander alike."
— G. Gordon Liddy, *Will* (p. 51)

"Everyone . . . bears within him a colossal charge of malice, just as a thundercloud bears its charge of electricity. It is not surprising that for a spetsnaz (soldier) war is just a beautiful dream, the time when he is at last allowed to release his full charge of malice."
— Viktor Suvorov

"The men are loading and firing with demonaical fury and shouting and laughing hysterically."
— unknown Union officer, speaking of Antietam

"Everyone is a moon, and has a dark side which he never shows to anybody."
— Mark Twain

"Kill without joy."
— John Minnery

"The only thing I feel when I kill is the recoil of my weapon."
— seen on an obnoxious T-shirt at a recent S.O.F. convention

"Get down with your bad self!"
— African American colloquialism

"Look through your subject's face and not at it. This will make you appear spiritless and empty hearted, sending no vibration for your subject to read. It will also cast an "empty" emotion over you. When you experience this empty emotion you will have no fear of being attacked."
— Edward Lewis, *Hostile Ground* (p. 5)

"(His) eyes gave him away — they told you what he was. If you studied his pupils you saw that they were as dead and lusterless as tiny brown tombstones; the eyes of someone who kills often and without conscience . . . a CIA agent I knew once called them 'executioner's eyes.'"
— Michael Levine, *The Big White Lie* (p. 31)

"For over ten years, my primary function was to kill — but I don't consider myself a 'bad guy' seeing as these skills were never misused; however, the indoctrination I received combined with all the shit I've been through really fucked up my programming — they call it PTSD, although I don't exhibit a lot of the symptoms of this disgusting weakness. What happens sometimes, if someone is attempting to physically intimidate me or if some truck starts tailgating me, or if I feel threatened in any significant way, It seems like my entire personality is shoved aside and something else suddenly appears in its place. This demonic self is either cold as ice or really pissed off, and it deals with hostile persons in a socially unacceptable manner. I try to keep the demon on a very short leash, but it's hard sometimes."
— anonymous (RWT)

"In violence, we forget who we are."
— Mary McCarthy, *On the Contrary*

"The youth had been taught that a man became another thing in a battle. He saw his salvation in such a change."
— Stephen Crane, *The Red Badge of Courage* (p. 28)

"Think of the situation like a computer would, in cold rational terms. Erase the opponent's face, his clothing, and his words . . . become ruthlessly calm and viciously calculating and turn off your emotions. You can deal with them later, after you've dealt with the attacker."
— Richard Ryan, *Master of the Blade* (p. 80)

"As your targeting mechanism locks onto your opponent's killzones, you tense ready to spring and fix him with a steady unwavering glare. Your face is flat and emotionless, as is your voice. You temporarily become a psychopath capable of killing another human being as if he were simply an annoying fly to be swatted. There is no need to shout, go into a fancy stance, or puff yourself up — that simply shows that you are afraid of him. Simply fix him with your stare and slowly declare your intentions in a low monotone: 'If you do not go away, I am going to kill you.' If you mean what you say, and truly intend to kill him, then something very unusual happens to your eyes. Your opponent looks into them and sees no warmth or fear there — only coldness and death. He sees that he is fucking with some inhuman thing that will neither retreat nor show any mercy."
— Jake Bishop (RWT)

"The epitome of skill among the most proficient navajeros in the gitano style is the ability to reach the state known as duende (DWEN-deh). The word duende literally means 'demon' or spirit.' Achieving this state — whether in dance or in knife combat — implies the presence of something magical or supernatural; that one is moving as if possessed. The state is more difficult to explain than to understand. . . . With his knife drawn, he does not follow any strict rules of steps or techniques; instead, his movements surge up as instinctive and spontaneous expressions of the moment. In essence then, achieving duende signifies a kind of possession by some mysterious force, driving the navajero to a lethally artistic display of ability that far exceeds the bounds of mere technique."
— James Loriega, *Sevillian Steel* (p. 59)

"There was a buzzing in his head and a red veil slid over his eyes as he turned, robot-like."
— C. R. Jahn, *Underground* (p. 240)

"It takes a certain something (or lack of something) to be able to look a man in the eyes as you're twisting a blade deep in his guts, or to methodically pump round after round into his center of mass without flinching. This is a valid, crucial, and widely misunderstood aspect of the Warrior's persona. You see, it is imperative that a Warrior be psychologically capable of performing such an act, however, it is equally imperative that these negative thoughts be suppressed if one is to be part of a civilized society. Only immature freaks and psychotic goblins fixate upon such negativity. Certain psychologists have dubbed this state of mind 'the demonic self.' Indicators that the demonic self is online are: expressionless face, unblinking eyes, color drains from skin, body temperature drops, and a surreal calmness permeates. For the duration of this state, an individual can no longer be considered a fellow human being. In a combat scenario, such an individual will be transformed into an unstoppable killing machine, totally focused on a single destructive goal. After a time, it will

be possible to enter this state instantly and at will — much like the act of flipping a switch.
— anonymous (RWT)

"Andrew Vachss speaks of the 'Ice God' in many of his Burke novels. This is a state of sociopathic transcendence in which fear of death — and indeed, all vestiges of human emotion — ceases to exist. Once communion with the Ice God has been achieved, he becomes a part of you forever; and although he abstains from interfering with your daily activities, he is always present, and can be accessed in a heartbeat if the need ever arises."
— Scribe 27 (RWT)

"Once a confrontation turns physical, the warrior's body, mind, and spirit fuse into an unthinking, unfeeling weapon. At this point, there are no considerations of honor, no thought of consequences. In this mode, the warrior will only think of destroying his enemy."
— Forrest E. Morgan, *Living the Martial Way* (p. 165)

"Release the fiend that lies dormant within you, for he is strong and ruthless and his power is far beyond the bounds of human frailty."
— Robert DeGrimston

OUTLAWS

"They branded us as outlaws. We know, as you, only outlaws can be free."
— excerpted from the introduction of *Hell's Angels Forever*

"You only carried a gun when you wanted to do business with it. That's a very disrespectful thing to do, carry a weapon into a meeting. Among criminals, they have their own code of ethics. If you and I are going to sit down and do a deal of stolen merchandise or dope and we're just in the talking stages of it, why do I need to have a gun at the table? I am either a cop or extremely paranoid about my own survival or I'm out to do something to you. Then nobody will deal with me and how am I going to make any money? So that's the reason you don't carry that weapon."
— anonymous, from Mark Baker's *Cops* (p. 136)

"The question of how you will respond to a confrontation with police at the scene of a crime, or in the immediate area, is one that must be examined carefully and thoroughly. Most often, this very real possibility isn't even considered, yet such a confrontation could create life threatening circumstances."
— Harold S. Long

"When the wind kicked up, I could smell the plants and it seemed unreal to me that this idyllic, starry night could at any moment be raided by a bunch of pissed-off, caffeine-wired, wife-beating federal agents, and we'd all spend the next ten or twenty years behind bars."
— Chris Simunek, *Paradise Burning* (p. 20)

"You should always strive to steer clear of any form of intoxicant. Booze and drugs can really fuck up your life . . . except for reefer . . . marijuana really gives you a mellower perspective of things . . . it really helped me to curb my violent impulses and self-destructive tendencies."
— Tony Miles

"I'm one with my gun,
I love it like my first son,
It protects me,
And makes sure that the jakes respect me."
— Talib Kweli, "Sharp Shooters"

"We do a job together. I don't know your real name. The only people that know the real names are the president and the treasury, for bail purposes. We do something together. They can put a polygraph on me, I still don't know your name. . . . They could ask me your real name . . . and I wouldn't know it."
— Edward Jackson, Pagans Motorcycle Club

"You fucked with Death, and now she's your wife . . ."
— overheard being spoken to the deceased at an open casket "one-percenter" funeral

"I got no love for a brother who comes to the party with no bud."
— "B-Real" of Cypress Hill

"There are a few good cops out there — most of the best cops, however, never intended to go into law-enforcement as a career — they might've originally been social workers, teachers, or graduate students before going through some sort of existential crisis (or something) which made them suddenly decide to enroll in the police academy -- and then they discovered that they really liked it. These individuals tend to reflect well upon their new profession, and usually do quite well at it. Conversely, those individuals who have 'always wanted to be a cop' often get involved with police work due to some deep rooted inadequacy which they hope to compensate for by acquiring the symbols of authority. Law-enforcement has always held a great attraction for bullies and other control freaks."
— anonymous (RWT)

"Let's say that you happen to find yourself in a situation where you might be considered a 'material witness' to a crime. Maybe someone who really fuckin' deserved it got whapped upside the head with a ballpeen hammer, or sumpthin. Anyway, the cops come around and ask you what happened, since (possibly due to the splatter marks) you were obviously in close proximity to the incident. What do you say? If you say, 'I ain't tellin' you shit,' then you can be jailed for obstruction of justice; if you exercise your 'right to remain silent,' you can be jailed as an accessory; if you say 'That guy with the bloody hammer didn't do it,' you'd be lying (which is dishonorable); and if you fucking rat someone out (especially if they were justified in their actions), then you are lower than dogshit and oughta be hammered on yourself! No, in a situation like this, it's usually best just ta calm down and say, 'Officer, my back was turned when this occurred, so unfortunately I didn't see nuthin."
— anonymous (RWT)

"He told me that if I was ever stranded on the side of the road, broke down or in trouble, and if a (Hell's Angel) came by, accept their help. Trust them. Nothing bad would come of it. They'd do me right. He even went on to say that if the politicians ran the country like the Club ran its chapters, we'd all be much freer. I think he admired their honor system and the fact that with bike riders, a handshake was a handshake and a deal was a deal."
— Barbara McQueen, speaking of her departed husband, Steve.

"The outlaw trail is like the path of the wolf: it teaches you much about life and gives you an understanding of how things work. It can also be an insane, lonely, and vicious path."
— Marc "Animal" MacYoung, *Pool Cues, Beer Bottles, & Baseball Bats* (pp. ix-x)

"It's good to be known as a thief when you go Inside. It's even better to be known as a killer, but only a certain kind. Like if you killed someone in a fight, that would be good. Or if someone paid you to do it. . . . But not every killing got you respect. The sick-in-the-head kids, they were nothings. Nobody was afraid of them. Like the one who chopped up his mother with an ax. Or the one who went to school with a rifle, and shot a bunch of other kids who were bullying him. After that kid got locked up, he still got bullied, only much worse. The kind of bullying they do in here."
— Andrew Vachss, *The Getaway Man* (p. 4)

"No-one knows what it's like,
To be the bad man. . .
To be the sad man. . .
Behind blue eyes."
— The Who, "Behind Blue Eyes"

"I suppose that in any well-ordered society people like us would be locked up or shot. But then you would have to get people like us to do the locking up and the shooting."
— Jim Morris, *War Story* (p. 158)

PEACE

"You dumbasses need to know that the alleged 'peace sign' is, in actuality, the depiction of a cursed amulet!!! Do you realize that, when it was officially adopted as the symbol of the peace movement its origin and true significance was completely unknown? The Fundies like to call it the 'cross of Nero,' but they are a bunch of ignoramuses. Do you want to know what this evil symbol really means? It is an ancient symbol known as 'the dead man's rune.' When you invert the protection rune, it becomes a curse, drawing to the bearer strife, harm, injury, illness, and persecution. Binding it within a circle increases its power. The leaders of this country belong to secret societies which practice ceremonial Teutonic magick, and, along with the neurological agent LSD, they used highly-placed infiltrators to thrust this cursed thing upon the peaceniks — the better to wipe them out!!!"
— Scribe 27 (RWT)

"Go placidly amid the noise & haste; and remember what peace there may be in silence."
— *Desdirada* (line one)

"To be prepared for war is one of the most effectual means of preserving peace."
— General George Washington

"If this endeavor of ours to arrive at peace fails, we have our armaments to fall back upon."
— Woodrow Wilson

"The more peace there is in us, the more peace there will be in our troubled world."
— Etty Hillesum

"Peace is the skillful management of conflict."
— Kenneth Boulding

"Many soldiers — tired by the rigidities of normal life — look back at violent moments of their war experiences despite the hunger and terror, as the monumental culminating experiences of their

lives."
— Joost van Meerlo

"It is worth noting that retired officers are amongst those professional groups with the highest rate of suicide, in part because the military values which they have acquired during their service often conflict with the values of civilian society."
— Richard Holmes

"They have not wanted Peace at all; they have wanted to be spared war — as though the absence of war was the same as peace."
— Dorothy Thompson

"Well, I have tried to be meek.
And I have tried to be mild,
But I spat like a woman,
And sulked like a child,
I have lived behind walls,
That have made me alone,
Striven for peace,
Which I never have known."
— Dire Straits, "The Man's Too Strong"

"While the Swiss believes in peace, and desires it above all else, his good sense tells him this is best assured by preparedness at all times."
— Colonel George Bell

". . . I am tired; my heart is sick and sad. From where the sun now stands I will fight no more forever."
— Chief Joseph of the Nez Perce

"Culture and Peace are the most sacred goals of humanity."
— Nicholas Roerich

"Who desires peace, let him prepare for war."
— Vegetius (4th c.)

"It seems to me that there are two great enemies of peace — fear and selfishness."
— Katherine Paterson, *The Horn Book*

"It's perfectly true that Israel wants peace. So did Hitler. Everybody wants peace. The question is, on what terms?"
— Noam Chomsky

"First keep the peace within yourself, then you can also bring peace to others."
— Thomas a Kempis (1420)

"They have not wanted Peace at all; they have wanted to be spared war — as though the absence of war was the same as peace."
— Dorothy Thompson, *On the Record*

"There can be no peace without law."
— Dwight D. Eisenhower

"The arts of peace are great,
And no less glorious than those of war."
— William Blake, *King Edward III*

"He had rid himself of the red sickness of battle. The sultry nightmare was in the past. He had been an animal blistered and sweating in the heat and pain of war. He turned now with a lover's thirst to images of tranquil skies, fresh meadows, cool brooks — an existence of soft and eternal peace."
— Stephen Crane, *The Red Badge of Courage* (p. 156)

LIFE

"You are enrolled in a full-time informal school called LIFE. Each day in this school, you will have the opportunity to learn lessons. You may like the lessons, or think them irrelevant and stupid."
— Seneca Wolf Clan Teaching Lodge

"Life itself is your teacher, and you are in a state of constant learning."
— Bruce Lee

"Human incarnation is not simply an opportunity to learn, but rather an obligation to participate in humankind's condition, purpose, and responsibilities."
— Anderson Reed, *Shouting at the Wolf* (p. 9)

"One of the greatest sins is the unlived life."
— John O'Donohue

"Dost thou love life? Then do not squander time, for that is the stuff life is made of."
— Benjamin Franklin, *Poor Richard's Almanac*

"All the things that used to bother me are so small and silly. I know what life is worth, now I've seen so much death."
— unknown Israeli paratrooper

"Life is a tragedy for those who feel, and a comedy for those who think."
— Jean de la Bruyere

"Life is the span of time appointed for accomplishment. Every fleeting moment is an opportunity,

and those who are great are the ones who have recognized life as the opportunity for all things."
— Manly P. Hall

"Human beings are afraid of dying. They are always running after something: money, honor, pleasure. But if you had to die right now, what would you want?"
— Taisen Deshimaru

"Dreams are real while they last. Can we say any more of life?"
— Havelock Ellis

"Life is real! Life is earnest!
And the grave is not its goal."
— Longfellow

"Life is not a spectacle or a feast; it is a predicament."
— George Santayana

"You've never lived until you've almost died. For those who have had to fight for it, life has a flavour the protected will never know."
— Theodore Roosevelt

"Everybody dies, but not everybody lives."
— Thomas Lynch

"All life is an experiment."
— Ralph Waldo Emerson

"It was easy to read the message in his entrails. Man was matter, that was (his) secret. Drop him out a window and he'll fall. Set fire to him and he'll burn. Bury him and he'll rot, like other kinds of garbage. The spirit gone, man is garbage."
— Joseph Heller, *Catch-22* (p. 554)

". . . the stoics regarded life as a difficult voyage in which most men are shipwrecked; they felt that man's only chance of escaping shipwreck was through reason and self-discipline."
— Colin Wilson

"Life is suffering."
— Buddha

"Although the world is full of suffering, it is also full of the overcoming of it."
— Helen Keller

"We are not human beings having a spiritual experience. We are spiritual beings having a human experience."
— Pierre Teilhard de Chardin

"Our truest life is when we are in dreams awake."
— Henry David Thoreau

"Life does not accommodate you, it shatters you. It is meant to, and it couldn't do it better. Every seed destroys its container or else there would be no fruition."
— Florida Scott-Maxwell, *The Measure of My Days*

"I am one of those people who just can't help getting a kick out of life — even when it's a kick in the teeth."
— Polly Adler, *A House Is Not a Home*

"Life is an illusion."
— Mata Hari, as she prepared to meet the firing squad in 1917

"Life was meant to be lived, and curiosity must be kept alive. One must never, for whatever reason, turn his back on life."
— Eleanor Roosevelt

"Life is either a daring adventure or nothing. To keep our faces toward change and behave like free spirits in the presence of fate is strength undefeatable."
— Helen Keller

"What, after all, is human life if not a continuous performance in which all go about wearing different masks, in which everyone acts a part assigned to him until the stage director removes him from the boards?"
— Erasmus

"Once weaned from the ephemeral craving for TV, most people will find they enjoy the time they spend reading. I'd like to suggest that turning off that endlessly quacking box is apt to improve the quality of your life as well as the quality of your writing."
— Stephen King, *On Writing* (p. 148)

"Life is better than death, I believe, if only because it is less boring, and because it has fresh peaches in it."
— Alice Walker

"Life, being sacred, demands our full participation."
— Starhawk, *Dreaming the Dark* (p. 42)

"Death belongs to life as birth does. The walk is in the raising of the foot as in the laying of it down."
— Rabindranath Tagore, *Stray Birds* (CCLXVII)

"What would the engineer say, after you had explained your problem and enumerated all of the dissatisfactions in your life? He would probably tell you that life is a very hard and complicated thing; that no interface can change that; that anyone who believes otherwise is a sucker; and that if you don't like having choices made for you, you should start making your own."
— Neal Stephenson, *In the Beginning . . . Was the Command Line* (p. 151)

"People say that what we're all seeking is a meaning for life. I don't think that's what we're really seeking. I think that what we're seeking is an experience of being alive, so that our life experiences on the purely physical plane will have resonances within our innermost being and reality, so that we actually feel the rapture of being alive."
— Joseph Campbell, *The Power of Myth*

PSEUDOSPECIATION

"Pseudospeciation is the ability to assign inferior and subhuman qualities to one's enemy."
— unknown

"Sometimes people denigrate others to justify maltreatment of them. To reassure ourselves that the things we do and the lives we lead are proper, we rationalize our actions. We can feel justified in discriminating, subjugating, enslaving, or even killing others, if we are able to convince ourselves that the other group is inferior, immoral, or less than human."
— from the textbook *Contemporary Social Problems*, 2nd edition (p. 257)

"Most people believe that it is wrong to kill another human being, yet we send our young off to war and expect them to rapidly change their beliefs and begin killing on command. To facilitate this change, we often use new words, commonly racist in nature."
— Col. John B. Alexander, Major Richard Groller, and Janet Morris, *The Warrior's Edge* (p. 24)

"To poison the mind of an individual against some other individual is an easy, all-too-common practice — so common that the phrase describing it is familiar in all languages. . . . Poisoning group minds against other groups is an equally familiar phenomenon. Common metaphors frequently conceal deep metaphysical truths. The term 'spellbinder' — originally applied only to an actual witch or sorcerer — has become a common appellation for the rabble-rousing orator. Baboon talk, direct in its appeal to the emotions, short-circuiting the mind and substituting 'feeling' for 'thinking' sets nations at each other's throats. Adolf Hitler was a bloodier witch and weaver of evil incantations than the foulest witch in any German fairy tale."
— William Seabrook, *Witchcraft* (p. 84)

"The key to success is the fact that most barroom brawlers and marauding motorists share a common failing: they're assholes."
— N. Mashiro, Ph.D.

"There is good clinical evidence for the assumption that destructive aggression occurs, at least to a large degree, in conjunction with a momentary or chronic emotional withdrawal."
— Erich Fromm

"The will to kill, the complete lack of sympathy and compassion, and no hesitation in killing the subject, is paramount. You must take his life as detachedly as you might swat a fly or crush an ant."
— John Minnery

"When I was killing the enemy I was killing a commie. . . . Oh, maybe the first time I saw a dead North Vietnamese I flinched a bit but after that they just became dead animals. It was either he'd shoot me or I'd shoot him and I wasn't shooting at a person. I was shooting at a bunch of ideologies."
— Simon Cole

"I've noticed that the putrid punks and other throwbacks who wander the streets of latter day civilization devise weapons quite similar in construction to stone axes and pikes . . . they are as deadly as the bludgeons and flint knives that earlier savages created from the shadows of their bestial and soulless minds."
— Fred Rexer, Jr.

"All these people start filing out of the bar — they're winos, street people, buzzards, lowlifes. They really are skeletons. Scumbags, street urchins; they're white, black; their teeth are rotted."
— Bill McCarthy

"Slime, sleaze, rejects. Crooked, bent, needing to straighten out. Rascals, hooligans, thieves, scoundrels. Corrupt, rotten, stinking. Shitheads, assholes. People with no respect for the law, the straight and narrow, the right way, the one way. People who don't fear God or man. Animals, perverts, dogs, mongrels, coyotes. Mixed-up, confused, crazy, insane, psychopathic. Wayward souls, lost souls, ingrates. Butchers, skull-bashers, cold-blooded murderers. Cold as ice — they'd rob their own mothers."
— Jerry Fjerkenstad

"They peep out from under cardboard crates, cursing me under their breath. They parade up and

down the street day after day, year after year, screaming at invisible foes. Their hearts are pumping, but their brains are stalled. Their minds are warped from booze, neglect, religion, and war. They contribute nothing to society. Their unnecessary lives are carried out on a dead-end street."
— Debbie Goad

"By thinking abstractly, and identifying your opponent as something 'subhuman' (for example: a goblin, troll, zombie, or caveman), it is possible to achieve a killer mindset in short order. By visualizing such a loathsome creature standing before you, you will automatically expect to be lied to and misdirected prior to your attempted victimization, so it is highly unlikely that you will be tricked or surprised. Furthermore, you will not hesitate to respond to a perceived threat, and you will strive to inflict maximum damage forthwith."
— C. R. Jahn, *Hardcore Self-Defense* (p. 12)

"When you have your boot on someone's neck, you have to justify it. The justification has to be their depravity."
— Noam Chomsky

WORLD WAR III

"Mankind must put an end to war, or war will put an end to mankind."
— this quote has been attributed to both John F. Kennedy and Martin Luther King Jr.

"It seems politically impossible for a capitalist democracy to organize expenditure on the scale necessary to make the grand experiment which would prove my case — except in war conditions."
— John Maynard Keynes

"World War III will be a guerilla information war, with no division between military and civilian participation."
— Marshall McLuhan

"While in theory there is nothing which is absolutely inevitable, in actuality there are things which are almost inevitable. People believe that wars happen in the future, whereas in reality they happen in the past; the fighting is only a consequence of many events which have already occurred. Viewed from this perspective, all the causes of the Third World War have already happened. There is therefore only a very remote possibility that the conflict itself will not take place."

— Osho

"I don't know what weapons will be used in World War III, but I do know World War IV will be fought with spears and clubs!"
— Albert Einstein

"There will be entirely new weapons. In one day more men will die than in all previous wars combined. . . . Gigantic catastrophes will occur. . . . The third great war will be the end of many nations."
— Stormberger (18th c.)

"The whole country will become so utterly desolated and depopulated that the crow of a cock shall not be heard, deer and other animals shall be exterminated by horrid black rain."
— Brahan Seer (1665)

"If only one-third of humanity will survive it is better!"
— Meishu-Sama (1955)

DISHONOR

"There are mistakes too monstrous for remorse . . ."
— Edwin Arlington Robinson

"When honour's lost, 'tis a relief to die;
Death's but a sure retreat from infamy."
— Samuel Garth

"There is a boundary in each man. He can eat crow and brown-nose to an extent. He can shuck the Man for a while, become a good "actor." But when a man goes beyond the last essential boundary, it alters his ontology, so to speak. It's like the small pebble that starts a landslide no-one can stop. You can betray the pigs until, lo, you've betrayed yourself. You want to survive so badly, to be free of violence so terribly, you will literally do anything after you start across that boundary. You'll allow anyone to order you around. You'll let your ma, wife, kids die just to stay alive yourself. You'll

wallow in the gutter of man's soul to live. You'll suck every cock in the cellhouse to "get along".
There is nothing you won't do."
— Jack Henry Abbott

"This is the punishment of a liar: He is not believed even when he speaks the truth."
— Babylonian *Talmud*

"Lying was not condemned as sin, but simply denounced as weakness, and, as such, highly
dishonorable."
— Nitobe, on Bushido

"There smites nothing so sharp, nor smelleth so sour
As shame."
— William Langland

"To do injustice is more disgraceful than to suffer it."
— Plato

"He will find ways to disrupt your family life or damage your standing at work. He will do things
like start painful rumors or manipulate people around you through lies and deception. His motive is
to get others to harm you for him. He doesn't care if you are harmed physically, emotionally, or
financially."
— Edward Lewis, *Hostile Ground* (p. 11)

"Mother, your eyes have gone suddenly cold,
And it wasn't what I was expecting.
Once I did think that I'd find comfort there,
And instead you've gone hard and suspecting. . ."
— Suzanne Vega, "Bad Wisdom"

"We should not pity or pardon those who have yielded to great temptation, or, perchance, great
provocation. Besides, it is right that our sympathies should be kept for the injured."
— Benjamin Disraeli

"Truthfulness has never been counted among the political virtues, and lies have always been
regarded as justifiable tools in political dealings."
— Hannah Arendt, *Crises of the Republic*

"Of course the ideal samurai was as rare as the courteous knight. In both Europe and Japan a satiric literature chronicles the misdeeds of these 'sacred' warriors. Sadistic cruelty, an exaggerated sense of personal honor, or just plain foolishness was the stuff of these satires."
— Robert Moore & Douglas Gillette, *The Warrior Within* (p. 84)

"I know that we all stumble down dark paths and we don't quite know what to make of life. But if you are reading this and you ever get to the point in your life where you want to fuck or murder a kid, forget prison. You've got to kill yourself."
— Dennis Miller, *Comic Relief* (p. 144)

"Having the thoughts is sick. Acting on those thoughts is evil."
— Andrew Vachss

"Lying is an accursed vice. It is only our words which bind us together and make us human. If we realized the horror and weight of lying, we would see it as more worthy of the stake than other crimes."
— Montaigne

"Remember the Oliver North trial? Even though years have passed, I can't figure that one out. He was dismissed from the military, right? But when he went to court he wore his uniform. Now I've been fired from a lot of jobs, but you don't see me tooling around in my Burger King outfit."
— Bob Goldthwait, *Comic Relief* (p. 178)

"Don't step on your dick."
— old biker sayin'

COWARDICE

"To see what is right and to not do it is want of courage."
— Confucius

"Lying is not so much an act of immorality as it is one of cowardice."
— Forrest E. Morgan

"A sword is useless in the hands of a coward."
— unknown

"Experience shows that in the overwhelming majority of cases the sadist is a coward, incapable of sacrificing himself."
— Victor Suvorov

"The attacker is generally a coward who either fights under the influence of alcohol or drugs or attacks from the rear, possibly with a weapon or an accomplice(s) or both."
— Geoff Thompson

"If you love wealth better than liberty, the tranquility of servitude better than the animating contest of freedom, go home from us in peace. We ask not your counsels or arms. Crouch down and lick the hands which feed you; may your chains set lightly upon you and may posterity forget that ye were our countrymen."
— Samuel Adams (1776)

"A cowardly man thinks he will live forever
If he can avoid fighting
But old age will give him no mercy
Though he be spared by spears"
— *Havamal*, verse 16, Plowright translation

"Despair and postponement are cowardice and defeat. Man were born to succeed, not to fail."
— Henry David Thoreau

"I've got no problem with pacifists — as long as they're willing to use limited violence against criminals who would deliberately harm those whose safety they're directly responsible for. If a man won't stand up to defend a woman or child, then he's nothing but a fucking coward — philosophical bullshit aside."
— anonymous (RWT)

"Ridicule is a weak weapon, when leveled at a strong mind; But common men are cowards and dread an empty laugh."
— Martin Farquhar Tupper

"A coward threatens when he is safe."
— Johann Wolfgang von Goethe

"Don't be a wussy!"
— Papa Titus

ASSOCIATES

"A man's friendships are one of the best measures of his worth."
— Charles Darwin

"Be courteous to all, but intimate with few; and let those few be well tried before you give them your confidence."
— George Washington

"Associate yourself with men of good quality if you esteem your own reputation; for 'tis better to be alone than in bad company."
— George Washington

"People should learn to see and avoid all danger. Just as a wise man keeps away from mad dogs, so one should not make friends with evil men."
— Buddha

"Call it a clan, call it a network, call it a tribe, call it a family. Whatever you call it, whoever you are, you need one."
— Jane Howard, *Families*

"To betray you must first belong."
— Harold Philby

"While honourable associates will enhance you, there are some who will only drag you down. It may be difficult to deal with such people because, being an honourable person yourself, you feel that you owe them loyalty for their friendship. This problem is not easily resolved. You may be able to lead by example, or talk them into improving themselves; you may find that you have to just start to distance yourself and gradually let them go their own way. You may have to tell them to get lost. . . . try not to waste your energy and wyrd on those who are unworthy."
— Sweyn Plowright, *True Helm* (p. 23)

"Sometimes people will make friends who engage in dangerous practices such as car-theft, shoplifting or periodic disruptive drunkenness. The person who travels with such a crowd while not engaging in any of these activities must know, in his deeper self, that he takes an awful chance of being arrested along with his friends and charged, even imprisoned, despite his innocence. People who travel with dangerous crowds are excitement junkies."
— Anderson Reed, *Shouting at the Wolf* (p. 174)

"O wise man, wash your hands of that friend who associates with your enemies."
— Saadi

"Always have distinguished friends. Never have fools for friends, they are of no use."
— Benjamin Disraeli

"Beware of the man who has no regard for his own reputation, since it is not likely he should have any for yours."

— George Shelley

"Every dunderhead needs a sidekick."
— Grandfather

". . . it is better not to become acquainted with men about whom you have formerly had some doubts. No matter what you do, they will be people by whom you will be tripped up or taken in."
— Yamamoto Tsunetomo, *Hagakure* (Wilson translation)

"True friends are like diamonds, precious and rare. False friends are like autumn leaves, found everywhere."
— Bruce Lee

PHILOSOPHY

"Without philosophy one should be little above animals."
— Voltaire

"Philosophy
Is a walk on the slippery rocks,
Religion
Is the smile on a dog."
— Edie Brickell, "What I Am"

"Try not to become a man of success, but rather a man of value."
— Albert Einstein

"As far as possible, without surrender, be on good terms with all persons."
— *Desdirada* (line two)

"Speak your truth quietly and clearly; and listen to others, even the dull & ignorant, for they too have their story."
— *Desdiada* (line three)

"Competition is natural to the ignorant; and cooperation is natural to the wise."
— Manly P. Hall

"The map is not the territory."
— Alfred Korzybsky

"Mistrust the people and they become untrustworthy."
— I Ching

"One of the reasons people stop learning is that they become less and less willing to risk failure."
— John W. Gardner

"The risk of insult is the price of clarity. To be clearly understood one must speak the simple, essential truth as plainly as he is able."
— Roy H. Williams

"Greatness requires the taking of risks. That's why so few ever achieve it."
— unknown

"So you will see how absurd is the whole structure that you have built, looking for external help, depending on others for your comfort, for your happiness, for your strength. These can only be found within yourselves."
— Krishnamurti

"Horror is that which we have not yet come to terms with."
— Ramsey Campbell

"Each experience teaches us a lesson."
— unknown

"Those who cannot remember the past are condemned to repeat it."
— Santayana

"Self-education makes great men."
— unknown

"Procrastination is the thief of time."
— Edward Young

"If you want to learn new things, you should try reading old books."
— unknown

"Quarrel is the weapon of the weak."
— unknown

"The great extension of our experience in recent years has brought to light the insufficiency of our simple mechanical conceptions and, as a consequence, has shaken the foundation on which the customary interpretation of observation was based."
— Niels Bohr

"You have to try and learn something new every day."
— Grandfather

"Procrastination is one of the worst things you can ever do."
— Grandfather

"Beware the fury of a patient man."
— Dryden, *Absalom and Achitophel*, I

"To waste time is to expend it thoughtlessly or carelessly. We all have time to either spend or waste and it is our decision what to do with it. But once passed, it is gone forever."
— Bruce Lee

"There are old bikers, and there are bold bikers, but there ain't no old, bold bikers."
— classic biker aphorism

"Shit Happens. . ."
— classic biker aphorism

"You can't polish a turd. . ."
— old hillbilly sayin'

"Don't piddle where you fiddle."
— seen on a bottlecap from "Magic Hat Brewing Company"

"Knowing others is wisdom, knowing yourself is Enlightenment."
— Lao Tzu

"Only after he has gained the trust of the common people does the gentleman work them hard, for otherwise they would feel themselves ill-used. Only after he has gained the trust of the lord does the gentleman advise him against unwise action, for otherwise the lord would feel himself slandered."
— Tzu-hsia

"There are three things which the gentleman values most in the Way: to stay clear of violence by putting on a serious countenance, to come close to being trusted by setting a proper expression on his face, and to avoid being boorish and unreasonable by speaking in proper tones."
— Confucius

"Human beings are afraid of dying. They are always running after something: money, honor, pleasure. But if you had to die now, what would you want?"
— Taisen Deshmaru

"The man who enjoys keenly, is subject to keen suffering; while he who feels but little pain is capable of feeling but little joy."
— *Kybalion*

"My religion is Kindness."
— the Dalai Lama

"Selfishness is the root of all evil."
— Scribe 27 (RWT)

"Wisdom is crystallized pain."
— Dr. Rudolf Steiner

"All that we are is the result of what we have thought. The mind is everything. What we think, we become."
— Buddha

"Human beings can alter their lives by altering their attitudes of mind."
— William James

"There are four things that come not back:
The spoken word,
The sped arrow,
The past life,
The neglected opportunity."
— Omar of Persia

"Do more than exist — live.
Do more than touch — feel.
Do more than look — observe.
Do more than read — absorb.
Do more than hear — listen.
Do more than listen — understand."
— John H. Rhoades

"Happiness is that state of consciousness which proceeds from the achievement of one's values."
— Ayn Rand, *Atlas Shrugged*

"The nine impediments that hinder the mind or consciousness from gaining tranquility are disease, mental sluggishness, doubt, carelessness, physical laziness, uncontrolled sensual craving, delusion, lack of perseverance and instability."

— Patanjali, *Samadhipada*, #30

"As a human being, you have no choice about the fact that you need a philosophy. Your only choice is whether you define your philosophy by a conscious, rational, and disciplined process of thought and scrupulously logical deliberation — or let your subconscious accumulate a junk heap of unwarranted conclusions, false generalizations, undefined contradictions, undigested slogans, unidentified wishes, doubts and fears, thrown together by chance, but integrated by your subconscious into a kind of mongrel philosophy and fused into a single, solid weight: self-doubt, like a ball and chain in the place of where your mind's wings should have grown."
— Ayn Rand, *Philosophy: Who Needs It?*

"THE ALL IS UNKNOWABLE. All the theories, guesses, and speculations of the theologians and metaphysicians regarding the inner nature of the ALL are but childish efforts to grasp the secret of the Infinite. Such efforts have always failed and will always fail, from the very nature of the task. And still more presumptuous are those who attempt to ascribe to the ALL the personalities, characteristics, and attributes of themselves, ascribing to the ALL the human emotions, feelings, and characteristics, even down to the pettiest qualities of mankind, such as jealousy, susceptibility to flattery and praise, and desire for offerings and worship. The ALL is Infinite Living Mind — the Illumined call it SPIRIT!"
— *Kybalion*

"Mountains cannot be your guru . . . . Are you able to have a little room where you can close the door and be alone? . . . That is your cave. That is your sacred mountain. That is where you will find the kingdom of God."
— Ram Gopal Babu, from *Autobiography of a Yogi* by Paramahansa Yogananda (p. 161)

"It hath been said that the continuation of the species is due to man's forgiving. Forgiveness is holiness; by forgiveness the universe is held together. Forgiveness is the might of the mighty; forgiveness is sacrifice; forgiveness is quiet of mind. Forgiveness and gentleness are the qualities of the Self-possessed. They represent eternal virtue."
— *Mahabharata*

"A human being should be able to change a diaper, plan an invasion, butcher a hog, conn a ship, design a building, write a sonnet, balance accounts, build a wall, set a bone, comfort the dying, take orders, give orders, cooperate, act alone, pitch manure, solve equations, analyze a new problem, program a computer, cook a tasty meal, fight efficiently, die gallantly. Specialization is for the insects."
— Robert Heinlein, *The Notebooks of Lazarus Long*

". . . any virtue becomes a vice unless it is balanced by its own opposite. Beauty, when unsustained

by strength, is vapid, lifeless. Power is insufferable when untempered by compassion. Honor, unless balanced by humility, becomes arrogance; and mirth, when not deepened by reverence, becomes mere superficiality."
— Starhawk, *The Spiral Dance* (p. 84)

"To the pure, all things are pure; to the base, all things are base."
— *Kybalion*

"Don't get involved in a threesome — someone always gets pissed off."
— Papa Titus

"Don't put yer food in the microwave — it turns it all backwards and shit."
— Scribe 27 (RWT)

"The only reason stereotypes exist is because they happen to be accurate so damn often."
— Spider 1%er

"Hell is other people."
— Jean-Paul Sartre

"Never forget what a man says to you when he is angry."
— Henry Ward Beecher, *Life Thoughts*

"Reading is to the mind what exercise is to the body."
— Richard Steele

"A man's got to know his limitations."
— unknown

"Estrangement permeates our society so strongly that to us it seems to be consciousness itself. Even the language for other possibilities has disappeared or been deliberately twisted. Yet another form of consciousness is possible. Indeed, it has existed from earliest times, underlies other cultures, and has survived even in the West in hidden streams. This is the consciousness I call immanence — the awareness of the world and everything in it as alive, dynamic, interdependent, interacting, and infused with living energies: a living being, a weaving dance."
— Starhawk, *Dreaming the Dark* (p. 9)

"The without is like the within of things; the small is like the large."
— Hermes Trimegistus

". . . our physical world of the senses is a mere illusion, a world of shadows, and he three-dimensional tool we call our body serves only as a container or dwelling place for Something infinitely greater and more comprehensive . . ."
— Holger Kalweit, *Dreamtime and Inner Space*

"I believe that the phenomenon is one of the ways through which an intelligence of incredible complexity is communicating with us symbolically. There is no indication that it is extraterrestrial. Instead, there is mounting evidence that it . . . (comes from) other dimensions beyond spacetime; from a multiverse which is all around us, and of which we have stubbornly refused to consider in spite of the evidence available to us for centuries."
— Jacques Vallee, *Dimensions* (p. 284-289)

"There is no reason why anyone cannot get an education if he or she wants it badly enough and is persistent. Most cities have libraries, and often state libraries will mail books to a reader. Books are available on every conceivable subject and there are many good 'how to' books from which one can learn the basics of a trade. . . .Our libraries are not cloisters for an elite. They are for the people, and if they are not used, the fault belongs to those who do not take advantage of their wealth. If one does not move on from what merely amuses to what interests, the fault lies with the reader, for everything is there."
— Louis L'Amour, *Education of a Wandering Man* (pp. 14, 192)

"Don't cry, children — it's Salisbury steak day!"
— "Chef," from the "South Park" cartoon

"I know that I know nothing."
— Socrates

ZEN

"The Way of the Sword and the Way of Zen are identical, for they have the same purpose — that of killing the ego."
— Yamada Jirokichi

"Zen is simply a voice crying, "Wake up! Wake up!"
— Maha Sthavira Sangharakshita

"So, instead of telling us what the problem is, Zen insists that our whole trouble is just our failure to realize that there is no problem. And, of course, this means that there is no solution, either."
— Bruce Lee

"Zen is not interested in high-flown statements; it wants its pupil to bite his apple and not discuss it."
— Anne Bancroft

"To know and to act are one and the same."
— samurai maxim

"To confuse the indivisible nature of reality with the conceptual pigeonholes of language is the basic ignorance from which Zen seeks to free us. The ultimate answers to existence are not to be found in intellectual concepts and philosophies, however sophisticated, but rather in a level of direct nonconceptual experience."
— Robert Sohl and Audrey Carr, *Games Zen Masters Play* (p. 15)

"Traditional karate derives much of its devastating speed from mental processes related to Zen Buddhism, concepts which can be understood by dedicated students but which cannot be expressed in words at all."
— N. Mashiro, Ph.D.

"This mental state (*mushin*, or "mind-no-mind") is the principle source of the traditional warrior's quick reactions, extra-sensory perception, and steely calm."
— Forrest E. Morgan

"Ideally, at some point you enter what servers call a "rhythm" and psychologists term a "flow state," where signals pass from the sense organs directly to the muscles, bypassing the cerebral cortex, and a Zen-like emptiness sets in."
— Barbara Ehrenreich, *Nickel and Dimed* (p. 33)

"There is a common experience in Tai Chi of seemingly falling through a hole in time. Awareness of the passage of time completely stops."
— Tom Horwitz

"Knowing others is wisdom, knowing yourself is Enlightenment."
— Lao Tzu

"Fuckit."
— unknown Ranger combat veteran from *The Deer Hunter*, by E.M. Corder

"When the swordsman stands against his opponent, he is not to think of the opponent, nor of his enemy's sword movements. He just stands there with his sword which, forgetful of all technique, is ready only to follow the dictates of the unconscious. The man has effaced himself as the wielder of the sword. When he strikes, it is not the man but the sword in the hand of the unconscious that strikes."
— Takuan

"Where Zen ends, asskicking begins."
— Richard Marcinko

"If you're going to change, you must KILL YOUR ENTIRE PREVIOUS LIFE — you must DIE to everything you have 'known'."
— The SubGenius Foundation

"Why have you fucked with my serenity?"
— "Chains," the main bad-guy from the great biker movie *Stone Cold*

"I'm here with, basically, nothing to say. And that's what I want to talk to you about tonight. Are you saying what you really mean to say? Do you even know what you're really thinking?"
— J. R. "Bob" Dobbs

". . . a car runs a red light right in front of you. Automatically, you jam on the brakes, tighten up and prepare for the possibility of a crash. During those actions, there were literally hundreds of physiological, psychological and emotional responses occurring in a patterned way, designed to effectively help you. If you had to 'think' . . . you would have had an accident."
— Heller & Steele, *Monsters and Magical Sticks* (p. 67)

"We should do only those righteous actions which we cannot stop ourselves from doing."
— Simone Weil, *Gravity and Grace*

"It all happened in a few seconds, but it felt like hours."
— Ralph "Sonny" Barger, *Ridin' High, Livin' Free* (p. 105)

"When the shit's going down, it's like you're in a time warp, or sumpthin.' You're speedin' down the freeway at 140 mph, and it seems like the other cars are barely movin' at all. Some fucker's charging at you with a naked blade, and it seems like he's runnin' in slow motion. I've actually seen bullets flying through the air just in time to move outta the way! Some folks'll say that sorta thing's 'impossible.' Maybe so, but I know what I've seen, and I know that other people have seen the same thing too. No eggheaded dipshit is gonna be able to convince me that I didn't see these things, because I did."
— anonymous (RWT)

"The most noticeable psychological effect is, as in sensory deprivation, one of the slowing down of time: second hands on clocks seem hardly to move. This sort of 'eternal present' is very much like a prolonged version of the way time can stand still in moments of great personal danger."
— Lyall Watson, *Supernature* (p. 241)

"The speed at which time passes depends on 'absorption,' that is, on how focused the mind is. The reason we assume that all time intervals are the same is that we have invented clocks that measure time as if that were the case — 60 seconds to a minute, 60 minutes to an hour. But in reality we experience time far more subjectively, so that at various times it seems to speed up, slow down, or stand still. In flow, the sense of time adapts itself to the action at hand."
— Mihaly Csikszentmihalyi, *Good Business* (p. 54)

"A mind free of thought,
merged within itself,
beholds the essence of Tao
A mind filled with thought,
identified with its own perceptions,
beholds the mere forms of this world"
— Lao Tzu, *Tao Te Ching, The Definitive Edition* (Star translation), Verse 1

"The idea behind the so-called empty mind is the surcease of all thought. Since we cannot create an empty mind by forcing out our thoughts, we do it by doing nothing at all. We make no attempt at forcing anything to happen to us, or to prevent anything from happening."
— Anderson Reed, *Shouting at the Wolf* (p. 176)

"I have learned that there is a space in my head where I can go where no one can get to me. Often when I'm on the street, that's where I am. I have learned to find open fields in the space of the seat on a bus."
— Henry Rollins, *The Portable Henry Rollins* (p. 242)

"The study of Zen teaches to live in the moment, and in reality it's all we really have, the here and now. . . . We exist in the fleeting moment. The past is gone the moment it is experienced and the future has yet to happen. . . . You must deal only with the present, moment by moment, second by second."
— Richard Ryan, *Master of the Blade* (p. 79)

"What does a fish know about the water in which he swims all his life?"
— Albert Einstein, *The World As I See It*

INDIVIDUALITY

"What we call 'normal' in psychology is really a psychopathology of the average, so undramatic and widely spread that we don't even recognize it ordinarily."
— Abraham Maslow

"Each (man) has his separate individuality and his priceless initiative which made him infinitely better than the clockwork soldier."
— unknown Australian sergeant

"We live, as we dream — alone."
— Robert Conrad, "Heart of Darkness"

"Shit, I don't like this white man's army. Teach us to shoot, but forget about the rest. You are wasting our time. They treat us like slaves. I don't mind fighting, but you can't make a windup toy out of me."
— John Lame Deer

"Public opinion, a vulgar, impertinent, anonymous tyrant who deliberately makes life unpleasant for anyone who is not content to be the average man."
— Dean W. R. Inge

"Precisely because the tyranny of opinion is such as to make eccentricity a reproach, it is desirable, in order to break through that tyranny, that people should be eccentric. Eccentricity has always abounded when and where strength of character has abounded; and the amount of eccentricity in a society has generally been proportional to the amount of genius, mental vigor, and moral courage it contained. That so few dare to be eccentric marks the chief danger of this time."
— unknown

"Originality and the feeling of one's own dignity are achieved only through work and struggle."
— Dostoevsky

"Few realize that the universe is made up of individuals in various stages of development, responsibility is consequently individual, and everything which man wishes to gain he must himself build and maintain."
— Manly P. Hall

"The nail that sticks out will be pounded down."
— Japanese proverb

"The strongest man in the world is he who stands most alone."
— Ibsen, *An Enemy of the People*, V

"When a true genius appears in the world, you may know him by this sign, that the dunces are all in a confederacy against him."
— Jonathan Swift, *Thoughts on Various Subjects*

"And some who turned away from life, only turned away from the rabble, they did not want to share well and flame and fire with the rabble."
— Friedrich Nietzsche, *Thus Spake Zarathustra*

"Great spirits have always encountered violent opposition from mediocre minds."
— Albert Einstein

"Children who know how to think for themselves spoil the harmony of the collective society which is coming where everyone is interdependent."
— John Dewey (1899)

"Imitation is a form of stealing: you are nothing but he is somebody, so you are going to get some of his glory by copying him."
— J. Krishnamurti

"Gradually, I became used to the idea that there were damned few groups around who wanted independent thinkers, and that most of the organizations I infiltrated or joined were likely to kick me out the second I started deviating from their party line."
— Isaac Bonewits

"If a man does not keep pace with his companions, perhaps it is because he hears a different drummer. Let him step to the music which he hears, however measured or far away."
— Henry David Thoreau

"If a man could understand all the horror of the lives of ordinary people who are turning around in a circle of insignificant interests and insignificant aims, if he could understand what they are losing, he would understand that there can be only one thing that is serious for him — to escape from the general law, to be free."
— G. I. Gurdjieff

"A man flattened by an opponent can get up again. A man flattened by conformity stays down for good."
— Thomas J. Watson, Jr.

"Do not choose to be wrong for the sake of being different."
— Lord Samuel

"To be alone is to be different, to be different is to be alone."
— Suzanne Gordon, *Lonely in America*

"Alienation produces eccentrics or revolutionaries."
— Jenny Holzer, *Truisms*

"There is little place in the political scheme of things for an independent, creative personality, for a fighter. Anyone who takes that role must pay a price."
— Shirley Chisholm, *Unbought and Unbossed*

"You won't have a future if you don't make one for yourself. It is as simple as that. If you accept the forms that be, then you are doomed, to your own ultimate blandness."
— John Lydon

"We are a group of complete individuals, and I mean individuals. Every one of us has a different reason for being who we are."
— Ralph "Sonny" Barger, *Ridin' High, Livin' Free* (pp. 184-185)

"The sage does not care whether or not anyone follows his teachings or ideas. To care would be to

have ego. The sage does what he has to, what he is 'told' to do by his own voices from within. If no-one even listens to him, he does not care. He has done his job and therefore fulfilled his reason for being."
— Erle Montaigue

"Since when was genius found respectable?"
— Elizabeth Barrett Browning, *Aurora Leigh*

"To be great is to be misunderstood."
— Ralph Waldo Emerson, *Self-Reliance*

"One can be instructed in society, one is inspired only in solitude."
— Johann Wolfgang von Goethe

"We must overcome the notion that we must be regular . . . it robs you of the chance to be extraordinary and leads you to the mediocre."
— Uta Hagen

"Self-respect has nothing to do with the approval of others."
— Joan Didion

"One must live the way one thinks or wind up thinking the way one has lived."
— Paul Bourget

"Whoever would make of himself a distinctive individual must be keen to perceive what he is not."
— Friedrich Schleiermacher

"Be a light unto yourself."
— Buddha's last words, 485 BC

PRECOGNITION

"Coming events cast their shadow before."
— Goethe

"Intuitive flashes are transient, spontaneous altered states of consciousness consisting of particular sensory experience or thoughts, coupled with strong emotional reactions . . ."
— Andrew Weil, *The Natural Mind*

"If you cannot imagine something, you also cannot predict it, nor protect against it."
— Gavin de Becker

"In order to know the future it is necessary first to know the present in all its details, as well as to know the past. Today is what it is because yesterday was what it was. And if today is like yesterday, tomorrow will be like today. If you want tomorrow to be different, you must make today different."
— G. I. Gurdjieff

"Perhaps I like to dwell on what might happen so as never to be surprised."
— Iain M. Banks, *Use of Weapons* (p. 124)

"The heightened cognition often shown by those — such as sailors, woodsmen, airmen and others — who live in relationship with natural forces . . . indicate the existence of influences which are present

for all of us, whether we know of them or not, whether we become conscious of them or not."
— Denning & Phillips, *Psychic Self-Defense & Well-Being* (p. 11)

"Trust your instincts. 'Intuition' can be the result of your subconscious comparing non-verbal cues to past experiences; your olfactory gland registering the nearly imperceptible trace of certain hormones being released; or possibly something even more subtle and incomprehensible, yet real nonetheless. Intuition often proves true — disregard it at your peril."
— C. R. Jahn, *Hardcore Self-Defense* (p. 37)

"There are three types of sweat: the sweat of strenuous labor, the sweat of fear, and the sweat of insanity — all of which have a separate and distinct aroma recognizable to the limbic brain."
— unknown

"Ask someone who's been in combat if he ever had a feeling that he was going to get hit right before a firefight. You'll be amazed at the number of stories you'll hear about people hitting the deck a split second before a bullet whizzes through where they just were. Some people even hear voices that say 'duck.'. . . If you've got this gift, listen to it! It can and will save your ass!"
— Marc "Animal" MacYoung, *Street E&E* (pp. 121-122)

"I had this sense of danger. I felt the sensation of something almost gripping me at the back of the neck. I turned around and there, about twenty yards away, was a chap in a uniform with a red star on his cap gazing hard at me. He was bringing his rifle up and I knew one of us was going to be killed. I shot him before he shot me, so I have lived to tell the tale."
— William Carter (referring to an incident in 1951 Malaya)

"Within one second prior to actual termination, a target would somehow seem to make eye contact with me. I am convinced that these people somehow sensed my presence at distances over one mile. They did so with uncanny accuracy, in effect to stare down my scope."
— Robert Hendrickson, USMC Scout/Sniper

"I have lived through a dozen or more such freak near-misses. But something has always saved me at the last moment. Maybe it was my guardian angel that alerted me. . . . I believe they telepathically warn people at such times when, unbeknownst to them, their lives are in grave danger. Some people hear and react to these warnings, others do not."
— Robert Bruce, *Practical Psychic Self-Defense* (p. 162)

"Intuition is not a close faculty or a quirky gift that some people have and some don't, but a natural sense that all living creatures are born with. Intuition is a partnership between the one who feels it and the all-life that sends signals to be felt. Intuition is a flow of energy between Spirit . . . and the

alert being who receives that flow and understands the messages within it. . . . In Western society, we are taught to ignore our psychic sense, and so most of us lose touch with it in early childhood."
— Anderson Reed, *Shouting at the Wolf* (p. 20)

"The warrior bets his life on his intuitive decision making. . . . In war fighting, it is a truism that certain people possess intangible qualities that make them good point men. . . . Successful point men have the intuition that leads their patrol safely through great danger. They simply 'feel' where ambushes are. They sense danger lurking in the bush. They know when to stop, proceed, or run. This sixth sense is renowned throughout the combat arms of fighting forces around the world."

— Col. John B. Alexander, Major Richard Groller, and Janet Morris, *The Warrior's Edge* (pp. 113-114)

"The warrior who is sensitive to synchronicity can generate luck. . . . To harness synchronicity, the warrior must become a focus of coincidence. Simple coincidence may be chance. Multiple coincidences linked by correspondence and interconnectedness are called luck — unless one is consciously trying to generate such coincidences. . . . The individual who applies the same techniques to life is using the warrior's edge to make precognition an ally. . . . The warrior manipulates coincidence to create luck. As any warrior knows, it doesn't matter how good you are if you aren't lucky."
— Col. John B. Alexander, Major Richard Groller, and Janet Morris, *The Warrior's Edge* (p. 108)

"Instinct is the sum of information collected by your senses that is not readily obvious to your conscious mind. It often produces a 'feeling' that something is wrong or right without a logical explanation. When you are uncertain what to do next or how to handle an opponent, rely on your gut feelings. The more experience you have in combat, the more reliable your instincts will be."
— Hanho, *Combat Strategy* (p. 16)

TRUTH

"The search for truth is neither new nor old . . . nobody is a founder in it, nobody is a leader in it. It is such a vast phenomenon that many enlightened people have appeared, helped, and disappeared."
— Osho

"I maintain that Truth is a pathless Land, and you cannot approach it by any path whatsoever, by any religion, by any sect . . . The moment you follow someone, you cease to follow Truth.
— Krishnamurti

"The truth is the one thing that nobody will believe."
— George Bernard Shaw

"They deem him their worst enemy who tells them the truth."
— Plato

"Statistics indicate that such sightings are indeed rare events, perhaps akin to the sighting of an extremely rare or unnamed species of bird (and how would you prove that on a walk through the mountains and woods you had sighted a California condor?) though not as rare as finding a coelacanth in the ocean depths."

— J. Allen Hynek

"I do not know what I may appear to the world; but to myself I seem to have been only like a boy playing on the seashore and diverting myself, now and then finding a smoother pebble or a prettier shell than ordinary, whilst the great ocean of truth lay all undiscovered before me."
— Sir Isaac Newton

"Once you see something as false which you have accepted as true, you can never go back to it."
— J. Krishnamurti (paraphrased)

"90% of everything is crap."
— "Sturgeon's Law"

"Even when one compromises, one should never compromise in regard to the basic truth."
— Jawaharlal Nehru

"Truth is the only safe ground to stand upon."
— Elizabeth Cady Stanton (1895)

"Not only are there many conflicting truths as there are people to claim them; there are equally multitudinous and conflicting truths within the individual."
— Virginia Peterson, *A Matter of Life and Death*

"Opposites are identical in nature, but different in degree; all truths are but half-truths; all paradoxes may be reconciled."
— *Kybalion*

"I am not afraid of the pen, or the scaffold, or the sword. I will tell the truth wherever I please."
— Mother Jones

"Just as some cheap magazines are deliberately written to generate fear in the public and to capitalize on that fear, some scientific reports are deliberate hoaxes designed to reinforce the credibility of our scientific, political, or military establishments. This is a fact of life, and it should not discourage one from the study of science. It does not necessarily mean that anyone is hiding some formidable truth. If the idea that science knows nothing about certain phenomena is unacceptable to the public, why should it be more easily acceptable to professional scientists?"
— Jacques Vallee, *Passport to Magonia* (p. 156)

"All truth passes through three stages. First, it is ridiculed. Second, it is violently opposed. Third, it is accepted as being self-evident."
— Arthur Schopenhauer

"Everything could be settled by speaking the truth. But now, people wouldn't know the truth if you spoke it. It only upsets them. It hurts their ego. And then you are their enemy."
— Grandfather Semu Huarte

"Without courage there cannot be truth, and without truth there can be no other virtue."
— Sir Walter Scott

"Few men have imagination enough for the truth of reality."
— Johann Wolfgang von Goethe

"YOU CAN'T HANDLE THE TRUTH!!!"
— "Col. Jessup," Jack Nicholson's character from *A Few Good Men*

"If you add to the truth, you subtract from it."
— *Talmud*

"All great truths began as blasphemies."
— George Bernard Shaw

"In an age of universal deceit, telling the truth becomes a revolutionary act."
— George Orwell

"Half a truth is often a great lie."
— Benjamin Franklin

"Knowledge is neither good nor evil. It is truth. How it is utilized, for good or evil, is the responsibility of the user."
— Anthony B. Herbert, *Military Manual of Self Defense* (p. 7)

"The small truth has words that are clear; the great truth has great silence."
— Rabindranath Tagore, *Stray Birds* (CLXXVI)

CIVILIZATION

"We are all born charming, fresh, and spontaneous — and must be civilized before we are fit to participate in society."
— Miss Manners (Judith Martin)

"Civilization means a society based upon the opinion of civilians. It means that violence, the rule of warriors and despotic chiefs, the conditions of camps and warfare, of riot and tyranny, give place to parliaments where laws are made, and independent courts of justice in which over long periods those laws are maintained."
— Winston Churchill

"I only know that he who forms a tie is lost. The germ of corruption has entered his soul."
— Joseph Conrad

"Something about servitude stills. Something about domestication stifles. The wolf, now the poodle, no longer howls. The wild boar lies on its side in the hog pen and grunts. The wildebeast stands in her stall placidly chewing her cud while she's milked dry. Domestication of man and beast muffles the cry of freedom and suffocates the spirit of liberty."
— Gerry Spence

"With an evil magic, the brainwashing transforms our children from the bright, the inquiring and the creative to mindless consumers, to empty-headed shoppers concerned chiefly with things, and the means by which to acquire things."
— Gerry Spence

"We are no longer alert. We continuously lie to our children and teach them to be liars. Easter bunnies, Santa Claus, denying what their senses tell them, these are all lies . . . If you're well educated you'll work to hurt people, you'll do the work of big institutions. You'll work to make alcohol, drugs, TV, schools, religion, things to put people's minds to sleep."
— Grace Spotted Eagle

"Nobody today is normal, everybody is a little bit crazy or unbalanced, people's minds are running all the time. Their perceptions of the world are partial, incomplete. They are eaten alive by their egos. They think they see, but they are mistaken; all they do is project their madness, their world, upon the world. There is no clarity, no wisdom in that!"
— Taisen Deshimaru

"Books are the carriers of civilization. Without books, history is silent, literature dumb, science crippled, thought and speculation at a standstill."
— Barbara Tuchman

"The glossy surface of our civilization hides a real intellectual decadence."
— Simone Weil, "The Power of Words"

"For the first time ever in the history of mankind, the wilderness is safer than 'civilization.'"
— Faith Popcorn

"It is alien to the Hopis to settle matters out of hand by majority vote. Such a vote leaves a dissatisfied minority, which makes them very uneasy. Their natural way of doing it is to discuss it among themselves at great length, and group by group, until public opinion as a whole has settled overwhelmingly in one direction."
— Oliver La Farge

"When someone stepped away from what was natural, the elders told him what was kind, what was right, what worked and what didn't. It was the job of the elders to make sure the people were straight with the universe, their job to leave order in this world before they went on to the next. In our time, we do not have elders; we have old people who do not know any more about living that we do and whose existence is increasingly burdensome to us and to them. . . . Without a link between us and the elders, there is no longer anyone to tell us we're on the wrong road. Nobody argues against our shallow life, nobody talks about a better time, because nobody alive now remembers a better time."
— Anderson Reed, *Shouting at the Wolf* (pp. 11-12)

"Books are the building blocks of civilization, for without the written word, a man knows nothing beyond what occurs during his own brief years . . ."
— Louis L'Amour, from *Education of a Wandering Man* (p. 195)

"The great ruler speaks little
and his words are priceless
He works without self-interest
and leaves no trace
When all is finished, the people say,
'It happened by itself'"
— Lao Tzu, *Tao Te Ching, The Definitive Edition* (Star translation), Verse 17

CARELESSNESS

"Do not be negligent, even in trifling matters."
— Miyamoto Musashi

"Unwatchfulness is the path of death."
— Buddha, 500 BC

"Those who are watchful never die; those who do not watch are already as dead."
— Buddha, 500 BC

"The most dangerous words are vain and lightly uttered words, because they are the voluntary abortions of thought."
— Eliphas Levi

"Complacency will kill you every time."
— Albert Tremblay

"Many little leaks may sink a ship."
— Thomas Fuller

"Don't get caught slippin'."
— popular gangsta sayin'

"There is, among New Age people, an astonishing lack of good sense and a dangerous Pollyanna attitude toward the realities of the occult. . . . When the door to the occult is opened, light and darkness spill out together. The idea that as long as we don't believe in evil it cannot harm us is disastrously wrong."
— Anderson Reed, *Shouting at the Wolf* (p. 254)

"The mundane realities of living and our failure to address them responsibly offer means of attack. We may habitually run out of money, ignore balding tires or overload the electrical wiring in our houses. We may let our teeth deteriorate or eat food that weakens instead of nourishes us. Attention to the facts of daily living and responsible care-taking in every aspect of our lives shuts the door on a multitude of ills."
— Anderson Reed, *Shouting at the Wolf* (p. 272)

THE MASSES

"We cannot trust . . . people who are nonconformists."
— Ray Kroc, former CEO of McDonald's

"Man would yield his sovereignty to an immense power; one that does not destroy, or even tyrannize, but one that serves to stupefy a people, reducing them to nothing better than a flock of timid and industrious sheep."
— Alexis de Tocqueville, *Democracy in America*

"The breathing dead emulate machines. Their work is mechanical. They relate more to the simulated

life on television than to their own species."
— Gerry Spence

"Zombies are the liberal nightmare. Here you have the masses, whom you would love to love, appearing at your front door with their faces falling off; and you're trying to be as humane as you possibly can, but they are, after all, eating the cat. And the fear of mass activity, of mindlessness on a national scale, underlies my fear of zombies."
— Clive Barker

"People in riots tend to act as one organism, the riot becoming some moving, twisting monster that sweeps along those in it in a sea of human emotions. There is a loss of individuality that many find very attractive. The riot itself becomes a cloak, a cover that protects the individual from being identified . . . Riots then become a convenient excuse for some humans to do everything they really wanted to do but never had the nerve to. It's carnival time where the mask of the riot provides anonymity."
— Eugene Sockut

"The chief preoccupation of a mass movement is to instill in its followers a facility for united action and self-sacrifice, and it achieves this facility by stripping each human entity of its distinctness and autonomy and turning it into an anonymous particle with no will and no judgement of its own. The result is not only a compact and fearless following but also a homogeneous plastic mass that can be kneaded at will."
— Eric Hoffer, *The True Believer* (p. 79)

"A few punks get out of hand, and the mob goes right with it. Even sheep can kick you to death when they stampede."
— Andrew Vachss, *Only Child* (p. 192)

"The minority, the ruling class at present, has the schools and press, usually the Church as well, under its thumb. This enables it to organize and sway the emotions of the masses, and make its tool of them."
— Albert Einstein

"Humankind cannot bear much reality."
— T.S. Elliot

"It seemed there were a thousand identical twins standing around with cans of Schlitz in their right hands. Each of the Thousanduplets was tall, with a flat, muscular stomach, a dark tan, and of course, blond hair down to his shoulders. Cocked at just the right angle at the front of their blond mops, as

you've already guessed, were sunglasses . . . They were concentrating on assuming 'cool' poses and making sure their sunglasses didn't fall off."
— Robert J. Ringer, *Looking Out For #1* (pgs 92-93)

"The People, your People, sir, is a Great Beast!"
— Alexander Hamilton

"The mass of the people, ignorant and easily swayed by violent passions, must have a strong arm over them for their own good. Otherwise, they would tear themselves and everything else to pieces."
— John McConaughy, *Who Rules America?* (p. 11)

"The conscious and intelligent manipulation of organized habits and opinions of the masses is an important element in a democratic society. Those who manipulate this unseen mechanism of society constitute an invisible government which is the true ruling power in our country."
— Edward Bernays

"(The masses) are ruled almost entirely by the minds and wills of other persons, whom they allow to do their thinking and willing for them. How few original thoughts or original actions are performed by the average person? Are not the majority of persons mere shadows and echoes of others having stronger wills or minds than themselves?"
— *Kybalion*

"The majority cares little for ideals or integrity. What it craves is display."
— Emma Goldman, *Anarchism*

"The collective intelligence of any group of people who are thinking as a 'herd' rather than individually is no higher than the intelligence of the stupidest members."
— Mary Day Winn, *Adam's Rib*

"Too many of our countrymen rejoice in stupidity, look upon ignorance as a badge of honor. They condemn everything they don't understand."
— Tallulah Bankhead

"'Mediocrity' does not mean an average intelligence; it means an average intelligence that resents and envies its betters."
— Ayn Rand, *The New Left*

"Great bodies of people are never responsible for what they do."
— Virginia Woolf, *A Room of One's Own*

"No written law has ever been more binding than unwritten custom supported by popular opinion."
— Carrie Chapman Catt (1900)

"A general state education is a mere contrivance for molding people to be exactly like one another; as is the mold in which it casts them is that which pleases the predominant power in the government. . ."
— John Stuart Mill

"Looking at all the brightly dressed college kids walking down the street makes me glad that I chose not to go that route. Hearing the shit they talk about is beyond belief. I can't understand how people of that age can be into such mindless bullshit. . . . I don't like college towns. The streets are full of people wearing the same clothes. It's like being stuck in a wine-cooler commercial and not being able to find the exit door."
— Henry Rollins, *The Portable Henry Rollins* (pp. 242-243)

"To prevent them from really thinking out anything themselves, we shall deflect their attention to amusements, games, pastimes, excitements, and people's palaces. Such interests will distract their minds completely from questions on which we might be obliged to struggle with them. Becoming less and less accustomed to independent thinking, people will express themselves in unison with us because we alone offer new lines of thought — of course through persons whom they do not consider as in any way connected with us."
— *Protocols*

"There's a whiff of the lynch mob or the lemming migration about any overlarge concentration of like-thinking individuals, no matter how virtuous their cause. . . . Whenever I'm in the middle of conformity, surrounded by oneness of mind with people oozing concurrence on every side, I get scared."
— P. J. O'Rourke, *Parliament of Whores* (p. 194)

". . . the observer would have to remark the docility of the masses — their pliability beneath the thumb of unscrupulous leaders, their credulity that made them believe almost anything poured into their ears."
— Stanton A. Coblentz, *From Arrow to Atom Bomb* (p. 417)

"To play on those millions of minds, to watch them slowly respond to an unseen stimulus, to guide their aspirations without their knowledge — all this whether in high capacities or in humble, is a big

and endless game of chess, of ever extraordinary excitement."
— Sidney Webb, founder of the Fabian Society, 1890

"Crowds are easily influenced and controlled, and it is well known that crowd violence can be orchestrated by a few key agitators. If an idea is presented to a crowd at the right time and in the right way, the crowd will act on the idea as a group, without thinking. Crowds will often do terrible things that no individual within the crowd would ever do alone."
— Robert Bruce, *Practical Psychic Self-Defense* (p. 122)

"Never underestimate the power of stupid people in large groups."
— unknown (oft attributed to Albert Einstein)

"It's too bad stupidity isn't painful. Then maybe some of these of these people would go get some help."
— Anton LaVey

"It is important to observe the normality of abnormal behavior, and to realize that it was in a hysterically deranged period of cultural history that the witch persecutions flourished."
— Julian Franklyn, *Death by Enchantment* (p. 17)

"What luck for the rulers that men do not think."
— Hitler

"The spectre of a polity controlled by the fads and whims of voters who actually believe that there are significant differences between Bud Lite and Miller Lite, and who think that professional wrestling is for real, is naturally alarming to those of us who don't."
— Neal Stephenson, *In the Beginning . . . Was the Command Line* (p. 60)

"The administration says the American people want tax cuts. Well, duh. The American people also want drive through nickel beer night. The American people want to lose weight by eating ice cream. The American people love the Home Shopping Network because it's commercial free."
— Will Durst

THE BEAST

"Hate is like acid. It can damage the vessel in which it is stored as well as destroy the object on which it is poured."
— Ann Landers

"Violent criminals are like nothing the average person has ever experienced. They are psychopaths, which means they release their anger and get their kicks from senselessly hurting or killing other people. Many of them don't care whether they live or die. They may sound and look like anyone else, they are often friendly, but that's only so they can get what they want — control over others, then the injuries begin."
— Sanford Strong, *Strong on Defense* (p. 30)

"The psychopathic violent criminal is not a movie character but a living beast who enjoys senseless acts of brutality — the maiming or killing of innocent people — to release his seething rage. . . . He attacks instantly and decisively, relying on surprise or subterfuge, either armed or bare-handed. He gives no quarter and cares little about being killed himself. This is what you may come up against."
— John Perkins, Al Ridenhour, and Matt Kovsky, *Attack Proof* (p. viii)

"Thieves are usually those who have something and want more. They steal not for food but for flashier clothes, a better watch, a handsome car. They steal for money to spend on flash, on women or drugs."
— Louis L'Amour, *Education of a Wandering Man* (p. 11)

"He sounded tough — the way a car with a bad muffler sounded fast."
— remembered line from an Andrew Vachss novel

"Despite a multitude of difference in their backgrounds and crime patterns, criminals are alike in one way: All regard the world as a chessboard over which they have total control, and they perceive people as pawns to be pushed around at will."
— Stanton E. Samenow

"A street criminal lives by a very basic philosophy: there are two types of people in the world, predators and food. The former are to be feared for the pain they can inflict, and the latter are to be victimized and used."
— Marc MacYoung and Chris Pfouts, *Safe in the City* (pp. v-vi)

"Although it is true with criminals in general, you should really consider a street addict as someone from an entirely different planet. . . . We're talking someone who was conditioned from childhood that the way to get what he wants or needs is to batter and abuse the weak and take it from them. You are not a person to an addict; you are a source for what he needs. . . . he's got nothing to do except

get high and watch for ways to get his drug money. In a real sense, his profession is being an addict and a thief. . . . In their world there are no boundaries except those enforced by violence. . ."
— Marc MacYoung and Chris Pfouts, *Safe in the City* (p. 88, 90)

"Street criminals get a rush knowing they are feared, a response they define as "getting respect." They look at average people as wimpy suckers who are there to frighten, take from, and to hurt."
— Loren Christensen

"When they see an easy target they react almost reflexively, giving little or no thought to the act."
— Loren Christensen

"They wake up every morning to a nothing day and a zero life. The poor uneducated, beaten, and forgotten. Nowhere near enough prisons to handle them. They're gone from the system, but they won't crawl under the nice clean streets and disappear."
— unknown

"Killing makes them feel big. Their sense of being alive comes from the fear they inspire, the pain they inflict, their survival while others are dead."
— unknown

"Some have decided not to be apprehended and will even charge against a drawn pistol rather than risk prison. One has no leeway against such predators, and they expect and give no quarter."
— Eugene Sockut

"Like with the psychopathic robot, a junkie high on drugs may become impervious to bullets. At last count, I read that 33 (9mm rounds) failed to stop one of these human sponges."
— Eugene Sockut

"Violent criminals often reflect startlingly peaceful exteriors."
— unknown

"That men should put an enemy in their mouths to steal away their brains! That we should, with joy, pleasance, revel and applause, transform ourselves into beasts!"
— unknown

"He believes profoundly in the depravity of human nature and knows (from his own experience) that in extreme conditions a man becomes a beast."

— Viktor Suvorov

"He is a walking time bomb that can be detonated at any moment by some tiny slight . . . Because he thinks someone's staring at him, he's ready to fight. (If) a motorist cuts him off . . . he speeds in pursuit intending to do the same to him."
— Stanton E. Samenow, *Straight Talk about Criminals* (p. 69)

"They joined gangs because they failed at school, had miserable home lives, were excluded from the job market, or knew that they qualified for only the most menial positions. Gangs provided a means of transcending these circumstances, of allowing adolescents to establish themselves as part of a "street elite," and to define a masculine identity in spite of the humiliations of everyday life. In gangs, adolescent males proved themselves, acquired respect and honor, and demonstrated their masculinity by humbling a foe. Violence arose out of the need to meet these intangible goals."
— Eric C. Schneider

"To achieve this state of control, they employ a range of linguistic and behavioral methods, like rhetorical questions, shame tactics, lies. Looking you straight in the eye, challenging, making themselves taller than you, intimidating, testing. Assuming a preaching style, using blanketing statements, asking questions, acting as instructor, treating you as student, giving you no room to respond, defining the power dynamic between you."
— Susan A. Phillips

"The rational faculties are clouded by strong drink, and the animal nature, liberated from bondage, controls the individual."
— Manly P. Hall

"EXPECT NO MERCY"
— a patch worn by many members of the Banditos outlaw motorcycle gang

"When you got a little kid with a gun that has a fuck it attitude, those are the most dangerous ones."
— anonymous, from *Wallbangin'* (p. 349)

"Once, that was what I wanted. No conscience. How I envied the sociopaths around me. Without moral and ethical baggage weighing them down, without the boundaries that restrain the rest of the world, they're the most efficient human beings on earth. You can kill them, but you can't hurt them."
— Burke, from *Pain Management* by Andrew Vachss

"Crackheads and speed freaks are violently unstable individuals, and their thought processes are so

scrambled that they tend to do things impulsively without considering the consequences of their actions. And not all the things they do are to get drug money either — they just do whatever the hell they feel like doing."
— anonymous (RWT)

"I don't have much compassion for some of these seemingly able-bodied mid-twenties, vaguely threatening, attitude laden guys who have decided that their personal statement is that they're going to give up on life at a very early stage of the game."
— Dennis Miller, *The Rants* (p. 75)

"Fancy thinking the beast was something you could hunt and kill! . . . You knew, didn't you? I'm part of you? Close, close, close! I'm the reason why it's no go. Why things are what they are."
— William Golding, *Lord of the Flies*

"Most violent men are failures."
— A. E. Van Vogt

". . . the basic characteristic of the criminal is not so much calculated wickedness as a kind of childish wilfulness."
— Colin Wilson (paraphrasing Yochelson and Samenow)

"The assistants . . . were tied up (as were several customers) . . . The bandits then forced everyone to drink a caustic cleaning fluid, which burned their mouths and throats. Then they were shot. The girl was raped before being shot. One of the bandits pushed a ballpoint pen into the ear of Mr Walker and kicked it into his head."
— Colin Wilson, *A Criminal History of Mankind* (p. 638)

"Fiends — you can tell a fiend a mile away. Somebody who looks like they lost a lot of weight, got on some raggedy clothes, they really don't care about theyself. They dirty all the time."
— "Maurice," 107 Hoover Crip

"We never killed nobody that I know of. We have put people in a coma, paralyzed them — stuff like that, but we ain't never killed nobody. Gave them brain damage."
— "N.A.," Compton Gangster BIC

"Chillin' on the corner on a hot Summer day,
Just me, my posse, and MCA,
Lotta wine, lotta beer, and a lot of cursin'

Twenty-two automatic on my person. . ."
— Beastie Boys, *Licensed to Ill*

"They're not 'white trash' — they're like white toxic waste!"
— Chris Rock

"I think playing with toy guns doesn't make you a killer. I believe ignoring your kids and giving them Prozac might."
— Ted Nugent

Most people who practice Satanism are Christian fundamentalists in drag."
— Isaac Bonewits

"He'd forgotten just how addictive crime can be. Repeat offenders are motivated more by withdrawal symptoms than necessity."
— Sue Grafton, *"H" Is for Homicide*

"Those who cannot live fully often become destroyers of life."
— Anais Nin

"Hungry people cannot be good at learning or producing anything, except perhaps violence."
— Pearl Bailey

"The fool shouts loudly, thinking to impress the world."
— Marie de France (12th c.)

"One attacks those who possess things that one does not possess. The attack is all the more savage because the one who attacks is destitute and the one who is attacked is well provided. The one who attacks always considers himself to be in the position of legitimate offence."
— Adrienne Monnier

"Persons who drop things from overpasses and walkways can usually be spotted behaving in a suspicious manner immediately prior to the act. Always be cautious of persons milling about aimlessly over a highway, especially if no protective chainlink fencing (sometimes referred to as an 'anti-drop barrier') is evident. These persons tend to favor large rocks and cinderblocks, which can easily crash completely through either the windshield or roof, resulting in serious injury or death."
— T. J. Steele (RWT)

"There are people that are so damaged that they are beyond all fear and are damn near unpredictable . . . Most of these people are killing themselves with drugs, but that takes too long . . . They are no longer human beings. I don't know any other way to describe them. There is something about them that causes an instinctive reaction of 'Wrong!' in normal people — not wrong in the sense of moral right and wrong, but wrong against nature and evolution . . ."
— Marc "Animal" MacYoung, *Violence, Blunders, and Fractured Jaws* (pp. 106-107)

"What causes opponents to come of their own accord is the prospect of gain. What discourages opponents from coming is the prospect of harm."
— Sun Tzu, *The Art of War*

"A man from hell is not afraid of hot ashes."
— Dorothy Gilman, *Incident at Badamya*

"In one series of interviews I spoke to four convicts, each of whom implied that he had committed more than a hundred muggings. I did not find these men to be irrational, violent, impulsive, or sadistic, but experienced them (remember, I saw them in a prison setting) as quiet, rational, and not psychotic. They were, however, singularly lacking in insight and frightening in their inability to relate to anyone's needs but their own. One man said, 'I am not a sadist. I don't beat people — only if they are slow in giving me my money.'"
— Dr. Martin Symonds, "Victims of Violence"

"Some murderers seem to kill for enjoyment, and a few become serial killers, killing again and again, seemingly for the love of it. These people seem to have no conscience at all. . . . Lack of conscience and remorse for wrongdoing are indicators of serious Neg contamination or possession."
— Robert Bruce, *Practical Psychic Self-Defense* (p. 160)

". . . the Amoral Thrill Cannibal is largely a prison phenomenon. Since the former republics of the Soviet Union do not carry out the death penalty much, they have tens of thousands of individuals facing incredibly long sentences with no hope of release. . . . By killing and eating the new guy, they figured they could at least vary their diet, come up with a new reason to kill someone, do a cursory study of anatomy, and have something new to talk about. They would also get a trip out of the prison for a court date and perhaps an evaluation period at a mental institution, which was bound to have better food and provide a glimpse of a nurse or two. From their perspective, their planning made sense."
— Shiguro Takada, *Contingency Cannibalism* (pp. 97-98)

"One thought consumes me,

The anger of lust denied
Covers me like darkness.
I have become a demon dwelling
In the hell of my dark thoughts,
Stormcloud of my desires."
— Seami Motokiyo, *The Damask Drum* (13th c.)

"Study shows that 8% of women and 2% of men have been stalked at some time."
— CNN news ticker

". . . but I do wonder, dear, if you've considered that there are those who are not merely unfortunate or deranged but actually evil."
— Elizabeth Ann Scarborough, *The Godmother* (p. 46)

"I don't like going out in the day. I can't take the sun. It's not good for me. I don't like all the ugly fucking people looking at me like they do. All I can do is dream of killing them. It would feel so good to just be able to shoot them like the pieces of shit that they are."
— Henry Rollins, *The Portable Henry Rollins* (pp. 227-228)

"Anger is short madness."
— Horace

THE PANTOMIME

"Every emotion expresses itself in the muscular system."
— Bruce Lee

"Gurdjieff stated that our movements are quite automatized. We have a fixed number of characteristic movements, gestures, postures, definitions of personal space, and the like, each keyed to certain situations and subpersonalities that bring them out."
— Charles T. Tart, *Waking Up* (p. 99)

"The face is the mirror of the mind. The human face is the subtle yet visual autobiography of each person."
— John O'Donohue

"People seeking to control others almost always present the image of a nice person in the beginning."
— Gavin de Becker

"The face tells us subtleties in feelings that only a poet can put into words."
— Paul Eckman

"It is inappropriate behavior that's relevant: a stare held too long, a smile that curls too slowly, a narrowing or widening of the eyes, a rapid looking away."
— Gavin de Becker

"One may smile, and smile, and be a villain."
— Shakespeare, *Hamlet*, 1, 5

"In dealing with men, female offenders frequently resort to flattery and seductive behavior. To gain sympathy with either sex, some female offenders appear to turn tears off and on virtually at will."
— Stanton E. Samenow

"Humility is a good thing, but overhumility is near to crookedness; silence is a virtue, but undue silence bespeaks a deceitful mind."
— unknown

"These guys get out of the joint, they come at you down the street, they look like gorillas. They swing their torsos when they walk; they look menacing . . . He's got the joint body, the prison strut. You can spot an ex-con in a second that way."
— anonymous, from Connie Fletcher's *What Cops Know* (p. 25)

"Ever notice two policemen talking to each other on the street? They never look at each other. One is always looking behind the other. They very seldom look each other in the eye. It's a survival mechanism. They want to know what's coming up at them."
— anonymous, from Connie Fletcher's *What Cops Know* (p. 18)

"If you see a woman rubberneck, she's usually a pickpocket or a whore. Whores rubberneck. They know what's going on. As a rule, whores know more about what's going on in the street than anybody. The guy whose head is on a swivel, the rubberneck, that's the guy who's probably looking to commit a crime. When you see a guy looking all around him, the trick is not to be seen by him, just to kind of lay back and let him look around, follow him to where he's going."
— anonymous, from Connie Fletcher's *What Cops Know* (pp. 24-25)

"Don't believe anything they say, especially if they say they don't want to fight . . . especially if they come closer rather than back away. Look out for ones who will touch you or put their arm around you, and never shake hands with them — it's the oldest trick in the book."
— Geoff Thompson

"Look for erratic eye movement, wide eyes, fidgeting, hand concealment, false smile, or pincer movement of companion(s)."
— Geoff Thompson (on precursors to an attack)

"You could see his bent little mind overextending itself, reading your insults, your fears straight from your brain, picking up on the thoughts you were too chickenshit to say."
— Chris Simunek, *Paradise Burning* (p. 72)

"Fake smiles are usually spotted easily, but if the subject is experienced at deception, it can be difficult to catch. A fake smile usually only shows the top teeth; natural smiles show both the upper and lower teeth."

— Edward Lewis, *Hostile Ground* (pgs. 14-15)

"As they talked, I was no longer hearing their words. I was watching the foam forming in the corners of their lips and the spray of saliva as their voices grew louder and more insistent."
— Michael Levine, *The Big White Lie* (p. 120)

"The study of psychology should be a history of the metamorphoses of men and women into their habitual Masks."
— Sigismundo Celine

"I have known a vast quantity of nonsense talked about bad men not looking you in the face. Don't trust that conventional idea. Dishonesty will stare honesty out of countenance any day in the week if there is anything to be got by it."
— Charles Dickens

"Become aware of body language. Your own and other people's. If you're explaining something important to your staff, try to convey some of your own urgency and enthusiasm; you'll diminish your effect if you're sitting rigidly, drawn tight together, with arms and legs crossed. . . . The body language that expresses confidence and authority is the easy, open stance, accompanied by direct eye contact with the other person. . . . If you stand up to address a seated person, you gain height and a certain amount of temporary power. But if you face the person directly, on his level (whether sitting or standing), you are more likely to establish communication."
— Cheryl Reimold

"Adopt a stance with the head erect, neither hanging down, nor looking up, not twisted. Your forehead and the space between your eyes should not be wrinkled. Do not roll your eyes nor allow them to blink, but slightly narrow them. With your features composed, keep the line of your nose straight with a feeling of slightly flaring your nostrils."
— Miyamoto Musashi, *The Book of Five Rings*

"Don't let your face or eyes give away your intention. If you can't depend on a dead pan poker face remaining that way, smile! Then make your move and carry it all the way through. If force is required, use enough to do the job, use it first and without hesitation."
— William H. Jordan, *No Second Place Winner* (p. 108)

"Your face, especially your eyes, mirrors your emotions. If you are tentative or nervous, frightened or apprehensive, the emotion is reflected in your expression and the way you look at someone. . . . When confronted by potential violence on the street, your face should be expressionless and your eyes watchful. . . . Keep your face as still and calm as possible. Don't try to do anything special with

your eyes by making them appear hard, cold, or haughtily staring. They should be opened, not narrowed, reflecting only that you are awake and alert."
— Joe Hyams, *Playboy's Book of Practical Self-Defense* (p. 59)

"A general reading of someone's face, especially their eyes, will usually give you a clue to what is in their minds. Attackers are usually tense, the muscles around the neck and shoulders are tight, the body rigid. Their movements are usually stiff because they are keyed up emotionally and therefore tense. Most attacks are preceded by a shove or physically aggressive move intended to intimidate you."
— Joe Hyams, *Playboy's Book of Practical Self-Defense* (p. 13)

"The smile, as most any tactic, has its risks. It must not appear foolish or project ridicule; nor should it look like an arrogant smirk."
— Myles Martel

"He liked to observe emotions; they were like red lanterns strung along the dark unknown of another's personality, marking vulnerable points."
— Ayn Rand, *Atlas Shrugged*

"An amateur in possession of a concealed weapon will often be seen adjusting its position when it shifts uncomfortably, or grazing his hand against it when he feels threatened."
— anonymous (RWT)

"Haggard and Isaacs suggested that these expressions, which they called 'micromomentary' expressions or 'micros,' are not intended as messages, consciously or unconsciously, but are leakage of true feelings. They may actually serve as a safety valve, permitting a person to express, very briefly, his unacceptable impulses and feelings."
— Flora Davis, *Inside Intuition* (pp. 57-58)

"The gesture is the thing truly expressive of the individual — as we think so will we act."
— Martha Graham

ACTIVISM

"Civil disobedience on grounds of conscience s an honourable tradition . . . and those who take part in it, may in the end be vindicated by history."
— Lord Justice Hoffman

"To violate the law is often the highest, most sacred duty that can devolve upon the citizen."
— Clarence S. Darrow

"Pie is the great equalizer. How wealthy or powerful are you with pie dripping off your face?"
— Rahula Janowski, on behalf of the Biotic Baking Brigade

"Anarchism is a game at which the police can beat you."
— George Bernard Shaw

"Anyone who challenges the prevailing orthodoxy finds himself silenced with surprising effectiveness."
— George Orwell

"Strict observance of the written law is doubtless one of the highest duties of a good citizen, but it is not the highest. To lose our country by a scrupulous adherence to written law would be to lose the law itself."
— Thomas Jefferson

"Never depend on government or institutions to create change. All significant social change in

human history was accomplished by individual action."
— Margaret Mead

"Avoid the faint-of-heart, the excessively paranoid, and the not-quite-thoroughly committed. Avoid the casual acquaintance you only see at a protest rally, especially the ones who "talk tough." Such people may well be police spies or agents provocateurs."
— Etta Place, *Ecodefense* (pg 237)

"Nonviolent actions are almost completely useless when deprived of media exposure."
— Antonio Negri

"Remember, there is a fine line between activism and just being a pain in the ass."
— Dennis Miller

"One has the right to be wrong in a democracy."
— Claude Pepper

"I presume that in general those who meddle with public affairs sometimes perish miserably and that they deserve it . . ."
— Voltaire, *Candide*

"Sitting in a circle singing Kumbaya isn't going to change anything."
— Ainsley Hargus

"Being fond of courage while detesting poverty will lead men to unruly behavior."
— Confucius

"The stakes . . . are too high for government to be a spectator sport."
— Barbara Jordan

"If I cannot air this pain and alter it, I will surely die of it. That's the beginning of social protest."
— Audre Lorde

"The master's tools will never dismantle the master's house."
— Audre Lorde

"The word 'revolution' is a word for which you kill, for which you die, for which you send the laboring masses to their death, but which does not possess any content."
— Simone Weil, *Oppression and Liberty*

"Most Americans have never seen the ignorance, degradation, hunger, sickness, and futility in which many other Americans live. . . . They won't become involved in economic or political change until something brings the seriousness of the situation home to them."
— Shirley Chisholm, *Unbought and Unbossed*

"The rich are never threatened by the poor — they do not notice them."
— Marie de France (12th c.)

". . . police have issued misinformation claiming unsubstantiated evidence of violent plans by protesters gathering for mass actions. The false information is then used as a pretext for unwarranted police actions. . . . many media outlets appear to have been predisposed to repeat information provided by police without fact-checking or seeking responses from the organizations accused. The damage to free speech and the mass protest movement has been extensive. In addition, activists are scared. Anyone who has been involved in the mass protest movement . . . has friends who have been brutalized at the hands of the system."
— Tim Ream

"The real troublemakers at the demonstrations are always a small minority — usually less than five percent — and they always seem to be able to magically slip away, ninja-like, sometime between when the gas grenades start getting fired into the crowd and when the police start putting everyone they can grab into flex-cuffs and loading them onto hot, crowded, bathroomless buses — where the captured activists will be made to sit until nearly everyone has pissed in their pants at least once. Humiliation is an even better means of aversive conditioning than gassing, beating, and jailing combined. Indeed, many demonstrators subject to this kind of treatment have dropped out of the movement altogether. It is not inconceivable that a handful of compensated federal intelligence 'assets' are deliberately perpetuating acts of criminal mischief by which law enforcement can justify 'collective punishment' of the entire crowd as a whole."
— Razor (RWT)

"The greater the resistance, the greater will be the force and scope of the state repression brought to bear upon the people. When resistance is at a high level, the enemy takes measures against the people. But treading lightly will not assuage the rulers. Violent repression is built into the status quo."
— Weather Underground, *Prairie Fire* (1974)

"Those who have joined the revolutionary left just to be trendy had better be careful not to involve themselves in something from which there is no going back."
— Baader-Meinhof Group, *Dans Konzept Stadtguerilla* (April, 1971)

"The declaration that our people are hostile to a government made . . . for themselves, and conducted by themselves, is an insult."
— John Adams

". . . my duty is to unify the people, 'cause to divide people is to destroy people, and destroy yourself, too."
— Peter Tosh

"Rights are never given, only asserted."
— Martin Luther King, Jr.

"The protests and people who indulge in the protests are completely misguided. . . . These protests are a complete outrage."
— Tony Blair

"Despite such amiable slogans as 'Make love not war,' the whole hippie movement was heavily loaded with hostility. It was Freaksville versus Squaresville, the counter-culture versus the establishment."
— Robert S. de Ropp, *Warrior's Way* (p. 287)

"Someone would move into a commune populated by sandal-wearing, peace-sign-flashing flower children and eventually discover that, underneath the facade, the guys who ran it were actually control freaks; and that, as living in a commune, where much lip service was paid to ideals of peace, love, and harmony had deprived them of normal, socially approved outlets for their control-freakdom, it tended to come out in other, invariably more sinister, ways."
— Neal Stephenson, *In the Beginning . . . Was the Command Line* (pp. 30-31)

"Some of the pipes are big enough to park a car in and some are the size of your finger, but all of them have told their secrets to my gas chromatograph. And often it's the littlest pipes that cause the most damage. When I see a big huge pipe coming right out of a factory, I'm betting that the pumpers have at least read the EPA regs. But when I find a tiny one, hidden below the waterline, sprouting from a mile-wide industrial carnival, I put gloves on before taking my sample. And sometimes the gloves melt."
— Neal Stephenson, *Zodiac* (pp. 30-31)

"The Earth is not dying, it is being killed. And the people who are killing it have names and addresses."
— Utah Phillips

"It is dangerous to be right when the government is wrong."
— Voltaire

FANATICISM:

"A fanatic is one who can't change his mind and won't change the subject."
— Winston Churchill

"Every reform movement has its lunatic fringe."
— Theodore Roosevelt

"Though they seem at opposite poles, fanatics of all kinds are actually crowded together at one end. It is the fanatic and the moderate who are poles apart and never meet."
— Eric Hoffer, *The True Believer* (#62)

"Passionate hatred can give meaning and purpose to an empty life. Thus people haunted by the purposelessness of their lives try to find a new content not only by dedicating themselves to a holy cause but also by nursing a fanatical grievance. A mass movement offers them unlimited opportunities for both."
— Eric Hoffer, *The True Believer* (#75)

"You think I want some farmer with a grenade pin for a brain blathering on about how the entire world is run by about five Jews from a luxury cave on Barbados? Well, frankly, yes, I do. The louder they bellyache, the better. Because then and only then — we know exactly where these people are. We can listen to them and, God forbid, actually communicate with them. This way they can't ferment like bad yeast and ooze out of the brew vat when we're not looking."
— Dennis Miller, *The Rants* (pgs 104-105)

"Manson became a hero of the west-coast 'underground' network. But the trial had the effect of convincing the rest of the world that the whole movement of social revolt was a form of mindless emotionalism whose arguments defied logic; it produced, in fact, precisely the kind of revulsion against the left that the McCarthy witch hunts had created against the right. In America, at least, the Manson family had discredited 'revolution.'"
— Colin Wilson, *A Criminal History of Mankind* (p. 630)

"To the fanatic, everything is black or white, curse or blessing, friend or foe — and nothing in between. He is immune to doubt and hesitation. He perceives tolerance as weakness."
— Elie Wiesel

"The trouble with our Texas Baptists is that we do not hold them under water long enough."
— William Brann, editor of *The Iconoclast*, who was shortly thereafter shot in the back by an irate Baptist, whom he managed to mortally wound with his own revolver before expiring (1898)

"Bennett's voice is the voice of an intolerant scold, narrow and shrill and mean-spirited, the voice of a man afraid of liberty and mistrustful of freedom. He believes that it is the government's duty to impose on people a puritanical code of behavior best exemplified by the discipline in place at an unheated boarding school. He never misses the chance to demand more police, more jails, more judges, more arrests, more punishments, more people serving millennia of 'serious time.'"
— Lewis Lapham

"Fundamentalists have never had too much respect for law and order."
— Isaac Bonewits

"In order to make sense of the brutal activities of the SS, it must be seen that its members were motivated, for the most part, not by sadism, but by sacrifice in a fanatical utopian cause which suspended normal judgement. . . . The master race was to be the culmination of a biological evolution. If 'inferior' races prevented these goals, the master race would be justified, by the 'natural law' of Darwinism, in doing whatever it needed to survive the harsh struggle for existence. . . . For the sake of being part of a utopian society which would usher in a golden age, he was willing to give

up personal liberty. . . .Though SS men were trained to be the first stage in a superhuman mutation, and already behaved as if they were supermen, they also exhibited a robotlike quality. Fearless and cruel, they were also capable of a cringing subservience to superiors."
— Dusty Sklar, *Gods and Beasts* (pp. 94-96)

"Crankish attacks on the freedom to read are common at present. When backed and coordinated by organized groups, they become sinister."
— Ursula K. Le Guin, *Dancing at the Edge of the World*

"The blessed Religion revealed in the word of God will remain an eternal and awful monument to prove that the best Institutions may be abused by human depravity; and that they may even, in some instances be made subservient to the vilest of purposes."
— George Washington

"Jesus said to be like children, but like 7th grade children? Cruel, gossiping liars and bullies that roam in packs and cliques, looking for weak and unsuspecting VICTIMS? If you're having the kind of fun that they can't experience, then you must be sinning — and in their eyes, Slack is the ultimate sin."
— The SubGenius Foundation, *Revelation X* (pg. 49)

"People on the whole are very simple-minded in whatever country one finds them. They are so simple as to take literally, more often than not, the things their leaders tell them."
— Pearl Buck, *What America Means to Me*

". . . the Pilgrims hardly let everyone 'worship God in his own way' once they arrived. They immediately set up a quasi-theocracy and expelled or imprisoned their own believers who spoke against ministers. . . . The Puritans to their north were even worse."
— James W. Loewen, *Lies Across America* (p. 385)

"If religion becomes a cause of enmity and hatred, it is evident the abolition of religion is preferable to its promulgation; for a religion is a remedy for human ills. If a remedy should be productive of disease, it is certainly advisable to abandon it."
— 'Abdu 'l-Baha (1912)

"You've seen an increase in career prosecutors that you didn't have 15 years ago, people who never practiced in the public sector. They sit in this lofty tower with a rather skewed vision of the world. They are on a divine mission, and everything that gets in their way is evil. The ends justify the means."

— Thomas Dillard

"Numerous religious extremists claim that a race war will soon begin, and have taken steps to become martyrs in their predicted battle between good and evil. Almost uniformly, the belief among right-wing religious extremists is that the federal government is an arm of Satan."
— excerpted from the FBI's Project Megiddo report

"Some delusional conspiracy nuts seem to think that simply lining up the object of their hatred in the crosshairs of a high powered rifle will magically reverse all the 'wrongs' the target in question is alleged to have committed. This is not so. Presidents of countries, CEOs of multi-national corporations, Chairmen of banking institutions, and Directors of large organizations are, almost invariably, nothing more than mere figureheads intended to take the blame for crimes committed by their handlers — an effigy for the rubes to huck tomatoes at, if you will. As Bobcat Goldthwait so eloquently put it, 'If you get a bad hamburger, you don't blame Ronald McDonald.' The true controllers tend to shun the spotlight."
— Razor (RWT)

"When there is One Right True and Only Way — Ours! — and everybody else is wrong, then those who are wrong are damned, and the damned are evil. We are excused from recognizing their humanness and from treating them according to the ethics with which we treat each other. Generally, the Chosen People set about the task of purifying themselves from any contact with the carriers of evil. When they are in power, they institute inquisitions, witchhunts, pogroms, executions, censorship, and concentration camps."
— Starhawk, *The Spiral Dance* (p. 189)

"The revolutionary is a doomed man. He has no interests of his own, no affairs, no feelings, no attachments, no belongings, not even a name. Everything in him is absorbed by a single exclusive interest, a single thought, a single passion — the revolution. In the very depths of his being, not only in words but also in deeds, he has broken every tie with the civil order and the entire cultured world, with all its laws, proprieties, social conventions, and its ethical rules. He is an implacable enemy of this world, and if he continues to live in it, that is only to destroy it more effectively."
— Sergey Nechaev, *Catechism of the Revolutionist* (1869)

"One man willing to throw away his life is enough to terrorize a thousand."
— Wu Ch'i (400 BC)

"After browsing through various hate group websites, you may notice a common denominator: Hate groups want the freedom to prevent others from exercising the same rights that they enjoy. If you look beyond the surface distinctions (skin color, national citizenship, religious affiliation. etc.) That hate groups use to identify their members, you'll see that hate groups are often more similar to each

other than they are to the people they're trying to recruit."
— Wallace Wang, *Steal This Computer Book 3* (p. 59)

"Have you noticed that most people who are against abortion are people you wouldn't want to fuck in the first place?"
— George Carlin

JUSTICE

"Kindness is the beginning and the end of the Law."
— *Talmud*

"Justice is . . . the conscience of the whole of humanity."
— Alexander Solzhenitsyn

"Justice cannot be for one side alone, but must be for both."
— Eleanor Roosevelt

"Fairness is what justice really is."
— Potter Stewart

"The administration of justice is the firmest pillar of government."
— George Washington

"The young man knows the rules, but the old man knows the exceptions."
— Oliver Wendell Holmes

"Man does not give rights. He only takes them away."
— Gerry Spence

"Laws are like spider webs. If some poor weak creature comes up against them — it is caught. But the bigger ones can break through and get away."
— Solon (630-555 BC)

"Under current law, it's a crime for a private citizen to lie to a government official, but not for the same official to lie to the people."
— Donald M. Frazer

"The game stayed the same: It was always about favors and friends, and who controlled the dough. Party labels were merely a way to keep track of the teams; issues were mostly smoke and vaudeville. Nobody believed in anything except hanging onto power, whatever it took."
— Carl Hiaasen, *Sick Puppy*

"The majority of defendants are provided with overworked, underpaid, and thoroughly apathetic public defenders, most of whom aspire for a better paying job in the office of the District Attorney, and jockey for the few available positions in that office by cooperating as much as possible with the prosecutors against whom they're paired in court."
— Wayne Henderson

"A conscientious law-abiding person might get arrested for inadvertently committing some minor infraction that is on the books but rarely enforced. In such a situation, one could say that an increased level of law enforcement led to identification of a crime (another officer might've ignored the offense or given a warning)."
— Stanton E. Samenow, *Straight Talk about Criminals* (p. 59)

"Search and seizure, the Miranda decision, all this kind of stuff, police have never cared about any of that. That's all bullshit. They testify however they want to . . . Who's there to say he didn't give the prisoner the Miranda warning? The prisoner? That's a joke."
— anonymous, from Mark Baker's *Cops* (p. 318)

"If you want to stay afterwards and face the authorities, good. I am sure you will enjoy your trial, especially when the opposing attorney points out to the jury how you, a trained killer, did attack and assault that poor mugger."
— John La Tourrette

"Some men are alive simply because it is against the law to kill them."
— Ed Howe

"Laws grind the poor, and rich men rule the law."
— Goldsmith

"Laws that do not embody public opinion can never be enforced."
— Elbert Hubbard

"You can't legislate intelligence and common sense into people."
— Will Rogers

"If we desire respect for the law, we must first make the law respectable."
— Louis D. Bradeis

"I proclaim that might is right, justice the interest of the stronger."
— Plato

"Laws are silent in time of war."
— Cicero (110 B.C.)

"The more laws, the less justice."
— Cicero

"Care should be taken that the punishment does not exceed the guilt; and also that some men do not suffer for offenses for which others are not even indicted."
— Cicero

"Let the punishment fit the crime."
— Cicero

"Moral law is an invention of mankind for the disenfranchisement of the powerful in favor of the weak. Historical law subverts it at every turn."
— Cormac McCarthy, *Blood Meridian* (p. 250)

"Watching the trust we had in the legal system disappear has been a sad, confusing experience . . . In the past, we revered the legal system as the backbone of democracy. Now we quite frankly fear it — its linguistic fog, the casualness of the brutal transactions, the sheer density of its unconcern."
— Dennis Miller, *The Rants* (p. 15)

"You may not believe a law is moral, but it might be wise to obey it out of the rational fear of what might happen to you if you didn't. Laws themselves don't keep people in line (except through intimidating slogans such as 'your duty,' 'law-abiding citizen,' etc.); it's the threat of violence — the guns behind those laws — that do the job. Therefore, it's perfectly rational to obey an immoral law if you feel your chances of getting caught are great enough, and the punishment duly severe, to warrant it."
— Robert J. Ringer, *Looking Out For #1* (pgs. 109-110)

"Punishments for capital crimes were almost never carried out. Such crimes and their punishments are on the books primarily as deterrents."
— Isaac Mozeson, Orthodox Judaic linguist

"The CIA in its pursuit of intelligence and influence, often courts the same powerful figures (DEA) pursued as criminals . . . and intelligence wins precedence over law enforcement. The highly connected tuxedo-clad criminal is left in place to provide intelligence to the United States — and drugs to its citizens."
— James Mills, *The Underground Empire*

"Law is anything which is boldly asserted and plausibly maintained."
— Aaron Burr

"What's really astounding about these brickheads who claim to be in touch with the original intent of

the founders is (1) none of them seem to have read what the founders wrote, from Thomas Jefferson's essays to Jamie Madison's notes, and (2) you know damn well that if they had been alive at the time of the American Revolution, they all would've been Tories."
— Molly Ivins

"The prohibition law, written for weaklings and derelicts, has divided the nation, like Gaul, into three parts — wets, drys, and hypocrites."
— Florence Sabin

"Why is the decision by a woman to sleep with a man she has just met in a bar a private one, and the decision to sleep with the same man for $100 subject to criminal penalties?"
— Anna Quindlen

"Petty laws breed great crimes."
— Ouida, *Wisdom, Wit and Pathos* (1884)

"That is what is so bizarre about the American legal system. Where else in the world would stealing from a phone booth be considered more serious than polluting the earth?"
— Laura Nader

"The contempt for law and the contempt for the human consequences of lawbreaking go from the bottom to the top of American society."
— Margaret Mead

"The vices of the rich and great are mistaken for error; and those of the poor and lowly, for crimes."
— Lady Marguerite Blessington (1839)

"Privilege is the greatest enemy of right."
— Marie von Ebner-Eschenbach

"For many persons, law appears to be black magic — an obscure domain that can be fathomed only by the professional initiated into its mysteries."
— Susan C. Ross, *The Rights of Women*

"(Law) is one part justice to nine parts expediency. Who needs it."
— Lucille Kallen, *Introducing C. B. Greenfield*

"A right which goes unrecognized by anybody is not worth very much."
— Simone Weil, *The Need for Roots*

"What does Mount Rushmore mean to us Indians? It means that these big white faces are telling us, 'First we gave you Indians a treaty that you could keep these Black Hills forever, as long as the sun would shine, in exchange for all the Dakotas, Wyoming, and Montana. Then we found the gold and took this last piece of land, because we were stronger, and there were more of us than there where of you, and because we had cannons and Gatling guns. . . . And after we did all this we carved up this mountain, the dwelling place of your spirits, and put our four gleaming white faces here. We are the conquerors.'"
— John Lame Deer

"There (have) been . . . literally thousands of instances of injustice where minor co-conspirators in cases, the lowest level participants, have been given the sentences that Congress intended for the highest kingpins. . . . the taxpayers are paying a fortune for excessive punishment. You know there's nothing conservative about punishing people too much. That's an excess. And it's just a waste. . . . There don't have to be drugs. All there have to be are witnesses who say, 'I saw the drugs,' or, 'He said there were drugs.' That's all you need."
— Eric E. Sterling

"Criminals are likely to say and do almost anything to get what they want, especially when they want to get out of trouble with the law. This willingness to do anything includes not only truthfully spilling the beans on friends and relatives, but also lying, committing perjury, manufacturing evidence, soliciting others to corroborate their lies with more lies and double-crossing anyone with whom they come into contact . . ."
— Stephen Trott

"To consider the judges as the ultimate arbiters of all constitutional questions is a very dangerous doctrine indeed, and one which would place us under the despotism of an oligarchy."
— Thomas Jefferson

"Because of what appears to be a lawful command on the surface, many citizens, because of their respect for the law, are cunningly coerced into waiving their rights, due to ignorance."
— *U.S. v. Minker* 350 U.S. 179, 187

"If a drug-free America is such a good idea, why aren't members of the House of Representatives taking drug tests? Why isn't the U.S. Senate pissing into jars on C-Span?"
— P. J. O'Rourke, *Parliament of Whores* (p. 119)

"This is the cynical truth about the War on Drugs. Officially-sanctioned factions within the National Security State allow drugs into the country, then domestic law enforcement agencies recruit informants to arrest the people who use them."
— Jim Redden, *Snitch Culture* (p. 199)

"Is anybody else indignant that we have a legal system where you can blow your mother's head off with a shotgun, and then upon advice of your legal council get a neatly trimmed haircut and wear a cable-knit sweater and actually have that matter in a court of law?"
— Dennis Miller, *Comic Relief* (p. 142)

"Revenge is a kind of wild justice."
— Francis Bacon, *Revenge*

"Our great cornerstone of democracy, the rule of law, has become a source of power and influence, not liberty and justice. I resent the insidious manipulations by those entrusted with such authority, but even more, I despise our deliberate ignorance and passive acceptance of these shackles on the American spirit. We have abdicated our freedom, literally our democracy, to the rule makers. Our institutions now serve these masters."
— Catherine Crier, *The Case Against Lawyers* (p. 5)

"Always take a jury trial. Your chances of a not guilty verdict are always greater, and there is always the chance of a hung jury or a reversal of the conviction in a higher court. . . . Your only real chance for an acquittal is to take a jury trial. . . . Court appointed attorneys could care less if you go to prison and are only there to make a show on the transcript to make the court records look all legal and official. . . . The system loves guys who sit in the courtroom nice and quiet while a mock-up trial is held right in their presence. . . . Your repeated objections and complaints about your attorney will open the doors for post-conviction relief. Stand up for yourself. You are probably the only one who will."
Harold S, Long, *Making Crime Pay* (p. 29, 34, 36)

"If the jury feels the law is unjust, we recognize the undisputed power of the jury to acquit, even if its verdict is contrary to the law as given by a judge, and contrary to the evidence."
— 4th Circuit Court of Appeals, *US v Moylan*, 1969

FREEDOM

"The greatest dangers to liberty lurk in insidious encroachment by men of zeal, well-meaning but without understanding."
— Justice Louis D. Brandeis

"Freedom of the press is limited to those who own one."
— A. J. Liebling

"A people or a class which is cut off from its own past is far less free to choose and to act as a people or class than one that has been able to situate itself in history."
— Peter Smith, *Ways of Seeing* (p. 33)

"Warriors never tolerate enslavement to anyone or anything."
— Forrest E. Morgan

"All laws which can be violated without doing anyone any injury are laughed at."
— Spinoza

"Men may be without restraints upon their liberty; they may pass to and fro at pleasure; but if their steps are tracked by spies and informers, their words noted down for crimination, their associates watched as conspirators — who should say that they are free?"
— Sir Thomas May

"Being socially proper is more important than possessing a fresh, uncompromised soul. Being acceptable to our neighbors is often more important than being acceptable to ourselves. The price of freedom is often rejection, even banishment."
— Gerry Spence

"A man without privacy is a man without dignity."
— Sir Zelman Cowen

"The Internet watches you while you're sleeping."
— From Mad TV's "Reading Railroad"

"If science produces no better fruits than tyranny . . . I would rather wish our country to be ignorant, honest, and estimable as our neighboring savages are."
— Thomas Jefferson (1812)

"A state of society where men may not speak their minds, where children denounce their parents to the police . . . such a state of society cannot long endure."
— Winston Churchill

"Is life so dear or peace so sweet as to be purchased at the price of chains and slavery?"
— Patrick Henry

"Liberty means responsibility. That is why most men dread it."
— George Bernard Shaw

"They that can give up essential liberty to obtain a little temporary safety deserve neither liberty nor safety."
— Benjamin Franklin

"Anyone who surrenders his arms because of a cry for public safety does not deserve freedom . . . No free man shall ever be debarred the use of arms . . . Laws that forbid the carrying of arms . . . disarm only those who are neither inclined nor determined to commit crimes."
— Thomas Jefferson

"Firearms stand next in importance to the Constitution itself. They are the American people's liberty teeth and keystone under independence. To ensure peace, security, and happiness, the rifle and pistol are equally indispensable. The very atmosphere of firearms everywhere restrains evil interference — they deserve a place of honor with all that's good."
— George Washington

"Prohibition . . . goes beyond the bounds of reason in that it attempts to control a man's appetite by legislation and makes a crime out of things that are not crimes . . . A prohibition law strikes a blow at the very principles upon which our government was founded."
— Abraham Lincoln

"When privacy is outlawed, only outlaws will have privacy."
— anonymous

"Assassination: the extreme form of censorship."
— George Bernard Shaw

"The rights of man, that Thomas Paine defended, were being assailed on every hand by selfishness, ambition, and tyranny."
— Manly P. Hall

"200 years ago, a gentleman carried a pistol with him wherever he went, and many respectable folks carried big knives as well. Our founding fathers grew vast fields of hemp, and cannabis was widely used for medicinal purposes. Carrying arms and smoking weed were socially acceptable activities. Nowadays, if you are 'stopped and frisked' and an unlicenced derringer or a well-packed bowl is found, you'll be branded as a criminal deviant and locked in a cage. Our rights of self-defense and self-medication have been stripped from us, and these unjust 'laws' will be enforced with physical violence."
— anonymous (RWT)

"The right of self-defense is the first law of nature; in most governments it has been the study of rulers to confine this right within the narrowest limits possible. Wherever standing armies are kept up, and the right of the people to keep and bear arms is, under any colour or pretext whatsoever, prohibited, liberty, if not already annihilated, is on the brink of destruction."
— St. George Tucker, *Blackstone's Commentaries* (1803)

"Eternal vigilance is the price of liberty."
— Wendell Phillips (1852)

"Is life so dear or peace so sweet as to be purchased at the price of chains and slavery? . . . I know not what course others may take; but as for me, give me liberty, or give me death!"
— Patrick Henry

"There is no inverse relationship between freedom and security. People with no rights are not safe from terrorist attack . . . The U.S. Constitution was written by men who had just been through a long, incredibly nasty war. They did not consider the Bill of Rights a frivolous luxury, to be in force only in times of peace and prosperity, put aside when the going gets tough."
— Molly Ivins

"The Swiss are most armed and most free."
— Machiavelli

"I don't agree with what you're saying — but I'll die for your right to say it."
— Bob Franks

"Today, those who enjoy the greatest freedom are those who have the wherewithal to buy it. At last, even freedom, has become a commodity, indeed, an item of luxury."
— Gerry Spense

"The great and direct end of government is liberty. Secure our liberties and privileges, and the end of government is answered. If this be not effectively done, government is an evil."
— Patrick Henry, speech against the U.S. Constitution, June 25, 1788

"We hear about constitutional rights, free speech and the free press. Every time I hear those words I say to myself, 'That man is a Red, that man is a Communist.' You never heard a real American talk in that manner."
— Frank Hague, Mayor of Jersey City, January 12, 1938

"If authority implies submission, liberation implies equality; authority exists when one man obeys another, and liberty exists when men do not obey other men. Thus, to say that authority exists is to say that class and caste exist, that submission and inequality exist. To say that liberty exists is to say that classlessness exists, to say that brotherhood and equality exist."
— Hagbard Celine

"Among the natural rights of the colonists are these: first, a right to life; secondly, to liberty; thirdly, to property; together with the right to support and defend them in the best manner they can. These are evident branches of, rather than deductions from, the duty of self-preservation, commonly called the first law of nature."
— Samuel Adams

"'Necessity' is the plea for every infringement of human liberty; it is the argument of tyrants; it is the creed of slaves."
— William Pitt (1783)

"In all that the people can individually do as well for themselves, government ought not to interfere."
— Abraham Lincoln

"I need no warrant for being, and no word of sanction upon my being. I am the warrant and the sanction."
— Ayn Rand, *Anthem*

"Freedom is fragile and must be protected.   To sacrifice it, even as a temporary measure, is to betray it."
— Germaine Greer

"Men would rather be starving and free than fed in bonds."
— Pearl Buck, *What America Means to Me*

"There are only two kinds of freedom in the world: the freedom of the rich and powerful, and the freedom of the artist and the monk who renounces possessions."
— Anais Nin

"When the freedom they wished for most was freedom from responsibility, then Athens ceased to be free and was never free again."
— Edith Hamilton, *The Greek Way*

"Liberty, as it is conceived by current opinion, has nothing inherent about it; it is a sort of gift or trust bestowed on the individual by the state pending good behavior."
— Mary McCarthy

"Individual rights are not subject to a public vote; a majority has no right to vote away the rights of a minority."
— Ayn Rand, *The Virtue of Selfishness*

"Despite the global nature of the World Wide Web, Washington is obsessed with finding ways to monitor and control it. Apparently the free flow of news, opinions and information makes politicians, bureaucrats and law enforcement officials nervous. . . . The purpose of this propaganda campaign is obvious — to create public support for government regulation of the Internet, including the power to monitor all transmissions and shut down those it deems offensive. . . . The corporate media has responded with lurid stories about online child molesters trolling for young victims, pedophiles swapping digital kiddie porn, and international criminals using encrypted e-mails to plot worldwide reigns of terror."
— Jim Redden, *Snitch Culture* (p. 161)

"It was the spirit of liberty which made our American civilization. That spirit made the Constitution. If that spirit is gone the Constitution is gone, even though its words remain. . . . Whatever that change may be, it must be clear of those confusions which impair the great safeguards of human liberty. There must never be confusion in the Bill of Rights, the balance of power, local government,

and a government of laws, not of men."
— Herbert Hoover

"We are free and prosperous because we have inherited political and value systems fabricated by a particular set of eighteenth-century intellectuals who happened to get it right. But we have lost touch with those intellectuals, and with anything like intellectualism, even to the point of not reading books anymore, though we are literate."
— Neal Stephenson, *In the Beginning . . . Was the Command Line* (p. 53)

"The only purpose for which power can be rightfully exercised over any member of a civilized community, against his will, is to prevent harm to others."
— John Stuart Mill, *On Liberty*

"When liberty is gone,
Life grows insipid and has lost its relish."
— Joseph Addison

"You have plenty of rights in this country, provided you don't get caught exercising them."
— Terry Mitchell, *The Revolutionary Toker*

"He that has gone so far as to cut the claws of the lion will not feel himself quite secure until he has also drawn his teeth."
— Charles Caleb Colton (1825)

"To make one's own rules is the highest freedom."
— Martin Heidigger

"Emancipate yourself from mental slavery . . ."
— Bob Marley

PATRIOTISM:

"All you have to do is tell the people they are being attacked, and denounce the pacifists for lack of patriotism and exposing the country to danger. It works the same in any country."
— Hermann Goering

"We must guard against the impostures of pretended patriotism, especially that patriotism which is the last refuge of scoundrels and which is so prevalent, so professional, and so well paid nowadays."
— George Seldes (1938)

"America's become a place where they wave a flag at you and expect your brains to go out the window."
— from an old copy of *Whisper*

"No man can be a patriot on an empty stomach."
— W. C. Brann, *The Iconoclast*

"How can a man be said to have a country when he has no right to a square inch of it?"
— Henry George, *Social Problems*

"Patriotism is the last refuge of a scoundrel."
— Johnson (Boswell's *Life* for the year 1775)

"A statesman is an easy man, he tells his lies by rote.
A journalist invents his lies, and rams them down your throat.
So stay at home and drink your beer and let the neighbors vote."
— William Butler Yeats

"Here's a good example of how the meaning of a word can change drastically over time. Fifty years ago, a 'patriotic' individual was perceived as someone, usually a former serviceman, who loved their country, flew the flag on national holidays, and was proud to sing the National Anthem. Nowadays, however, the word 'patriot' implies that someone is a violently deranged, ultra-right-wing fanatic with a stockpile of illegal weapons and a seething hatred for minorities, foreigners, liberals,

teenagers, and the Federal Government. It has become an accusation rather than a compliment."
— anonymous (RWT)

"The budget should be balanced. Public debt should be curtailed. The arrogance of officialdom should be tempered, and assistance to foreign lands should be curtailed, lest Rome become bankrupt."
— Cicero (110 B.C.)

"The great fear in the hearts of these men of all nationalities was the same — the dread of awakening to the Individual Spirit within them through which they would see that all their cherished patriotic ideals were no more than a deadly tissue of dreams."
— Trevor Ravenscroft, *The Spear of Destiny* (p. 137)

"To some people, not only was my book out of order, my whole life was out of order — there was something unpatriotic, subversive, dangerous, in my criticism of so much that went on in this society."
— Howard Zinn, *You Can't Be Neutral on a Moving Train* (p. 3)

"We should behave toward our country as women behave toward the men they love. A loving wife will do anything for her husband except stop criticizing and trying to improve him. We should cast the same affectionate but sharp glance at our country."
— J. B. Priestley

"It's kinda difficult to be patriotic when our 'elected officials' keep pissing on our heads and tell us it's raining."
— anonymous (RWT)

"American patriotism is generally something that amuses Europeans, I suppose because children look idiotic saluting the flag and because the constitution contains so many cracks through which the lawyers may creep."
— Katharine Whitehorn

"It is high time that we had lights that are not incendiary torches."
— George Sand (1863)

"I question whether I want to be integrated into America as it stands now, with its complacency and materialism, its soullessness."

— Paule Marshall

"When fascism comes to this country, it's going to be wrapped in an American flag."
— Huey Long (early 1930's)

"A machine organization took charge of the fountains of public information, supervised the molding of mass psychology, and saw that the people were permitted to read only such statements as would inflame their minds with warlike frenzy and kindle their hatred of the foe."
— Stanton A. Coblentz, *From Arrow to Atom Bomb* (p. 394)

"We hold these truths to be self-evident, that all men are created equal, that they are endowed by their Creator with certain unalienable Rights, that among these are Life, Liberty and the pursuit of Happiness. That to secure these rights, Governments are instituted among Men, deriving their just powers from the consent of the governed. That whenever any Form of Government becomes destructive of these ends, it is the Right of the People to alter or to abolish it, and to institute new Government, laying its foundation on such principles and organizing its powers in such form, as to them shall seem most likely to effect their Safety and Happiness."
— *Declaration of Independence*, 1776

"It's an obscene comparison, but there was a time in South Africa when people would put flaming tires around people's necks if they dissented. In some ways, the fear is that you will be neck-laced here, you will have a flaming tire of patriotism put around your neck."
— Dan Rather

"We are not content with negative obedience, not even with the most abject submission. When finally you surrender to us, it must be of your own free will."
— George Orwell, *1984*

"A free people must have a government that embodies the ideals of that people. . . . A suicidal national government, a government that seems bent on devouring its people rather than nurturing them, forfeits our allegiance."
— Ernest Callenbach, *Ecotopia Emerging* (pg. 252)

"As for the Pledge of Allegiance, I choose not to say it. I salute the flag each morning as a symbol of what this country is supposed to be, but I can't say the Pledge. I am sorry to say that I don't believe this country offers liberty and justice for all. I will continue to work toward that end, but until I see it happening, I will not say the Pledge."
— "Ms. Finney," from *The Cat Ate My Gymsuit,* by Paula Danzinger (p. 111)

"While you may be pledging allegiance to some noble idea, don't let that blind you to the fact that your cherished group, organization, or country may also have a questionable and immoral history as well."
— Wallace Wang, *Steal This Computer Book 3* (p. 60)

"The true citizenship is to protect the flag from dishonor — to make it the emblem of a nation that is known to all nations as true and honest and honorable. And we should forever forget that old phrase — 'my country, right or wrong, my country!'"
— Mark Twain

PARANOIA

"The problem with any group is that if you do not belong, it becomes a 'they.' The word itself has power, a collective authority: for some mysterious reason, 'they say' carries more weight than 'we say.' 'They' provokes unease, if not paranoia ('They're out to get me.')."
— Christine Andreae, *Grizzly* (p. 108)

"We cannot absolutely know that all these exact adaptions are the result of preconcert. But when we see a lot of framed timbers, different portions of which we know have been gotten out at different times and places and by different workmen — Stephen, Franklin, Roger, and James, for instance — and we see these timbers joined together, and see they exactly make the frame of a house or a mill, all the tenons and mortises exactly fitting, and all the lengths and proportions of the different pieces exactly adapted to their respective places, and not a piece too many or too few, not omitting even scaffolding — or, if a single piece be lacking, we see the place in the frame exactly fitted and prepared yey to bring such piece in — in such a case we find it impossible not to believe that Stephen and Franklin and Roger and James all understood one another from the beginning, and all worked upon a common plan or draft drawn up before the first blow was struck."
— Abraham Lincoln, Speech at Springfield, June 16th, 1858

"It's not paranoia if they're really out to get you."
— unknown

"It's not paranoia, that's not it. But I watch people."
— anonymous, from Connie Fletcher's *What Cops Know* (p. 167)

"Every friend can be a potential enemy, and every enemy a potential friend."
— unknown

"I learned long ago that the only person I could count on was myself."
— unknown

"Offer not your right hand easily to anyone."
— Pythagoras

"Paranoia is a state of heightened awareness. Most people are persecuted beyond their wildest delusions."
— Claude Steiner

"Don't trust, don't beg, don't fear."
— Spetsnaz credo (originated in Soviet prisons centuries ago)

"Everyone and everything was feared. The neighbors in your building, the caretaker in your building, your own children. People lived in fear of their co-workers, those above them, those beneath them, and those on the same level. They feared oversights or mistakes on the job, but even more they feared being too successful, standing out."
— Ovesyenko, on Stalin's Great Purge

"I say it has gone too far. We are dividing into the hunted and the hunters. There is loose in the United States today the same evil that once split Salem Village between the bewitched and the accused and stole men's reason quite away. We are informers to the secret police. Honest men are spying on their neighbors for patriotism's sake. We may be sure that for every honest man two dishonest ones are spying for personal advancement today and ten will be spying for pay next year."
— Bernard De Voto (1949)

"Drink nothing without seeing it; sign nothing without reading it."
— Spanish proverb

"Never attribute to malice that which is adequately explained by stupidity."
— Arthur Bloch

"If They want to take you out discretely, They likely won't shoot you with a sniper rifle or plant a bomb under your car — not when it's so much simpler just to either run you over or bump you off the road. If you live in the city, perhaps you'll be fatally 'mugged.' Maybe your bedroom will fill up with ether one night — it'll knock you right out, and the fire will eliminate any evidence. If They

want to discredit you, a syringe full of cocaine hydrochloride solution squirted up your nostril will make your heart explode within minutes — or They could substitute a massive dose of LSD to fry your brains and land you in an institution. If They really want to get nasty, They've been known to contaminate cushions and mattresses with plutonium dust and spray the contents of refrigerators with concentrated pesticide — this can result in liver failure or rare forms of cancer, and an overworked medical examiner will likely attribute your untimely death to natural causes."
— Jake Bishop (RWT)

"Project Coast included the development of a bizarre range of biological agents and delivery systems for individual murders that would have been the envy of the Borgias. There were cholera organisms by the millions and anthrax planted in the gum of envelopes, into the filters of cigarettes, and inside chocolates. There was thallium and ricin and organo-phosphates; there was snake venom, paratyphoid, Plague, Hepatitis A, HIV, and the terrible Ebola and Marburg viruses. There was botulinum toxin secreted inside beer bottles and Salmonella germs hidden in sugar. Most of the 'bugs' were freeze-dried, where possible, for more effective use."
— Tom Mangold and Jeff Goldberg, *Plague Wars* (p, 255)

"The toxic information is spreading. There's no way to contain it. Your only choice is to destroy the credibility of that person. You have to put a stain on his character. And what's the worst stain a guy can have right now? Being linked to terrorism. So you blow up the guy's house and say it was a bomb factory. . . . Even if the guy survives, no one will ever believe him."
— Neal Stephenson, *Zodiac* (p, 219)

"The informants changed the entire culture of the movement, it started out very open and trusting, but, after we realized we had been infiltrated, people became paranoid, fearful, and distrustful. Before too long, the movement became just like the society it was protesting."
— Stew Albert, in reference to the peace movement of the 60s

"Particularly significant has been the high-level penetration we have achieved of Klan organizations. At the present time, there are 14 Klan groups in existence. We have penetrated every one of them through informants (and) currently are operating informants in top-level positions of leadership in seven of them."
— excerpted from a letter from the FBI to a White House assistant, dated September 2. 1965

". . . according to criminal justice experts, many of the people who have been convicted on drug charges are innocent. The pressure to snitch is so great that a large number of informants simply make up accusations against friends, associates — even family members — to escape the long mandatory minimum sentences."
— Jim Redden, *Snitch Culture* (pp. 195-196)

"There is no War on Crime. There is no War on Drugs. There is no War on Terrorism. There is no War on Youth Violence. There is only the ongoing effort by the federal government to collect as much information on as many people as possible. Domestic law enforcement initiatives are merely excuses to increase the amount of spying on the American people."
— Jim Redden, *Snitch Culture* (p. 60)

"By the end of the school year which included the Columbine shootings, over 3 million students had been suspended or expelled, many for doing or saying things which had never been considered a problem before. . . . During the last few weeks of the school year, American Civil Liberties Union offices across the nation were swamped with complaints from students and their parents. . . . many schools across the country spent the summer months developing new snitch programs. . . . A category called 'Early Warning Signs of Violence' urges parents and students to turn in students for such normal adolescent behavior as 'social withdrawal' and 'low interest in school.'. . . Students who express 'intolerance for difference or prejudicial attitudes' are also supposed to be reported, along with any who have 'inappropriate access to, possession of and use of firearms.'"
— Jim Redden, *Snitch Culture* (pp. 135-137)

"Once an entry is made into official computer files, nothing can dislodge it."
— *San Francisco Chronicle*, May 11, 1993

"Even if you use a file-shredding program consistently, law enforcement officials can always use a variety of computer forensic tools to pry out any secrets your deleted files may be hiding. So how can you protect your computer from their prying eyes? Basically, you can't. While you can make recovering data harder by periodically purging your cache directory and only storing files on removable disks (such as floppy or ZIP disks) and physically destroying them afterwards, just remember that everything you do on your computer can be recovered and examined later."
— Wallace Wang, *Steal This Computer Book 3* (p. 260)

"Observe the street prior to leaving home to see if your house is being watched. . . . When checking to determine if you are being followed, do not turn around in a conspicuous manner. Instead, casually glance to the rear while crossing the street, lighting a cigarette, unfolding a newspaper, entering or leaving a shop."
— Major H. Von Dach, *Total Resistance* (p. 113)

"The material to be passed would be placed in a magnetic key box, the kind you can buy at any auto parts store. To load the drop, you just stuck the magnetic box to the underside of the pay phone's shelf while making a call or looking up a number. The box is always stuck in a predetermined spot on the shelf. . . . The 'loader' makes his 'load' signal as he departs. . . . No one needs to know the identity of anyone else, especially between cells, and in the event of capture and interrogation, it helps minimize the knowledge any one operator can give up."
— Eric L. Haney, *Inside Delta Force* (p. 132)

"If you find a listening device or something you think might be, first of all, leave it alone for now. Don't say anything to alert the listener that you have found it. . . . never assume that it is the only one. Always assume that there are others. . . . Look for surveillance vans. Is there always a van parked near you? Or a panel truck or a pickup with a camper? . . . If you see a van pull up and stop, watch it for a while. If the driver doesn't get out and go somewhere, then someone is probably watching someone. Use binoculars to watch them, but don't let them see you. See if they seem to be there in shifts."
— M. L. Shannon, *Don't Bug Me* (pp. 44-45, 69)

"You should be wary of unanticipated, odd-shaped, or odd-colored packages mailed to you. These may be devices used by someone who is trying to identify you — you would be easy to spot walking out of the building with this unusual package."

— Anonymous, *New I.D. in America* (p. 55)

"The tactics by law enforcement agencies in the past have been to arrest these high profile artists on gun violations. Leaving them in a 'Catch-22' situation to violate parole by defending themselves. Or leaving them defenseless, making them easy prey . . ."
— Mutulu Shakur

". . . this heightened vigilance can become paranoia. In this state a man's perceptions are amplified like an overloaded electronic system. We start to short-circuit. We experience danger where there is none, or exaggerate present dangers."
— Robert Moore & Douglas Gillette, *The Warrior Within* (p. 111)

"On Monday, Attorney General John Ashcroft issued a terrorism warning asking all Americans to be on high alert this week. Then on Friday, he announced that the period of high alert would be extended indefinitely. I think I speak for all Americans when I say, 'Bitch, I can't be any more alert than I already am, okay?' I'm opening my mail with salad tongs; I take my passport in the shower with me; I am watching so much CNN I am having sex dreams about Wolf Blitzer."
— Tina Fey, on *Saturday Night Live's* "Weekend Update"

"Every family in Amerika should prepare themselves for terrorist attack."
— Tom Ridge, extolling the virtues of plastic wrap and duct tape (as well as promoting hysteria) on a recent Department of Heimland Defense television commercial

". . . she was terribly frightened, already depressed, acutely conscious of all her physiological

processes, and imagining all sorts of things. That's the way it always begins. If you become acutely conscious of your visceral organs and functions — heart, kidneys, respiration — no matter how sound they are, they'll soon begin to bother you. Add ordinary fear, and you'll be ill. Add superstitious terror, and you'll crack up completely."
— William Seabrook, *Witchcraft* (p. 93)

"My own information is that the IMF and World Bank were taken over by a space alien named Larry. It's obvious that 'Larry' Summers, once World Bank chief economist, later US Treasury Secretary, is in reality a platoon of extraterrestrials sent here to turn much of the human race into a source of cheap protein."
— Greg Palast, *The Best Democracy Money Can Buy* (p. 48)

"I love my country, but I fear my government."
— seen on a bumpersticker

"Evil beings can create an aura of peace around themselves and their homes. It is not a real peace, but a projection, done intentionally so as to encourage others to relax in their presence and trust them. Other evil ones have no charisma at all. They may be so dull, so lifeless, as to be remarkable only for their drabness. This keeps them hidden. . . . Religion is often a cover for evil. What safer disguise for evil than to present itself as a nun, a missionary? . . . Anyone can be evil, and no-one and nothing is beyond evil's reach. Our naive attitude regarding particular religions and certain professions, such as counselors, those who give free meals to the homeless, and other apparently blameless endeavors, gets us into trouble all the time."
— Anderson Reed, *Shouting at the Wolf* (pp. 72-74)

"Man is engaged all his life in bitter warfare with a million energies that conspire to kill him. Let him rest upon his weapons, let him relax his vigilance, let him commit his defense to the Power that has organized the attacking forces, and he is gone."
— Ambrose Bierce, *The Devil's Advocate*

"Everyone is a killer
I look at all of them now
I search out their eyes
I let them know that I'll kill them back
They take one look and they know I mean it
I lock the door behind me
Everything that moves begs me to attack it . . .
Now I walk the streets like a secret animal . . .
The one who fucks with me
Will lose his throat
He'll have no idea what he's fucking with

I live on the outskirts of humanity
I am scarred for the rest of my time here
That's all it is to me
Time left here
Time spent walking the city filth
Breathing in and out and keeping my teeth sharp
Waiting for something horrible to happen again."
— Henry Rollins, *The Portable Henry Rollins* (pp. 147-148)

DEFIANCE

"A rebel is simply someone who says "no.""
— unknown

"One should respect public opinion in so far as it is necessary to avoid starvation and keep out of prison, but anything beyond this is voluntary submission to an unnecessary tyranny."
— Bertrand Russell

"No law can be sacred to me but that of my nature."
— Ralph Waldo Emerson

"What though the field be lost?
All is not lost; th' unconquerable will,
And study of revenge, immortal hate,
And courage never to submit or yield."
— Milton, *Paradise Lost*

"They've got us surrounded again, the poor bastards."
— General Creighton W. Abrams

"I've got 'em right where I want 'em — surrounded *from the inside*."
— Sgt 1st Class Jerry "Mad Dog" Shriver

"Before a standing army can rule, the people must be disarmed, as they are in almost every kingdom in Europe. The supreme power in America cannot enforce unjust laws by the sword, because the whole body of the people are armed, and constitute a force superior to any band of regular troops that can be, on any pretense, raised in the United States."
— Noah Webster (1888)

"We would rather die on our feet than live on our knees."
— Franklin D. Roosevelt

"I'd rather die,
Than give you control!"
— Trent Reznor, "Head Like a Hole"

"You'll never take me alive, coppers!"
— paraphrased from innumerable low-budget gangster movies

"More than 2,000 heavily armed German soldiers and police were backed by tanks and artillery. The 700 to 750 ghetto fighters had a few dozen pistols and hand grenades. Yet in three days of street battles, the Germans were unable to defeat the Jewish combatants."
— from a plaque at the U.S. Holocaust Memorial Museum

"Whenever the legislators endeavor to take away and destroy the property of the people, or to reduce them to slavery under arbitrary power, they put themselves into a state of war with the people who are thereupon absolved from any further obedience."
— John Locke (1690)

"Don't believe the Church and State, and everything they tell you;
Believe in Me, I'm with the High Command . . ."
— Mike and the Mechanics, "Silent Running"

"A poet will even face death when he sees his people oppressed."

— Carolina Maria de Jesus

"I always slept in my clothes, for I never knew what might happen. Not even my incarceration in a damp underground dungeon will make me give up the fight in which I am engaged for liberty and for the rights of the working people. To be shut from the sunlight is not pleasant but . . . I shall stand firm. To be in prison is no disgrace."
— Mother Jones

"There was one of two things I had a right to, liberty or death; if I could not have one, I would have the other; for no man should take me alive."
— Harriet Tubman

"No-one attacks me with impunity."
— motto of Scotland, as well as the "Order of the Thistle"

"Go ahead! Send your ninjas against me! I got sumpthin' for 'em . . ."
— Jazzman, into a phone he believed was tapped, on a really bad day

"There are approximately 20,000 high-speed pursuits each year — of these, 40% terminate when the fleeing suspect crashes his vehicle. Every day, an average of one fleeing suspect dies as a result of his vehicle crashing."
— statistics provided by The Learning Channel (paraphrased)

"Mandatory gun registration would make instant criminals out of millions of law-abiding citizens. Confiscation laws could lead to civil war. The American people own more than 250 million handguns and rifles of all kinds, including hundreds of thousands of fully automatic machine guns. Firearms can be found in nearly half of all households, with a large share in rural areas. Many gun owners would undoubtedly refuse to go along with such laws."
— Jim Redden, *Snitch Culture* (p. 231)

"Whoever lays their hand on me is a usurper and a tyrant; I declare them to be my enemy . . . government is slavery. Its laws are cobwebs for the rich and chains of steel for the poor. To be governed is to be watched, inspected, spied on, regulated, indoctrinated, preached at, controlled, ruled, censored by persons who have neither wisdom nor virtue. It is in every action and transaction to be registered, stamped, taxed, patented, licensed, assessed, measured, reprimanded, corrected, frustrated. Under pretext of the public good it is to be exploited, monopolized, embezzled, robbed, and then, at the least protest or word of complaint, to be fined, harassed, vilified, beaten up, bludgeoned, disarmed, judged, condemned, imprisoned, shot garroted, deported, sold, betrayed,

swindled, deceived, outraged dishonoured, that's government, that's its justice, that's its morality!"
— Pierre Joseph Proudhon (1848, Paris)

"If their assaults be verbal, their defense must be likewise verbal; if the sword be drawn against them, they may also take up arms and fight either with tongue or hand, as occasion is: yea, if they be assailed by surprisals, they may also make use both of ambuscades and countermines . . ."
— "Junius Brutus" (Duplessis Mornay), *Vindiciae contra Tyrannos* (1579)

"There are two chief motives which induce men to attack tyrannies — hatred and contempt. Hatred of tyrants is inevitable, and contempt is also a frequent cause of their destruction. . . . Even the friends of a tyrant will sometimes attack him out of contempt; for the confidence which he reposes in them breeds contempt . . ."
— Aristotle, *Politics Book V*

"NEVER AGAIN!"
— J.D.L. Motto

"When you say, 'Jump!', we say, 'Go fuck yourself.'"
— seen on a button worn by a disgruntled employee

"With self-awareness emerging you can perceive the quality of sensory deadness television induces, the one-dimensionality of its narrowed information field, and arrive at an awareness of boredom. This leads ti channel switching at first and eventually to turning off the set. Any act that breaks immersion in the fantastic world of television is subversive to the medium, because without the immersion and addiction, its power is gone. Brainwashing ceases. As you watch advertising, you become enraged."
— Jerry Mander, *Four Arguments for the Elimination of Television* (p. 311)

"Why are the people rebellious?—
Because those above them meddle in their lives
That's why they're rebellious"
— Lao Tzu, *Tao Te Ching, The Definitive Edition* (Star translation), Verse 75

"QUESTION AUTHORITY"
— seen on a bumper sticker

"DIPLOMACY"

"Words are powerful tools for a warrior, for they literally shape our world. We therefore learn how a warrior approaches the correct use of words."
— Theun Mares

"Sometimes being responsible means pissing people off."
— Gen. Colin Powell

"The only graceful way to accept an insult is to ignore it; if you can't ignore it, top it; if you can't top it, laugh at it; if you can't laugh at it, it's probably deserved."
— Russell Lynes

"When you have nothing to say, say nothing; a weak defense strengthens your opponent, and silence

is less injurious than a weak reply."
— Charles Caleb Colton

"Never forget the power of silence, the massively disconcerting pause that goes on and on may at last induce an opponent to babble and backtrack nervously."
— Lance Morrow

"You start by saying no to requests. Then if you have to go to yes, OK. But if you start with yes, you can't go to no."
— Mildred Perlman

"Grasp the possibility that a truly tough and worthy competitor knows not only how to fight but also when to quit."
— Jeffery Z. Rubin

"If people wish for peace, they should cease the pin-pricks that precede cannon-shots."
— Napoleon Bonaparte

"You can avoid a lot of fights by realizing that the other guy isn't intentionally being an asshole by not seeing things your way. A sizable hunk of the time the guy literally can't understand what your point is. It's not that he's stupid, it's just that his brain operates along totally different lines."
— Marc "Animal" MacYoung, *Fists, Wits, and a Wicked Right* (p. 57)

"Matters of great concern should be treated lightly."
— Yamamoto Tsunetomo, *Hagakure* (Wilson translation)

"At times of great trouble or disaster, one word will suffice. At times of happiness, too, one word will be enough. And when meeting or talking with others, one word will do. One should think well and then speak."
— Yamamoto Tsunetomo, *Hagakure* (Wilson translation)

"He who overcomes men understands them."
— Lao Tse, *The Book of Tao*, LXVIII (6th c. B.C.)

"You can't reason with a drunk. You can lie, bullshit, con, and trick one, but you can't reason with one."
— Marc MacYoung, *A Professional's Guide to Ending Violence Quickly* (p. 205)

"To subdue an enemy without fighting is the greatest of skills."
— Sun Tzu, *Art of War*

"Your greatest weapon is in your enemy's mind."
— Buddha

"If you want to hurt them . . .
Tell them the truth always
When you meet them
Stare deep into their eyes
Take those who wish to dominate you
Turn the game around and play it on them
Don't spare them a thing
Make sure you tell them about the blood and the pain
They can say what they want
You will trigger all their responses
It's all blood and death from here
You won't be kept waiting long."
— Henry Rollins, *The Portable Henry Rollins* (p. 141)

INCARCERATION

"We live in a society of laws. Break them and you face the consequences. Use force when you shouldn't, or use excessive force, and you may find yourself living with the very people you were trying to defend against."
— Richard Ryan, *Master of the Blade* (p. 13)

"Record number of 6 million Americans incarcerated during 2001. 1 out of every 32 Americans is currently either incarcerated or under court mandated supervision."
— from CNN news ticker

"U.S. violent crime (excluding murder) at lowest rate since first tracked in 1973."
— from CNN news ticker

"I hereby sentence you to a term of no fewer than four years, to be served at a Federal pound-you-in-the-ass Prison."
— archetypical judge from a dream sequence near the end of *Office Space*

"When you take everything away from a human being, including his personal dignity, then he has nothing left to lose. He becomes extremely dangerous."
— Dr. John Salazar

". . . it is well known that there is an extraordinarily high death rate (even suicide rate) among all confined animals. This is especially true of the more intelligent ones, such as dolphins and monkeys. There is an even higher lethargy rate, as a visit to any zoo reveals."
— Jerry Mander, *Four Arguments for the Elimination of Television* (p. 121)

"Unfortunately, the rulers of any system cannot maintain their power without the constant creation of prohibitions that then give the state the right to imprison — or otherwise intimidate — anyone who violates any of the state's often new-minted crimes. . . . In the name of correctness, of good health, or even of God — a great harassment of the people-at-large is now going on. Although our state has not the power to intimidate any but small, weak countries, we can certainly throw most Americans in prison for violating the ever-increasing list of prohibitions."
— Gore Vidal, *Dreaming War* (p. 175)

"Even if you come in with a real good charge on you, if you don't have friends Inside, you'll probably have to fight a couple of times. The charge doesn't always tell the story, so people test you. You don't have to win when you fight, but you have to keep fighting until somebody stops it. And if you come in without any friends, everybody watches you. They want to see what kind of a person you are. After they find out, different things happen, depending."
— Andrew Vachss, *The Getaway Man* (p. 14)

"Jail is nothing more than a pain in the ass. The threat of being sent to jail is like threatening to send someone to his room. Often it is the cost of doing business. Many prefer staying in jail to facing the complexities of life in the world."
—Marc "Animal" MacYoung

"How would you like to be forced all the days of your life to sit beside a stinking, stupid wino every morning at breakfast? Or for some loud fool in his infinite ignorance to be at any moment able to say (slur), "Gimme a cigarette, man!" And I just look into his sleazy eyes and want to kill his ass there in front of God and everyone."
— Jack Henry Abbott

"Everyone has this badass attitude that made it very uncomfortable. Every single confrontation led to a fight. There was nowhere to run and nowhere to hide — you had to back up your words with violence."
— "Reymundo Sanchez," *My Bloody Life* (p. 271)

"Whilst we have prisons it matters little which of us occupies the cells."
— Bernard Shaw

"The most difficult part of prison to accept is that no-one in the system or out on the streets could care less what is happening to the human beings that are living in these places. No-one cares how you feel, no-one cares about your health or your state of mind."
— Harold S. Long

"One thing about prison labor: there is no shop steward or Labor Department to take a grievance to. If the foreman is pissed off at you and wants to spit at you or slap you or destroy your output, there's no a lot you can do about it."
— Sara Paretsky, *Hard Time* (p. 396)

"When we were in jail, I met a lot of my enemies. And when they didn't have a gun, boy they were quiet . . . They can't hide in jail. You can't run and hide, let me tell you, you can't. There ain't no way."
— anonymous, from *Wallbangin'* (p. 159)

"Prison is so much more dangerous than the street that inmates must be ready at all times."
— Susan A. Phillips

"I was twenty when I went in, thirty-one when I come out. You don't count months and years — you don't do time that way. You gotta forget time; you gotta not give a fuck if you live or die. You gotta get to where nothin' means nothin'."
— James Caan, in *Thief*, Screenplay by Michael Mann

"It is unnatural and degrading to cage a man like a beast. It serves no purpose but to strip a man of his dignity, twisting him in an attempt to make him conform to the whims of a sick and blatantly corrupt system. No good ever comes of this. Either the inmate assumes the identity of a beaten dog — afraid of his own shadow — or he is forced to protect his dignity with the threat of violence. Either way, the inmate becomes resentful, not respectful, of authority, and loses whatever respect he might've had for it as a direct result of his incarceration."

— anonymous (RWT)

"Before our white brothers came to civilize us we had no jails. Therefore we had no criminals. You can't have criminals without a jail. We had no locks or keys, and so we had no thieves. If a man was so poor that he had no horse, tipi or blanket, someone gave him these things."
— John Lame Deer

"They kept us blindfolded and would not allow us to speak. If we tried to speak they would hit us with the butt of a gun . . . We had our hands tied; escape was virtually impossible because we were so well guarded. We disrobed right down to our skivvies and we were barefoot . . ."
— William Lawrence, USN (POW 1967-1973)

"If punishment has no effect to diminish or prevent crime, then no danger would be incurred to dismiss our jailers and jurors and close our prison doors."
— Clarence S. Darrow

"Through a year or more of sensory and psychological deprivation, prisoners are stripped of their individual identities in order that compliant behavior patterns can be implanted, a process of mortification and depersonalization."
— Report on the U.S. Penitentiary at Marion, John Howard Association Report, October 1987, (p. 1)

(The purpose of a HSU (High Security Unit) style facility is to)". . . reduce prisoners to a state of submission essential for their ideological conversion. That failing, the next objective is to reduce them to a state of psychological incompetence sufficient to neutralize them as efficient, self-directing antagonists. That failing, the only alternative is to destroy them, preferably by making them desperate enough to destroy themselves."
— from the ACLU sponsored report, *Effects of Confinement in HSU*, by Dr. Richard Korn

"Hitler instituted slave labor, which often was equivalent to execution. Laborers were routinely beaten to death or died of cold, untreated illness, or starvation. The penalty for 'loafing' or any refusal of work was hanging."
— Hershman & Lieb, *A Brotherhood of Tyrants* (p. 186)

"Anybody out on the yard at night alone was shot. If you ran in the yard, you were shot. If you fought in the yard, both of you were shot, no warning. When shit happened in Folsom, they'd kill you on the spot, then sort things out later."
— Ralph "Sonny" Barger, on Folsom Federal Penitentiary's questionable policies during the early 70s, from *Hell's Angel* (p. 194)

"I am convinced that imprisonment is a way of pretending to solve the problem of crime. It does nothing for the victims of crime, but perpetuates the idea of retribution, thus maintaining the endless cycle of violence in our culture. It is a cruel and useless substitute for the elimination of those conditions — poverty, unemployment, homelessness, desperation, racism, greed — which are at the root of most punished crime. The crimes of the rich and powerful go mostly unpunished."
— Howard Zinn, *You Can't Be Neutral on a Moving Train* (p. 150)

"And remember, if 'Big Luther' tells you to 'touch yer toes,' just say NO . . ."
— Jazzman, just prior to a brother's sentencing

"The sight of a cage is only frightening to the bird that has once been caught."
— Rachel Field, *All This and Heaven Too*

"You have put me in here as a cub, but I will come out roaring like a lion, and I will make all hell howl!"
— Carry Nation (1901)

"Jail and prisons are designed to break human beings, to convert the population into specimens in a zoo — obedient to our keepers, but dangerous to each other."
— Angela Davis

"The character and mentality of the keepers may be of more importance than the character and mentality of the kept."
— Jessica Mitford, *Kind and Unusual Punishment*

"Inmates live in fear. The informal organization of prison is a pecking order, with the stronger and better organized inmates preying on the weaker ones. This preying takes many forms, such as expropriation of food, tobacco, and other personal property. It can also involve sex."
— Jack Luger, *Improvised Weapons in American Prisons* (p. 20)

"With the passing of time, the criminal will forget the reason for his crime; it is best to execute him on the spot."
— Yamamoto Tsunetomo, *Hagakure* (Wilson translation)

"You can get raped and killed here. Addicted and imprisoned. Saturated and intimidated. Isolated and condemned. You might not get what you deserve but you'll get something that hurts."
— Henry Rollins, from *The Portable Henry Rollins* (p. 205)

"Stay out of jail."
— Alfred Hitchcock (advice to young writers)

POLICE STATE:

"The state calls its own violence law, but that of the individual crime."
— Max Stirner

"We can't allow a locked-down surveillance society to be institutionalized by media-incited people or career-building politicians. We can't let the land of the free become 'Fortress America,' where what's left of liberty is frisked, x-rayed, fingerprinted, digitized, thermal-imaged, retina-scanned and strip-searched."
— Wayne LaPierre

"If its purpose is to create one of the highest crime rates in the world — and thus to provide permanent fodder for demagogues who decry crime and promise to do something about it — it is achieving that end. If its purpose is de facto repeal of the Bill of Rights, victory is in sight."
— Steven Duke, referring to the "War on Drugs" in an article submitted to *National Review*

"Simply put, the government's 'war on drugs' hysteria is a thinly disguised campaign to invade private homes, steal property and assert control over private citizens."
— Kenn Thomas

"If you (smoke marijuana) in this country you cease to have any human rights. They can manhandle you, imprison you, take your car, your home, your children . . ."
— Vlad the Inhaler

"The people who cut down the ganja are devils! Devils! If you dance, you are a dancer. If you pick up the garbage, you are a garbage man. If you do the devil's work, you are the devil."
— Rasta Tex

"Protective Custody is an act of care."
— the despicable Heinrich Himmler, attempting to veil the true nature of the Concentration Camps through propaganda

"CIA officials wanted the (Stinger) missiles to fall into the hands of terrorists. The downing of one or more commercial aircraft would justify their existence and expansion, as well as 'justifying' imposing Draconian security measures upon the American people."
— Rodney Stich, *Defrauding America* (p. 267)

"A frequent charge for sentencing innocent people to prison is charging them with the federal crime, misprision of felony. Anyone who knows of a federal crime and who does not promptly report it to a federal judge or other federal tribunal is guilty of this crime."
— Rodney Stich, *Defrauding America*(p. 487)

"The federal government now has the audacity to say that members of a family are members of a conspiracy, little children are members of a conspiracy."
— Gerry Spense (in reference to the Weaver trial)

"The inescapable message of much of the material we have covered is that the FBI jeopardizes the whole system of freedom of expression which is the cornerstone of an open society . . . At worst it raises the specter of a police state . . . in essence the FBI conceives of itself as an instrument to prevent radical social change in America . . . the Bureau's view of its function leads it beyond data collection and into political warfare."
— Thomas I. Emerson, Yale Law Professor (1971)

"The constitution and all citizen's rights were immediately abolished. . . . Labor unions were outlawed and replaced by a fraudulent national union. Censorship and the total extinction of free speech were celebrated with great bonfires of books. Germany's prisons filled with those who had openly opposed Hitler; concentration camps would soon swallow the overflow."
— Hershman & Lieb, *A Brotherhood of Tyrants* (p. 69)

"Comrades, we are not uncovering conspiracies, we are fabricating them. We are persecuting and killing people on the basis of unfounded and slanderous charges."
— Drovyanikov of the Leningrad NKVD (who was shortly thereafter executed for "treason"as a result of this statement)

"Very few people knew the real dimensions of what was happening. Most trials were secret and it was illegal to seek any information about them. The NKVD kept many imprisonments and executions hidden even from surviving family members, either by saying the arrested had been transferred or by claiming that the missing had been exiled without the right to send letters. Deaths due to torture were officially attributed to natural causes: murders were disguised as accidents or suicides."
— Hershman & Lieb, *A Brotherhood of Tyrants* (pp. 113-114)

"I'd do as I please, act high-handed and regal,
'Cause when you're a G-Man there's nothing illegal."
— Harold Rome, from "The G-Man Song" (1937)

"Police, I learned over the years, are like soldiers, normally good-natured people, but part of a culture of obedience to orders and capable of brutal acts against anyone designated as 'the enemy."
— Howard Zinn, *You Can't Be Neutral on a Moving Train*

"Man's dominance is pathological. His control is compulsive and ill . . . Power is an unfortunate

palliative for the insecure."
— Gerry Spense

"They would take you to a secret sub-basement of a military or government building, where they would methodically savage your body and brain with the latest 'advances' in torture methods, designed to inflict the maximum pain a human can tolerate without losing consciousness or dying, until you named all the other 'leftists' you knew. You would then be 'disappeared' from the face of the earth, and these men would pay a visit to everyone you had named."
— Michael Levine, on the estimated 25,000 desaparecidos of Argentina, from *The Big White Lie* (p. 29)

"The main enemies of the revolution were union leaders, student leaders, journalists, progressive clergy, political activists, and just ordinary Bolivians who happened to be in someone's gunsight. Thousands were herded into sports stadiums in a style reminiscent of the 1973 Chilean coup, from where special groups were selected for torture and execution."
— Michael Levine, on the "Cocaine Coup" masterminded by fugitive Nazi war criminal Klaus Barbie, from *The Big White Lie* (p. 59)

"If a skilled polygraph examiner wants you to fail, you fail. I don't care how truthful you think you are. One of the things you've got to be wary of is if they try to change questions at the last minute — if they try to make them so general in scope that you have to fail. They might say, for instance, 'Have you ever taken anything that doesn't belong to you since you've been (employed here)? You could fail if you once took home some paper clips or a pen. If . . . you already suspect that you're being set up, why even agree to a test that can only hurt you?"
— "Ken," a former government polygraph examiner

"So the inhabitants of Thessalonica were invited to games in the circus — seven thousand of them — and then the doors were closed and the soldiers were given the signal for a massacre. It took three hours, and at the end of that time all the citizens were dead."
— Colin Wilson, *A Criminal History of Mankind* (p. 234)

"If science produces no better fruits than tyranny . . . I would rather wish our country to be ignorant, honest and estimable as our neighboring savages are."
— Thomas Jefferson (1812)

"Gentlemen do not read each other's mail."
— Henry L. Stimson

"The dream of every leader, whether a tyrannical despot or a benign prophet, is to regulate the

behavior of his people."
— Colin Blakemore

"Yes, we can successfully overthrow the governments of Third World countries by means of covert operations, but we always replace those governments with repressive regimes. Their collective record of murder, torture, theft, and abuse is a disgrace to this country and everything we want it to stand for."
— Molly Ivins

"There is an interesting resemblance in the speeches of dictators, no matter what country they may hail from or what language they may speak."
— Edna Ferber, *A Kind of Magic*

"But I have noticed this about ambitious men, or men in power — they fear even the slightest and least likely threat to it."
— Mary Stewart, *The Crystal Cave*

"The war on crime has gotten to the point that all these offices are stuffed to the gills with resources. They have to justify their existence. They go out and make things crimes that weren't even crimes 10 years ago."
— Thomas Dillard

"The deal Tredwell cut with the government is typical of professional informants. He was not only paid a regular salary, but received bonuses for every bust he helped set up. In addition, as long as he was informing, the government allowed Tredwell to continue dealing drugs, and to break a number of other state and federal laws, too."
— *United States of America v. Rance Preston*, CR 92-155 RE, USDC Oregon

"Children will be instructed to report any unfriendly remarks made about the regime. The final goal is to have an informer (the child) in each family so that parents and sisters and brothers will be watched. . . . Attempts will be made to misrepresent and change history. Efforts will be made to degrade and neutralize all former democratic institutions and principles. . . . Such words as peace, freedom, democracy will be so twisted and distorted that the younger generation will no longer know what they really mean."
— Major H. von Dach, *Total Resistance* (p. 135)

"Nothing is more offensive to the average citizen than the notion of children informing the authorities on their parents. Child-snitches are a tool of totalitarian regimes, such as Nazi Germany

and the former Soviet Union. Americans generally regard the idea of the state using children to monitor their parents as morally repugnant, even though it happens all the time."
— Jim Redden, *Snitch Culture* (p. 20)

"Arguing that criminals and terrorists were infesting the information superhighway, the government wants to wiretap every phone, computer, and fax machine."
— Jim Redden, in reference to Projects ECHELON and CARNIVORE, from *Snitch Culture* (p. 42)

"Putting surveillance cameras everywhere, monitoring random conversations, and turning local law-enforcement into black-armored tactical teams would be a lot more acceptable if the laws were just and government officials were trustworthy."
— Jake Bishop (RWT)

"When we deny something, we create it — or at least, we create the conditions in which it can grow and flourish, precisely because there is no resistance. In Nazi Germany, it was not the resistance to fascism that allowed the spread of Anti-Semitism and led to the death camps, it was the widespread denial, the refusal to admit that such things could happen."
— Starhawk, *Dreaming the Dark* (p. 98)

"One reason America has been moving so effortlessly into a post-constitutional, post-democratic era has been the willingness of the mass media to terrorize the public with stories and images of a country out of control. The work that more primitive societies once did with government ministries and state broadcasting is now done voluntarily, primarily by television networks. Programs glorifying extreme police actions are daily fare, sending the subliminal message that control by cop is a normal form of government and anesthetizing viewers against violence, much as is done with troops to ready them for battle."
— Sam Smith, *Progressive Review*, September 21, 1999

"It's the militarization of Mayberry. This is unprecedented in American policing, and you have to ask yourself, what are the unintended consequences?"
— Peter Kraska

"The more a police officer thinks of himself as a soldier, the more likely he views the citizen as the enemy."
— James Fyfe

"The line between a free society and a police state is usually broached in small steps."
— Roger Pilon

". . . it has been proven beyond contradiction that the CIA were principal importers of Crack Cocaine and Cocaine period into the hood, initiating the newly created drug laws that were blatantly racially motivated to set into motion tactics of genocide to destroy and lock away our brothers and sisters for the rest of their lives."
— Mutulu Shakur

"COINTELPRO was out to do more than prevent a Communist menace from overtaking the United States, or keep the Black Power movement from burning down cities. COINTELPRO was out to obliterate its opposition and ruin the reputations of the people involved in the antiwar movement, the civil rights movement, and the rock revolution."
— John Holmstrom

"Show them as scurrilous and depraved. Call attention to their habits and living conditions, explore every possible embarrassment. Send in women and sex, break up marriages. Have members arrested on marijuana charges. Investigate personal conflicts or animosities between them. Send articles to the newspapers showing their depravity. Use narcotics and free sex to entrap. Use misinformation to confuse and disrupt. Get records of their bank accounts. Obtain specimens of handwriting.. Provoke target groups into rivalries that may result in death."
— leaked intelligence memorandum submitted for the record before the Senate Intelligence Committee on 26APR76

"He discovered that by boring into an individual's skull with a surgical pick and severing the prefrontal cortex from the rest of the brain he could make the most troublesome patients docile. . . . In the 1950s the procedure's popularity continued and it became a tool, like the McCarthy hearings, to stamp out cultural undesirables. So accepted was its use for this purpose that the surgeon Walter Freeman, the most outspoken advocate for the procedure in the United States, wrote unashamedly that lobotomies 'made good American citizens' out of society's misfits, 'schizophrenics, homosexuals, and radicals.'"
— Michael Talbot, *The Holographic Universe* (p. 4)

"The principal type of surgical intervention which has been practiced is known as prefrontal lobotomy, and consists in the removal or isolation of a portion of the prefrontal lobe of the cortex. It recently has been having a certain vouge, probably not unconnected with the fact that it makes the custodial care of many patients easier. Let me remark in passing that killing them makes their custodial care still easier."
— Norbert Wiener, *Cybernetics*

"Don't resist an illegitimate arrest. You'll beat it in court if the arrest is improper, but you'll make it legitimate if you resist."
— E. X. Boozhie, *The Outlaw's Bible* (p. 303)

"The golden rule of police interrogation is: absolutely nothing said by police interrogators will be the truth."
— Ragnar Benson, *Ragnar's Guide to Interviews, Investigations, and Interrogations* (p. 56 — paraphrased)

"If you are scared, you are powerless. If you are always wondering when they are going to come and get you, your soul will wither away and your life of freedom will be meaningless."
— Sheldon Charrett, *The Modern Identity Changer* (p. 124)

"There's a wonderful sense of duty and responsibility on the part of most people. Otherwise, the whole system fails. You can't do it by having a policeman at the door or having a truant officer check up on every employee to make sure they really are sick. You work on the basis of trust. That's how the world runs. And, when you don't have that trust, then the world comes apart."
— Richard DeVos

"The SS order was a state within a state, not subject to national law, with its own laws, courts, and judges. A curtain separated Himmler's empire from the outside world; other Germans, no matter how lofty their position, could not penetrate it. SS men were discouraged from contact with others. Concentration-camp guards could not be stationed near home, were shifted to new locations every three months, and could never be transferred to street duty."
— Dusty Sklar, *Gods and Men* (p. 98)

"They were suspiciously very ready with the Patriot Act as soon as we were hit. Ready to lift *habeas corpus*, due process, the attorney-client privilege. They were ready. Which means they have already got their police state."
— Gore Vidal, *Dreaming War* (p. 192)

"They say that the people who listen to bugs for a living are all thirty-five-year-old men who still live with their mothers. That was the image I kept in my own mind. Some kind of balding, spare-tired paleface in wirerims, sitting at a desk, monitoring my life and worrying about the carburetor on his Chevette. I didn't care what he heard, because if he didn't know by now that I wasn't a terrorist, he'd never figure it out."
— Neal Stephenson, *Zodiac* (pp. 125-126)

"While it appeared, in all of the pogroms, that decent people were tracking down bad ones in order to save the world from evil, precisely the opposite happened. In the tortures and murders, primary evil was the instigator because it was the beneficiary. The men and women who were jailed, ostracized, tortured and murdered for being witches were not the evil ones; the evil ones were behind

these persecutions. . . . It was a banquet for evil, arranged by evil, and served up by the human race in a frenzy of fear and ignorance."
— Anderson Reed, *Shouting at the Wolf* (pp. 66-67)

"The final, and the desperate effort of any reactionary regime to preserve the economic-financial status-quo, can be called Fascism provided it acts according to the Fascist pattern — and that means, that to be Fascist it must employ violence, it must use armed force, it must if necessary impose itself through armed seizure of power and armed maintenance of power. This has been proved true elsewhere; it is the pattern for Fascism in America. . . . It is always money and power that control Fascism. The backers of Fascism everywhere are the industrialists, manufacturers, big businessmen, the bankers."
— George Seldes (1938)

"Nothing was so frequently discoursed of as the propriety of employing, for a good purpose, the means which the wicked employed for evil purposes; and it was taught, that the preponderancy of good in the ultimate result consecrated every mean employed . . ."
— John Robison, *Proofs of a Conspiracy Against all the Religions and Governments of Europe, Carried on in the Secret Meetings of Free Masons, Illuminati, and Reading Societies* (Edinburgh, 1797)

"They will close their eyes to everything because we will promise them to return all the liberties taken away, after the enemies of peace have been subjugated and all the parties pacified. Is it worth while to speak of how long they will have to wait?"
— *Protocols*

"Assassination: the extreme form of censorship."
— George Bernard Shaw

LESS THAN LETHAL

"Radio-frequency weapons that impair the nervous system might have uses in commando operations, anti-terrorist actions, and what the Pentagon calls 'low level conflicts' when more deadly weapons are being held back."
— Dr. Robert Beck

"These frequencies fall precisely within the psychoactive range of neuronal synchronization or brainwave entrainment, where subjects experience states from increased anxiety to extreme disorientation and even unconsciousness."
— Robert C. Beck

"Several 'disabling technologies' employ high-intensity strobe lights that flash at or near human brain-wave frequency, causing disorientation and nausea."
— Paul Evancoe

"A thermal gun would have the operational effect of heating the body to 105 to 107 degrees Fahrenheit, thereby incapacitating any threat, based on the fact that even a slight fever can affect the ability of a person to perform even simple tasks. This approach is built on four decades of research relating radio frequency exposure to body heating. A seizure gun would use electromagnetic energy to induce epileptic-like seizures in persons within the range of a particular electromagnetic field. The magnetophosphene gun is designed around a biophysical mechanism which evokes a visual response and is thought to be centered in the retina . . ."
— John Alexander

". . . microwave radiation has frequently been cited as being responsible for non-thermal effects in integrated central nervous system activity. The behavioral consequences most frequently reported have been disability, listlessness and increased irritability."
— National Bureau of Standards, Law Enforcement Standards Laboratory

"When a part of your brain receives a tiny electrical impulse from outside sources, such as vision, hearing, etc., an emotion is produced — anger at the sight of a gang of boys beating an old woman, for example. The same emotion of anger can be created by artificial radio signals sent to your brain by a controller. You could instantly feel the same white hot anger without any apparent reason."
— Walter Bowart, *Operation Mind Control* (pp. 261-264)

"Hoffman-La Roche, a pharmaceutical company in Nutley, New Jersey, was the Army's source for a new psychoactive compound, quinuclidinyl benzilate: BZ. This is a drug with even more profound effects than LSD, effects that last for about three days — but that have been known to last for six weeks. One Army doctor noted of BZ that, 'During the period of acute effects the person is

completely out of touch with his environment.'"
— Alex Constantine

"I saw some very frightening films of soldiers who had been given BZ. The guys were reduced to catatonics. They would just sit there, drooling, with no control over their bodily functions unless they were given commands, like 'get up,' or 'put your helmet on.'"
— Arnold Rothman

"The capability of communicating directly with humans by pulsed microwaves is obviously not limited to the field of therapeutic medicine."
— Dr. James Lin, *Microwave Auditory Effects and Applications*

"A 1976 DIA report mentions 'anti-personnel applications' of pulsed microwaves that carry 'sounds and possibly even words which appear to be originating intercranially.'"
— Paul Brodeur, *The Zapping of America: Microwaves, Their Deadly Risk, and the Cover-Up* (p. 295)

"Experiments had produced some communications equipment that far exceeded the ability to broadcast defeat into the minds of the enemy. It is not only capable of producing auditory hallucinations, but visual hallucinations as well."
— Harlan Girard, in a 1991 NATO address on emergent technologies

". . . potential uses include dealing with terrorist groups, crowd control, controlling breaches of security at military installations, and antipersonnel techniques in tactical warfare. In all of these cases the EM systems would be used to produce mild to severe physiological disruption or perceptual distortion or disorientation. In addition, the ability of individuals to function could be degraded to such a point that they would be combat ineffective. Another advantage of electromagnetic systems is that they can provide coverage over large areas with a single system. They are silent and countermeasures to them may be difficult to develop . . ."
— Lt Col. David J. Dean, *Low-Intensity Conflict and Modern Technology* (pp. 249-251)

"External stimulation of the brain by electromagnetic means can cause the brain to be entrained or locked into phase with an external signal generator. Predominate brain waves can be driven or pushed into new frequency patterns . . . which then cause changes in brain outputs in the form of thoughts, emotions or physical condition."

— Dr. Nick Begich, *Angels Don't Play This HAARP* (p. 137)

". . . advanced infrasound generators designed for crowd control have been tested by France and

other nations. The devices emit very low-frequency sound waves that can be tuned to cause disorientation, nausea, and loss of bowel control."
— Alvin and Heidi Toffler, *War and Anti-War* (p. 129)

"Fascinated by the phenomenon, Gavraud decided to build machines to produce infrasound so that he could investigate it further. In casting around for likely designs, he discovered that the whistle with a pea in it issued to all French gendarmes produced a whole range of low-frequency sounds. So he built a police whistle six feet long and powered it with compressed air. The technician who gave the giant whistle its first trial blast fell down dead on the spot. A post-mortem revealed that all his internal organs had been mashed into an amorphous jelly by the vibrations."
— Lyall Watson, *Supernature* (p. 93)

"Laser rifles are no fantasy. They can damage enemy optical and infrared equipment. Used against people, they can flash blind them temporarily. They can also do permanent harm, depending on the power used and whether the targeted person is using optical equipment like night vision goggles, which might amplify the light."
— Alvin and Heidi Toffler, *War and Anti-War* (pp. 130-131)

"When we must incapacitate people as well as equipment, calmatives or sleep agents mixed with DMSO can curb violence and limit casualties wherever full NBC gear is not worn. In anti-terrorist actions, counterinsurgency, ethnic violence, riot control, or even in select hostage situations, calmative agents offer an underrated tactic whose effectiveness depends only on modern precision and area delivery systems."
— U.S. Global Strategy Council

"(There allegedly was) a United States government study into the feasibility of using holographs as weapons. . . . The simplest way to describe a holograph is that cris-crossing laser beams create a 3-D image capable of being seen from all angles. This technology opens the possibility of projecting images into the sky in order to affect the minds of anyone seeing the images."
— Lung & Prowant, *The Black Science* (pp. 159-160)

"With the right electromagnetic field, for example, you might be able to produce the same effects as psychoactive drugs."
— Capt. Paul Tyler

"U.S. agents were able to destroy any person's reputation by inducing hysteria or excessive emotional responses, temporary or permanent insanity, suggest or encourage suicide, erase memory, invent double or triple personalities inside one mind . . ."
— Mae Brussell

"This agency [DARPA] is not aware of any research projections, classified or unclassified, conducted under the auspices of the Defense Department, now ongoing, or in the past, which would have probed possibilities of utilizing microwave radiation in a form of what is popularly known as 'mind control.' We do not foresee the development by DARPA of weapons utilizing microwaves and actively being directed toward altering nervous system functions or behavior. Neither are we aware of any of our own forces . . . developing such weapons."
— George H. Heilmeier, director of Defense Advance Research Projects Agency, in response to a 1977 Congressional inquiry

"KILL YOUR TELEVISION!":

"Television is a communication medium that effortlessly transmits huge quantities of information not thought about at the time of exposure."
— Herbert Krugman

"A monopoly on the means of communication may define a ruling elite more precisely that the celebrated Marxian formula of 'monopoly on the means of production.' Since man extends his nervous system through channels of communication like the written word, the telephone, radio, etc., he who controls these media controls part of the nervous system of every member of society. The contents of these media become part of the contents of every individual's brain."
— Hagbard Celine

"Look at the way most of us relax. We come home after work, exhausted. We turn on the TV — a reflex. We sit there passively hour after hour, barely moving except to eat. We receive but we do not transmit. Identical images flow into our brains, homogenizing our perspectives, knowledge, tastes, and desires."
— Kalle Lasn, *Culture Jam* (p. 11)

"The images enter you and are recorded in memory whether you think about them or not. They pour into you like fluid into a container. You are the container. The television is the pourer. . . . It is total involvement on the one hand — complete immersion in the image stream — and total unconscious detachment on the other hand — no cognition, no discernment, no notations upon the experience one is having."
— Jerry Mander, *Four Arguments for the Elimination of Television* (p. 204)

"The images seem to pass right through me, they go way inside, past my consciousness into a deeper level of mind, as if they were dreams."
— Jack Edelson

"Corporate America determines what electronic primary experiences our children shall have, where,

on any given evening, we shall travel and what we shall see, and from what perspective. It decides what news we shall hear, what blood on what streets, what deaths, what crimes, what scandals. It is frightening to realize that corporations with mind-altering electronics possess the power to control 250 million mostly unsuspecting subjects."
— Gerry Spence, *From Freedom to Slavery* (p. 146)

"The immensely rich and powerful corporations of this country can buy access to the public mind, can form public taste, and can create public opinion. These corporations can invade our minds and change our likes or dislikes, our ideas, our values, and even our personalities."
— Gerry Spence, *From Freedom to Slavery* (p. 147)

"In modern parlance to become the subject of hypnosis is to become spell-bound, and because all human beings are both affectible and suggestible, all are subject, more or less, to hypnotic influence."
— Julian Franklyn, *Death by Enchantment* (p. 14)

"Television is by nature the dominator drug par excellence. Control of content, uniformity of content, repeatability of content make it inevitably a tool of coercion, brainwashing, and manipulation. Television induces a trance state in the viewer that is the necessary precondition for brainwashing."
— Terrence McKenna, *Food of the Gods*

"Television can synchronize the mental processes of hundreds of millions of people simultaneously."
— Dr. Chris Gross

". . . television is a medium that tends to portray the world as left and right, good and bad, black and white. There is little time for the all-important grays where real life exists."
— Catherine Crier, *The Case Against Lawyers* (p. 219)

"That televised commercials influence the food choices, preferences, and demands of children — particularly younger children — has been well understood since the early 1970s. Researchers consistently have linked snack choices and food requests to televised commercials, especially to those repeated frequently. The conclusion from such studies seems inescapable: television advertising works well and is especially effective for the most frequently aired commercials such as those for sugared cereals, candy bars, and soft drinks."
— Marion Nestle, *Food Politics* (p. 182)

"But a hypnotic state is harmful to those often subjected to it; a negative psychological effect ensues

that in time deranges the brain cells. Hypnotism is trespass into the territory of another's consciousness."
— Paramahansa Yogananda, *Autobiography of a Yogi* (p. 57)

"If you accept the existence of advertising, you accept a system designed to persuade and to dominate minds by interfering in people's thinking patterns. You also accept that the system will be used by the sorts of people who like to influence people and are good at it. No person who did not wish to dominate others would choose to use advertising, or choosing it, succeed in it."

— Jerry Mander, *Four Arguments for the Elimination of Television* (p. 45)

"With an evil magic, the brainwashing transforms our children from the bright, the inquiring and the creative to mindless consumers, to empty-headed shoppers concerned chiefly with things, and the means by which to acquire things."
— Gerry Spense

"Advertising may be described as the science of arresting the human intelligence long enough to get money from it."
— Stephen Leacock

"When you are watching TV, you are experiencing mental images. As distinguished from most sense-deprivation experiments these mental images are not yours. They are someone else's. Because the rest of your capacities have been subdued, and the rest of the world dimmed, these images are likely to have an extraordinary degree of influence. Am I saying this is brainwashing or hypnosis or mind-zapping or something like it? Well, there is no question that someone is speaking into your mind and wants you to do something."
— Jerry Mander, *Four Arguments for the Elimination of Television* (p. 169)

"A meme (rhymes with "dream") is a unit of information (a catchphrase, a concept, a tune, a notion of fashion, philosophy or politics) that leaps from brain to brain. Memes compete with one another for replication, and are passed down through a population much the same way genes pass through a species. Potent memes can change minds, alter behavior, catalyze collective mindshifts and transform cultures. Which is why meme warfare has become the geopolitical battle of our information age. Whoever has the memes has the power,"
— Kalle Lasn, from *Culture Jam* (p. 123)

"And shall we just carelessly allow children to . . . receive into their minds ideas for the most part the very opposite of those which we should wish them to have when they grown up?"
— Plato, *The Republic, Book II*

EMPIRE:

"You can either have Republic or Empire, but you cannot have both."
— James Madison

"Their dogma holds that it is moral to take first and most from the weakest and the poorest, and that it is laudable to create classes of people based on wealth, not virtue."
— Gerry Spense

"Their concern for the rights and needs of others shrank to the vanishing point while their egos expanded to infinity. Everything and everyone belonged to them, existing only to satisfy their desires, which increased exponentially."
— Hershman & Lieb, *A Brotherhood of Tyrants* (pp. 198-199)

"Of all the contrivances of the aristocracy, next to the usurpation of the judiciary, and thus turning the most potent engine of the people's government against themselves, their unions in the shape of incorporate monopolies are the most subtle, and the best calculated to promote the ends of the few, the ignorance, degradation, and slavery of the many."
— Frederick Robinson (1834)

"I've always resented the smug statements of politicians, media commentators, corporate executives who talked of how, in America, if you worked hard you would become rich. The meaning of this was that if you were poor you hadn't worked hard enough."
— Howard Zinn, *You Can't Be Neutral on a Moving Train* (p. 165)

"The corporation cannot be ethical. Its only responsibility is to turn a profit."
— economist Milton Friedman

"Corporations have neither bodies to kick nor souls to damn."
— Andrew Jackson

"When punished, the corporation never repents. Nor is it jailed, for, as we have observed, these corporations do not exist in any physical sense so they cannot, in fact, be punished. As concerns justice, those invisible entities are, for reasons not at all clear, in most ways above the law and remain immune to the operation of justice."
— Gerry Spense

"The idea that the poor are poor because they are lazy, and that the rich are rich because they are not, is part of the dogma of free enterprise and leaves half the world famished and in rags."
— Gerry Spense

"The Chinese (role) exchanges have been brutal: scholars sent away from their books to do manual labor, peasants called to the city to run computers, and the like. . . . For the sake of freeing people from the toils of bureaucracy, the Cultural Revolution treated people with contempt for their differences in ability and interest. To be free was to make no discriminations."
— Richard Sennett, *Authority* (p. 184)

"If one is guided by profit in one's actions, one will incur much ill will."
— Confucius

"Galton derived the word eugenics from the Greek 'eugenes' meaning 'well born.' This aggrandizement of the privileged class was one of the reasons why eugenics research found ready support from the monied in both America and Europe; it justified their disdain for and parasitism of 'the masses.'"
— Jim Keith, paraphrasing Stefan Kuhl

"Ambition breeds competition and therefore destroys people. A society based on greed and acquisition has always within it the spectre of war, conflict, suffering."
— J. Krishnamurti

"For the first time in the history of the world, every human being is now subject to contact with

dangerous chemicals, from the moment of conception until death."
— Rachel Carson, *Silent Spring*

"Capitalism and altruism are incompatible; they are philosophical opposites; they cannot co-exist in the same man or in the same society."
— Ayn Rand, *For the New Intellectual*

"Fascism should rightly be called corporatism, as it is a merge of state and corporate power."
— Benito Mussolini

"Workers are treated like criminal fifth graders."
— anonymous, from *Going Postal* by Don Lasseter (p. 300)

"A man who wants money, power, position, is perpetually occupied with it."
— Krishnamurti, *The Network of Thought*

"He who has the gold makes the rules."
— *The Golden Rule*, author unknown

"In one sense, McWorld itself is a theme park — a park called Marketland where everything is for sale and someone else is always responsible and there are no common goods or public interests and where everyone is equal as long as they can afford the price of admission and are content to watch and to consume. . . . Infantilism is a state of mind dear to McWorld, for it is defined by 'I want, I want, I want' and 'Gimme, gimme, gimme,' favorites from the Consumer's Book of Nursery Rhymes."
— Benjamin R. Barber, *Jihad vs. McWorld* (pp. 136 & 93)

"During what's been called the 'Mexican economic miracle' of the last decade, their wages have dropped 60%. Union organizers get killed. If the Ford Motor Company wants to toss out its work force and hire super cheap labor, they just do it. Nobody stops them. Pollution goes on unregulated. It's a great place for investors."
— Noam Chomsky, on NAFTA

"A business or a big corporation is a fascist structure internally. Power is at the top. Orders go from top to bottom. You either follow the orders or get out."
— Noam Chomsky

"What makes work alienating is the hierarchical structure in which our efforts, our pace, our needs, our sense of timing, our connection with our own bodies' rhythms and with our friends and co-workers, are all shaped to serve somebody else's ends. When we are valued only as objects, for the most mechanical of our abilities, when our work serves the ends that seem meaningless or even harmful to us, we are alienated."
— Starhawk, *Dreaming the Dark* (p. 145)

"For the peasant-laboring classes, however, discipline and hard work led, at best, to bare survival. The work ethic was used by the monied classes to impose discipline on the laborers and the poor. Idleness was sinful . . . Charges of idleness also justified low wages. . ."
— Starhawk, *Dreaming the Dark* (p. 211)

"Now let us consider . . . a drug capable of making people happy in situations where they would normally feel miserable. Such a drug would be a blessing, but a blessing fraught with grave political dangers. . . . a pharmacological method of making people love their servitude, and producing . . . a kind of painless concentration camp for entire societies."
— Aldous Huxley

"Capitalism survives by forcing the majority, whom it exploits, to define their own interests as narrowly as possible. This was once achieved by extensive deprivation. Today in the developed countries it is being achieved by imposing a false standard of what is and what is not desirable."
— Peter Smith, *Ways of Seeing* (p. 154)

"The Devil no doubt has some interest in cultural despair, Satan chic, and demonic rock groups, but he must be much more enthusiastic about nuclear armament, gulags, and exploitive imperialism . . ."
— Jeffery Burton Russell, *Mephistopheles* (p. 257)

"The leaflet says that workers in the burger chains are paid low wages and accuses you of tempting your customers with food too high in fat, sugar and salt and too low in vitamins to be healthy. Do you: (a) ignore your critics . . .: (b) hire private detectives to infiltrate their meetings and spy on their private lives; or (c) sue for libel, spending $15 million trying to silence two people with a combined income of $12,000 a year? In McLibel, the legal farce that just closed in London, the correct answers are (b) and (c)."
— *New York Times*, June 20, 1997: A1, A9.

"A man in debt is so far a slave."
— Ralph Waldo Emerson

"Like everything else bureaucrats desire to keep track of, human beings have been serialized. Once

established, your Social Security Number is the serial number that stays with you for the rest of your life. . . . Though it may be true that the SSN was not designed as a general identifier (I have my doubts), it is certainly erroneous to state that it has not become one. . . . Identity documents are the tools of tyranny. Big Brother's ability to control our movements, track our whereabouts, and mold our habits allows for the production of die-cast citizens and the destruction of the individual."
— Sheldon Charrett, *The Modern Identity Changer* (pp. 36-37, 133)

"The hidden hand of the market will never work without a hidden fist."
— Thomas Friedman

"To the capitalist, profit-oriented mind, there is no outrage so great as the existence of some unmediated nook or cranny of creation which has not been converted into a new form that can then be sold for money. . . . A forest of uncut trees is nonproductive. A piece of land which has not been built upon is nonproductive. Animals living wildly are nonproductive."
— Jerry Mander, *Four Arguments for the Elimination of Television* (p. 117)

"Since corporations have no souls and no commitment to the human race, corporations will always commit wrongs in their unquenchable quest for profit. The corporate structure may be a necessary evil to gather the capital required to carry on business, but the corporate structure, itself, is inherently evil. It is evil in the same way that a person without a conscience is evil. Psychologists call such persons 'sociopaths.'"
— Gerry Spence, in *From Freedom to Slavery* (p. 71)

"My guess is that the indignities imposed on so many low-wage workers — the drug tests, the constant surveillance, being "reamed out" by managers — are part of what keeps wages low. If you're made to feel unworthy enough, you may come to think that what you're paid is what you are actually worth. It is hard to imagine any other function for workplace authoritarianism."
— Barbara Ehrenreich, *Nickel and Dimed* (p. 211)

"You are asking me to believe in a world that does not recognize merit, or striving, or a heroic ideal, but instead rewards duplicity and sneakery and whoever is fastest to watch out for their own self-interest. A world where there is no justice! What sort of world is that?"
— Peter David, *Sir Apropos of Nothing* (p. 378)

C.O.G. (Corporate Occupation Government):

"They've eliminated the middleman. The corporations don't have to lobby the government anymore. They are the government."
— Jim Hightower

"There is something profoundly undemocratic about a 'corporate' state run by only a few without the informed consent and participation of the many."
— Ralph Nader (1976)

"The State is the absolute reality and the individual himself has objective existence, truth and morality only in his capacity as a member of the State."
— Hegel

"Everyone is mentally, physically, and genetically programmed to serve the World State. It exists to control the mind and feelings of the individual and impart an artificial sense of achieving his full potential."
— Cyberpunk manifesto

"Some of the biggest men in the United States, in the field of commerce and manufacture, are afraid of something. They know that there is a power somewhere so organized, so subtle, so watchful, so interlocked, so complete, so pervasive, that they had better not speak above their breath when they speak in condemnation of it."
— Woodrow Wilson, *The New Freedom*

"Single acts of tyranny may be ascribed to the accidental opinion of a day; but a series of oppressions, begun at a distinguished period, and pursued unalterably through every change of ministry, too plainly prove a deliberate systematical plan of reducing us to slavery."
— Alexander Hamilton

"We shall have a world government whether or not you like it, by conquest or by consent."
— James Warburg, Testimony to Senate sub-committee, February 17, 1950

"The money power preys upon the nation in times of peace and conspires against it in times of adversity. It is more despotic than monarchy, more insolent than autocracy, more selfish than bureaucracy. I see in the near future a crisis approaching that unnerves me, and causes me to tremble for the safety of my country. Corporations have been enthroned, an era of corruption will follow, and the money power of the country will endeavor to prolong its reign by working upon the prejudices of the people, until the wealth is aggregated in a few hands, and the republic is destroyed."
— Abraham Lincoln

"Our revolution has made me feel the full force of the axiom that history is fiction. I am convinced that coincidence and conspiracy have produced more heroes than genius and virtue."
— Maximilien Robespierre, 1792

"The history of the world is the history of the warfare between secret societies."
— Ishmael Reed

"What is History but a fable agreed upon?"
— Napoleon Bonaparte

". . . we have limitless resources and the people yield themselves with perfect docility to our molding hands. The present educational conventions fade from our minds and, unhampered by tradition, we work our will upon a grateful and responsive rural folk."
— Frederick T. Gates, chairman of Rockefeller's GEB (1904)

"I had always assumed that textbooks were based on careful research and designed to help children

learn something valuable. I thought that tests were designed to assess whether they had learned it. What I did not realize is that educational materials are now governed by an intricate set of rules to screen out language and topics that might be considered controversial or offensive. Some of this censorship is trivial, some is ludicrous, and some is breathtaking in its power to dumb down what children learn in school."
— Diane Ravitch, *The Language Police* (pg. 3)

"And somehow or other, quite anonymous, there were the directing brains who coordinated the whole effort and laid down the lines of policy which made it necessary that this fragment of the past should be preserved, that one falsified, and the other rubbed out of existence."
— George Orwell, *1984*

"Bureaucracy, the rule of no one, has become the modern form of despotism."
— Mary McCarthy

"Its specific nature . . . develops the more perfectly the more the bureaucracy is 'dehumanized,' the more completely it succeeds in eliminating from official business, love, hatred, and all purely personal, irrational, and emotional elements which escape calculation."
— Max Weber

"Everywhere the weak loathe the powerful before whom they cower and the powerful treat them like flocks of sheep whose wool and flesh are to be sold."
— Voltaire, *Candide*

"There is only one institution that can arrogate to itself the power legally to trade by means of rubber checks: the government. And it is the only institution that can mortgage your future without your knowledge or consent: government securities (and paper money) are promissory notes on future tax receipts, i.e., on your future production."
— Ayn Rand, *Philosophy: Who Needs It?*

"Power travels in the bloodlines, handed out before birth."
— Louise Erdrich, *Tracks*

"Keynesianism is the highest form of phoney economics yet developed to our benefit. The highly centralized, mixed economy resulting from the policies advocated by Lord Keynes for promoting 'prosperity' has all the characteristics required to make our rule invulnerable . . . Keynesianism rationalizes this omnipotent state which we require, while retaining the privileges of private property on which our power ultimately rests."
— Anonymous, *The Occult Technology of Power* (pg. 18)

"When it comes to imperialism, there is much that left and right can agree on. Imperialism means government repression at home, violations of international law abroad, the exploitation of the weak by the strong and the destruction of different national cultures and traditions."
— George Szamuely

"He mocks the people who proposes that the government shall protect the rich that they in turn may care for the laboring poor."
— Grover Cleveland

"The elite are an insular, clannish clique, given to raging idiosyncracies and immense deposits of superstition. Their insulation from the rest of the world which we inhabit, has rendered them emotionally undeveloped, incapable of loving, of caring, of giving . . ."
— Anonymous, *Secret & Suppressed* (p. 234)

"The world is divided into three kinds of people — a very small group that makes things happen, a somewhat larger group that watches things happen, and a great multitude that never knows what has happened."
— Dr. Nicholas Murray Butler

"The real rulers in Washington are invisible and exercise their power from behind the scenes."
— Justice Felix Frankfurter, U.S. Supreme Court

"So you see . . . that the world is governed by very different personages to what is imagined by those who are not themselves behind the scenes."
— Benjamin Disraeli

"The world isn't run by weapons anymore, or energy, or money. It's run by ones and zeros — little bits of data — it's all about electrons. . . . There's a war out there, a world war. It's not about who has the most bullets; it's about who controls the information — what we see and what we hear, how we work and what we think. It's all about information."
— "Cosmo", from the movie *Sneakers*

"Everything is politics . . ."
— Talib Kweli, "Sharp Shooters"

"Bow down before the One you serve,

You're going to get what you deserve. . ."
— Trent Reznor, "Head Like a Hole"

"Again, wealth is power, and to power it belongs more or less to be unfeeling, arrogant, tyrannical. To many people the privilege of oppressing the weak, and next to that, the privilege of being indifferent to their oppressions, is one of the most comfortable luxuries of a condition of ease. The cry of Mr. Pickwick's assailants, 'Hit him again, he's got no friends,' is apt to be the cry alike of the rich and of the rowdy vulgar."
— John Gorham Palfrey (1851)

"Though rank-and-file members were not individually evil, they were blinded and corrupted by a persuasive ideology that justified treason and gross immorality in the interest of the subversive group. Trapped in the meshes of a machine-like organization, deluded by a false sense of loyalty and moral obligation, these dupes followed orders like professional soldiers and labored unknowingly to abolish free society, to enslave their fellow men, and to overthrow divine principals of law and justice."
— David Brion Davis, "Some Themes of Countersubversion"

". . . as so many governments before it, it will become despotic as the people become so corrupted as to need despotic government, being incapable of any other."

— Benjamin Franklin, speaking in favor of the Constitution (1787)

"In public services, we lag behind all the industrialized nations of the West, preferring that the public money go not to the people but to big business. The result is a unique society in which we have free enterprise for the poor and socialism for the rich."
— Gore Vidal, *Dreaming War* (p. 129)

". . . war encourages debt and taxes, the known instruments for bringing the many under the domination of the few. In war, too, the discretionary power of the executive is extended . . . and all the means of seducing the minds are added to those of subduing the force of the people."
— James Madison

"See how magnificent the courts have become
The women are dressed in colorful gowns
The men carry well-crafted swords
Food and drink overflow
Wealth and finery abound
Yet in the shadow of all this splendor
the fields grow barren

the granaries are empty
I say this pomp at the expense of others
is like the boasting of thieves after a looting"
— Lao Tzu, *Tao Te Ching, The Definitive Edition* (Star translation), Verse 53

"The Black Lodge uses weak men, destructive men, selfish and greedy men as puppets to be their tools and instruments. Often such human beings have no idea of the vastness of the evil ways in which they are involved."
— Viola Neal, *Through the Curtain* (p. 289)

"You belong to your father the devil and you willingly carry out your father's desires. He was a murderer from the beginning and does not stand in truth, because there is no truth in him. When he tells a lie, he speaks in character, because he is a liar and the father of lies."
— John 8:44

"The Devil's best trick is to persuade us that he does not exist."
— Baudelaire

CURRENT EVENTS:

"To announce that there must be no criticism of President, or that we are to stand by the President, right or wrong, is not only unpatriotic and servile, but is morally treasonable to the American public."
— Theodore Roosevelt

"Fortunate is the man who knows how to read the signs of the times, for that man shall escape many misfortunes, or at least be prepared to understand the blow."
— Hermes Trismegistus (c. 1st century A.D.)

"Don't listen to our enemies or the weak sisters in our own ranks who accuse us of all sorts of purposeful atrocities around the world. If we were what our enemies said we were, Afghanistan would be a smouldering and uninhabited moonscape. Iraq would be the same, and quite possibly

several other places on the map would be in similar shape."
— Eric L. Haney, *Inside Delta Force* (p. 323)

"The CIA is not an intelligence agency. In fact, it acts largely as an anti-intelligence agency, producing only that information wanted by policymakers to support their plans and suppressing information that does not support those plans. As the covert action arm of the President, the CIA uses disinformation, much of it aimed at the U.S. public, to mold opinion. It employs the gamut of disinformation techniques from forging documents to planting and discovering weapon caches. But the major weapon in its arsenal of disinformation is the 'intelligence' it feeds to policymakers. Instead of gathering genuine intelligence that could serve as the basis for reasonable policies, the CIA often ends up distorting reality, creating out of whole cloth 'intelligence' to justify policies that have already been decided upon. Policymakers then leak this 'intelligence' to the media to deceive us all and gain our support."
— from the introduction of *Deadly Deceits* (p. xi), by 25 year Agency veteran and Intelligence Medal recipient, Ralph W. McGehee

"Central Intelligence Agency operatives . . . had been feeding totally fictitious stories to 200 newspapers, 30 news services, 20 radio and television outlets and 25 publishers, all foreign owned. These stories, sometimes concerning fictitious guerrilla movements, would be reported as real in these countries and then would be picked up by the American media. . . . The purpose of the false stories was to manipulate information so that foreign governments and our government would think some event was happening when it wasn't or vice versa. Policy decisions would be made based on this information. Public understanding would be distorted. The course of world politics would be altered."
— Jerry Mander, *Four Arguments for the Elimination of Television* (pp. 293-294)

"The discrepancies between official representations and official realities in the conduct of foreign affairs . . . stand out starkly in documents already available. Other documents that bear on the subject, running into the thousands, are known to exist, but they are still under the seal of secrecy. What they will reveal, if all of them are ever unsealed, can only be a matter of conjecture for the general public and students of history."
— Charles A. Beard (1948)

". . . genuine conspiracies have seldom been as dangerous or as powerful as have movements of countersubversion. The exposer of conspiracies necessarily adopts a victimized, self-righteous tone which masks his own meaner interests as well as his share of responsibility for a given conflict. Accusations of conspiracy conceal or justify one's own provocative acts and thus contribute to individual or national self-deception. Still worse, they lead to overreactions, particularly to degrees of suppressive violence which normally would not be tolerated."
— David Brion Davis, *The Fear of Conspiracy* (p. 361)

". . . the nation's leaders have increasingly come to feel that certain decisions must be made by them alone without popular consent, and in secret, if the nation is to survive."
— Wise & Ross, *The Invisible Government* (p. 6)

"The very word 'secrecy' is repugnant in a free and open republic, and we are as a people inherently and historically opposed to secret societies, to secret oaths and to secret proceedings. We decided long ago that the dangers of excessive and unwarranted concealment of pertinent facts far outweighed the dangers which are cited to justify it. Even today there is little value in insuring the survival of our nation if our traditions do not survive with it."
— John F. Kennedy, April 27, 1961

"The age in which we live can only be characterized as one of barbarism. Our civilization is in the process not only of being militarized, but also being brutalized."
— Alva Myrdal

"We have no quarrel with the _____ people."
— A well known presidential code-phrase, used many times in the past, which roughly translates as, "We're about to bomb your monkey asses into the Stone Age."

"The whole aim of practical politics is to keep the populace alarmed (and hence clamorous to be led to safety) by menacing it with an endless series of hobgoblins, all of them imaginary."
— H. L. Mencken

"Fear is what makes the field fertile for the 'planting' of hypnotic suggestions . . ."
— Heller & Steele, *Monsters & Magical Sticks* (p. 21)

"The problem with defense is how far you can go without destroying from within what you are trying to defend from without."
— Dwight D. Eisenhower

"Pay no attention to the man behind the curtain. . ."
— L. Frank Baum, *The Wizard of Oz*

"The age of virtuous politics is past,
And we are deep in that of cold pretence.
Patriots are grown too shrewd to be sincere;
And we too wise to trust them."
— William Cowper, *The Task*

"War is just to those to whom war is necessary."
— Titus Livius, *History*

"Sometimes the minority cannot prevail except by force; then it must determine whether the prevalence of its will is worth the price of using force."
— William F. Buckley, Jr.

"Fascism is government by the few and for the few. The objective is seizure and control of the economic, political, social and cultural life of the state. . . . They maintain themselves in power by use of force combined with propaganda based on primitive ideas . . . by skillful manipulation of fear and hate and by false promise of security."
— U.S. War Department (1945)

"When the realistic freedom of dialogue and public discourse is restricted in any society, the quality of satire increases. . . . When the culture decays and the communications media decay, then something (like "Weekend Update") on Saturday Night Live shines."

— Ralph Nader

"Curs'd is the man, and void of law and right,
Unworthy property, unworthy light,
Unfit for public rule, or private care,
That wretch, that monster, that delights in war:
Whose lust is murder, and whose horrid joy
To tear his country, and his kind destroy! . . ."
— Homer, *The Iliad,* Nestor's speech from Book IX, translated by Alexander Pope

"At times some governments do, in fact, want war even in the absence of external threat. Many leaders are not risk-aversive but thrive politically on high risk. For them, nothing succeeds like crisis."
— Alvin and Heidi Toffler, *War and Anti-War* (p. 250)

". . . someone who 'has to win' will habitually go to extremes that would make all but the most fanatical flinch away . . . In extreme cases, this fixation exists in spite of how much damage the person causes or even what it might cost him to do it! . . . You need to realize that he is totally committed, and all the normal safety checks we rely on other people having are off line."
— Marc MacYoung, *A Professional's Guide to Ending Violence Quickly* (p. 12)

"(This has the potential to be) a war without end. This President has an open-ended war on terrorism."
— Stephen Colbert, from "The Daily Show with Jon Stewart"

". . . constant injustice, plundering, and atrocious corrupt practice on the part of the tyrant form the surest and most speedy remedy against tyrannic government. The more guilty and villainous the ruler is and the further he goes in open abuse of his unlimited wrongful authority, the more he will leave room for hope that the people will at last resent it, will listen and understand, and becoming inflamed with a passion for the truth will solemnly put an end forever to so violent and irrational a form of government."
— Vittorio Alfieri, *Della Tirannide*, Vol. II, Chap. 7

"It was always a mistake for cities to integrate their responses to nuclear/chemical attacks with biological terrorist attacks. You have got to separate the biological side. The disciplines involved are completely different. . . . There's going to be a lot of panic, there will be civil unrest, people will break into pharmacies to get medicines, there will be problems burying the dead, we've looked at scenarios, and yes, they include, in extremis, the possible use of lime pits and crematoria."
— Jerome Hauer, Director of NYC Office of Emergency Management

"The huge populations of the industrial countries were living in a fool's paradise, refusing to face facts though the facts were obvious to anyone. A crash was inevitable. We were running out of everything: fossil fuels, metals, forests, arable land. . . Our huge extravagant American agriculture was nothing but a factory for turning oil into food. Stop the oil and you stop the tractors. Stop the tractors and you stop the food production. Stop the food production and people starve. They will not starve quietly. The chaos could be as bad as that created by the Mongol invasions. We were facing a period of destruction and grave danger. It made sense to prepare."
— Robert S. de Ropp, *Warrior's Way* (p. 323)

"In the false belief that industrial growth will provide benefits to the poor and unemployed, we provide tax breaks to aid industrial growth. Meanwhile, with our own taxes, we feed the growing number of hungry and poor, who are blamed for the rising taxes. We pay for what is being taken away from us."
— Jerry Mander, *Four Arguments for the Elimination of Television* (pp. 144-145)

"Now the rulers are filled with clever ideas
and the lives of the people are filled with hardship
So the nation is cursed"
— Lao Tzu, *Tao Te Ching, The Definitive Edition* (Star translation), Verse 65

"If we believe absurdities we shall commit atrocities."
— Voltaire

"If voting could change the system, it would be illegal."
— unknown

EXTREME ANECDOTES

OPEN YOUR EYES!

"You must choose:
Do you wish to see (perceive) nothing, or do you want to see things as they really are?
It is not hard to see things as they really are, it is simply a matter of tearing down walls, ridding oneself of defenses and presumption, rendering oneself vulnerable, an idiot, a fool.
But it is not easy to see things as they really are, because it is painful, it is real, it requires response, it's an incredible commitment.
To go nine-tenths of the way is to suffer at every moment utter madness.
To go all the way is to become sane.
Most people prefer blindness.
But most people are a dying race."

— Paul Williams

THE MAN IN THE ARENA

"It is not the critic who counts, not the one who points out how the strong man stumbled or how the doer of deeds might have done them better. The credit belongs to the man who is actually in the arena, whose face is marred with sweat and dust and blood; who strives valiantly; who errs and comes short again and again; who knows the great enthusiasms, the great devotions, and spens himself in a worthy cause; who, if he wins, knows the triumph of high achievement; and who, if he fails, at least fails while daring greatly, so that his place shall never be with these cold and timid souls who know neither victory nor defeat."

— Theodore Roosevelt

THE WARRIOR PATH

"Our culture must not omit the arming of the man. Let him hear in season that he is born into the state of war, and that the commonwealth and his own well-being require that he should not go dancing in the weeds of peace, but warned, self-collected and neither defying nor dreading the thunder, let him take both reputation and life in his hand, and with perfect urbanity dare the gibbet and the mob by the absolute truth of his speech and the rectitude of his behavior."
— Ralph Waldo Emerson

THE MASSES ARE LIKE MACHINES

"What do you expect? People are machines. Machines have to be blind and unconscious; they cannot be otherwise, and all their actions have to correspond to their nature. Everything happens. No-one does anything. 'Progress' and 'civilization', in the real meaning of these words, can appear only as a result of conscious efforts. They cannot appear as a result of unconscious mechanical actions. And what conscious effort can there be in machines? And if one machine is unconscious, and so are a thousand machines, or a hundred thousand, or a million. And the unconscious activity of a million machines must necessarily result in destruction and extermination. It is precisely in unconscious involuntary manifestations that all evil lies. You do not yet understand and cannot imagine all the results of this evil. But the time will come when you will understand."

— G. I. Gurdjieff

THE MASSES ARE LIKE INSECTS

"Cities are like hives in which humans scuttle frantically about like insects. Nearly identical housing projects, condominiums, and high-rises form the shell of the hives, with congested streets and tracks being like the chemical trails. The metaphorical 'insects' of the hive, unlike true insects, lack a hive mind; in fact, they seem to lack any willingness to co-operate or help one another in the absence of threats or rewards. The drones and workers dredge through tedious and demeaning jobs, usually spending their non-working time entranced in front of their televisions, partaking of mind-numbing intoxicants, sleeping fitfully and dreamlessly, or mindlessly reproducing to ensure the cycle of despair continues. The pathetic denizens of the hive cannot leave, as they have become too dependant upon it; bound to their jobs by invisible chains and unable to conceive of a world without the conveniences of mass-transit and free delivery."

— Scribe 27 (RWT)

THE COMPUTER IS WATCHING YOU

"When technology reaches a certain level, people begin to feel like criminals. Someone is after you, the computers maybe, the machine-police. You can't escape investigation. The facts about you and your whole existence have been collected or are being collected. Banks, insurance companies, credit organizations, tax examiners, passport offices, reporting services, police agencies, intelligence gatherers. Devices make us pliant. If they issue a print-out saying we're guilty, then we're guilty. But it goes even deeper, doesn't it? It's the presence alone, the very fact, the superabundance of technology, that makes us feel we're committing crimes. Just the fact that these things exist at this widespread level. The processing machines, the scanners, the sorters. That's enough to make us feel like criminals. What enormous weight. What complex programs. And there's no-one to explain it to us."

— unknown

SOCIETY DOESN'T TOLERATE DISRUPTION

"Let us pretend that you are an ape, and that you have been born into an unusually large group of, say, a hundred or more of your kind . . . this is your society. In most societies, everyone has their place; if you do not know your place, you will soon be put where society feels you belong — usually near the bottom. In this society, there is one maximum leader, the 'Alpha'; and several of his assistants, the 'Betas'; and everyone else is subservient to the leaders and one another based on a sort of 'pecking order.' It is a society of bullies. Whomever is strongest and most feared rules, and whomever is not quite as strong is permitted to harass and attack those weaker than himself. Whatever apes are too passive, weak, or ill to defend themselves will be at the bottom of the pecking order.

Now let us pretend that your ape, for whatever reason, is at the lower end of the pecking order. However, not only is he resentful of his mistreatment by others, but he is significantly more intelligent than most of them. Using his intelligence, he crafts a sort of long dagger from a discarded broken animal bone. Now when the dominant greyback Alpha no longer receives homage in the form of submissive and fearful gesticulation (averting the eyes, exposing the buttocks for mounting, ect.), he flies into a murderous rage and lunges, only to have the needle point of the sharp bone tool plunged through his eye and into his brain. As the Alpha drops dead, is your ape the new king? No. Even if he is able to fend off, or even kill, the attacking Betas with his magic sword, he will not sway the masses. Why? Because he was once like them and still is, in many ways. He is not inclined to rule as a tyrant, and if he sets down his weapon his strength will be gone. Aren't the apes happy with their newfound freedom? On the contrary, they will be fearful and confused, and as soon as your ape falls asleep, as he eventually must, they will take up the weapon and kill him with it. Then, the strongest and most aggressive survivor will take over as king, and society will return to normal. In most societies, there is no place for one such as your ape. If he cannot be rendered powerless in some way, he must be exiled, imprisoned, or killed. He will never be accepted or assimilated unless be changes into that which he despises. Society does not tolerate disruption."

— Scribe 27 (RWT)

MAD DOG SHRIVER

"Mad Dog Shriver was twenty-eight years old and, according to one SOG veteran, 'the quintessential warrior loner, antisocial, possessed by what he was doing, leading the best team, always training, constantly training.'

Shriver rarely spoke and walked around camp for days wearing the same clothes. In his sleep he cradled a loaded rifle, and in the NCO club he'd buy a case of beer, open every can, then go alone to a corner and drink them all. Although he could not care less about decorations, he'd been awarded a

Silver Star, five Bronze Stars, and the Soldier's Medal.

Shriver was devoted to the Montagnards. He spent all his money on them and collected food, clothes, whatever people would give, to distribute in Yard villages. He taught the Yards how to play an accordion, the most sophisticated musical instrument they'd ever had. Mad Dog even built his own room in the Montagnard barracks so he could live with them. 'He was almost revered by the Montagnards,' O'Rourke says.

Shriver's closest companion was a German Shepherd he'd brought back from Taiwan and named Klaus. One night Klaus got sick on beer some recon men fed him and crapped on the NCO club floor; the men rubbed his nose in it and threw him out. Shriver arrived, drank a beer, removed his blue velvet smoking jacket and derby hat, put his .38 revolver on a table, then dropped his pants and defecated on the floor. 'If you want to rub my nose in this,' he dared, 'come on over.' Everyone pretended not to hear him, except one man who'd fed Klaus beer and who urged the recon company commander to intervene. The captain laughed in his face, saying, 'Hey, fuck you, pal.'"

— excerpted from *SOG* by John L. Plaster (p. 247)

DISPOSABLE HEROES

"If the truth be known, the Army went out of its way to find guys like me — ass-kicking 'Nam vets who ran the woods and lived on the edge — and systematically weeded them out of the service.

Why?

Because we were misfits.

We didn't fit the mold. We just didn't fit in. We were renegades used to operating independently, with few people pulling our strings. We disregarded the established rules and created our own. I take that back — there were no rules for us . . . But that attitude surely was out of place in a peacetime environment, and the thought of keeping guys around who were distainful of authority and might not toe the line was a little too much for the Army to deal with. So the hard-core guys were sent packing. Fortunately for me I had the medal, which gave me too much visibility to be fucked with completely, so I was spared the axe, though not the hassles.

A noncombat lifestyle was everything I'd feared. It was very boring. It was unbelievably slow-paced. And worst of all, my free-wheeling, do-as-I-damn-well-please lifestyle had come to an end . . .

I felt like I'd been put on a leash. The Army had taken a high-performance engine and drastically untuned it. Not only had my activities been severely curtailed, but the special status that I Once enjoyed quickly evaporated. I was no longer that unique individual who did the dangerous job most others were reluctant to do. Since cunning, sharpshooting, and bravery were no longer required in my new environment, I had nothing to set me apart from the crowd. I quickly found that the Medal of Honor was more a novelty than anything else to most noncombat soldiers, and really had no place in a peacetime Army. My extensive combat skills and ass-kicking abilities were no longer needed, appreciated, or even wanted."

— Franklin D. Miller, *Reflections of a Warrior* (pp. 198-199)

DON'T BE A DUMBASS

"Never leave a potentially deadly weapon where unauthorized hands may find it. Never insert your finger into the trigger guard until the actual use of a weapon seems imminent; a fall, or the muscle-tightening reaction to a sudden noise, can result in an accidental discharge . . . Never touch a firearm while under the influence of alcohol, or display one at an occasion when liquor is flowing. Never allow yourself to become embroiled in a squabble while you are carrying a gun, be it caused by an insult to your wife, an argument in traffic, or any similar situation. Never let it be known to anyone outside your immediate household . . . that you carry a gun. Never make remarks to the effect that you will "kill any sonofabitch who breaks into my house/hooks my kid on drugs/tries to steal from my store," etc. If such a killing situation ever occurs, testimony in court will show that you seemed pre-occupied with the idea of killing real or imaginary criminals, especially if you've made such remarks frequently. If circumstances were such that your reactions could be considered to have been too hasty, such testimony would imply that you were excessively pre-disposed toward using your gun."

— Massad Ayoob, *In The Gravest Extreme* (p. 121)

BULLET WOUNDS: TV VERSUS REALITY

"In TV and motion pictures, the bullet is often portrayed as a very discreet piece of metal. When it strikes a bad gut, it produces a round, red polka dot approximately the diameter of a pencil. There is usually very little blood and never an exit wound. Good guys are regularly shot in the arm, shoulder or leg and are up and around in no time . . . Bullets aren't sharp. They don't drill neat holes in flesh. Bullets rip and tear. When they hit bone, lead slugs don't produce neat fractures. Bones are burst and splintered. No longer able to support body weight, the jagged end of a bone is sometimes jabbed up and out through the skin as gravity pulls the flesh down. Flattened into an irregular shape by the impact, but unspent, the bullet tumbles off and away through the body, often bursting out with a fist-sized ball of meat at an odd angle and a remarkable distance from where it entered . . . If the heart does not stop right away, that organ can pump most of the blood the body contains through the wound and out onto the ground in a matter of minutes."

— Mark Baker, *Cops* (pp. 168-169)

GETTING SHOT SUCKS

"A high powered bullet through the complex of shoulder bones and muscles will leave the arm crippled for life. The same with a leg. The possibility of death from hemorrhage or shock is present with any bullet wound. A bullet in the side or abdomen can fatally damage liver, kidneys, and other organs. People don't always recover completely from serious gunshot wounds, even if they do survive initially. Damage can be lingering — 'he was never any good after he was shot' is a common description — and the results of the wound can radically shorten the natural life span."

— Massad Ayoob, *In the Gravest Extreme* (p. 24)

IF I WERE TO SHOOT YOU IN THE BELLY

"If I were to shoot you in the belly with a small caliber handgun, what do you think would happen? Do you think you would drop to the floor in a clean white shirt and expire quietly after saying a few final words? Do you think you would take the shot bravely, wrestle the gun away, apprehend me for the authorities, and see your photo on the front page of tomorrow's newspaper, smiling in your hospital bed as you receive a medal from the mayor? No, such things occur only in the fantasy world of television, but a great many people, inundated by repeated exposure to such lies, tend to believe that violence is drama.

Let me tell you the ugly truth. If I were to shoot you in the belly, first, you would shit your pants. You would fall to the ground, doubled up in agonizing pain. You would bleed great quantities of smelly dark brown blood. As your stomach fills with blood, you would vomit copious amounts. As your lifeblood drains away, soaking into the carpeting, your core body temperature would plummet, causing you to shiver uncontrollably. Unless the abdominal aorta is punctured, there may be hours of suffering before you die.

If you are rescued by paramedics, stabilized for transport, and immediately brought into the operating room, you will not be patched up and quickly released. First, your intestines will be placed in a pile alongside you where they can be examined while the abdominal cavity is thoroughly rinsed in hopes of averting peritonitis. If you were shot with a high velocity hollowpoint, shot repeatedly, or are just unlucky enough to have multiple ruptures of the gastrointestinal tract, the surgeons won't even bother trying to patch you up. Your entrails will go in the hospital dumpster, and you will shit in a colostomy bag for the rest of your weak, sickly, frightened, lonely, and pain-ridden existence.

Violence is not a game, nor is it a cartoon. Violence is sickeningly real, it hurts, it ruins lives, and it has lasting medical, psychological, legal, and social repercussions. Violence is not something to be toyed with, it is something to be avoided through whatever means necessary. Violence is not fun."

— anonymous (RWT)

OF EYEBALLS AND JELL-O

"It's quite unlikely that your finger will actually penetrate the eyeball. If it does, it only gets wet. It's no slimier than gelatin.

There will be large amounts of blood, and the criminal whose eyes you gouge will scream like a banshee. The pain and shock are enough that many people will actually pass out when their eyeballs are ruptured. It's tough to live with afterward, but when you realize that it's your life and your eyeballs on the line, if you don't do it first, you can do it if you know beforehand that you're capable.

I have put my thumbs into eyes, and I know what it feels like for my thumb or my index finger to pierce the tough sclera (outer eye membrane) and gouge through the aqueous tissue beneath. It's no ickier than grabbing a handful of Jell-O out of the refrigerator or pulling the gizzard out of your family's Thanksgiving turkey."

— Massad Ayoob, *The Truth About Self-Protection* (p. 243)

SPADES AND MEN

"The infantry spade does not have a folding handle, and this is a very important feature. It has to be a single monolithic object. All three of its edges are as sharp as a knife. It is painted with a green matt paint so as not to reflect the strong sunlight. It is practically impossible to describe in words how they use their spades . . . In the hands of a spetsnaz soldier the spade is a terrible noiseless weapon . . . The first thing he has to teach himself is precision: to split little slivers of wood with the edge of his spade or to cut off the neck of a bottle so that the bottle remains whole. He has to learn to love his spade and have faith in its accuracy. To do that he places his hand on the stump of a tree with his fingers spread out and takes a big swing at the stump with his right hand using the edge of the spade. Once he has learned to use the spade well and truly as an axe he is taught more complicated things . . . A soldier armed with nothing but the spade is shut in a room without windows along with a mad dog, which makes for an interesting contest. Finally a soldier is taught to throw the spade as accurately as he would use a battle-axe . . . If it lands in a tree it is not so easy to pull out again . . . (The enemy) will rarely see the blade coming, before it lands in the back of his neck or between his shoulder blades, smashing the bones . . . (They) work with spades more surely and more accurately than they do with spoons at a table."

— Viktor Suvorov, *Spetsnaz*

GROWLING

"Why not growl? The wolf is in all of us. The hunter. The warrior. Growl like the wolf. The sound is not a shallow scraping in the throat. Take a breath and force the sound from deep down into the chest. Can you feel it reverberate in the lower lobes of your lungs? Can you hear the growl, the universal growl? The growl of alpha wolves standing face to face in the moonlight. It is the growl of ancient man confronting the enemy. It is the growl of a million ancestors who abide in our genes. It is a growl out of the pit of your being, a growl from under the heart itself. The sound is a powerful sound.

Can you feel the power? The stomach tightens when the sound is made. The stomach tightens in preparation for battle. The stomach, the diaphragm, force the sound upward and out. How does the power feel?"

— Gerry Spence, *How to Argue and Win Every Time* (pp. 163-164)

MEDITATION ON THE CORPSE

"The Buddhist Sutra of Mindfulness speaks about the meditation on the corpse: meditate on the decomposition of the body, how the body bloats and turns violet, how it is eaten by worms until only bits of blood and flesh still cling to the bones, meditate up to the point where only white bones remain, which in turn are slowly worn away and turn into dust. Meditate like that, knowing that your own body will undergo the same process. Meditate on the corpse until you are calm and at peace, until your mind and heart are light and tranquil and a smile appears on your face. Thus, by overcoming revulsion and fear, life will be seen as infinitely precious, every second of it worth living."

— Thich Nhat Hanh

YOUR COMPUTER IS ALIVE!

"It was as if from the year 1947 to 1980 a fundamental paradigm shift in the ability to process information took place. Computers themselves almost became something like a silicon-based life-form, inspiring the carbon-based life-forms on planet Earth to develop them, grow them, and even help them reproduce. With computer-directed process-control programs now in place in virtually all major industries, software that writes software, neural-network-based expert systems that learn from their own experience in the real world, and current experiments under way to grow almost microscopically thin silicon-based chips in the weightless environment of earth orbit may be the forerunner of a time when automated orbital factories routinely grow and harvest new silicon material for microprocessors more sophisticated than we can even imagine at the present. Were all this to be true . . . would not the natural development stream, starting from the invention of the transistor, have carried us to the point where we achieve a symbiotic relationship with the silicon material that carries our data and enables us to become more creative and successful?"

— Phillip Corso

JUST PISS IN THE CUP . . .

"Throughout history, Americans have held the legal tradition that one could not give up one's Constitutional rights — and if someone was stripped of these protections, then he or she was being victimized. By 1989, if you sign up for an extracurricular activity in school or apply for a minimum wage job, you could be asked to forego your right to privacy, protection from self-incrimination, Constitutional requirements of reasonable grounds for search and seizure, presumed innocence until found guilty by your peers, and that most fundamental right of all: personal responsibility for one's own life and consciousness. By 1995, the supreme court upheld that these intrusions into your privacy were constitutional! . . . Submission to the humiliation of having your most private body parts and functions observed by a hired voyeur is now the test of eligibility for private employment, or to contract for a living wage."

— Jack Herer, *The Emperor Wears No Clothes* (pp. 71, 87)

TRIAL BY JURY

"'Jury nullification of the law' is a traditional right dating back to the Magna Carta and was intended by America's founding fathers as the final test a law must pass before it gains the authority to punish violators. John Adams, our nation's second president, in 1771 said of the jury, 'it is not only his right, but his duty . . . to find the verdict according to his own best understanding, judgement, and conscience, though in direct opposition to the direction of the court' . . . Due to special interest pressure, juries have been misinformed of their right to judge law as well as fact for almost 100 years. Jurors now swear in their oaths to judge only the facts of the case according to the law as dictated to them by the judge. The majority of judges will not allow attorneys to tell jurors of their power to say "no" to unjust laws. In most cases juries are no longer allowed to hear the defendant's motives. Fully informed juries are essential for justice, rebuilding respect for the law, protection of individual rights and control of the government by people."

— The Fully Informed Jury Association (FIJA)

POLICE STATE

"In our own time, police randomly search groups of (usually minority) adolescents, engage in mass sweeps of inner-city blocks, blockade neighborhoods, create databases of gang members and associates, and target gang leaders for arrest and incarceration. So far, these tactics have not proven particularly effective in controlling gangs. Instead, they increase alienation among adolescents, violate civil rights, and, if anything, tend to promote identification with gangs and assist their internal cohesion. Moreover, they belie the promise of more sensitive 'community policing' and, because of their lack of discrimination between gang members and non-gang members, they further the feeling of inner city residents that they are under siege with as much to fear from the police as from gang members."

— Eric C. Schneider, *Vampires, Dragons, and Egyptian Kings* (p. 260)

"BLAZE OF GLORY"

"If a criminal is convinced he is cornered, he might choose to go down in what he would perceive to be a blaze of glory rather than face the ignominy of surrendering and being imprisoned, perhaps for life. Seeing no way to escape, this individual might assert himself in the final moments by trying to take someone down with him. An alternative is to kill himself. Either way, true to form, he strives one last time to remain in control of whatever happens to him. He will end his own life rather than allow someone else to do it."

— Stanton E. Samenow, *Straight Talk about Criminals* (p. 83)

WETWORK

"What I need you two fellas to do is take those cleaning products and clean the inside of the car. And I'm talking fast, fast, fast. You need to go in the back seat, scoop up all those little pieces of brain and skull. Get it out of there. Wipe down the upholstery — now, when it comes to upholstery, it don't need to be spic and span, you don't need to eat off it. Give it a good once over. What you need to take care of are the really messy parts. The pools of blood that have collected, you gotta soak that shit up. But the windows are a different story. Them you really clean. Get the Windex, do a good job . . . I need blankets, I need comforters, I need quilts, I need bedspreads. The thicker the better, the darker the better. No whites, can't use 'em.. We need to camouflage the interior of the car. We're gonna line the front seat and the back seat and the floorboards with quilts and blankets. If a cop stops us and starts stickin' his big snout in the car, the subterfuge won't last. But at a glance, the car will appear to be normal."

— "Winston Wolf," from *Pulp Fiction* by Quentin Tarantino

"THE REVOLUTION WILL NOT BE TELEVISED"

"There are a whole lot of delusional clowns who seem to think that staging a protest, participating in a march, or passing around a petition will actually make a difference . . . such activities seldom show any positive results (and only to a very limited degree when they do). True, everyone with open eyes can easily see that things are horribly wrong, but boldly standing up and announcing such to the largely apathetic masses generally only succeeds in directing a lot of unwelcome scrutiny at oneself, whilst the issue remains ignored.

Reading Socialist and Communist propaganda can have a strong influence on earnest individuals who've recently been made aware of the deplorable state of affairs — these writings place the blame for all of the world's ills solely upon the greed of the 'Capitalist oppressors,' and offer 'solutions' which may seem reasonable in theory, yet consistently fail miserably in practice. More adventurous types may even delve into the murky fantasy world of 'Conspiracy Theorism' literature, which places the blame for all of society's ills upon an elite sinister cabal composed of: Freemasons, Zionists, Satanists, extraterrestrials, or even 'Reptilian shapeshifters' (dependant upon which work of fiction you've happened upon) — these fables make entertaining reading, but are often seized upon by unstable minds desperate for the 'Truth.'

What is truly scary is the fact that certain groups of demented individuals have actually banded together in disorganized armed clans, 'training' for the day when everyone will suddenly 'rise up' to make war against the 'enemy from within.' — these folks are totally fucking nuts. Believe you me, people — there is no fucking way that anyone — not even a heavily armed guerilla army with over a million hardcore soldiers — would ever have a chance of overthrowing the government of a contemporary superpower. Their resources (manpower, weaponry, intelligence, propaganda, logistics, and the willingness to engage in total war) are far too vast, and their power structures are firmly entrenched. 'They' can take whatever steps are necessary (tanks, helicopter gunships, ultrasonics, laser blinders, nerve gas, bioweapons, tac-nukes, etc.) to quell a domestic disturbance during a state of emergency (and will be free to either deny, or fail to disclose, the methodology used), and no mere "light infantry" could hope to withstand such an onslaught. The only circumstances by which such a mass uprising could have any small chance of success would be immediately following the apocalyptic devastation of a possible Third World War."

— anonymous (RWT)

MI VIDA LOCA

"Pride, that's what most of us die for. Respect and pride . . . We ain't taught to sit there and say, 'Okay, let's take a deep breath and count to ten.' It doesn't work for us like that. If you get into an argument with somebody, you better be ready to die . . . that's what gets 90 percent of these people killed. It's your pride and your love. Your love for what you represent . . . Pride is what draws people to the gang. Because there is nothing like being around people who have something to be proud of. Pretty soon, you want to be proud of something too. And you look around at your life and realize that you have nothing that can match what they have. So you pay the price, you get jumped in (intitiated into the gang), and maybe you get into a situation where you have to spray gunfire at someone's house one night — or drive the car for the gunman . . . Representing is a practice that is public in nature. It shows your homeboys and your enemies who you are and what you stand for. Representing can take many forms: warfare, tattooing, graffiti, clothing — even when homeboys hang out on a certain corner they represent their neighborhood."

— anonymous, from *Wallbangin'* (pp. 116-117)

ELITISM

"Like in American society is not fair. This sort of elitist behavior may have its beginnings in adolescence, but it is definitely existent in all of American society. It is self-perpetuating, the elitist class in the social stratification is learned and internalized to the point at which there will always be a dominant social elite, and that class will always take measures to ensure a constant and consistent membership. It may not be as apparent as it is in adolescents, but it still exists. The older children and adults are better social actors, and they are able to euphemize their elitist activities, and disguise them as normal social interaction. The problem that helps this behavior to continue is the duality of me, and you. It is instilled in us by society. We internalize it and make it a subconscious habituation, it is me and us, and what we want, against you and what you might do to prevent that which we want. This is the basis of all conflict, and try as progressive thinkers may, we cannot seem to alleviate this pattern of dualism."

— Donna Eder

OVERPOPULATION:

"One of the greatest sources of violence on the planet is unwanted, uncared for, unloved children. Such children as they grow older are not only typically angry and prone to violence, but are potential time-bombs that can capriciously explode and destroy whatever is around them. A world is being created that is full of people without hope, often driven by hatred and envy, who do not care about their own lives, let alone yours. How can such people really care if life on this planet continues or not? The worldwide increase in population coupled with an increasing discrepancy between haves and have-nots creates more and more people without hope. When a large segment of the population lives without hope, it is dangerous for everyone."

— Joel Kramer & Diana Alstad, *The Guru Papers* (p. 373)

MY RIFLE:

"This is my rifle. There are many like it, but this one is mine. My rifle is my best friend. It is my life. I must master it as I must master my life. My rifle, without me, is useless. Without my rifle, I am useless. I must fire my rifle true. I must shoot straighter than my enemy, who is trying to kill me. I must shoot him before he shoots me. I will . . . My rifle and myself know that what counts in war is not the rounds we fire, the noise of our burst, nor the smoke we make. We know that it is the hits that count. We will hit . . . My rifle is human, even as I, because it is my life. Thus, I will learn it as a brother. I will learn its weaknesses, its strengths, its parts, its accessories, its sights, and its barrel. I will ever guard it against the ravages of weather and damage. I will keep my rifle clean and ready, even as I am clean and ready. We will become part of each other. We will . . . Before God I swear this creed. My rifle and myself are the defenders of my country. We are the masters of our enemy. We are the saviors of my life. So be it, until there is no enemy, but Peace!"

— The Creed of the United States Marines

"WHAT'S THAT YOU'VE GOT IN YER HAND?"

"You might think that some of the signs, like being set up or stalked by an attacker, might be obvious; however, depending upon the skill and cunning of your attacker, they can be surprisingly subtle. It would be impossible to describe all the indicators here, but one of the key things to look for is the positioning of people around you. Be wary of people trying to flank you, move behind you, place you between them, or cut off your avenues of escape. Look for people whose hands are cupped or unnaturally stiff, like something is held in them, or concealed from view behind the back or in a pocket. Most importantly, don't let anyone get too close to you, where they might be able to move on you before you can react. If someone starts to move close, try to position your back against a wall and put something between you and him as an obstacle to an advance. At the very least, tell him to back off so you can have enough distance between you to react if he makes a move. If he doesn't listen and keeps coming, draw your blade and prepare for all hell to break loose.

— Michael D. Janich, *Knife Fighting: A Practical Course* (pp. 98-99)

RIGIDITY:

"We can pass more laws, write more detailed rule books, establish more customs, paint more 'No U-Turn' signs, and so on, to cut down the variability in human behavior that can create problems. 'Well-behaved,' 'predictable,' 'rigid,' 'mechanical' people make the system run more smoothly: choose your favorite adjective. At its extreme, nothing is required of people other than following the rules. And, as the old joke says, "Everything that is not required is forbidden!" The rules are external environmental rules (like 'No U-Turn' signs) or internalized psychological rules ('Decent people never even think of doing X'). For best results, both kinds of rules need to be backed up by rewards for following them, as well as by the strength of mindless habit. . .

If we want a smoother, more efficient, less dangerous world, then, one direction we can take is to make people more like machines, machines with lots of mechanical intelligence. You can also spend great effort and use lots of resources in designing the world so that it is mechanically impossible to violate the rules. Many parking lots now have concrete dividers or green belts that prevent you from driving diagonally across them when they are empty. The other direction is to increase genuine intelligence, including the discovery and cultivation of the uniquely human aspects of intelligence that are not mechanical.

The unfortunate truth about people is how machinelike we can become. . . Right and wrong ways are set up and rules to implement them are established. Goodness then becomes a matter of following the rules.

The problem with trying to create a rule to cover everything is that reality frequently gets more complex than the rules can handle, or changes faster than the rules change. Yet many people keep mechanically following the rules, feeling virtuous about it but actually destroying themselves and others."

— Charles T. Tart, *Waking Up* (pp. 29-30)

"THE SECRET ARTS:"

"There are two major reasons for genuine growth practices to be secret. First, a given practice may be capable of producing such powerful effects that if you are not prepared for them, they could harm you or others. They are dangerous in the hands of the unprepared . . . The second reason why some of these practices have sometimes been secret has to do with your readiness to respond, the "shock value" they might have in requiring a radical reorientation. . . Secrecy is a useful way of handling these problems. If most techniques were secret, you wouldn't have the blunting effect of knowledge of so many you never really tried, or the attitude caused by the residues of many failure experiences from half-heartedly trying some. The presentation of a new growth technique would command far more of your attention than it does now. If, in addition, you had to prove yourself worthy of having a technique revealed to you, not to mention the 'glamour' of being sworn to secrecy, even more attention would be given to the technique. It would have more surprise value, be more of an attention-getting shock. The result is that you would give a great deal of energy and attention to practicing the technique, and it would have a much greater chance of affecting you. For most growth practices, the old rule holds: it works if you work.

The last two decades have been a time of drastic change, though. Many of the 'secret' techniques of spiritual paths are now available in paperback at your corner bookstore. We must deal with the dulling that comes from knowing so many techniques and the probability that it makes it harder to respond appropriately to new techniques. This is advantageous in some ways: secrecy appealed to parts of our minds that were more interested in power and glamour than in growth, for example, so there is now less feeding that part of us."

— Charles T. Tart, *Waking Up* (pp. 177-179)

OVERCOMING FEAR:

"Overcoming fear does not mean eliminating fear. Courage is not the absence of fright, but the ability to act in spite of it. Reports of people having performed amazing acts of heroism reveal that they commonly felt fear — even terror. But they performed in spite of their fear. Being afraid in a dangerous situation is a normal reaction, it is not cowardice. Refusing to fight is not cowardice either.

There are only three choices open to you when faced with the threat of attack on the street:

You can run away (situation permitting);

You can fight;

You can submit to a beating.

If you feel, as I do, that it is less dignified to get into a fight than to take off, you can run away from a fight without loss of self-esteem, especially if you know that you can win. If you are cornered and cannot run away, the decision to fight or to submit to a beating can have completely different meanings for different people. Although I respect as valid and brave the non-violent attitude of those who feel it is more dignified to submit to a beating than to fight, it is not a choice I would make, and it is not very likely a choice you would make or you would not be reading these pages. Therefore, if cornered, your choice is between fighting to defend yourself and keep your self-respect or failing to fight and losing your self-respect.

You must prepare yourself mentally as well as physically to fight to defend yourself correctly if danger threatens. Correct behavior is no secret. There are easily recognizable traits of confident behavior, as easily recognizable as traits of demoralized behavior. You can imitate confident behavior. If you imitate it regularly, others will respond to your way of behaving and not to your inner doubts about yourself. The very act of behaving in a confident manner will eventually increase your self-respect and give you the courage to continue to behave in ways which inspire confidence. It is a self-nourishing cycle.

Here are a few specific manners of confident behavior you can imitate: Keep your head and body erect when you speak to anyone. Avoid lowering your eyes or looking at the ground — an abject, self-despising mannerism. If you do not have the confidence to look a person in the eye, look at his ear. To look at an ear you must keep your head up and this gives the impression that you are looking into the face. Even when you are considerably shorter than the person you are talking to, keep yourself drawn up to your full height. Do not diminish yourself; show yourself at your best.

At all times, and especially in a trouble situation, keep your voice firm and speak clearly. Many of my students have avoided a fight simply by having said to a bully, 'Leave me alone. I don't want to fight, but if you insist on fighting, you will get hurt.' Pleading for mercy with a streetfighter is a waste of time. Cowering only convinces him that you are an easy mark and increases his sadistic pleasure. If you cannot speak quietly and firmly say nothing at all. Keep quiet when you have nothing to say. Foolish chatter is not a sign of confidence. It is a sign of fear."

— Bruce Tegner, *Instant Self-Defense* (p.7)

BLIND FAITH:

"Do not put faith in traditions, even though they have been accepted for long generations and in many countries. Do not believe a thing on the authority of one or another of the Sages of old, nor on the ground that a statement is found in the books. Never believe anything because probability is in its favor. Do not believe in that which you yourselves have imagined, thinking that a God has inspired it. Believe nothing merely on the authority of your teachers or of the priests. After examination, believe that which you have tested for yourselves and found reasonable, which is in conformity with your well-being and that of others."

— The Buddha

INDENTURED SERVITUDE:

"Enlisting in the armed forces is definitely not for everyone. Enlistees literally sign away all their civil rights, and enter into a contemporary form of indentured servitude. If you have a problem with your boss, you will not have the option of quitting, or even speaking your mind freely — insubordination can be punished by: loss of rank (and reduction in pay), confinement to quarters, being forced to perform unpleasant (and often unsafe) tasks, or — in extremis — incarceration in a Federal penitentiary. Combine compulsory obedience to orders with an abundance of petty regulations enforced by inept (and often seemingly irrational) drones, and you are looking at an authoritarian culture only a few small steps removed from a prison society."

— anonymous (RWT)

CONTEMPORARY SERFDOM:

"When we speak of disciplinary government, we are not referring simply to the juridical and political forms that organize it. We are referring primarily to the fact that in a disciplinary society, the entire society, with all its productive and reproductive articulations, is subsumed under the command of capital and the state, and that the society tends, gradually but with unstoppable continuity, to be ruled solely by criteria of capitalist production. A disciplinary society is thus a factory-society. Disciplinarity is at once a form of production and a form of government such that disciplinary production and disciplinary society tend to coincide completely . . . It is precisely when the disciplinary regime is pushed to its highest level and most complete application that it is revealed as the extreme limit of a social arrangement, a society in the process of being overcome."

— Michael Hardt & Antonio Negri, *Empire* (p. 243)

F.T.W :

"Even though, at one time or another, many folks considered me to be an "outlaw," I've always respected and obeyed approximately 85% of all the laws. However, (as most people would agree) 10% of the laws we're subject to on a daily basis have been rather poorly thought out, and seem to be enforced only selectively. The primary motivation of these (often paternally or religiously based) statutes seems to be simply to demean and oppress the general populace through regimentation and fines. The other 5% I couldn't abide by are so Draconian as to be counter-productive due to the fact that their inherent stupidity, unfairness, and bias instils such resentment and antipathy in the masses. Since I strongly disagree with these laws, and since I seem to have no representation in the legislative process, I feel (as do many others) that these wrongful laws should not apply to me. The fact that so many of them (including 'victimless crimes' and other seemingly minor offenses) carry such heavy penalties is tantamount to an act of violent aggression against the underclasses by the power-elites."

— anonymous (RWT)

"MIND WAR":

"MindWar must be strategic in emphasis, with tactical applications playing a reinforcing, supplementary role. In its strategic context, MindWar must reach out to friends, enemies, and neutrals alike across the globe — neither through the primitive "battlefield" leaflets and loudspeakers of PSYOP nor through the weak, imprecise, and narrow effort of psychotronics — but through the media possessed by the United States which have the capabilities to reach virtually all people on the face of the Earth. These media are, of course, the electronic media — television and radio. State of the art developments in satellite communication, video recording techniques, and laser and optical transmission of broadcasts make possible a penetration of the minds of the world such as would have been inconceivable just a few years ago . . . it can transform the world for us if we have but the courage and the integrity to guide civilization with it.

MindWar must target all participants if it is to be effective. It must not only weaken the enemy; it must strengthen the United States. It strengthens the United States by denying enemy propaganda access to our people, and by explaining and emphasizing to our people the rationale for our national interest in a specific war . . . Unlike PSYOP, MindWar has nothing to do with deception or even with "selected"— and therefore misleading — truth. Rather it states a whole truth that, if it does not now exist, will be forced into existence by the will of the United States . . . the MindWar operative must know he speaks the truth, and he must be personally committed to it. What he says is only a part of MindWar; the rest — and the test of its effectiveness — lies in the conviction he projects to his audience, in the rapport he establishes with it. . .

There are some purely natural conditions under which minds may become more or less receptive to ideas, and MindWar should take full advantage of such phenomena as atmospheric electromagnetic activity, air ionization, and extremely low frequency waves . . . (Extremely Low Frequency (ELF) waves: ELF waves (up to 100 Hz) are naturally occurring, but they can also be produced artificially (such as for the Navy's Project Sanguine for submarine communication). ELF-waves are not normally noticed by the unaided senses, yet their resonant effect upon the human body has been connected to both physiological disorders and emotional distortion. Infrasound vibration (up to 20

Hz) can subliminally influence brain activity to align itself to delta, theta, alpha, or beta wave patterns, inclining an audience toward everything from alertness to passivity. Infrasound could be used tactically, as ELF-waves endure for great distances, and it could be used in conjunction with media broadcasts as well.)"

— excerpted from: *From PSYOP to MindWar: The Psychology of Victory*, a declassified military document by Colonel Paul E. Vallely and Major Michael A. Aquino

"ARE YOU PARANOID???":

"Intellectual respectability required mental health, and it was becoming evident to me by then that "mental health" consisted of trusting everyone about everything as much as possible — and, for good measure, poking fun at anyone who didn't. Especially to be trusted were the mass media, whose owners and personnel were not to be regarded as minions of the Establishment because, as they themselves used to attest with confidence, there was no Establishment in the United States of America. Only foreigners and paranoids believed (otherwise)."

— Kerry Thornley

"YER DIFFER'NT FROM US . . . LET'S GIT 'IM!":

"It is precisely here . . . that the culture of the individual has been reduced to the most rigid and absurd regimentation. It is precisely here, of all civilized countries, that eccentricity in demeanor and opinion has come to bear the heaviest penalties. The whole drift of our law is toward the absolute prohibition of all ideas that diverge in the slightest from the accepted platitudes, and behind that drift of law there is a far more potent force of growing custom, and under that custom there is a national philosophy which erects conformity into the noblest of virtues and the free functioning of personality into a capital crime against society."

— H. L. Mencken (1919)

THE ECONOMIC MODEL:

"To make a short story of it all, it was discovered that an economy obeyed the same laws as electricity and that all of the mathematical theory and practical and computer know-how developed for the electronic field could be directly applied in the study of economics. This discovery was not openly declared, and its more subtle implications were and are kept a closely guarded secret, for example that in an economic model, human life is measured in dollars, and that the electric spark generated when opening a switch is analogous to the initiation of a war."

FREEDOM IS SLAVERY:

"Every civilization has had slavery as an essential element of its economy — including our own. Have you attained the "American Dream" by making payments on your own home? But who owns your home, really? If you're still making payments, who owns your car? Washer/dryer? Refrigerator/freezer? Big screen TV? Just stop making payments and see what happens. Let's say you've paid off your car, paid off your home. What happens if you don't pay your property taxes on time, or pay car insurance? What if you suddenly take ill? Ever hear of indentured servitude? Before the Civil War, free men who needed money could sell themselves into slavery for a period of time, usually seven years. Most Americans are way over their heads in debt. Daily they sell themselves into slavery — in forty hour weeks, eight hour shifts, if they can find them.

What has all this got to do with the media? The people who direct and control the world's financial resources are, to a very large extent, the same people who control and direct the world's media. Networks, cable stations, studios, theater chains, publishing consortiums, newspapers, are owned by a handful of people, and those people either own the banks or are owned by the banks.

Electronic and print media are a pacification program run by the Happyface Fun Enforcers. There is an ideal mental/emotional state for rabid consumerism, and that is the state of glad that the media promotes. The shock cuts and nervous camera succor a short attention span; so short, in fact, that your brain becomes a sieve, short-circuiting memory and logic. You are on IV TV, awaiting the next in-flow of shock or pacifying hypnotic to keep you hooked into the consumerist foodchain."

— Jim Keith

THE HISTORY OF UNKNOWN MEN:

"All the petty princes of Europe in medieval times had their Merlins, wise old men who in many instances were the actual rulers of the State. It is obvious that if these counselors were bound together by some common purpose their collective power would be considerable. And they were bound together, in the secret society of unknown philosophers, moving the crowns of Europe as on a mighty chess board. Men of this calibre bring about the mutations of empire. It is the general opinion that revolutions begin with the common people, but this is not true; the benevolently informed always guide and direct public opinion . . .nearly all great causes are furthered by mysterious and obscure persons who receive little or no credit for the part which they have played . . . In an old book of rules used by the brothers of the secret orders, is the following: 'Our brothers shall wear the dress and practice the customs of those nations to which they travel so that they shall not be conspicuous or convey any appearance that is different or unusual. Under no condition shall they reveal their true identity, or the work which they have come to accomplish; but shall accomplish all things secretly and without violating the laws or statutes of the countries in which they work.'"

— Manly P. Hall, *The Secret Destiny of America* (pp. 97, 171-72)

"DO YOU GLOW IN THE DARK?":

"Many commercial laundry detergents contain chemical "brighteners" that increase the reflectivity of clothing (ever notice your sleeves glowing under a "black light"?). Avoid these when washing clothes to be used in secretive activities. Only actual laundry soap, like Ivory, will leave you with the wonderfully dull and dingy look while still getting out those telltale body odors. All detergents will increase the reflectivity of your clothing, and will make you more visible to night vision devices . . . Beware of ultraviolet brighteners in your clothing. These chemicals, which are now in all laundry detergents, make you glow in the dark to (someone) equipped with night vision equipment. This problem is so serious that the US military specifies that no brighteners be used in the manufacture or cleaning of combat fatigues. A commercial remedy is readily available in the hunting supply market. Hunters are trying to reduce their visibility to animals whose eyes are far more receptive to ultraviolet light than is the human eye. "U-V Killer" (and a detergent called "Sport Wash") can be found in better sporting goods and hunter supply stores."

— "The Invisible Man" and "Strix," from *Ecodefense* (pp 253-54, 273)

"SEMIMARTIAL LAW":

"Foreign wars brought the temporary impositions of a semimartial law, notably through curbs of the freedom of press and the freedom of assembly, but the domestic wars have created a permanent state of semimartial law. For example, the Fourth Amendment to the Constitution, prohibiting the State from conducting 'unreasonable' searches and seizures, has been dramatically curtailed while the powers of the police have been equally extended. Drug and gang-related 'profiles' are now commonly accepted as sufficient criteria for the police to stop and search citizens. Adequate suspicion has been defined almost exclusively along racial and cultural lines . . . In general, the recent decline of the Bill of Rights has served to reinforce the traditional federalist project to strengthen the powers of the State against the danger of social disorder. A rising militarism on both foreign and domestic soil, then, and increasing recourse to a politics of social alarm, fear, and racism show the emergence of some fascistic elements of the State and the tendency toward the institution of a police state."

— Michael Hardt & Antonio Negri, *Labor of Dionysus* (pp. 242-43)

TROLLS LEERING AT THE WOMENFOLK:

"One place homeless men would often watch women was along a jogging trail in one of the city's parks adjacent to the river. Here, on warm afternoons, they would drink beer and call out to women who jogged or walked along the trail or came to the park to sun themselves. Most of the women moved nervously by, ignoring the overtures of the men. But some responded with a smile, a wave, or even a quick 'Hi!' Starved for female attention, the homeless men are quick to fantasize, attributing great significance to the slightest response. One Saturday afternoon, for example, as we were sitting by the jogging trail drinking beer with Pat Manchester and Ron Whitaker, we noticed several groups of young women who had laid out blankets on the grassy strip that borders the trail. Pat and Ron were especially interested in the women who were wearing shorts and halter tops. Pat called out for them to take their tops off. It was not clear that they heard him, but he insisted, 'They really want it. I can tell they do.' He suggested we go over with him to 'see what we can get,' but he was unwilling to go by himself . . . Occasionally, the women glanced toward us with apprehension, and Pat always acted as though it was a sign of interest."

— David Snow and Leon Anderson, *Down on Their Luck*

POSTMODERN SOCIAL REALITY:

"Some students of contemporary social life maintain that we have entered a new epoch of human history. Current modes of transportation and electronic means of communication have profoundly altered social life. We may now watch television programs on Kenya in the morning, telephone someone in Japan that afternoon, send a computer message to someone in Israel later, and fly to the Bahamas for a weekend that evening. Such travel and communication expands and multiplies networks of social interaction and relationships. It exposes us to numerous and often clashing versions of reality. Moreover, the diverse array of goods and services sold in the marketplace enable us to create collages of such diverse realities. We may dress like a New England woodsman, courtesy of L.L. Bean, in our Chicago apartment with Southwestern decor, while listening to rap music and feasting on Thai food. We see a kaleidoscope of realities on television, on city streets, and during our travels. Under these conditions, it is difficult to believe that any human reality is inevitable. Even supposedly authoritative experts are suspect. They often disagree and quickly change their minds. Nothing seems certain. This is what many students of social life call the postmodern condition. Some welcome it while others condemn it, but they all agree that human social life and experience is profoundly changing right before our eyes. They also agree that students of social life who ignore those changes will be left behind."

— Spencer Cahill, *Inside Social Life*, 3rd edition (p. 289)

CHURCH OF THE HOLY THUNDER!!!

"In my belief system, guns/firearms have divine symbolism — like the knife is to the Sikh, the Balisong is to the Filipino, and the cross is to the Christian. I dare anyone to abolish my religious rights with such a cavalier attitude as to make a joke of it! If so, I know how the court system works — I, too, know the way of the serpent. I think civil action is fine, but step on my rights with your trampling feet of clay and die outright for it, you fool. 'Don't tread on me, for my venom is pure fire.' . . . If they say that guns are bad, then it is also my right to say that Guns are DIVINE!!! Guns as religious artifacts are my right as per freedom of religion! I assert that guns are indeed religious artifacts — free from persecution, prohibition, or witch hunts of any type!"

— Master-at-Arms James Keating (slightly edited), from: www.combattech.com

"THE MAN" OWNS YOUR ASS!

"In 1968, one person working full-time at the minimum wage would come pretty close to the federal poverty level for a family of four (so if someone else in the family worked part-time, that family would be over the poverty line). Today, that same full-time, minimum-wage job takes a worker up to just 56% of the poverty line.

Who makes up the difference? We do, through food stamps, the Earned Income Tax Credit and other programs designed to help the working poor. In effect, we're subsidizing employers so that they can pay less than a living wage.

The Federal Reserve Board tries to keep the pool of unemployed workers above 5%, so as not to fuel inflation (it does that by raising or lowering interest rates to slow down or speed up the economy). Unemployment above 5% guarantees that there will be plenty of competition for jobs at below-subsistence wages. But there's a steadily growing pool of even cheaper labor — the nation's prison population.

Since 1990, thirty states have legalized contracting prison labor to private firms. Inmates are now employed booking reservations for TWA, doing data entry for the Bank of America and restocking shelves for Toys 'R' Us. Not only do prisoners work for much lower wages than people on the outside, but they have virtually no way to organize or strike. For an employer, it's the best of all possible worlds.

The US imprisons more of its citizens than any other nation on earth, and prison construction is growing by leaps and bounds. This great boon to the construction industry results from mandatory minimums for nonviolent drug offenders, the tough new "three-strikes" laws (the California version alone is costing $5.5 billion a year, five times what was estimated), and the roundup of illegal aliens.

In fact, as of 1995, the largest employer of illegal aliens in the US was Unicor, a $500 million-a-year company that pays prison laborers between .23 and $1.15 an hour to make clothing and furniture for the US government."

— Mark Zepezauer, *Take the Rich Off Welfare* (pgs 124-125)

"I'VE GOT YOUR 'TAX CUT' RIGHT HERE!"

"Back in the 1950s, US corporations paid 31% of the federal government's general revenues. Today, they pay just 11%. . . . Taxes that corporations don't pay have to be raised by taxing individuals. Not by taxing all individuals indiscriminately, of course — that would be un-American. A series of tax 'reforms' that began in 1977 have cut the rate paid by the richest Americans nearly in half, while Social Security taxes — which are paid overwhelmingly by ordinary wage earners (and not paid at all on income over $62,700) — have steadily risen.

Not surprisingly, these tax changes have contributed to a widening gap between rich and poor. Between 1983 and 1989, 99% of the increase in American's wealth went to the top 20% of the population, and 62% of it went to the top 1% of the population (currently made up of families whose net worth is $2.35 million or more). Income disparity in the United States is now the widest it's been since the crash of 1929, and it continues to grow.

The total net worth of that top 1% is now wqual to the total net worth of the bottom 90% of the population! In other words, the 2.7 million Americans who are worth 2.35 million or more have as much money as the 240 million Americans who are worth $346,000 or less.

Wherever you look on the economic ladder, the rich are getting richer. The wealth of the top 20% has increased while the wealth of the bottom 80% has decreased. Within that top 20%, the top 5% have gotten richer than the bottom 15%. Within that top 5%, the top 1% have gotten richer than the bottom 4%. Within that top 1%, the top 1/4% have gotten richer than the bottom 3/4%.

And so it goes, right up to the 400 wealthiest Americans. In the eight years from 1980 to 1987, their average net worth tripled."

— Mark Zepezauer, *Take the Rich Off Welfare* (pgs 10-11)

THE POPULACE PERSECUTES CRUSADER RABBITS

"Guerrilla and underground movements have seldom enjoyed the backing of a majority of the populations around them, even in countries occupied by foreign armies. Typically, such movements have been regarded as dangerous jabs at authority which often result in heavy reprisals against persons either not involved in the armed opposition or involved only against their will. . . . such forces often operated in a hostile environment. Usually, widespread support for resistance movements has emerged only when it appears they might succeed in actually displacing existing authority, or if they seem balanced on the edge of military victory."

— Perry Biddiscombe, *Werwolf!* (p. 4)

THE EMASCULATED WARRIOR

"If you are out in a bar and some drunk asshole comes up and spits in your girlfriend's face, and you bust about three or four of his teeth out, you will be arrested, charged with felony assault, and incarcerated — even if you have ten witnesses and the drunk guy apologizes and refuses to press charges! (In this case — if you have no prior record — the felony could be reduced to a misdemeanor which means you'll serve a couple months in jail (possibly only weekends, if you're lucky), be put on probation for three years, and be required to pay for the creep's medical bills.) If some crackhead with a meat cleaver breaks into your family's dwelling at four AM, and you spray him across your livingroom carpet with a couple rounds of 12 gauge buckshot, then call 911 and report the incident to the local constabulary, all the firearms in your house will be seized and you will be hauled off to jail charged with murder. (After paying several thousand dollars in legal fees, you will probably get your property back and the charges dropped — provided you could legally possess a firearm in the first place.) If you find out that the boyfriend of your three-year-old's babysitter has been jerking off into your kid's mouth, and you feel that a year in jail, counseling, and probation is too lenient for a baby-raping piece of shit and decide to administer justice yourself, you will be put in prison for the next eight to twenty-five years, because even though a 'jury of one's peers' would probably sympathize with you, the prosecution would bully the partially informed jurors into thinking they had no other option than to convict you for the maximum allowable penalty.

The government wants all of its citizens to be 'civilized' in dealing with criminal activities. This means that one's natural aggressive survival instincts must be suppressed and the citizen be totally dependant on law-enforcement officers for his personal protection. No citizen in New York State is permitted to carry any sort of weapon on the street. According to legislation, 'weapons' are not limited to firearms, knives, and exotic martial-arts garbage. Anything that could conceivably be used as a weapon is prohibited. For example: mace, electronic stun guns, slapper coshes, and telescopic steel whips are all non-lethal self-defense items which are carried by numerous women for protection from attackers. It is impossible to kill or even seriously injure someone with one of these toys — they are designed to provide a weaker individual with an opportunity to flee from a stronger attacker and nothing more, however, all are illegal in New York (NOTE: pepperspray was recently made legal to possess by persons over the age of 18 with no criminal history, but you have to show ID and fill out a form in order to purchase it). If you are pulled over by the police and you happen to have a jack handle, tyre iron, hammer, or crescent wrench on the floorboards, the policeman can cite 'probable cause' to search you and your vehicle, confiscate your tool, and arrest you for 'Criminal Possession of a Weapon' because the tool would meet the criteria for being a 'dangerous instrument.' If you have a cane or walking-stick and are not lame or elderly, you can have your cane taken away from you and be thrown in jail if the cop decides he doesn't like the looks of you. If you kick someone during a physical altercation, your sneaker ('shod foot') would even be classified as a 'weapon' under New York's statutes! What sort of self-defense items (other than a legally possessed handgun — for which carry permits involve a tedious and expensive application process — after which many folks who are legally entitled to receive one are often arbitrarily denied without any explanation) are available to the law-abiding New York State resident then? Well, it looks like we've got a choice between a whistle and an airhorn!"

— anonymous (RWT)

THE POWER PRINCIPAL

"Elizabeth I ascended the throne soon after her 25th birthday. At court, by careful observations, she developed the style that later became her motto, which translates into: 'I see and am silent.'

She learned self-possession from practicing her observations. She also discovered that public power was a derivative of some overmastering idea about which all people agree, and is a force accrued from some transcendent principal.

She learned that such power can only be held if one becomes the embodiment of the idea oneself. She learned that prior to holding such power one must deny oneself certain luxuries that might disperse potency and principle . . . something she wished to get done early in life.

She also learned that those who share in one's power are thus bound by need, but can become resentful if the source of power recedes, or dangerous if they begin to fear exile.

She learned that true power is concerned only with the maintenance of itself, and answers only to its source, and that power in itself can never spoil or be corrupted.

She saw how the carful cultivator of power always stores extra power in reserve and uses the power of others at every opportunity in an effort to conserve his own. She also saw that others would gladly waste their small bits of power on one's behalf if they were sufficiently enthralled.

She learned that power grows in silence, by not doing, gathering to itself more of itself. She learned that it must be used by deliberation. But above all, she learned that power is merely the strength of a systematic self-delusion on the part of the masses about the absolute importance of some grand idea that no one has ever seen."

— summary of "A Meditation on Power" by A. Bartlett Giamatti

IS FROGGY GONNA JUMP?

"Telltale signs of a potentially assaultive subject include extreme pacing, the inability to keep his arms or hands in one position, wide stance, jutting chest, erect body posture, fixed eyes, speaking to himself, rapid speech, changes in speech volume, refusing to cooperate, looking at you out of the corner of his eye, the inability to maintain a relaxed facial expression, and leaving the area and then returning to stalk you or another intended victim. Bent legs or a bobbing motion are signs that the subject is preparing to spring at you. Long pauses in the middle of a sentence could be a sign that the subject is contemplating an attack. Pacing behind you or outside your vision (i.e., in a blind spot) are signs of a possible sneak attack. If a subject looks you over from the top of your head down to your feet, he may be sizing you up for an attack. Hitting a fist into the open palm, having a tense body, or rubbing a clenched fist with the opposite hand are intimidation gestures."

— Edward Lewis, *Hostile Ground* (p. 15)

THE "WAR ON LOGIC"

"Now I'm not pro-drug. They obviously cause a lot of damage. But I am pro-logic, and you're never going to stop the human need for release through altered consciousness. . . . Our displeasure with someone hell-bent on self-ruination through drug use seems really disproportionate to its direct impact on us. And as a matter of fact, we amplify that impact when we attempt to enforce unenforceable laws. It not only costs us billions but puts us in harm's way as addicts are driven to crime as a means to an end. Why do we chase druggies down like villagers after Karloff? Let them legally have what they already have and defuse the bomb. You know, I think the hysteria about drugs is oftentimes baseless, . . . fruitless, and patently hypocritical. . . . We seem to be willfully turning away from reality, and from logic might I add, to punish people who in many instances are doing an extremely fine job of punishing themselves . . . let's save the money we're wasting trying to regulate other people's private lives. . . . They are going to do with their lives what they want to do, whether you like it or not. There is nothing you can do about it that won't break the bank, overcrowd the prisons, or corrode an already oxidized judicial system."

— Dennis Miller, *The Rants* (pp. 34-37)

ARMED NEUTRALITY

"The Swiss always has his rifle at hand. It belongs to the furnishings of his home . . . That corresponds to ancient Swiss tradition. . . . the Swiss soldier lives in constant companionship with his rifle. He knows what that means. With this rifle, he is liable every hour, if the country calls, to defend his hearth, his home, his family, his birthplace. The weapon is to him a pledge and sign of honor and freedom. The Swiss does not part with his rifle."

— Philipp Etter

SWITZERLAND FLIPS ADOLF THE BIRD!

"Switzerland was the only country in Europe that had no single political leader with the authority to surrender the people to the Nazis. On Swiss soil there were no Jewish victims, no Gestapo jurisdiction and no slave labor for the German war machine. Every man in Switzerland had a rifle in his home. Switzerland was the only European country which proclaimed that, in the event of invasion, any announcement of surrender was to be regarded as enemy propaganda, and that every soldier must fight to the last cartridge and then with the bayonet."

— Stephen P. Halbrook, *Target Switzerland* (p. ix)

"HERR DOPPELGANGER"

"The monster who occupied Heinrich Himmler, the world's most unlikely tyrant, achieved the pinnacle of personal power over life and death over the people of Germany under the guise of safeguarding their interests and protecting the Nation from non-existent enemies!

The vessel for this role of mass enslavement and mass extermination of millions of innocent people had to be a man without an Ego, a soulless zombie totally incapable of the experience of love or of any human motive. And this is exactly what Heinrich Himmler was, an anti-human in a human body. One cannot even call Himmler a soul imprisoned and possessed by evil as was the case of Adolf Hitler. For in Himmler there was no self-conscious soul to be possessed, only a body and brain to be occupied and bent to inhuman purposes. . . .

The most prominent feature in the working of the Doppelganger is an endless capacity to counterfeit and dissemble, to make something look what it is not, and to feign benign reasons and moral justification to cover up evil motives.

The whole Nazi regime was built up on such practices. For instance, Adolf Hitler achieved personal power through such a counterfeit law, the so-called 'Enabling Law', by which (he) gained complete independence from both President and Reichstag. The actual title of this law, which Hitler secured by burning down the Reichstag to prove the existence of dangerous enemies of the state, was 'Law for Removing the Distress of People and Nation'. In this manner the power of all other political parties, state institutions, and the Trades Unions was eliminated overnight. The application of the same law on an individual level extinguished the personal liberty of every single German in the Reich."

— Trevor Ravenscroft, *The Spear of Destiny* (pgs. 295, 306)

THE THIEF OF TIME

"(Time is) the most precious commodity we have. I always view my time as divided into infinite moments or transactions or contacts. Anyone who steals my time is stealing my life because they are taking my existence from me. As I get older, I realize that time is the only thing I have left. So when someone comes to me with a project, I estimate the time it will take me to do it and then I ask myself, 'Do I want to spend weeks or months of what little time I have on this project? Is it worth it or am I just wasting my time?' If I consider the project time-worthy I do it.

I apply the same yardstick to social relations. I will not permit people to steal my time. I have limited my friends to those people with whom time passes happily. There are moments in my life — necessary moments — when I can't do anything but what is my choice. The choice of how I spend my time is mine, and it is not dictated by social convention."

— Stirling Silliphant

DIGNIFIED PACIFISM (HAS ITS LIMITATIONS)

"The only reason men fight is because they are insecure; one man needs to prove that he is better or stronger than another. The man who is secure within himself has no need to prove anything with force, so he can walk away from a fight with dignity and pride. He is the true martial artist — a man so strong inside that he has no need to demonstrate his power.

The point of achieving proficiency in any martial art is to be able to walk away from a fight rather than to win it. But you will walk with shoulders erect, pride in your bearing, knowing inside what the outcome of the battle would have been had you wished to precipitate it. And the attitude of confidence will be communicated to your antagonist, who will realize that he narrowly escaped defeat."

— Ed Parker

LEGISLATION AS VIOLENCE

"To say that laws are necessary to protect individuals sounds all right until you realize that most laws interfere with the freedom of individuals — particularly the endless number of absurd victimless-crime laws on the books. How can any group of people — whether it calls itself a government or any other name — know what's good for you when you have desires, ambitions, needs, beliefs and standards different from anyone else's? How can they act in your best interest when they don't even know you? Only you can decide what's best for you; anyone who tries to do it for you, through force, is an aggressor and is in violation of natural law."

— Robert J. Ringer, *Looking Out For #1* (p. 240)

"WHAT IS HISTORY BUT A FABLE AGREED UPON?"

"There is an Establishment history, an official history, which dominates history textbooks, trade publishing, the media and library shelves. The official line always assumes that events such as wars, revolutions, scandals, assassinations, are more or less random unconnected events. By definition events can NEVER be the result of a conspiracy, they can never result from premeditated planned group action. An excellent example is the Kennedy assassination when, within 9 hours of the Dallas tragedy, TV networks announced the shooting was NOT a conspiracy, regardless of the fact that a negative proposition can never be proven, and that the investigation had barely begun.

Woe betide any book or author that falls outside the official guidelines. Foundation support is not there. Publishers get cold feet. Distribution is hit and miss, or non-existent. . . .

Times have changed. The weaknesses, inconsistencies and plain untruths in official history have surfaced . . . . it is rare to find a thinking reader who accepts official history. Most believe it has been more or less packaged for mass consumption . . .

. . .The only reasonable explanation for recent history in the United States is that there exists a conspiracy to use political power for ends which are inconsistent with the Constitution.

This is known by the official historians as the 'devil theory of history,' which again is a quick, cheap device for brushing facts under the rug. However, these critics ignore, for example, the Sherman Act, i.e., the anti-trust laws where conspiracy is the basic accepted theory. If there can be a conspiracy in the marketplace, then why not in the political arena? Are politicians any purer than businessmen?"

— Antony C. Sutton, *America's Secret Establishment* (pgs. 1, 3)

"COERCION IS ALWAYS ASSOCIATED WITH SECRECY"

"Secret political organizations can be — and have been — extremely dangerous to the social health and constitutional vitality of a society. In a truly free society the exercise of political power must always be open and known.

Moreover, organizations devoted to violent overthrow of political structures have always, by necessity, been secret organizations. Communist revolutionary cells are an obvious example. In fact, such revolutionary organizations could only function if their existence was secret.

In brief, secrecy in matters political is historically associated with coercion. Furthermore, the existence of secrecy in organizations with political ambitions or with a history of political action is always suspect. Freedom is always associated with open political action and discussion while coercion is always associated with secrecy."

— Antony C . Sutton, *America's Secret Establishment* (p. 185)

THE "MAKE-BELIEVE" WARRIOR

"There are few things in the world I can conceive as being more instantly ludicrous than a prosperously middle-aged lump of pudgy Euroamerican verse-monger, an apparition looking uncannily like some weird cross between the Mall-O-Milk Marshmallow Man and Pillsbury's Doughboy, suited up in a grotesque mismatch combining pleated Scottish tweeds with a striped Brooks Brother's shirt and Southwest Indian print vest, peering myopically along his nose through coke-bottle steelrim specs while holding forth in stilted and somewhat nasal tonalities on the essential virtues of virility, of masculinity, of being or becoming a 'warrior.' The intrinsic absurdity of such a scene is, moreover, compounded by a factor of five when it is witnessed by an audience — all male, virtually all white, and on the whole obviously well-accustomed to enjoying a certain pleasant standard of material comfort — which sits as if spellbound, rapt in its attention to every nuance of the speaker, altogether fawning in its collective nods and murmurs of devout agreement with each detail of his discourse."

— Ward Churchill, "Indians 'R' Us?"

DIRTY POOL AT THE PICKLE FACTORY

"The CIA has many media personnel on its payroll to plant stories or discredit charges against it. The Agency secretly pays out large sums of money for articles and books to be written on the CIA's behalf. Its control over the media is like a Wurlitzer, orchestrating and manipulating all segments of the written or broadcast media. The CIA uses taxpayer funds to control reporters and publishers of newspapers, magazines, and books. . . . (p. 175)

Instead of the CIA being primarily an intelligence gathering and coordinating agency acting under the National Security Council, the CIA has become so powerful that it can destroy any politician who seriously questions its activities. This is especially true when combined with the criminal misuse of power by Justice Department attorneys and federal judges.

The average American is unaware of the gravity of the CIA's criminal activities, thanks to the orchestrated coverup and disinformation by the establishment media. The corrupt mindset has existed for years. Initiating wars, as in Vietnam, and assassination operations, as in Vietnam and Central America, are routine. Engaging in drug trafficking in foreign countries and the United States, a key reason for the world-wide proliferation of drugs, is the type of criminal activities this dangerous agency considers proper. . . .

Although the CIA is not permitted by law to operate within the United States, it has done so. It has engaged and is engaging in many forms of criminal activities against the American people. Through fronts, cutouts, and proprietaries, the CIA has defrauded all types of U.S. financial institutions, including savings and loans, banks, and insurance companies. . . . (p. 231)

It is standard practice for the CIA to use contract employees and mercenaries to carry out CIA activities within the United States and abroad, and in this manner fraudulently deny any involvement. Another standard practice is for the CIA to conspire with Justice Department attorneys to charge covert employees with violating federal law, and seek long prison sentences so as to silence or discredit them. . . . (p. 238)

In its bag of dirty tricks, the CIA has promoted pedophilia for the purpose of blackmailing and controlling people, especially those in high government positions. . . . (p. 547)

Their power . . . reaches into every home in America . . . It is the power which shapes and molds the mind of virtually every citizen . . . The mass media form for us our image of the world and then tell us what to think about that image. . . . Employing carefully developed psychological techniques, they guide our thought and opinion . . . Most Americans fail to realize that they are being manipulated. . . . Every point on the permissible spectrum of public opinion is acceptable to the media masters — and no impermissible fact or viewpoint is allowed any exposure at all, if they can prevent it." (P. 581)

— Rodney Stich, *Defrauding America*

"WE DON'T NEED NO STEENKING BADGES!"

"Regardless of the unattractiveness or noisy militancy of some private citizens or organizations, the Constitution does not permit federal interference with their activities except through the criminal justice system, armed with its ancient safeguards. There are no exceptions. No federal agency, the CIA, the IRS, or the FBI, can be at the same time policeman, prosecutor, judge and jury. This is what constitutionally guaranteed due process is all about. It may sometimes be disorderly and unsatisfactory to some, but it is the essence of freedom . . . I suggest that the philosophy supporting COINTELPRO is the subversive notion that any public official, the President or a policeman, possesses a kind of inherent power to set aside the Constitution whenever he thinks the public interest, or 'national security' warrants it. That notion is postulate of tyranny."

— Congressman Don Edwards (1975)

AGENT PROVOCATEUR

"Probably the most-well-known agent provocateur was Thomas Tongyai, known as Tommy the Traveler. Tongyai, who was paid by both the FBI and local police, spent over two years traveling among colleges in western New York state urging students to kill police, make bombs and blow up buildings. He supplied students with radical speakers, literature and films, tried to organize an SDS chapter at Hobart College, organized SDS conferences in Rochester and urged students to participate in the Weatherman 'Days of Rage' in Chicago in October, 1969. Tongyai constantly talked violence, carried a grenade in his car, showed students how to use an M-1 rifle and offered advice on how to carry out bombings. After some students at Hobart College apparently took his advice and bombed the Hobart ROTC building, and Tongyai's cover was exposed, the local sheriff commented, 'There's a lot of difference between showing how to build a bomb and building one.' As a result of disturbances connected with Tongyai's activities on the Hobart campus, nine students and faculty faced criminal charges, but Tongyai was cleared by a local grand jury and went on to become a policeman in Pennsylvania."

— Robert J. Goldstein, *Political Repression in Modern America*

TRAITORS BEWARE!

"See the old man at the corner where you buy your papers? He may have a silencer equipped pistol under his coat. That extra fountain pen in the pocket of the insurance salesman who calls on you might be a cyanide gas gun. What about your milk man? Arsenic works slow but sure. Your auto mechanic may stay up nights studying booby traps. These patriots are not going to let you take their freedom away from them. They have learned the silent knife, the strangler's cord, the target rifle that hits sparrows at 200 yards. Traitors beware. Even now the cross hairs are on the back of your necks."

— anonymous, taken from a death threat post card sent to many "leftist" activists by the "Minutemen" domestic terrorist group during 1970

BREAKING MEN'S MINDS

"In order to produce marked changes in behavior, it is necessary to weaken, undermine, or remove supports for old attitudes. I would like you to think of brainwashing not in terms of . . . ethics and morals, but in terms of the deliberate changing of human behavior by a group of men who have relatively complete control over the environment in which the captives live. . . (These changes can be induced by) isolation, sensory deprivation, segregation of leaders, spying, tricking men into signing written statements which are then shown to others, placing individuals whose will power has been severely weakened into a living situation with others more advanced in thought reform, character invalidation, humiliations, sleeplessness, rewarding subservience, and fear." (emphasis added)

— Dr. Edgar Schein, in a 1962 address to all federal penitentiary wardens

THE SHAPE OF THINGS TO COME

"A pattern is emerging in which the 'attitude adjustment' represented by police and prison becomes a normative rather than exceptional experience of power in the U.S. If the present dynamics of spiraling police power and state sanctioned secrecy, proliferating penal facilities and judicial abandonment of basic constitutional principles is allowed to continued unabated, it is easily predictable that upwards of 20% of the next generation of Americans will spend appreciable time behind bars . . . any hint of politically 'deviant' behavior will likely be met with more-or-less immediate arrest, packaging as a 'criminal' by the FBI and its interactive counterparts in the state and local police, processing through the courts and delivery to one or another prison for an appropriate measure of behavior modification. The social message — 'don't even think about rocking the boat, under any circumstances' — is both undeniable and overwhelming. . . . (COINTELPRO) will have moved from covert and relatively selective or 'surgical' repression of dissent to the overt and uniform suppression of political diversity. . . (which would amount to) outright social pacification and maintenance of a rigid social order. . . . concern with questions of police power and the function of prisons has been consigned mainly to lawyers and a scattering of researcher-activists whose work has been typically viewed as 'marginal,' esoteric,' and even 'paranoid' . . . the posture of far too many people on the left suggests they are (ambivalent) . . . . This is readily borne out by the number of progressives who have rallied nationally to the cause of removing assault rifles and other semi-automatic weapons from the hands of the populace, while doing nothing to confront the rampant proliferation of SWAT capabilities among police forces throughout the country. Another choice indicator may be apprehended in the range of ostensibly progressive individuals and groups which have lately queued up to 'take back streets' they never had in the first place, righteously endorsing a government-sponsored 'war on drugs' entailing unprecedented police prerogatives to engage in no-knock entry, warrantless search and seizure, the routine 'interdiction' of people of color driving along the nation's highways, uncompensated impoundment of personal property, massive applications of physical and electronic surveillance, the use of preventive detention on a wholesale basis, and myriad other abridgements of civil rights and liberties which would have remained unthinkable just five years ago."

— Ward Churchill, *The COINTELPRO Papers* (pp. 324-325)

PARANOIA WILL DESTROY YA

"The tyrant recruits his countrymen in his crusade against those he suspects might oppose him. He uses unceasing propaganda to incite mass hysteria and witch hunts, transforming the nation into an army of informers, starting an undeclared civil war of hunters against prey.

His paranoia may infect his country, spreading racism, religious intolerance, and persecution of specific people and groups. Obsessed with vengeance, the tyrant delights in torture and annihilation. Concentration camps and genocide are the final solution, the balm for his burning anxieties. . . .

Tyrants, in their monstrous egoism and frenzied fears, are willing to destroy the world rather than submit to defeat."

— D. Jablow Hershman & Julian Lieb, M.D., *A Brotherhood of Tyrants* (p. 201)

THE ICEMAN COMETH

"The enemy is subhuman.
They are to be terminated. . .
And it doesn't really matter how I feel.
I no longer feel.
Blood turns to ice water, pumping through my veins.
Eyes glass over, changing from blue to steely grey.
Face is cold,
Expressionless. . .
Meditation.

Clear your mind, so it is as a blank slate.
Kill without joy. . .
Without revulsion. . .
Without any feeling whatsoever. . .
Numb yourself.
There is plenty of time for sorrow later. . .
But the dreams! They won't let me alone!"

— excerpted from an untitled poem by Jake Bishop

MARK OF THE BEAST

"We shall all be considered 'World Citizens' and shall be issued 'Worker Cards' that will help keep track of everyone's movements, expenditures and activities. There shall be one World currency, which shall primarily be composed of digitalized 'credits' on one's Worker Card account. Eventually the Worker Card shall be replaced with a non-transferable, unreproducible and unlosable form of identification, such as computerized records of palmprints and retinas or even a UPC barcode indelibly tattooed with ultraviolet ink in one's flesh. No funds can then be transferred from one party to another without government knowledge/approval. This will effectively wipe out the black market economy, which will be forced to resort to the barter system. Furthermore, any (or all) account(s) may be 'frozen' at any time, making access to funds for various transactions impossible, plus an alert could be transmitted to the Enforcement Branch as to your present location. All transactions of every conceivable nature will be closely monitored by Artificial Intelligence, which will immediately red flag any anomaly for government administrators, who will then examine the suspect transaction and decide whether to alert the Enforcement Branch. New 'advances' in communication technology (such as miniaturized computers/pictophones) will serve as combination homing beacons/listening devices. Every person on the planet will be under computerized scrutiny for any evidence of 'disloyalty.'"

— excerpted from the anonymously published *Prophesy File*, which was distributed to a number of underground groups in the Summer of 1991

"I'LL GIVE UP MY UZI WHEN THEY PRY IT FROM MY COLD DEAD FINGERS"

"All firearms will be declared contraband, with possession of a gun being considered the highest level of treason and grounds for summary execution, as civilian gun owners will all be classified as violent subversive criminals (first, guns will be ordered to be turned in to the proper authorities in exchange for compensation in the form of 'credits,' then a short amnesty period will be declared so 'dawdlers' have no excuse not to turn in their guns, finally a 'General Warrant' shall be issued and Enforcement Branch agents throughout the former United States will simultaneously launch a mass raid versus the digitalized listing of known gun owners suspected of non-compliance. After the mass gun raids, any civilian found in possession of a firearm will obviously be a terrorist and the government will show no mercy towards them). Hunting will have been outlawed due to mass outbreaks of deadly wildlife plagues which are easily transmitted to persons who handle carcasses or eat meat. Target shooting will have been reviled as 'violent and anti-social behavior' and totally banned. Self-defense will not be a legitimate excuse either, as all World Citizens will have a 'duty' to respect the rights of others, as well as an 'obligation' (non-compliance being a punishable offense) to immediately report any wrongdoings to the proper Authority figures. All forms of 'weapon' (including: knives, bludgeons, pepperspray, bows, BB guns, and slingshots) will be prohibited, as well as toys which either look like guns, or are believed to 'encourage violence' (i.e., 'action figures,' footballs, darts, etc.). Books, magazines, and comics which depict the use of weapons will be declared 'subversive literature' and burned in massive bonfires (as well as any other materials deemed antagonistic to the new worldview). Possession of any form of contraband (or failure to report those known to possess contraband — even an antique cap gun rusting away in someone's attic), or even being in the same place where contraband is discovered, will be considered irrefutable proof of disloyalty. There will be no juries and no appeals process."

— excerpted from the anonymously published *Prophesy File*

GENOCIDE

"Overpopulation is considered a serious threat to mankind, and steps are being taken to reverse the process. Ways to control population growth include: genocide, sterilization or reduction of the average lifespan through various environmental stressors. Genocide may occur as a result of: war, riots, plague, famine (caused primarily by economic manipulation), 'ethnic cleansing,' cataclysmic weather conditions (which may be artificially induced) or mass poisoning. Sterilization may be encouraged through: cash (or 'credit') disbursements, mandatory eugenics programs, or chemicals surreptitiously introduced into the food/water supply (perhaps the most popular corporate-sponsored soft drink or fast food sandwich?). Reduction of the average lifespan can be caused by repeated (if not constant) exposure to toxins (i.e., pollution, solvents, fumes, mysterious food additives, or prescribed medications) and radiation (primarily electromagnetic), resulting in a variety of stress-related ailments, cancers and energy imbalances. Population controls are already being practiced (conspicuous examples of possible officially sanctioned genocide programs could include: Chile, Argentina, Bolivia, Columbia, Peru, Brazil, Haiti, Rwanda), and many more are expected to be introduced in the near future."

— excerpted from the anonymously published *Prophesy File*

WHY WHORES AREN'T EVIL

"We must accept that, sad as it may be, many people do not merit sex on a regular basis as a result of either visual unpleasantness or social ineptitude. These persons often channel their repressed sexual energy in an unacceptable or self-destructive manner. Depression is common, which can lead to alcoholism, drug use or perversion. Many clients of the Nevada brothels are disabled veterans who are unfairly shunned by most women in our image-conscious society. Are we, as a society, going to deny legions of ugly, stupid and awkward people what Maslow considered a basic need? What often happens is that one of these 'rejects,' feeling sad and unloved, pairs up with a like reject whom he or she finds dull and unattractive but a convenient partner for coitus, and then because the Fundamentalists whom these rejects follow shun contraception they inflict upon society a sizable brood of miniature rejects — in which they instil their twisted sheeplike 'values,' and the cycle is thus doomed to repeat itself exponentially. Many individuals would be deeply offended by what I have just said, and would vehemently deny the truth of my statement, but it is a sad fact that many unattractive individuals marry one another simply as an excuse to have sex with someone, are often unhappy with their choice of a mate, and usually have an above average amount of ill cared for children who tend to become burdens upon society later in life (if not predatory criminals). If a safe, legal, and socially acceptable opportunity to sate one's sexual appetites existed, I believe that many of these marriages, and the ensuing broods of delinquents, would not occur."

— anonymous (RWT)

"EXTERMINATE ALL THE BRUTES!"

"If any man was a habitual criminal, I am one. In my lifetime I have broken every law that was ever made by both God and man. If either had made any more, I should very cheerfully have broken them also. The mere fact that I have done these things is quite sufficient for the average person. Very few people even consider it worthwhile to wonder why I am what I am and do what I do. All that they think is necessary to do is catch me, try me, convict me and send me to prison for a few years, make life miserable for me while in prison and turn me loose again . . . If someone had a young tiger cub in a cage and then mistreated it until it got savage and bloodthirsty and then turned it loose to prey on the rest of the world . . . there would be a hell of a roar . . . But if some people do the same thing to other people, then the world is surprised, shocked and offended because they get robbed, raped and killed. They done it to me and then don't like it when I give them the same dose they gave me."

— the demonic serial killer Carl Panzram, *Killer, a Journal of Murder* (ed. by Gaddis & Long)

THE MEN BEHIND THE CURTAIN

"Winston Churchill called it 'The High Cabal.' Colonel L. Fletcher Prouty, JFK's Director of Covert Operations for the Joint Chiefs of Staff, called it 'The Power Elite.' Others knew it as 'The Enterprise,' 'The Council,' 'The Committee,' and other names. But no matter what it was called, the organization that has pulled the political strings of government since before World War I in not only the U.S., but Europe, Russia and Japan, exists. It is resident in four major areas of international affairs: the international banking community; certain, selected boardrooms of major corporations; cells within the command structure of the military services of the most powerful of countries; and within the secret corridors of the covert intelligence community. It is an all-powerful organization that makes its own laws as needed, disregarding any that happen to be objectionable, utilizes the covert intelligence services of virtually every major country as footsoldiers during peacetime, and their military machines in times of war.

Such an elite and powerful organization requires highly educated, extremely qualified, and very loyal individuals to fill its upper echelon ranks. The astute student of history will note that during the past eighty years, many of the same names appear over and over within the administrations of the upper levels of government. Often these names are not in the forefront of historical events, but certainly involved in a staff or advisorship position. It is these people who truly control the fate of the nation — and the other nations of the world. And it is these people who are consistently awarded key positions and promotions, and continue to serve within the hallowed halls of government from one administration to the next without fear of replacement. It is this resiliency and continued success in ascension that, even though they attempt to hide behind other, more visible figures, identifies them for what they are: members of The Power."

— Craig Roberts, *Kill Zone* (pp. 149-150)

HOLLYWOOD "HEROES"

"In modern Western culture, we are surrounded by what we are told are warrior images. GI Joe stuff. Heroic Hollywood figures played by actors like Eastwood, Stallone, Willis, and Schwartzenegger. Gladiators solving all of the world's problems with fists and firearms. I'm not such an idealist that I believe that I could do my job as a police officer without occasionally using force to manage the violence of criminals. But there is a big difference between using only as much force as is necessary and the excessive force and destruction that are characteristic of these Hollywood crime dramas, If I let myself behave in this violent manner, I would be no better than the criminals that I deal with. Force isn't the answer. Too often it simply breeds more bloodshed in the form of vendetta and revenge. This Hollywood 'warrior' stereotype is incomplete and unbalanced."

— Kerr Cuhulain, *Wiccan Warrior* (p. 6)

THE "RIGHT MAN"

"He is a man driven by a manic need for self-esteem — to feel that he is a 'somebody.' He is obsessed by the question of 'losing face,' so he will never, under any circumstances, admit that he might be in the wrong. . . . the Right Man is an 'idealist' — that is, he lives in his own mental world and does his best to ignore aspects of reality that conflict with it. Like the Communists' rewriting of history, reality can always be 'adjusted' later to fit his glorified picture of himself. . . . The Right Man hates losing face; if he suspects that his threats are not being taken seriously, he is capable of carrying them out, purely for the sake of appearances. . . . the central characteristic of the Right Man is the decision to be out of control, in some particular area. We all have to learn self-control to deal with the real world and other people. But with some particular person — a mother, a wife, a child — we may decide that this effort is not necessary and allow ourselves to explode. But — and here we come to the very heart of the matter — this decision creates, so to speak, a permanent weak-point in the boiler, the point at which it always bursts. . . . What is so interesting here is the way the Right Man's violent emotion reinforces his sense of being justified, and his sense of justification increases his rage. He is locked into a kind of vicious spiral, and he cannot escape until he has spent his fury. . . . The Right Man feels that his rage is a storm that has to be allowed to blow itself out, no matter what damage it causes. But this also means that he is the slave of an impulse he cannot control; his property, even the lives of those he loves, are at the mercy of his emotions."

— Colin Wilson (paraphrasing A. E. Van Vogt), *A Criminal History of Mankind* (pp. 67-70)

THE EPITOME OF DETACHMENT

"In reprisal for Resistance activity in the area, the Germans rounded up all the inhabitants and made them go to the marketplace. The women and children were herded into the village church. No one was alarmed at this stage — the Germans were laughing and joking, and playing with the babies. Then, at a signal from a captain, the soldiers in the square opened fire on the men and massacred them all. The church was set on fire and the women and children burned alive. The children who managed to stumble out were thrown back into the fire. A Swiss who described the massacre remarked, 'I am convinced these Elite Guards did not feel the slightest shade of hatred against the French children when they held them in their arms. I am equally convinced that, if a counter order had arrived . . . they would have continued to play daddy.' But the SS men were 'under orders,' and the order had the effect of a hypnotist's command. They 'blocked out' the reality of the women and children, and 'did their duty.' A confidence trickster swindles his victims in much the same way; he may actually feel genuinely friendly towards them as he lulls them into a state of trustfulness, yet the basic intention remains unchanged."

— Colin Wilson (on the massacre at Oradour-sur-Glane in June 1944), *A Criminal History of Mankind* (p. 35)

"ONE IN TWENTY"

"Dominance is a subject of enormous interest to biologists and zoologists because the percentage of dominant animals — or human beings — seems to be amazingly constant. Bernard Shaw once asked the explorer H. M. Stanley how many other men could take over leadership of the expedition if Stanley himself fell ill; Stanley replied promptly: 'One in twenty.' 'Is that exact or approximate?' asked Shaw. 'Exact.' And biological studies have confirmed this as a fact. For some odd reason, precisely five percent — one in twenty — of any animal group are dominant — have leadership qualities. During the Korean War, the Chinese made the interesting discovery that if they separated out the dominant five percent of American prisoners of war, and kept them in a separate compound, the remaining ninety-five percent made no attempt to escape."

— Colin Wilson, *A Criminal History of Mankind* (p. 72)

FIRE OF THE GODS

"Gunpowder was invented in China some time around the year 1000, and seems to have been used for fireworks, but not, so far as we know, for destructive purposes. It is interesting to speculate how the discovery came about. Its chief ingredient is nitre — saltpetre. And in Europe at least its discovery came about by a rather curious process. Walls of farm buildings were often built with mud in which the hardening ingredient was cattle dung. Men would go and urinate against these walls, with the consequence that white streaks would form on the wall. This was nitre — potassium nitrate. Someone no doubt tried the experiment of tossing some of this crystalline substance on a bonfire, and observed that it made the wood burn with a new fury — it releases oxygen. The next step, which was probably made by some Chinese alchemist — for they had been at work trying to make semi-magical drugs and elixirs since the fifth century B.C. — was to find that, in certain proportions, nitre, sulphur and powdered charcoal will burn with a single bright flash, or — if confined in a tube — explode. So the Chinese made fireworks, and the Mongol hordes of Genghis Khan seem to have learned about it from them and brought gunpowder to the west when they invaded the Kharismian empire in 1218 A.D. By about 1250 the Arabs had invented the first gun, a bamboo tube reinforced with metal bands which would fire an arrow. And so man's most dangerous invention before the atomic bomb reached Europe around 1300, and helped to blow apart the last remnants of the Middle Ages."

— Colin Wilson, *A Criminal History of Mankind* (p. 298)

"KNOW ALIGNMENT!!!" (AD&D 2nd Level Clerical Spell)

"The alignments possible for characters are described below:

Chaotic Evil: The major precepts of this alignment are freedom, randomness, and woe. Laws and order, kindness, and good deeds are disdained. Life has no value. By promoting chaos and evil, those of this alignment hope to bring themselves to positions of power, glory, and prestige in a system ruled by individual caprice and their own whims.

Chaotic Good: While creatures of this alignment view freedom and the randomness of action as ultimate truths, they likewise place value on life and the welfare of each individual. Respect for individualism is also great. By promoting the gods of chaotic good, creatures of this alignment seek to spread their values throughout the world.

Chaotic Neutral: Above respect for life and good, or disregard for life and the promotion of evil, the chaotic neutral places randomness and disorder. Good and evil are complimentary balance arms. Neither are preferred, nor must either prevail, for ultimate chaos would then suffer.

Lawful Evil: Creatures of this alignment are great respecters of laws and strict order, but life, beauty, truth, freedom, and the like are held as valueless, or at least scorned. By adhering to stringent discipline, those of lawful evil alignment hope to impose their yoke upon the world.

Lawful Good: While as strict in their prosecution of law and order, characters of lawful good alignment follow these precepts to improve the common weal. Certain freedoms must, of course, be sacrificed in order to bring order; but truth is of highest value, and life and beauty of great importance. The benefits of this society are to be brought to all.

Lawful Neutral: Those of this alignment view regulation as all-important, taking a middle road betwixt evil and good. This is because the ultimate harmony of the world — and the whole of the universe — is considered by lawful neutral creatures to have its sole hope rest upon law and order. Evil or good are immaterial beside the determined purpose of bringing all to predictability and regulation.

Neutral Evil: The neutral evil creature views law and chaos as unnecessary considerations, for pure evil is all-in-all. Either might be used, but both are disdained as foolish clutter useless in eventually bringing maximum evilness to the world.

Neutral Good: Unlike those directly opposite them (neutral evil) in alignment, creatures of neutral good believe that there must be some regulation in combination with freedoms if the best is to be brought to the world — the most beneficial conditions for living things in general and intelligent things in particular.

True Neutral: The "true" neutral looks upon all other alignments as facets of the system of things. Thus, each aspect — evil and good, chaos and law — of things must be retained in balance to maintain the status quo; for things as they are cannot be improved upon except temporarily, and even then but superficially. Nature will prevail and keep things as they were meant to be, provided the "wheel" surrounding the hub of nature does not become unbalanced due to the work of unnatural forces — such as human and other intelligent creatures interfering with what is meant to be.

Naturally, there are variations and shades of tendencies within each alignment. These descriptions are generalizations only. A character can be basically good in its "true" neutrality, or tend towards evil."

— Gary Gygax, *Advanced D&D Player's Handbook*, 1st ed. (pp. 33-34)

SUBGENII RANKIN' ON THE "CON"

"We've been wrong about two major things. Our leaders don't 'mean well,' and they aren't stupid.

They've succeeded in creating a world of financial control in what looks like private hands, dominating all nations through world economy . . . but those 'private hands' are not the hands of the human Insiders and it isn't money they grasp for.

The Conspiracy has many noble, ignorant patriots duped into swallowing hook, line and sinker the fallacies that either 'Communism' or 'Capitalism' is the Big Threat, but either way it's the same power elite in control.

The same ones who promulgated the Red Scare and the Commie Witch Hunts also financed the Russian Revolution. Those who rule Russia and China don't believe in Communism any more than those who rule America believe in Capitalism. Both are only two arms of a very unholy octopus indeed.

(This slamming of Capitalism may be a shock coming from the 'megacapitaliast' Church of the SubGenius, but all we really preach is free enterprise, which hasn't been seen in this country in 100 years except on the most piddling scale.)

They aren't readying us for takeover — THAT'S already HAPPENED. ONE WORLD GOVERNMENT IS HERE. It just isn't obvious yet. But any day now the media will have people not only prepared for the realization, but welcoming it. One World Government is 'hip.'

They WON the political battle long ago. Politically, they've conquered the world, from the KKK to the Libertarian Party to the Kremlin and the Pentagon.

Now they want our SLACK.

Oh, their World Government plans are humanitarian enough . . . they don't want to make us miserable, they just don't want us to be happy.

Most of the traps have already been sprung.

For instance, even you think we're kidding.

They effectively erased private property for the middle class and are working on erasing the middle class itself. They dissolved the foundations of the family. They keep the individual's choices for lifestyle within an increasingly narrow range. All humans are numbered from birth and thus tracked through education, military service, taxes, medical requirements, retirement benefits, and especially BANKS, all the way to death.

They control all natural resources and business, all systems of transport, all major entertainment sources. Through the deliberate fomenting of wars, revolutions, depressions, and epidemics, it's easy for them to eliminate all competition and deliver the coup de grace to free enterprise.

And it was so damn easy it's PATHETIC. They created a Central Bank and called one of its main branches 'the Federal Reserve.' That monster bank is the real U.S. Government — the duly-elected one in Washington being a soap-opera opiate for the masses, a stageful of bad stand-up comics propped up for the rubes to throw things at.

There's no Constitution — there's just the MONEY. The 'U.S. Government' has to borrow from the Federal Reserve, which really means from international banking. Our supposed leaders are in debt to themselves, and, worse, to their secret bosses.

This is literally true: there's a big 'Men's Club' to which belong all major politicians from all major parties, plus the heads, directors, editors and superstar personalities of ALL THE MAJOR NETWORKS, MAGAZINES AND NEWSPAPERS. In this Club they can all meet to agree on how to explain things.

Sounds like kook-talk, huh? That's because they're always one jump ahead of you. THEY ENGINEERED THE SPREAD OF CRAZY CONSPIRACY THEORIES, because even though many of the theories are true, they still sound crazy: the Rockefeller Conspiracy, the C.F.R., The Round Table, the Bilderbergers, the JFK 'cleanup,' ALL OF IT.

The C.F.R. and the Trilateral Commission: oh, they're bad guys, alright, but compared to the REAL controllers they're just the clerks at the front desk. They're just the sales force of a far larger 'company.' Sure, they have more control than any sane American ever dreamed possible, but they themselves are more controlled than THEY ever dreamed possible."

— The SubGenius Foundation, *The Book of the SubGenius* (pp. 92-93)

MONEY SUCKS!

"You must understand that money itself is worth nothing. It is only a tool. Yet, because The Conspiracy controls its printing, They extract great life energy from those who worship it.

Until we rid ourselves of the artificially-induced obsession with the colored pieces of paper themselves, we are still slaves to Their conditioning. If you worry about its lack you are theirs, for they make far more off your hours of labor than you do. If you were paid what you're worth, they'd go broke. (They are not really obsessed with money, but with TIME — your time. They are Time Junkies who vampirize your minutes and days until you are nearly drained of Slack.)

To break this vicious cycle of exploitation, you must purge yourself of all respect for paper money. DEBASE THE FALSE GODS of the Federal Reserve. Make a game of its destruction; feel righteous pleasure as you draw on it, write on it, shred it. Make it useful for something real."

— The SubGenius Foundation, *The Book of the SubGenius* (p. 141)

THE "INVISIBLE GOVERNMENT"

"'INVISIBLE GOVERNMENT' is a phrase for which it would be difficult to formulate a dictionary definition without sacrifice of accuracy to brevity. It may perhaps be best described as the political and economic control of the community . . . by groups who are careful to evade the responsibility which should always accompany power. They operate behind a mask of puppets in politics and business, and these must take the blame in courts of law, and before the bar of public opinion, for any errors in the technique of knavery.

To this end, our law-administration and, to a certain extent, even our ethics have been twisted in order to make the servant more responsible than the master. For example, when it comes to light that a public officer has been directly or indirectly corrupted by men of wealth, or by the higher officials of a great corporation, the prosecuting authority will almost invariably ignore or immunize the true authors of the corruption in order to crush the instrument. Of the men who bribed Secretary Fall to make over to them hundreds of millions of dollars in Government oil lands, not one was convicted; nor has their standing in the business or financial world been in the slightest degree impaired. Fall went to the penitentiary. There are scores of such cases in our history."

— John McConaughy, *Who Rules America?* (p. 1) 1934

"GOVERNMENT BY INJUNCTION"

"If a judge signs an order restraining a citizen, or a group of citizens, from doing certain things, no matter how much their legal and Constitutional rights permit them, they must immediately desist or go to jail for contempt of court, while the legal rights of the question are being threshed out in a tangle of writs and appeals. The peculiar viciousness of this method lies in the fact that, in many cases, time acts automatically against the citizen so restrained. By the time he has established his rights, he has lost his cause."

— John McConaughy, *Who Rules America?* (p. 304)

"SHIT HAPPENS"

"History demonstrates that men have often built imposing, elaborate cities, flourished in them for hundreds or even thousands of years, then deserted them to live in simple grass huts on their perimeters. Wars and natural calamities often played a part in this pattern, of course. Great cultures have risen and then died out. Men returned to simpler ways of life. It is a natural order of things. A thousand years from now people may be living in thatched shacks in New Jersey and on Long Island within full view of the decaying towers of Manhattan. They may tell the children about the peculiar ancients who built the towers as part of the strange religion which worshiped the great god Money."

— John A. Keel, *Our Haunted Planet* (p. 65)

DUTY

"When all is stripped away

And honor lies in the dust
Dignity burned to ashes, hope drowned
Vanity tattered in the wind
Trust a dim memory of a forgotten dream
When even pain deserts you
And senses merge and blur
Sounds a dull thunder of dark water
All colors grey, tastes all bitter
Your fingers mute, your cries lost
Eyes unseeing and unseen
When you stand stripped to the bone
With nothing
Utterly alone
Still I am with you
Call to me, I come to you
Sleep in my arms, I carry you
To bear you up when you sink
To force the air into your mouth
When you hunger after death
You cannot escape too freely
Your duty"

— received by Donald Tyson via automatism whilst meditating on the rune *Nyd*

TRUTH

"What is stronger than Truth?
No work of stone can survive it
No lying words dispose it
Truth endures to the end of things
All else is fleet and passes away
All that subsists is Truth
Cruel dart that pierces every shield
Without pity, without remorse
Truth is, it cannot be other
What dares defy it is destroyed
Slayer of false dreams and false hope
Hard master, but equal in justice
All must serve, all are slaves
Truth is the highest King
Who holds all honor bound
Truth is Lord, holy Truth
Disdain all lesser powers
In pain is wisdom, in loss is triumph

I the herald, speak His Word"

— received by Donald Tyson via automatism whilst meditating on the rune *Tyr*

TEMPORARY INSANITY

CP: "I remember having the option of going crazy or not. I could just let myself go and go that way. . . . I had no idea that it was a temporary possibility. To me it was an all-out choice, either I'm going to go crazy or I'm not. I was in the hospital at the time. I never thought I could just walk over there for a little while and take a look around and come home."

HS: "A lot of people don't know that. That's something I learned from working with a guy named Marty Lane. . . . he was probably one of the best with schizophrenics. He taught me how to literally go in — he was a psychiatrist, a medical doctor, but he was a shaman, he wasn't a fucking psychiatrist — he showed me how to go in where schizophrenics and catatonics are at. Go right in the same place with them and come right back out. I've gone crazy a few times. I know how to go there and come back, and that's important. . . . That's an important revelation, that there is a moment you face, knowing you can just step into that twilight zone. That you've got that choice. Some choose to do it and don't come back, and some just say I don't think I'm going to go there."

— conversation between Chris Pfouts and Harley Swiftdeer, as related in the former's book, *Lead Poisoning* (pp. 164-165)

"KNOW YER PLACE, BOY!"

"Shame has taken the place of violence as a routine form of punishment in Western societies. The reason is simple and perverse. The shame an autonomous person can arouse in subordinates is an implicit control. Rather than the employer explicitly saying 'You are dirt' or 'Look how much better I am,' all he needs to do is his job — exercise his skill or deploy his calm and indifference. His powers are fixed in his position, they are static attributes, qualities of what he is. It is not so much abrupt moments of humiliation as month after month of disregarding his employees, of not taking them seriously, which establishes his domination. The feelings he has about them, they about him, need never be stated. The grinding down of his employees' sense of self-worth is not part of his discourse with them; it is a silent erosion of their sense of self-worth which will wear them down. This, rather than open abuse, is how he bends them to his will. When shame is silent, implicit, it becomes a patent tool of bringing people to heel."

— Richard Sennett, *Authority* (p. 95)

"IF I AIN'T HAPPY, AIN'T NO-ONE HAPPY!"

". . . when treated aversively people tend to act aggressively or to be reinforced by signs of having worked aggressive damage. Both tendencies should have had evolutionary advantages, and they can easily be demonstrated. If two organisms which have been coexisting peacefully receive painful shocks, they immediately exhibit characteristic patterns of aggression toward each other. The aggressive behavior is not necessarily directed toward the actual source of stimulation; it may be 'displaced' toward any convenient person or object. Vandalism and riots are often forms of undirected or misdirected aggression. An organism which has received a painful shock will also, if possible, act to gain access to another organism toward which it can act aggressively."

— B. F. Skinner, *Beyond Freedom & Dignity* (p. 27)

A CASHLESS SOCIETY OVERNIGHT???

"The Federal Reserve is a secretive privately-owned corporation which is not held accountable to any government agency through the common practices of utilizing inspectors and oversight committees. This is puzzling, since they alone guarantee the negotiability of all of America's paper currency — which is NOT backed by our depleted gold reserves at Fort Knox, but rather by a somewhat insubstantial system of 'interest, loans, and credit' which give these 'Notes' their constantly fluctuating value.

In a hypothetical (though admittedly unlikely) scenario in which the corporation known as the 'Federal Reserve' (which is NOT part of the Federal government) were to suddenly and unexpectedly dissolve (how could this happen? I don't know specifics, but bear with me nonetheless), all of their 'Federal Reserve (promissary) Notes' would immediately become worthless scraps of paper. Only coins (which are minted by the U.S. government and not regulated by the Federal Reserve) would continue to retain their negotiable value!

This means that, unless you had a credit card, debit card, checking account, or sacks of dollar coins, you would be UNABLE TO BUY AND SELL. The resultant 'cashless society' would effectively eliminate any illusion of privacy pertaining to the transfer and distribution of funds! Not only would 'investors' be unable to hide certain assets from the government anymore, but the illegal 'black market' economy would be virtually decimated overnight! An unlikely scenario, but a scary thought nonetheless."

— "Mr. Y." (excerpted from a pseudonymous correspondence)

MANIFESTO

"Man has the right to live by his own law — to live in the way that he wills to do: to work as he will: to play as he will: to rest as he will: to die when and how he will.

Man has the right to eat what he will: to drink what he will: to dwell where he will: to move as he will on the face of the earth.

Man has the right to think what he will: to speak what he will: to draw, paint, carve, etch, mold, build as he will: to dress as he will.

Man has the right to kill those who thwart these rights."

— Aleister Crowley, *The Equinox: A Journal of Scientific Illuminism*, 1922

SUBMISSION TO AUTHORITY

"All authority is a function of coding, of game rules. Men have risen again and again armed with pitchforks to fight armies with cannon; men have also submitted docilely to the weakest and most tottery oppressors. It all depends on the extent to which coding distorts perception and conditions the physical (and mental) reflexes.

It seems at first glance that authority could not exist at all if all men were cowards or if no men were cowards, but flourishes as it does only because most men are cowards and some men are thieves. Actually, the inner dynamics of cowardice and submission on the one hand and of heroism and rebellion on the other are seldom consciously realized either by the ruling class or the servile class. Submission is identified not with cowardice but with virtue, rebellion not with heroism but with evil. To the Roman slave-owners, Spartacus was not a hero and the obedient slaves were not cowards; Spartacus was a villain and the obedient slaves were virtuous. The obedient slaves believed this also. The obedient always think of themselves as virtuous rather than cowardly."

— Hagbard Celine

PRIDE AND PREJUDICE

"The besetting sins of the Right-hand path are pride, and the tendency to set oneself apart from humanity. What better way of doing this than to claim that one's own race comes from the heavens, all others from the dirty earth? The more fanatical the quest for purity, the worse the consequences for anyone who gets in the way. If Aryans alone can tread the path to Deliverance, those who are disqualified by blood, race, or caste from this high destiny are an unfortunate nuisance, to be shunned, enslaved, or exterminated, while the masters set their steely eyes in nostalgia for the cold purity of their Hyperborean home.

The corresponding fault of those who take the Left-hand path is to misunderstand the famous motto of Aleister Crowley's Thelema: 'Do what thou wilt shall be the whole of the Law.' In a sense, but a very precise and restricted one, this implies freedom from ethical restraints. But it is all too tempting to identify one's 'will' with one's basest impulses of indulgence and selfishness. Hitler invariably acted as if everything were permitted him: no amount of suffering and death mattered so long as it served his purposes, and he set an example of how a whole people can be willed into a frenzy of hatred and nationalism. The second part of the motto of the Left-hand path, 'Love is the law, love under will,' became for the Nazis: 'Hatred is the law, hatred under will' — a powerful formula indeed.

The inescapable historical parallel to all of this is to be seen in the innumerable cruelties committed by Christians against Jews, pagans, witches, heretics, and each other: a disgrace to the Solar tradition, as the Nazis are to the Polar. Yet many of the worst offenders were pious, and believed themselves to be sincere Christians; some of them were even mystics. All this goes to show that any religious tradition can do more harm than good, unless it is tempered by the simple humanity and compassion that come more readily to women than to men. When the Dalai Lama says with his characteristic smile, 'My religion is Kindness,' he is pointing the way to the Golden Age more surely than any priest, shaykh, or esoteric pundit."

— Joscelyn Godwin, *Arktos* (p. 175)

A "PSYCHOTIC RANT"

"A major Ahrimanic stratagem in the battle for the earth is exploitation of the neurotic deference inculcated in human beings towards the forms of 'authority.' Modern humans are all too willing and ready to be reassured and diverted from significant matters by generals, presidents, doctors and spokesmen for learned societies.

Where the existing neurotic mechanisms in these processes are insufficient, vulnerable human beings in positions of authority run the risk today of being placed under various forms of psychic control. Etheric tunings, via advanced radionic-type instruments, are in all probability employed to this end from the unseen. The victims think, voice, write, and otherwise place into earthly currency, the misleading falsehoods that the Ahrimanic powers wish to have disseminated as part of their own continuing concealment. . . .

Political corruption in America has reached unprecedented levels. Political corruption is simply the expression, in and through the body politic, of the corruption poured into the souls of men by the Ahrimanic powers. . . . Just as destructive power has extended to a world scale and made the occult manipulation of leaders of signal importance — all humanity being effected — so on a smaller scale within America itself has Federal power become total power. . . .

The President is deceitful concerning his income tax. The verbal environment in the innermost sanctum of the White House, the political and spiritual center of America, becomes saturated with constant profanity. The power of words is never underestimated by persons of occult knowledge. If a man uses constant profanity he creates for himself a psychic environment that is profane. If he surrounds himself with profane men, their profane force is added to his. Soon there is created a profane center wherein flourish unseen beings with profane motives. . . . Such processes as these, opening American life and fortune to control by the powers of darkness, created America's downskidding fortunes and descent from grace and respect in the world."

— Trevor James Constable, *The Cosmic Pulse of Life* (pp. 385-387)

"PILLBOY'S GOT A GUN!!!"

"The symptoms that 'educators' are treating with drugs may in fact have nothing to do with congenital brain defects, as they have argued, but with a number of other less mysterious factors including:

— Poor nutrition, fostered by parents either too poor, irresponsible, or dumbed down themselves to provide decent food for their kids; encouraged by a criminal food production industry more intent on moving cheap, sugar-coated, chemically-dyed, pesticide-poisoned swill than in providing healthy food. Sugar, pesticides, and chemical additives may be a key factor in causing what is termed ADD and ADHD.

— Television and other media. Kids are estimated to watch six hours per day of an electronic medium deliberately designed to foster a short attention span, with quick three-to-five second visual cuts purposely stimulating the kind of artificial agitation that induces a child to respond to commercials. Is it any wonder that these kids have a short attention span?

— Another negative aspect of the pop media is the abundance of sexual and violent images disseminated via TV, movies, hyper-violent video games, and music with violent/sexual 'gangsta' ghetto rap. There are many studies showing that when television is introduced to a community that violent acts double over the course of a few years. . . .

— Little parental contact with kids at all. The prevailing economy is designed so that both parents usually have to slave full time, leaving very few moments for contact with the kids. The situation of the single parent family is usually worse.

— Finally, there is a problem with the nature of public schooling itself, which does not challenge children to learn or to think creatively, but instead indoctrinates them to conform to their prison-like surroundings. . . .

There is no indication that the drugging of children is going to diminish in the near future. Quite the contrary."

— Jim Keith, *Mass Control: Engineering Human Consciousness* (pp. 26-29)

INDOCTRINATION

"I always wondered why the teachers just threw the knowledge at us when we were in school, why they didn't care whether we learned it or not. I found that the knowledge which they had made into a cabala, stripped of its terms and the private codes, its slang, you could learn in a few weeks. It didn't take 4 years, and the 4 years of university were set up so that they could have a process by which they could remove the rebels and the dissidents. By their studies and the ritual of academics the Man has made sure that they are people who will serve him. . . . Some of these people with degrees going around here shouting that they are New Negroes are really serving the Man who awarded them their degrees, who has initiated them into his slang and found them 'qualified,' which means loyal."

— Ishmael Reed, *Mumbo Jumbo* (p. 37)

THE NATURE OF INTELLIGENCE

"Intelligence is the capacity to discern, to understand, to distinguish; it is also the capacity to observe, to put together all that we have gathered and to act from that. . . . Intelligence demands doubting, questioning, not being impressed by others, by their enthusiasm, by their energy. Intelligence demands that there be impersonal observation. Intelligence is not only the capacity to understand that which is rationally, verbally explained but also implies that we gather as much information as possible, yet knowing that that information can never be complete, about anybody or anything."

— J. Krishnamurti, *The Network of Thought*

POWER PLAYS

"When I argue, I face power, the power of the Other. It is the Other's power that I wish to overcome and that I fear. I am therefore fascinated by power and I wish to trace its source. If I understand power, if I understand its nature and where it abides, if I understand how to get it and how to resist it, I will have attained great power of my own. I want power. I need power to win . . .

Power is first an idea, first a perception. The power I face is always the power I perceive. Let me say it differently. Their power is my perception of their power. Their power is my thought. The source of their power is, therefore, in my mind.

The power others possess is the power I give them. Their power is my gift. I give them all the power in the universe, as, indeed, the faithful give to God, or I give them no power at all, as, indeed, is the quantum of power we too frequently allot to our children. If I have endowed the Other with power that the Other does not possess, then I face my own power, do I not? My own power has become my opponent, my enemy. On the other hand, if the Other possesses power, but I do not perceive the Other's power as effective against me, he has none — none for me."

— Gerry Spence, *How to Argue and Win Every Time* (pp. 32-33)

ADAPTABILITY

"A human being should be able to change a diaper, plan an invasion, butcher a hog, conn a ship, design a building, write a sonnet, balance accounts, build a wall, set a bone, comfort the dying, take orders, give orders, cooperate, act alone, pitch manure, solve equations, analyze a new problem, program a computer, cook a tasty meal, fight efficiently, die gallantly. Specialization is for insects."

— Robert Heinlein, *The Notebooks of Lazarus Long*

"POPULAR DELUSIONS AND THE MADNESS OF CROWDS"

"Various beliefs can be implanted in many people after brain function has been sufficiently disturbed by accidentally or deliberately induced fear, anger, or excitement. Of the results caused by such disturbances, the most common one is temporarily impaired judgement and heightened suggestibility. Its various group manifestations are sometimes classed under the heading of 'herd instinct,' and appear most spectacularly in wartime, during severe epidemics, and in all similar periods of common danger, which increase anxiety and so individual and mass suggestibility."

— Dr. William Sargent, *Battle for the Mind*

"THE ACT OF BOOK-BURNING REVEALS THE CREATURE FOR WHAT IT IS"

"Books cannot be killed by fire. People die, but books never die. No man and no force can put thought in a concentration camp forever. No man and no force can take from the world the books that embody man's eternal fight against tyranny. In this war, we know, books are weapons."

— Franklin D. Roosevelt

"SKELL TV!"

"In the very near future, a computer technology will make possible alternatives to imprisonment. The development of systems for telemetering information from sensors implanted in or on the body will soon make possible the observation and control of human behavior without actual physical contact. Through such telemetric devices, it will be possible to maintain twenty-four-hour-a-day surveillance over the subject and to intervene electronically or physically to influence and control selected behavior. It will thus be possible to exercise control over human behavior and from a distance without physical contact. The possible implications for criminology and corrections of such telemetric systems is tremendously significant."

— Barton L. Ingraham and Gerald W. Smith, "The Use of Electronics in the Observation and Control of Human Behavior and its Possible Use in Rehabilitation and Control"

"THIS IS FOR YOUR OWN GOOD . . ."

"Because of the intensifying economic decline it is inevitable that more and more jobless will go beyond the limits of the law to satisfy their needs. There are probably upwards of 30 percent of our population who are permanently impoverished . . . And once these 30 percent become convinced that the democratic process is not working for them, they become desperate and may resort to violent means. There is a rising radicalism in their midst and there is an 'uppitiness' among the Black and Chicano prisoners which prison officials find intolerable. To subdue them, the authorities are using new methods. They're employing the psychiatric armamentarium and a new technological too set — what has come to be known as psycho-technology. Under the guise of therapeutic behavior modification they're applying anything from Anectine and other aversive drugs to psychosurgery."

— Dr. Isidore Ziferstein

"IT'S TRUE! YOU HAVE NO BRAIN!"

"The fanatic is stubborn, obstinate, dogmatic: Everything for him is black or white, curse or blessing, friend or foe — and nothing in between. He has no taste for or interest in nuances. Does he seek clarity? Driven by irrational impulses, he wants everything to be visible and necessarily clear.

The fanatic simplifies matters: He is immune to doubt and to hesitation. Intellectual exercise is distasteful, and the art and beauty of dialogue alien to him. Other people's ideas or theories are of no use to him. He is never bothered by difficult problems: A decree or a bullet solves them . . . immediately. The fanatic feels nothing but disdain toward intellectuals who spend precious time analyzing, dissecting, debating philosophical notions and hypotheses. What matters to the fanatic is the outcome — not the way leading there.

And more: The fanatic derides and hates tolerance, which he perceives as weakness, resignation, or submission. This is why he despises women: Their tenderness is to him a sign of passivity. The fanatic's only interest is in domination by fear and terror. Violence is his favorite language — a vulgar language filled with obscenities: He doesn't speak, he shouts; he doesn't listen, he is too busy yelling; he doesn't think, he doesn't want anyone to think.

In other words, the fanatic, intoxicated with hatred, tries to reduce everybody to his own size.

He has a goal and is willing to pay any price to achieve it. Or more precisely: He is ready to make others pay any price to achieve it."

— Elie Wiesel

THE ESSENCE OF WARRIORSHIP

"Warriorship is a personal and individual path. It is a path which deals with all aspects of life. The essence of warriorship is the process of fulfilling one's potential. The ways towards warriorship are many, and they are all hard. Few ever go far, though all benefit. This is a commitment to a life of discipline and development in mind, body, and soul. The true warrior is an athlete, a scholar, a poet, a magician, a priest, and a skilled lover.

As a part of warriorship, the combat principles you learn can be applied to all areas of life. Discipline, flexibility, strategic thinking, and the ability to stay calm and see the larger perspective. These along with physical fitness, allow the warrior to succeed in any endeavor. This is what makes a true warrior. Skill in battle is of little use if you do not have a life worth fighting for."

— Sweyn Plowright, *True Helm* (pp. 2 & 58)

"DIPLOMACY FOR BADASSES"

"Simply by saying a few words, in a certain tone of voice, it is possible to alter and /or manipulate the energy of another. This phenomenon could be called 'Non-Verbal Communication combined with Deep Linguistics,' 'Psychotherapy,' or even 'Magick' — but whatever you choose to call it, it works great for defusing hostilities (especially when dealing with the emotionally unbalanced). Conversely, it is also possible, through the usage of different words and tones, to so unbearably antagonize another that it is virtually guaranteed that the situation will degenerate to the point of actual physical violence. Due to these facts, it is imperative that your most experienced diplomat should always be the designated speaker for the group in the event of a potentially hostile confrontation (or potentially sensitive 'Public Relations' issue) — and everyone else needs to know to keep their fucking mouths shut.

— Scribe 27 (RWT)

THE GREAT WURLITZER

"There is no such thing at this date of the world's history, in America, as an independent press. You know it and I know it. There is not one of you who dares to write your honest opinions and if you did, you know beforehand that it would never appear in print. I am paid weekly for keeping my honest opinion out of the paper I am connected with. Others of you are paid similar salaries for similar things, and any of you who would be so foolish as to write honest opinions would be out on the streets looking for another job. If I allowed my honest opinions to appear in one issue of my paper, before twenty-four hours my occupation would be gone.

The business of journalists is to destroy the truth, to lie outright, to pervert, to vilify, to fawn at the feet of Mammon, and to sell his country and his race for his daily bread. You know it and I know it, and what folly is this toasting an independent press?

We are the tools of rich men behind the scenes. We are jumping jacks — they pull the strings and we dance. Our talents, our possibilities and our lives are all the property of other men. We are intellectual prostitutes."

— John Swinton, in his "toast" to the New York Press Club in 1953.

THE "WARRIOR" CONTRASTED AGAINST THE "FALSE WARRIOR"

"Simply put, warriors choose to walk a separate path, different from others. They take the risk of standing alone and speaking up when others are silent. A vital component of ethical behavior is feeling obligated to do what is right. To feel obligated, one must not only care but be willing to pay the hard price that comes in wrestling with one's own conscience. Warriors are self-actuated. They project consequences into the future and think, plan, and live long range. Warriors take personal control over their lives rather than be passive spectators and the victims of events occurring around them. . . .

Although true warriors are difficult to find, many people want to become warriors and begin walking the path, but they allow their energy to be taken from tem and their light to dim. You can see it in their eyes. They want the rewards, but they are no longer willing to pay the price to fill the lamp with the kind of oil that keeps it from growing dim. They have lowered their self-esteem and feel a constant need to prove themselves to others."

— Larry F. Jetmore, *The Path of the Warrior* (p. 65)

THE WARRIOR PATH

Follow this path if you are to be a warrior and share your light with others. But tread carefully! We become what we pretend to be!. . .

It's not easy to become a warrior. It's even more difficult to remain a warrior after becoming one. Many answer the call of the drums, but few are able to sustain the strength of character necessary to march to them. There are many labyrinths, traps, and dragons along the path to the way.

Courage and inner fortitude are required to overcome the difficult and sometimes painful obstacles along the path a warrior must travel. Abuse of power and self-diminishing behavior are traps that snare and draw a would-be warrior off the path. We are often seduced by illusions of power bestowed upon us by the titles, promotions, or credentials we receive. These outward symbols quickly lose their luster unless placed on a foundation of self-worth. Because we often close our hearts to the people in our lives, many would-be warriors suffer the penalty of loneliness while surrounded by heaps of gold. Temptation and suffering for the sake of others are tests each person on the path to becoming a warrior must face. The voice and comfort of the herd is loud and strong. Although a warrior is sometimes joined by others, the walk is often the high and lonely path of the nomad. True warriors do not cower at the opinions of others, but feel themselves accountable to a higher tribunal than man.

All who walk the path have the freedom to choose where their steps will take them. There are many different paths but only one 'way.' Warriors accept total responsibility for their thoughts, behaviors, deeds, and actions. This is known as decision making."

— Larry F. Jetmore, *The Path of the Warrior* (pp. 103, 106-107)

COP OR CREEP?

"The law enforcement officer, mindful of his responsibility to the whole community, shall deal with individuals of the community in a manner calculated to instill respect for its laws and its police service. The law enforcement officer shall conduct his official life in a manner such as will inspire confidence and trust. Thus, he will be neither overbearing nor subservient, as the individual citizen has neither an obligation to stand in awe of him nor a right to command him. The officer will give service where he can and require compliance with the law. He will do neither from personal preference or prejudice but only as a duly appointed officer of the law discharging his sworn obligation."

— Article VII of the "Canons of Police Ethics" adopted by the International Association of Chiefs of Police in 1957

THE LAW OF SYNCHRONICITY

"Two or more events happening at 'the same time' are likely to have more associations in common than the merely temporal; very few events (if any) ever happen in 'isolation' from other events; 'there is no such thing as a mere coincidence.' In point of fact, if you ever manage to pin a professional debunker against a wall (be careful, they get nasty when cornered), you will find that the word 'coincidence' is a scientific term of exorcism, which is used to banish away unwanted demons of implied causality. Naturally, the word 'synchronicity' is from Carl Jung's research, even though the concept shows up all over the globe."

— Isaac Bonewits, *Real Magic* (p. 208)

GENTLEMANLY CONDUCT

"The forbearing use of power does not only form a touchstone; but the manner in which an individual enjoys certain advantages over others is the test of a true gentleman. The power which the strong have over the weak, the magistrate over the employed the educated over the unlettered, the experienced over the confiding, even the clever over the silly; the forbearing and inoffensive use of all the powers or authority, or a total abstinence from it, when the case admits it, will show the gentleman in a plain light. The gentleman does not needlessly and unnecessarily remind an offender of a wrong he may have committed against him. He can only forgive; he can forget; and he strives for that nobleness of self and mildness of character which imparts sufficient strength to let the past be but the past."

— General Robert E. Lee

THE "CONSPIRACY" EXPOSED!!!

"Things didn't just 'get' this way. Not even humans could cause this much trouble by accident. It had to be PLANNED. It's a CONSPIRACY. It is THE Conspiracy. . . .

One can endlessly explore the world of conspiracies, intricately detailing its works, mapping its eddies and flows, its secret, subtle currents, its dangers — but one risks succumbing to its apparent friendliness and charm. For it contains within it so many infinitely varying conspiracies of fanatics that there's BOUND to be a conspiracy JUST FOR YOU to sink into forever! There are certainly plenty to go around . . .

The conspiracy we truly hate, the real Conspiracy, isn't one of those fiendishly clever ones. It doesn't even know it's a conspiracy. It can't. It's a faceless confederacy of dunces, so vast and broad that it underlies all the lesser conspiracies and permeates all human reality. Quite the opposite of devious, it dominates by merely exploiting the overall, mealy-mouthed, chickenbutt-kissing 'Code of Normality' (or CON) of ALL the Pinks, norm-worms and mere-humes at large. But there is no more insidious and subtle a weapon as that.

The Conspiracy has no face; we know it only by its desires — a great Mirror of Disfigurement, it reflects what's wrong with everyone. Politics and the petty squabbles of nations are only part of what The Conspiracy manipulates. It is MUCH BIGGER than gods and demons, Republicans and Democrats, or Presidents and interlocking corporate directorates; it's everything from the school bully to the wimp principal, from Mom and Dad to the Bobbie in the woodpile. More than anything else, The Conspiracy is an attitude — a fear — a PINKNESS, a cancer of the imagination, the hatred of the real, the yearning for 'cuteness,' the eagerness to obey . . .

The Conspiracy is not vengeful. It has nothing against you PERSONALLY; you're being persecuted and hobbled by people who couldn't care less who you are. The hive automatically protects itself from evolution by negating any individual member whose circuits are too 'resonant.'. . .

The modern Conspiracy hive functions just like the old Mayan hives, with smug priests, brutal warrior castes and larval masses quivering in mortal fear of nature and power. . . .

Immersion in the TV reality . . . makes people paranoid and isolated. While simultaneously uniting them with common imagery and fantasies, it cuts them off from reality. . . . TV distorts what we are; we aspire to become what it shows . . .

Television both integrates the culture and destroys literacy, reducing us to a homogeneous mass of photon-dependant P-heads. Pinks aren't sentient enough to disengage their sense of reality from the products being sold to them. They are their tennis shoes, jackets, drugs, favorite shows and stars -- and the Con, rather than protecting the minds and psyches of the undiscerning, childlike Pinks, exploits that weakness. Everything, including 'news' and 'fact,' is reduced to 'entertainment' geared to the lowest common denominator — irrelevant sound bites and factoids made to seem meaningful. . . .

In the normal job world, the Conspiracy keeps you on the tightest leash possible. They would completely deprive you of Slack if they could, but, out of necessity, to keep you alive for another year, they grudgingly give you Sundays, sometimes Saturdays, sometimes a whole week out of your life for that minimum life-sustaining drop of False Slack. . . . Somewhere along the line, (you) receive some pitiful modicum of Slack, or else (you) would die. HOW MUCH Slack (you) receive is what the Conspiracy tries so hard to control. They want to ration it out to you, drop by drop, as with an eyedropper, so you'll always be at Their mercy, carrying out Their evil whim.

Their arbitrary 'laws' extend unquestioned into every minuscule aspect of your private life. Every last vestige of Slack, even the act of standing around doing nothing, is regulated. Notice that "loitering" isn't illegal only in stores and restaurants, but even so-called public sidewalks, parks, everywhere. You've got to keep moving. For that matter, you can be thrown in jail for "vagrancy," the inability to produce a driver's license, passport or money. We are not legal life forms without a shell of paper and cloth defining our bodies. The only place you can legally cease moving is in your own home. . . .

They listen to you through your telephone without its even being off the hook, and record you through satellites that can peer down on any street, anywhere. The only legal drugs are alcohol and other reality-numbing tranquilizers; most forms of sex are crimes. Exercise of instincts must be suppressed for Their system to work. No one who is getting due Slack is really going to feel like saluting a flag or dying for God and Company.

They kick your door in any time they want to. All they have to yell is 'DRUGS!' and your spouse is in jail, your kids are farmed out to the state, your car and house are suddenly Theirs. They can walk up to you anywhere today and say, 'Excuse me, can we see your wallet, please? Hmm, you have a lot of cash here. We'll have to confiscate it — you fit the profile of someone who might be a drug dealer.'

The fake 'war on drugs' is eroding every last bit of freedom we've managed to wring out of the sons of bitches since 1776. We've spent 200 years trying to make 'we the people' include someone besides the white land-owning aristocracy, and now that we're finally beginning to do it, they're going over to the other end of the Constitution and telling us what rights we don't have. Everything that is not forbidden is proscribed."

— from *Revelation X* (pp. 17-18, 22), by The SubGenius Foundation

THE TELEVISED CORPORATE MINDFUCK CAMPAIGN

"In my vision of a perfect world, advertising — as it now exists — would be classified as a punishable offense. Through silly catch-phrases (memes) and high-tech computer imagery (which could easily conceal prohibited subliminals), inferior products are wrongfully being misrepresented by unscrupulous marketeers. Impressionable teenagers are being told that they won't 'fit in' unless they display the appropriate brand names. Elders are being frightened into purchasing questionable heath-care items, monitoring systems, and 'insurance' coverage that they don't need. Even home mortgages and prescription pharmaceuticals are being advertised on the TV! Remember, lying is not a criminal offense (as long as an actual 'fraud,' as defined by law, does not occur), so these advertisements cannot be trusted! For examples: Pontiac vehicles, Gateway computers, and Red Devil paint are still being purchased by gullible dupes for no discernable reason other than that they 'liked the commercials' — even if the product being sold is crap, by spending a few million on TV marketing you can ensure that people will buy it! And the most abominable thing about this false advertising is that the majority of TV commercial messages have deliberately been engineered to make them attractive to children! As a result of this incessant media bombardment, our culture has become far more ignorant, materialistic, and shallow — and now the multi-nationals are attempting to inflict this mindless consumerism on the rest of the world as well (which is, perhaps, the primary reason why our enemies are so hostile to America). If our country was not being run by soulless multi-national corporations, the majority of advertising executives would be thrown in padded cells where they would be subject to 18 hrs of continuous TV commercials every fucking day! For sustenance, they could have all the Coca-Cola, McFood, and candy bars they wanted — but nothing else. After 4 months of incarceration, the executives probably wouldn't have been 'rehabilitated' (i.e., transformed into ethical citizens), but they certainly would have 'learned their lesson,' and perhaps would be ready to be released back into society — with the understanding that if they were convicted of a second offence, they'd be looking at an 8 month sentence next time! What was their crime? Insulting the public sensibilities. Sure, the masses might be stupid, but it oughta be a crime for corporate predators to exploit their naivete for commercial gain (or other, more sinister, reasons)."

— anonymous (RWT)

"BOW DOWN BEFORE THE ONE YOU SERVE . . ."

"The media likes to portray all violent criminals as 'sociopaths.' By definition, a sociopath (or psychopath) is nothing more than an extremely selfish person with no ethical boundaries (honor, conscience, etc.) and no emotional rapport with other human beings (except, perhaps, from the sadistic joy derived from watching them suffer). The true sociopath is a demonic egomaniac that thrives on the accumulation of power, which he (or she) uses almost exclusively for the subjugation of the weak. By this definition, only about a third of all incarcerated violent offenders (a demographic which includes many 'first offenders') could be considered sociopaths (indeed, many have close emotional ties with friends and family, and only use violence impulsively — usually when either desperate or impaired). However, using this definition, the vast majority of 'respected' salesmen, evangelists, attorneys, politicians, and corporate executives can be seen as they truly are — psychopathic predators who repeatedly victimize others through deliberate premeditated acts."

— Scribe 27 (RWT)

BUG-EYED RETICULAN SODOMITES DO NOT EXIST!!!

"Like many of my colleagues in the field, I have become convinced that the U.S. Government, as well as other governments, was very much involved in the UFO business. This involvement is not limited to the kind of data collection that is the normal responsibility of intelligence agencies. It extends to the close monitoring of the UFO organizations themselves and, in some cases, to the staging of false sightings and the occasional leaking of false documents. It is not my business to interfere with such activities. The belief in extraterrestrials, like any other strong belief, is an attractive vehicle for some mind control and psychological warfare activities. I do not believe that any government has the answer to the UFO problem, although several governments must have the proof of its reality."

— Dr. Jacques Vallee, *Confrontations* (pp. 21-22)

GETTING BAKED WITH "NON-LETHAL" WEAPONRY

"In recent years the major powers have done much development of their own in the area of beam weaponry. Microwave technology is now used under the general acronym HPM (high-power microwave) to jam or burn the electronic hardware of enemy missiles, aircraft, and tanks.

Generators for the types of beams used in the new weapons include magnetrons and klystrons, as well as newer devices with names like gyrotron and vircator (virtual cathode oscillator). Vircators are especially relevant here. They operate in the pulse mode at demonstrated powers up to twenty gigawatts.

An obvious biological effect of microwaves is that they heat tissue. Brain temperature changes of only a few degrees have been shown to cause convulsions, unconsciousness, and amnesia in rats. Even weaker microwave pulses, too weak to heat animal tissue, can have serious effects by disturbing cell membranes. . . .

In his review of the field, Dr. Keith Florig, an expert on policy issues involving ionizing and non-ionizing radiation, notes that 'HPM weapons that merely stun the nervous system temporarily seem, like short-acting chemical agents, to be more humane than lethal force. . . . HPM weapons that blind, burn, or bake people to death are likely to be viewed as an abhorrent addition to the arsenal.' . . . Interestingly, Dr. Florig remarks that 'the difference between a disabling and a lethal (force) is largely one of range. So it would be hard to show that a weapon intended to disable could not be lethal at close range.'"

— Dr. Jacques Vallee, *Confrontations* (pp. 229-230)

DECLINING TO DUEL

"Sir:

I have two objections to this duel matter. The one is lest I should hurt you; the other, lest you should hurt me. I do not see any good it would do me to put a bullet through any part of your body. I could make no use of you when dead for any culinary purpose, as I could a rabbit or a turkey . . . for though your flesh might be delicate and tender, yet it wants that firmness and consistency which takes and retains salt. At any rate, it would not be fit for long sea voyages. You might make a good barbacue, it is true, being of the nature of a racoon or an opossum, but people are not in the habit of barbacuing anything human now. As to your hide, it is not worth taking off, being little better than that of a two-year old colt. As to myself, I do not much like to stand in the way of anything that is harmful. I am under the apprehension that you might hit me. That being the case, I think it most advisable to stay at a distance. If you want to try your pistols, take some object — a tree or a barn door — about my dimensions, and if you hit that, send me word. I shall then acknowledge that if I had been in the same place you would have killed me in a duel."

— John Breckinridge, from a private correspondence (late 1790s)

IMPROVISED WEAPONS CAN BE FUN!

"Weapons can be used without it being final! People often think 'lethal' when they think of weapons. Any tool that is used to aid and abet knocking the shit out of someone is considered a weapon! Capisce? You have to widen your definition of what constitutes a weapon. In my time, I have been clobbered by or attacked with hairbrushes, a pot, rope, scissors, beer bottles, pens, a cat, tables and chairs, pool cues, shuriken, playing cards, keys, razor blades, rocks, a candleholder, shoes, a cup of Coke, and, of course, chains. I have used leaves, dirt, the water from a dog dish, a shirt, a belt, trash cans, paint scrapers, beer, orange juice, spit, and many of the things I previously listed, to open conversations. Many of these things serve to knock you off balance or mildly hurt you so you'll choke and your attacker can get in there with something more serious."

— Marc "Animal" MacYoung, *Pool Cues, Beer Bottles, & Baseball Bats* (pp. 3-4)

DEMON IN A BOTTLE

"I pretty much quit drinking about seven years ago. Being half Irish and half Cherokee, my genetics are such that alcohol doesn't sit well with me. I can down an entire liter of vodka, and it'll fuck me up, but the scary part is that I won't fall down, pass out, or yak — it's like I'm turbocharged, or something, and I just don't give a fuck. I can be kicked back, all happy and shit, then someone says something stupid or starts eye-fucking me, and the next thing you know, I've kicked a table full of drinks in his face and started beating him over the head with a lamp. For an insult I would've simply laughed off if sober, I'd be inclined to slit someone from asshole to eyeball when I'm 'in my cups.' And I'm pretty much unstoppable in this capacity — I've been punched full-force in the face by people three times my size, had chairs and pool cues broken across my back, and even took lead from a small caliber handgun without even feeling it. If I've been drinkin', I will not back down from anyone, regardless of how many opponents I might be up against. On several occasions, large groups of pissed-off rednecks have decided to retreat rather than take me on, and I have never gotten my ass kicked — ever. It was like the 'Legend of the Drunken Master,' or some shit, but I finally realized that if I continued to drink vodka by the quart, eventually I'd wind up either dead or in prison, so I decided to quit. Nowadays, if I'm at a social function where I'm expected to drink, I'll make my second bottle of beer last the whole night — because I know that once I finish that third drink, I'll just keep drinking till it's all gone — and there's probably gonna be casualties."

— anonymous (RWT)

SCENE FROM A TAVERN KNIFEFIGHT . . .

"'So you like to hurt people, huh?' Hanse breathed, gliding across the floor as he closed the distance between them. Kat's knife flipped and rolled in a silver blur — the suit blinked, mesmerized. Half a heartbeat later his forehead was slashed open and the Imada high-hollow blade had stabbed completely through his forearm, twisting as it retracted. The broken bottle clattered to the barroom floor, useless. Hanse's Red Bird shattered his knee joint and he fell. Flipping balisong, he buried it deep in the fucker's chest to run the gears. As he slammed it into second he noted the lack of resistance and realized that he'd fucked up . . . the knife wasn't open. He reeled as frantic thoughts flooded his mind and it suddenly dawned on him what he was doing: Shit, I'm really wasted . . . I almost killed this fuck in front of all these witnesses . . . lucky thing I flipped it one too many times . . . can't let him get up! Holding balisong closed in his fist, he used it to mash the fucker's face. Job finished, he slid the streamlined weapon into the back pocket of his reinforced 550's — knifefighting jeans. He could clean the blood off later.

'Fuckin' jerk . . . come back here again, I'll make you disappear.' He spat on him, kicking him in the groin."

— C. R. Jahn, *Underground* (pp. 163-164)

"THE MOVIE"

"This is a difficult concept for many people to grasp, but it is one of the most powerful methods of self-improvement we know of. It has its basis in certain occult teachings, but there is no "magic" involved — except for the results. In the original teachings, one is told about the many invisible beings which we encounter every day, and how people who lead interesting lives tend to attract these beings, which may even feel compelled to intervene on our behalf in time of need. Positive behavior attracts positive beings, and negative behavior attracts negative beings. We thought that this was an interesting concept, but decided to alter it in order to make it more suitable for defensive applications. Simply think of yourself as the protagonist in an ongoing movie about your life. The movie is put on hold while you're sleeping (except for the occasional interesting 'dream sequence'), but is being viewed by an unseen audience at all other times — until shortly after your eventual demise. Your control over the script is limited primarily to the dialogue and actions of your character. You will decide how he (you) reacts to various crisis situations — will he proceed calmly and bravely, or will he instead scream like a girl and run away? The choice is yours — and the audience is watching. Is your character interesting, or is he boring? Is he likable, or is he despicable? Will your story be an adventure, a drama, a comedy, a tragedy, a romance, a combination of the above, or something altogether different? If you do not like your character, feel free to transform him into something more suitable for your purposes. Make sure your character always is presentable in appearance, and conducts himself in a proper manner — even when he thinks no-one's looking. Always try to do the right thing, proceed with valor, and don't behave like an idiot (through giving in to: rage, pettiness, dishonesty, lechery, or other forms of immaturity). Above all, don't bore your audience! No-one wants to waste their time watching some pathetic, stoop-shouldered, procrastinating, slothful, wage-slave mope! Don't be afraid to do what you want, stand up for yourself, and live up to your full potential . . . after all, it's only a movie!"

— C. R. Jahn, *Hardcore Self-Defense* (pp. 15-16)

FREEWHEELIN'

"A common misconception is that evasion requires driving at unsafe speeds and ignoring red lights and 'one-way' signs . . . nothing could be further from the truth. Whether on city streets or back roads, you seldom want to exceed 60 mph. If you go too fast, you cannot negotiate sharp turns, nor can you compensate for unexpected obstacles or the stupidity of other drivers. If your vehicle is low to the ground and you are being pursued by a vehicle with a high center of gravity (such as a 'sport utility vehicle'), you can put more distance between your vehicles by accelerating through sharp curves and taking unexpected turns which a more top-heavy vehicle would need to slow down for to avoid tipping. The only time speeds in excess of 100 mph are permissible is when you are being pursued on a well-maintained, multi-lane highway and feel you have a good chance of safely outdistancing your tail (for example, you are driving a new sports car and they are in a rusted out pickup truck with bald tires). You do not want to drive beyond your abilities or your car's capabilities. Once you wreck, the chase has most likely come to an end."

— T. J. Steele (RWT)

MAMMON'S MINIONS AT WORK

"Yet although full employment is a public good, it is not a corporate good. Business efficiency dictates downsizing, which means capital-intensive production, and capital-intensive production means labor-minimizing policies. Translated into English this means firing as many permanent workers as possible and eliminating their costly benefit and pension packages. In their place appear machines, robots, and multiplying (so-called) 'temporary' jobs, which are actually long-term jobs without long-term contracts, long-term security, or long-term benefits. . . . a large percentage of the new class that makes up the second sector of the poor, the indigent, and the unemployed are flotsam and jetsam on the tides of privatization: workers who have been sloughed off by a system that is more profitable to its new private owners without them."

— Benjamin R. Barber, *Jihad vs. McWorld* (pp. 27 & 251)

ALTAR OF THE SHEEPLE

"Films are McWorld's preferred software, but television rather than the cinema is its preferred medium; for with television, McWorld goes one-on-one, the solitary individual and cyberspace confronting one another in exquisite immediacy — with the screen as the perfect nonmediated (im-mediate) medium. Where cinema is limited in time and space, television is a permanent ticket to ceaseless film watching anytime, anywhere. It is a private window on McWorld — providing personal access via computers, satellites, cable, and phone lines to information sources, data collections, shopping centers, banking facilities, and the now almost notorious Internet — that welter of interlinked computers and interactive bulletin boards and video games and information banks and videomarketers and ordinary users that will one day (we are told) replace more or less every other kind of interaction in our lives."

— Benjamin R. Barber, *Jihad vs. McWorld* (pg. 100)

"VECTORS — IT'S WHAT'S FOR DINNER . . ."

"The prion is a mystery to science. It is not a parasite, bacterium, or even a virus — it is a microscopic crystal which somehow replicates within a living host organism, forming an extensive crystalline structure which burrows numerous holes throughout the brain of its victim. It is always fatal, and is most commonly transmitted by ingesting the flesh of an afflicted animal. Several rare diseases known to be prion related include: Creutzfeld-Jakob disease, Kuru, and the infamous 'Mad Cow' (Bovine Spongiform Encephalopathy) disease. Somehow, a rare prion-based disease has reportedly reached epidemic proportions within the deer and elk population of the Mid-West.

Allegedly, this rare disease of carnivores has not only somehow been introduced into an exclusively herbivorous population (most likely through deliberately contaminated feeding stations — prions have an indefinite 'shelf-life' and are indifferent to extremes of heat and cold), but it allegedly is capable of spreading to every wild deer and elk throughout Amerika, which is compelling Mid-Westerners to discard frozen venison and massacre their entire deer and elk population. It is now potentially fatal to eat venison! Furthermore, the exotic 'West Nile Virus' (which, although potentially fatal, usually only results in flu-like symptoms) has now reportedly reached epidemic proportions amongst our nation's bird population. Consider that if the CDC declares that the consumption of wild game constitutes 'a clear and present danger to the public health,' hunting will be outlawed. Once hunting is outlawed, citizens (excuse me — subjects) will thereby forfeit their right to possess sporting firearms 'for the public good.' Assault weapons and handguns have already been demonized by the media as 'guns which are only good for shooting people' — soon, they may feel the justification to similarly disparage your deer rifle (already referred to as a 'vest buster') and shotgun. Oh, you think that they'll let you keep your trusty double-barrel for shooting skeet? Don't fucking count on it! The way this country is going, in another five years the possession of an unloaded .22 single-shot rifle might be all they need to brand someone as a 'terrorist.'"

— Jake Bishop (RWT)

FUEL FOR THE WAR MACHINE

". . . from the mind-made magical qualities of gold, other mind-made qualities took birth, so that a small quantity of the metal came to be treasured as the equivalent of a day's work, of a plot of land, of a yoke of oxen, of a house or a boat or of sorely needed food. Thus commerce and magic began to mingle, and the artificial value given to gold found expression in ancient Sumer in gold currency. Not that there was any natural relationship between the dense, glittering metal and the objects it would purchase, the services it would command, and the sacrifices it would entail; it was merely that the mind of man provided the link, and conferred prestige and piled power upon him who could dig or buy, extort or steal enough of the favored substance. With such an incentive, the path was paved for small-scale and large-scale quarreling over gold.

Thus we see how the artificially inflamed beliefs and desires behind one metal have given a fiery prod to the acquisitive impulse, and have been responsible for wave after wave of warfare. It is known, of course, how large a part the lust for gold has had in stimulating bloodthirsty raids among scores of peoples . . . and how — most important of all — it nourished a spirit of callousness and of violence that tended towards war's indefinite propagation, somewhat as a fire will tend to indefinite burning, so long as fuel remains."

— Stanton A. Coblentz, *From Arrow to Atom Bomb* (pp. 60-61)

ATTITUDE

"The longer I live, the more I realize the impact of attitude on life. Attitude, to me, is more important than fact. It is more important than the past, than education, than money, than circumstances, than failures, than successes, than what other people think or say or do. It is more important than appearances, giftedness or skill. It will make or break a company . . . a church . . . a home. The remarkable thing is we have a choice everyday regarding the attitude we will embrace for that day. We cannot change our past . . . we cannot change the fact that people will act in a certain way. We cannot change the inevitable. The only thing we can do is play on the one string we have, and that is our attitude . . . I am convinced that life is 10% what happens to me and 90% how I react to it."

— Charles Swindoll

THE FOURTH BRANCH OF GOVERNMENT

"Consider the current balance between the states and Washington. We have reached the point where the federal government dictates to states details of their traffic regulations, holding as carrot the federal share of highway appropriations. States can no longer stand up to the federal government even on minutiae like tests required for neighborhood-based water providers or the required staffing ratio for home-based daycare centers.

Or consider the relative power of the three branches of government. From the Woodrow Wilson administration, the federal government has grown even stronger. It now looms as by far the largest employers in the U.S. Within that executive, some political scientists claim that a fourth branch — the CIA, National Security Council, and other covert agencies — has developed in the last thirty years. The Constitution cannot save democracy when officials in the FBI, CIA, State Department, and undercover agencies determine not only our policies but also how much the people, the Congress, and perhaps even the President need to know about them."

— James W. Loewen, *Lies Across America* (pp. 360-361)

SOULLESSNESS EQUATED WITH JOB SECURITY

"Huge enterprises, either in the public or the private sector, are run on bureaucratic principles which are fundamentally anti-democratic, particularly as they stifle free expression. It is not surprising, then, that they become unmanageable and obsolete in their gargantuan proportions. Vast institutions are incapable of give-and-take informal decision making or spontaneity. People within them communicate by memo — written, usually, in 'in-house' code. Policy decisions and procedures emanate from the top and are accepted as gospel. The person at the peak of the corporate or bureaucratic ladder is czar, and, as such, is automatically right. Those below him either agree or are wrong. There is virtually no internal criticism. This is the principle of hierarchical infallibility, and a whistle-blower had better have an independent income. The rote numbness which pervades bureaucracy causes people to lose their sense of what is right and wrong or even what is likely to happen. Thus, they become unthinking robots who, knowing their expected demeanor, and protecting their livelihoods, operate as mindless functionaries. . . . Like business enterprises, government agencies arrive at decisions by relying upon established procedure and information, supporting conclusions long since determined. Job protection is no small factor in this practice with risk or innovation being nothing short of astonishing. The result? Hackneyism and stagnation. . . . The drones of corporate and government complexes hold their loyalty to the institution or organization — not to a real community. Thus, they form a kind of supra-community apart, and see all the world around them as existing for their own use and benefit. This pattern easily absorbs elected officials. Legislative bodies are thoroughgoingly bureaucratic. Problems are referred to committees for study and recommendation, and the resultant studies are often filed and forgotten. Obeisance must be paid to 'higher-ups,' and the best way to keep one's job and expect advancement is to avoid controversy, to play the game by established rules. As long as decision makers in the private and public sectors continue to put job security ahead of real creativity and problem solving, they are not serving the public."

— Richard Cummings, *Proposition Fourteen* (pp. 15-16, 20)

MODELS OF REALITY:

"Here is a quick and dirty survey of the theoretical reality maps used by many on the leading edge of physical thought in engineering, physics, and government to approach extraordinary phenomena in a rational context.

1.) The electromagnetic (EM) model suggests that we are biological transceivers attuned to the psychic frequencies. This model is favored by Soviet and Eastern European scientists. Here, geophysical wave processes such as geoseismic and infrasonic waves are considered potential carriers for human mind/body communications.

2.) The anthropic model postulates that human minds shape the reality they observe, that we order the random processes of the universe with our consciousness.

3.) The quantum-mechanical model suggests that the mind prefers recognizing static moments of 'reality' but also interacts with wave phenomena on a continual basis. Thus, consciousness has access to the future and the past as well as the present.

4.) The holographic model suggests that human consciousness transforms frequency and amplitude information into intelligible sensory impressions.

No one knows which, if any, of these models is the correct one. No one knows for certain how consciousness interacts with the phenomenal world."

— Col. John B. Alexander, Major Richard Groller, and Janet Morris, *The Warrior's Edge* (p. 111)

WARRIORSHIP DEFINED:

"The key attributes of the warrior are will and patience. . . . The warrior acts decisively and strategically while seeking self-mastery and self-awareness, continually conscious that life is fragile and death waits at the end of it. What tenets shape the warrior's beliefs?

Moral courage: a stringent code that values honor and struggle for a cause.

Willingness to risk: the warrior knows he may not always win; he is prepared to spend his life for his beliefs.

Devotion: the warrior chooses a noble cause that instills in him devotion to duty and serves the human family.

Decisiveness: the ability to recognize correct action, take that action, and accept responsibility denotes a warrior.

The warrior 'aims to follow his heart, to choose consciously the items that make up his world, to be exquisitely aware of everything around him, to attain total control, then act with total abandon. He seeks, in short, to live an impeccable life.'"

— Col. John B. Alexander, Major Richard Groller, and Janet Morris, *The Warrior's Edge* (pp. 18-19)

"GIMMIE SOME SUGAR . . .":

"The use of granulated sugar for treatment of infected wounds is recommended by some as a treatment of first choice. Sugar has been called a nonspecific universal antimicrobial agent. Based on its safety, ease of use, and availability, sugar therapy for the treatment of infected wounds is very applicable to the needs of the (medic). . . . As with any traumatic wound, the wound is first irrigated and debrided. . . . Once bleeding is under control, deep wounds are treated by pouring granulated sugar into the wound, making sure to fill all cavities. The wound is then covered with a gauze sponge soaked in povidone-iodine solution. . . . In a few hours, the granulated sugar is dissolved into a 'syrup' by body fluid drawn into the wound site. Since the effect of granulated sugar upon bacteria is based upon osmotic shock and withdrawal of water that is necessary for bacterial growth and reproduction, this diluted syrup has little antibacterial capacity and may aid rather than inhibit bacterial growth. So to continually inhibit bacterial growth, the wound is cleaned with water and repacked at least one to four times daily (or as soon as the granular sugar becomes diluted) . . . A variety of case reports provide amazing data supporting the use of sugar in treating infected wounds. . . . Odor and secretions from the wound usually diminished within 24 hours and disappeared in 72 to 96 hours from onset of treatment."

— Hugh L. Coffee, *Ditch Medicine* (pp. 47-48)

"THIS CHEST WOUND SUCKS!!!":

". . . the wound site (be it the result of a bullet or a knife) must be dressed with an occlusive dressing. . . . The purpose of the occlusive dressing is to prevent air from entering the chest through the wound, with the possible consequence of a pneumothorax. The dressing can consist of any material that will ensure an airtight seal over the wound (e.g., aluminum foil, plastic wrap, Vaseline gauze). The traditional technique is to tape down all four sides of the dressing. The last edge is taped down after the patient exhales forcefully. The dressing should be large enough to cover at least 2 inches past the wound on all four sides. If tape won't stick to a wet or bloody chest, large trauma dressings can be held down with cravats that surround the chest. If an exit wound is present, as is common with a gunshot wound, it must be covered too. . . . a flutter valve dressing may be applied over the wound site to prevent the development of a tension pneumothorax. With the flutter valve, one corner of the occlusive dressing is left untaped. As the patient inhales, the dressing will seal the wound. With exhalation, the free corner acts as a flutter valve to release air that is trapped in the chest."

— Hugh L. Coffee, *Ditch Medicine* (pp. 68-69)

DEATH TO TYRANTS!:

"For in exceptional circumstances that which is commonly held to be wrong is found on reflection not to be wrong. I shall illustrate my meaning by a special case which, however, has a general bearing. There is no greater crime than to murder a fellowman, especially a friend. Still who would say that he commits a crime who assassinates a tyrant, however close a friend? The people of Rome, I tell you, think it no crime, but the noblest of all noble deeds. Did expediency here triumph over virtue? No, virtue followed in the train of expediency. . . . There can be no such thing as fellowship with tyrants, nothing but bitter feud is possible: and it is not repugnant to nature to despoil, if you can, those whom it is a virtue to kill; nay, this pestilent and godless brood should be utterly banished from human society. For, as we amputate a limb in which the blood and the vital spirit have ceased to circulate, because it injures the rest of the body, so monsters, who, under human guise, conceal the cruelty and ferocity of a wild beast, should be severed from the common body of humanity."

— Cicero, "No Fellowship with Tyrants"

PSYCHOTRONIC TECHNOLOGY AND THE "SAUCER PEOPLE" HOAX:

"I believe there is a machinery of mass manipulation behind the UFO phenomenon. It aims at social and political goals by diverting attention from some human problems and by providing a potential release for tensions caused by others. The contactees are part of that machinery. They are helping to create a new form of belief: an expectation of actual contact among large parts of the public. In turn this expectation makes millions of people hope for the imminent realization of that age-old dream: salvation from above, surrender to the greater power of some wise navigators of the cosmos. . . .

However, if you take the trouble to join me in the analysis of the modern UFO myth, you will see human beings under the control of a strange force that is bending them in absurd ways, forcing them to play a role in a bizarre game of deception. This role may be very important if changing social conditions make it desirable to focus the attention of the public on the distant stars while obsolete human institutions are wiped out and rebuilt in new ways. Is this the deeper meaning of the UFO 'deception'? Are the manipulators, in the final analysis, nothing more than a group of humans who have mastered a very advanced form of power? . . . Let me summarize my conclusions thus far. UFOs are real. They are an application of psychotronic technology; that is, they are physical devices used to affect human consciousness. They may not be from outer space; they may, in fact, be terrestrial-based manipulating devices. Their purpose may be to achieve social changes on this planet."

— Jacques Vallee, *Messengers of Deception*

"WHAT'S YER PROBLEM, PROFESSOR???":

"The research in this book is harmless in itself, and deals with subjects that many people find interesting. Yet it can provoke surprisingly intense emotions. Some people become angry at, or scornful of, anyone who takes these phenomena seriously. Why? Some people find psychic phenomena of no interest, which is fair enough. Most people are not very interested in the scientific study of the behavior of cuttlefish, or research into the genetics of mosses. Yet no one becomes emotionally antagonistic to cuttlefish or moss research. Is it simply a matter, then, of hostility to new ideas? This may be a partial explanation, but some areas of contemporary scientific speculation seem far more radical, and yet excite little or no opposition. Some physicists, for example, postulate that there are countless parallel universes besides our own. Few people take these ideas seriously, but no one gets angry about them. Even speculations about time travel through 'wormholes' in space-time are considered a legitimate field of inquiry within academic physics, rather than a branch of science fiction. . . . The only remaining explanation is that the existence of psychic phenomena violates powerful taboos. These phenomena threaten deep-seated beliefs, especially the belief that the mind is nothing but the activity of the brain. For people who identify science and reason with the materialist philosophy, they arouse fear. They seem to threaten reason itself; if they are not kept at bay, science and even modern civilization seem to be endangered by a tidal wave of superstition and credulity. Hence they have to be denied outright, or dismissed as unscientific and irrational. . . . These taboos are strongest among intellectuals, and are actively upheld by many academics. . . . Although people with these attitudes usually call themselves skeptics, they are not genuine skeptics. They are usually believers in a worldview that excludes psychic phenomena. Some try to deny or debunk any evidence that goes against their beliefs. The most zealous behave like vigilantes policing the frontiers of science. The Greek word skeptis, the root of our word, means 'inquiry' or 'doubt.' It does not mean denial or dogmatism. The effect of these taboos has been to inhibit research and to suppress discussion in the academic world in general, and within institutional science in particular."

— Rupert Sheldrake, *The Sense of Being Stared At* (pp. 7-9)

"THIS IS AS IT IS, AS IT ALWAYS HAS BEEN, AND AS IT ALWAYS SHALL BE!":

"Our culture engages historians, sociologists, psychiatrists and the media to . . . impose upon us a common view of reality. The reason for this imposing of socially-approved views is fear: As a culture we are afraid that unless we can force the majority of us to comply with particular givens, everything we have achieved and everything we believe we understand will unravel. The truth is that without the continual reinforcement of commonly held cultural views of 'reality,' most of our beliefs and some of our ways of living would unravel. . . . In fairness, we need to understand that there can never be a common view of reality because each of us is capable of seeing only so much and no more. . . . a commonly-held world view is not a possibility, not now and not ever. . . . We are stuck with the social illusions into which we are born. . . . From this evolution-of-illusion we get politics, religion, fads and all manner of cultural blindness. We pass our blindness down from one generation to another until it becomes so firmly entrenched in daily life that nobody asks whether this or that aspect of our social belief system might simply be wrong.

— Anderson Reed, *Shouting at the Wolf* (p. 142-143, 148)

OPERATION MINDCRIME:

"What is sanity? Let us start with what sanity is not. Sanity is not blindly accepting anyone else's version of reality or anyone's view of how we ought to live. . . . Sanity is the acceptance of our own experiences and perceptions in the face of 'proof' from other people and social institutions that our views are 'wrong' because they do not match the views held by others. . . . We invented psychiatry. . . after psychiatry entered mainstream western life, a terrible shift occurred. A tool became a weapon. One no longer had the option of using the techniques of psychological theories on himself if that was right for him. Suddenly the tools of psychiatry were being used on us instead of for us, and we no longer had any choice about it — or anything to say about its validity. . . . In reading about the Salem trials, I have found an impressive resemblance to the ways in which psychiatrists today deal with questions of sanity and mental illness. The underlying transaction, in Salem and in our society, pits an afflicted person against a self-appointed 'expert' who cannot truly comprehend either the affliction of the afflicted. Despite his inability to understand the alleged aberration or the person manifesting it, he passes life-threatening judgements on both. He is inadequate to do this, but our society requires his services every time someone is violent, misaligned, or simply eccentric. . . . What do we truly comprehend about psychiatric beliefs and the laws that derive from them? Not much. Yet our society allows the testimony of mental health authorities to send people to jail or to mental institutions. We allow those we place in authority to induce us to forsake our personal, valid experiences if our perceptions displease or confound the authorities. . . . Our society's relationship with the disturbed has not changed in three hundred years. In Salem, nothing effective was done for the afflicted, and the accused were killed for unobservable behavior. Today, people are shunned or incarcered for the 'crime' of being incomprehensible to a psychiatrist. The same dynamic is at work now as was then. . . . What, then, do we achieve by turning (people) over to our uneducated, possibly uncaring, mental health 'authorities'? We don't care about (people). We care to maintain ourselves in a state of passivity. Our freedom is lost to us

— lost by our own doing."

— Anderson Reed, *Shouting at the Wolf* (p. 142, 147, 152, 154-155)

"PAIN IS A SIGNAL":

"All pain is a signal that there is something that's out of balance. Pain is a signal. It's like a fire alarm. Real quick analogy, see if this makes sense to you: If all of a sudden a fire alarm goes off here, we don't sit around drinking our Dr. Peppers, and I don't go over and cut off the alarm so we can finish our conversation. Nor do I go over and stuff pillows around it to get it to shut up. And I don't cut the wires. I go and find out why the goddamn alarm went off. Doctors cut the alarm; that's surgery. Or they'll stuff pillows around it; that's medication. Or they'll shut it off, which is long, extended treatment. That's the three methodologies that medical practice uses, none of which acknowledge what pain is. Pain is a signal that must be acknowledged, that you know your body has been put into a traumatic state, therefore you have to change whatever the cause was for the effect of the trauma."

— Harley Swiftdeer, excerpted from an interview by Chris Pfouts in *Lead Poisoning* (pp. 157-158)

THE CONTROLLERS DO LOVE TO RUB YER NOSE IN IT . . .

"In this America we are taught to put self-interest first, to compete, to better ourselves as individuals. And so we are controlled by promises and threats — controlled at a level so deep that we are rarely conscious of it. . . . Going to jail . . . is an experience that can teach us more about consciousness than a hundred growth seminars. For in jail we experience the controls of our culture directly. We see their naked operation, unclothed by the usual niceties. Power-over is a vise, a clamp that holds us with our hopes and fears. For there are always privileges to be won if we behave, and there is always somewhere worse they can put us, something they can do to us or take away from us, if we refuse to be controlled. So we are caught. In jail we cannot escape knowledge of this control: the system itself has devised a thousand minor rituals, a thousand petty rules to drive the lesson home again and again.

So the purpose of cuffing our hands behind our backs is not to prevent us from attacking the police; it is to acquaint us with the extent of our helplessness. The purpose of the airless, windowless holding tanks, with their open toilets that can only be flushed from outside by the guards is to make us aware, when we are taken to a more decent place, that we can always be returned to a place that is worse. The purpose of stripping us to search us, of having us bend over, spread our cheeks, and cough is not really to discover if we have contraband stuck up our assholes, it is to teach us that humiliation is the favorite weapon the system has devised against the self.

We come out of jail angry, on fire with rage that does not retreat, because as we look around us, day by day, we see the same vise in operation. . . . the prison, the mental hospital, stand as representations of the worse place — where they can take us if we resist control. Yet it is not that most of us live in constant fear of being carted off to jail, but rather that the jail is a symbol of the thousand petty rituals of punishment we face in our jobs, our homes, on the streets. There are endless ways — from the boss's reprimand to the headwaiter's sneer to the look on the grocery clerk's face when we pull out our food stamps, for the culture to confirm our lack of worth."

— Starhawk, *Dreaming the Dark* (pp. 94-96)

"HE WHO FORMS A TIE IS LOST":

"I see that you are wearing a tie. Do you know the origin of the tie? Don't feel bad, as no-one else seems to know either — yet no-one questions the fact that nearly all corporate and government employees are mandated to wear a tie under penalty of termination! Why do you think that is? There are many kinds of tie. Some men like to proclaim their status in the community by wearing a tie with the distinctive pattern of a military regiment or an Ivy League university, while others will flaunt their wealth by spending hundreds of dollars to purchase a single hand-painted silk tie. A man's tie-tack can show that he belongs to a respected fraternal order, that he once served with a particular military unit, or that he can afford a three carat gemstone. A bright red tie supposedly infers 'power' and virility. Certain exclusive cliques like to tie their ties with specific and complex knots, so as to distinguish them from the masses. In the American Southwest, those free-thinking nonconformists are fond of wearing bolo 'string-ties.' It is all the same. That silly piece of colored cloth around your neck is a symbol of your inferiority. It is a constant reminder that you have been 'put in your place.' This humiliating mark of subjugation is a slip-knot attached to a convenient handle, a noose around your neck, a leash for a dog, a garrote if you will. Although it rarely happens, your 'betters' can reach out at any time to pull that loop taut, cutting off your air supply, your voice, and even the critical bloodflow to your brain. To toy with you, they could use it to yank you up out of your chair and swing you around the room. The tie is a symbol of your enslavement. But hey, don't most corporate CEOs wear ties? Don't most religious leaders wear ties? How about the President of the United States? Who makes them wear the tie? Who do they take their orders from? The tie is a veiled threat. I would never wear a tie. It is contrary to my religious beliefs."

— Scribe 27 (RWT)

WAR ON FREEDOM:

"So we got us a war on drugs? War, all right — but not on drugs. Think the government would cut their own throats? The war's been going on for a long, long time, and'll go on for a long time to come. War's still going on, but the good guys have already lost. Started a long time ago, like I said, in World War II. OSS cut a deal with Lucky Luciano for the mafia to control Italian waterfronts after we invaded Italy. Maybe you heard of the heroin network they set up — the French Connection? Luciano got the stuff from Turkey, processed it in Marseilles and Sicily. OSS (the CIA) and French Secret Service got the stuff to America. I mean — look, all you've got to do is look. The United

States goes into Europe and the Middle East, the country gets flooded with heroin. We go into Southeast Asia, they declare a war on drugs. Cut off the Marseilles supply. The heroin and the hashish and the opium start coming in from the Golden Triangle, shipped through 'Air America,' the CIA's bogus airlines. We shift attention to South America and Central America. Suddenly heroin's not the problem. Suddenly everyone's doing cocaine. Ne we got us a war on the Mendellin Cartel? Ri-i-ight. I hear heroin's making a comeback. Grown in Afghanistan. Now doesn't the Company happen to be in Afghanistan, helping all those hill rebels overthrow the Soviet puppet government? Funny how the traditional cash crop of those hill rebels is opium poppies. Funny how the Mendellin Cartel was buying weapons for the Company to supply the Contras with. Funny how the Golden Triangle opium lords are all Chinese refugees. Ex-Kumintang. Funny how the Company was using 'em against the reds, back in the old days. And on and on, all the way back to Luciano. Don't make the mistake of thinking the Company thinks for itself. They might have carte blanche, sure. I think it was their idea to flood the country with LSD back in the 60's just to test the stuff — but they don't give the orders. They don't call the shots. They're told what to do. America's not a fit place to live anymore. See, I know who's behind the drugs. And I know why. You've got to look for the money. Let's say you've got people who need their operations funded. They go to Congress for the money, and what happens? What happens is they've got to tell people what the money's for. If you're trying to keep things secret, that's not such a hot idea. So you've got to get lots of money from somewhere. Hidden money that nobody can find. Money that won't stop coming. Drug money. So they got money, and I think that's all they wanted when they started. I don't think they figured out the side benefits at first — but they're smart. Didn't take them long. See, they had to sell the drugs to somebody. Heroin, cocaine, marijuana, whatever. So who's most likely to buy 'em? They ended up at the fringes of American society — the people who're most likely to be trouble somewhere down the line. I'm talking your blacks, your hippies, whatever. They start using the stuff, makes 'em feel like they're being defiant. Shaking a fist at 'the man.' And pretty soon their energies are all focused on drugs. Usin' 'em, figuring where the money'll come to buy 'em. Sellin' 'em, 'cause that's where the money is — and 'the man' is where the money's going to! Hell, you got kids focused on drugs, they ain't about to get political. Too busy financing gutter capitalism. They make sure everyone associates minorities with drugs. Racism goes up, 'decent white folk' get nervous. People start demanding more police, more laws, more jails. Keep 'em down. You get armies used to acting as cops, society tightens up. It's easier for them to control things when everybody's afraid. Y'know, Vietnam sort of shut down their right to drop armies anywhere in the world. War on communism? Passe' stuff. War on terrorism? Can't keep that going forever without looking wimpy. But a war on drugs? Ah! You've got to use all your resources. Got to give intelligence back the power to operate anywhere, without question. Got to make sure the President can put troops anywhere in the world, without question. Got to declare war on your own people, teach 'em to be snitches. Test 'em without giving them a choice. And every patriotic citizen lines up to go along with the crackdown. America's become a place where they wave a flag at you and expect your brains to go out the window. And anyone who stands up to say what's really going on gets accused of being 'soft on drugs.' And you know what the best part is? The bigger the war on drugs, the higher the price goes, and the more money it's worth. A war on drugs? That's a laugh. An excuse for repression, that's what it is. There's a war on drugs, all right, but the only thing they really fight for is like, who brings the stuff in . . . and who ends up with the money."

— Steven Grant, as adapted from the work of John Judge and transcribed in *Whisper* # 36 (May 1990)

"THOU SHALT NOT SUFFER A _____ TO LIVE!!!"

". . . why did they persecute Witches? Church history is a history of persecution. The Witch burnings were not an isolated phenomenon; they must be seen in the context of centuries of blood and terror. . . . The Witch persecutions were different in several important ways from the persecution of Jews and heretics. To begin with, they were directed primarily, although not exclusively, against women . . . Witches were not an alien ethnic-religious group . . . Nor were they a clearly delineated alien sect . . . with a clearly defined doctrine and organization. . . . Anyone — especially any woman — could be accused of being a Witch. Witchcraft was defined as a special crime to which the ordinary rules of evidence did not apply. . . . a noted French witch-hunter and intellectual actually favored the use of children as witnesses because they could be persuaded more easily to give evidence against the accused. . . . The persecution of Witches undermined the unity of the peasant community and contributed to its fragmentation. . . . The persecutions encouraged, spawned, paranoia. . . . Witches also made convenient scapegoats, diverting the anger and rage of the poorer classes to these other members of their own class. . . .

The Witch persecutions were tied to another of the far-reaching changes in consciousness . . . The rise of professionalism in many arenas of life meant that activities and services that people had always performed for themselves or their neighbors were taken over by a body of paid experts, who were licensed or otherwise recognized as being the guardians of an officially approved and restricted body of knowledge. . . . Many of the charges against Witches and heretics can be seen as charges of giving or receiving 'Brand-X' grace, one that lacked the official seal of approval; of transmitting knowledge without approval. Witches' powers, whether used for harming or for healing, were branded as evil because they came from an unapproved source. . . . Knowledge itself began to be an 'intangible commodity.' It was something to be sold only to those who could afford to buy it."

— Starhawk, *Dreaming the Dark* (pp. 186-187, 196, 199)

DIFFERENT SIDES OF THE SAME COIN . . .

"The so-called Left-Right political spectrum is our creation. In fact, it accurately reflects our careful, artificial polarization of the population on phoney issues that prevents the issue of our power from arising in their minds. The Left supports civil liberties and opposes economic or entrepreneural liberty. The Right supports economic liberty and opposes civil liberty. Of course neither can exist fully (which is our goal) without the other. We control the Right-Left conflict such that both forms of liberty are suppressed to the degree we require. Our own liberty rests not on legal or moral 'rights,' but on our control of the government bureaucracy and courts which apply the complex, subjective regulations we dupe the public into supporting for our benefit."

— Anonymous, *The Occult Technology of Power* (pg. 19)

COINTELPRO

"Too many people have been spied upon by too many Government agencies and too much information has been collected. The Government has often undertaken the secret surveillance of citizens on the basis of their political beliefs, even when those beliefs posed no threat of violence or illegal acts on behalf of a hostile foreign power. The Government, operating primarily through secret informants, but also using other intrusive techniques such as wiretaps, microphone 'bugs,' surreptitious mail opening, and break-ins, has swept in vast amounts of information about the personal lives, views, and associations of American citizens. Investigations of groups deemed potentially dangerous — and even of groups suspected of associating with potentially dangerous organizations -- have continued for decades, despite the fact that those groups did not engage in unlawful activity. Groups and individuals have been harassed and disrupted because of heir political views and their lifestyles. Investigations have been based upon vague standards whose breadth made excessive collection inevitable. Unsavory and vicious tactics have been employed — including anonymous attempts to break up marriages, disrupt meetings, ostracize persons from their professions, and provoke target groups into rivalries that might result in deaths. Intelligence agencies have served the political and personal objectives of presidents and other high officials. While the agencies often committed excesses in response to pressure from high officials in the Executive branch and Congress, they also occasionally initiated improper activities and then concealed them from officials whom they had a duty to inform."

— summation of the Church Committee report, released in April 1976

"DON'T BUG ME!"

"Electronic surveillance technology has advanced significantly in recent years. All cell phone and e-mail communications are being randomly monitored, as are most conversations over cordless phones, walkie-talkies, CB radios, shortwave radios, and public payphones. If a government agency wants to tap your phone, they can have it done directly through the telephone company. If a government agency wants to bug your house, they have the capability to monitor your conversations through your unmodified telephone, cable box, or modem (as long as they're plugged into the wall jack) without any need to physically gain entry. Laser bugs can monitor conversations by sensing the vibrations of a window pane — but these toys are mostly considered obsolete, nowadays. Undercover agents can have audio, and even video, transmitters concealed on their persons (i.e., the lapel camera) — and if a skilled operative can gain access to your home for even a few moments (through a variety of ruses), these transmitters can be successfully installed (or a small amount of contraband can be hidden, to be seized later). Automobiles are incredibly easy to gain entrance to (provided you have the proper tools), and a permanent transmitter can be attached to the wiring under your dashboard. If you need to relay sensitive data to another individual, it is advised that you write it down on a notepad, then, after the 'conversation' is terminated, the paper (as well as the sheet directly under it, which will retain an impression), can be destroyed by either burning it in an ashtray, or tearing it to shreds and flushing it down the toilet."

— Jake Bishop (RWT)

OTHER PEOPLE'S PROBLEMS . . .

"Try to avoid making other people's problems your own. Especially if you are known to be a good fighter or are unusually large, 'friends' (especially women) will try to convince you to fight people for them. If you like them, and they claim to have been threatened with violence, it is tempting (and perfectly normal) for you to want to help them — but be aware that you could be walking into a trap! Sometimes this takes the form of their provoking a confrontation while you are out with them, then expecting you to 'step in' and pound somebody. Other times they will fill your ears with tales of their enemy's nefarious deeds (which are often fabricated or blown out of proportion) in order to enrage you to the point of making him 'pay' for his crimes against your friend. My advice to you is not to get involved, if it can reasonably be avoided. If your 'friend' goes around disrespecting people he or she wants to watch you fight, or if your date is flirting with guys when you're not looking in hopes that one of them does something in front of you to provoke a violent confrontation, then I strongly suggest that you cut the asshole loose and look for a new friend."

— anonymous (RWT)

"DON'T BE AN ASSHOLE!!!"

"Resist the urge to 'correct' total strangers who you believe are fucking up. If someone is fucking up and: 1.) You don't know them; 2.) The situation does not involve you; 3.) You are in no apparent danger; and 4.) You can leave the area without repercussions; then I strongly suggest that you either ignore the jerk or leave. Walking up to a stranger and saying, 'I don't like the way you're acting, you asshole,' is known as starting trouble, which makes you not only a troublemaker but a meddlesome do-gooder as well — and if you get your teeth kicked out you deserve it for being stupid. Furthermore, you must make a point to keep your opinions about other people to yourself. If you pass someone on the street who has green hair and a ring in their nose, don't laugh in his face or go, 'Lookit the fuckin' weirdo.' Nor should you voice your ignorant views about 'welfare scum leeching off the system' when you see the person ahead of you at the checkout is paying for their groceries with food stamps. If you go around acting like an asshole and talking shit to total strangers, sooner or later you're gonna say the wrong thing at the wrong time to the wrong person, and may well find yourself sitting on the floor trying to stuff your intestines back in. Avoid trouble instead of provoking it!!!"

— anonymous (RWT)

THE POLECAT TOTEM

"In observing the habit patterns of Skunk, it is easy to notice the playfulness and nonchalance of its natural behavior. The 'I-dare-you' attitude of this four-legged creature commands you, as the observer, to respect its space by mere reputation alone. Skunk is teaching you that by walking your talk and by respecting yourself, you will create a position of strength and honored reputation. The carriage of your body relates to others what you believe about yourself. There is no need to bully, aggravate, torment, or overpower other beings when your sense of 'self' is intact. As with Skunk, the resonant field of energy around your body is relayed through the senses. Self-esteem permeates the body's energy, and is instantly recognized on an extrasensory level by others. Learn to assert, without ego, what you are. Respect follows. Your self-respectful attitude will repel those who are not of like mind, and yet will attract those who choose the same pathway. . . . it repels those who will not respect (your) space.

— Jamie Sams and David Carson, *Medicine Cards* (p. 65)

GOING 150 MPH ON THE INTERSTATE WITH A PSYCHOTIC DIPSHIT

"In my youth, I may have been a wee bit delusional. I used to think that I was unkillable, that I could pretty much do whatever the fuck I wanted, that I was living in an Action/Adventure movie, and that my car was a spaceship. Yes, you heard me correctly, a spaceship. No, I didn't eat acid, and I wasn't a fucking Trekkie — but I did play a lot of Dungeons & Dragons and videogames (it was the 80s). In the daylight, it was just an ordinary car, but after the sun went down and the instrument panel lit up, I was in the cockpit of a fighter jet from a Science Fiction movie. I would go into a Zen trance, merging with the bucket seat, steering wheel, and pedals — becoming one with my 'ship' as it zoomed scant inches over the landscape — totally focused on the road, the traffic, and everything that was within my sphere of influence. I was the Captain, and my word was law. Myself; my Co-Pilot, Chewbacca; and our Bombardier, Onion, all wore leather flight jackets and created a specialized jargon — which served to reinforce our shared delusion. Seat belts became 'G-force restraint harnesses,' the CB radio became a 'communications module,' and the Dan Wesson Super-Magnum between the seats became a 'blaster.' After a few tokes and a slug of Jim Beam, we were good to go! 70 - 90 mph was considered 'cruising speed,' 100 mph was 'Warp 1,' 120 mph was 'Warp 2,' and anything over 140 mph was referred to as 'hyperspace.' If we didn't enter hyperspace at least once, the mission was considered a failure. On our missions we encountered beacons and bogeys, cargo transports and cornfields, and sometimes were pursued by Empire Interceptors. On the occasions when we picked up hitchhikers or stranded motorists, they were generally referred to as 'unfortunate passengers,' and although they occasionally freaked out, they were usually treated with the utmost of courtesy and respect. We had many an adventure, and even compiled a handwritten 'flight manual' which included over a hundred specialized terms, tips on high speed evasive driving, 'rules of engagement' for encounters with enemy vessels (of which there were many), and other socially unacceptable information of a similar nature. It is truly amazing that we aren't all dead."

— T. J. Steele (RWT)

GOT MORE GUNS THAN YOU CAN SHOOT?

"For years, lotsa folks have been recommending that we 'bury our guns.' Not all of them, of course — just the extra ones you won't need right away. Handguns and military-style autoloaders are specifically mentioned, as these are the weapons deemed most likely to be criminalized and confiscated at a future date. Besides, realistically, you really don't need several M-1 carbines or AK-47s laying around your house anyway — what if you were burglarized, or experienced a structure fire? Having all of your guns (as well as money and important documents) in one place is both irresponsible and foolish. And if you happen to own an illegal weapon of some sort, only a criminal or a dumbass would store it in his home! On many occasions, people have been convicted of weapons charges after a fire investigator discovered the charred remnants of a sawed-off shotgun or antique SMG which had been so cleverly concealed in some 'secret hiding place,' now reduced to ashes. Any guns you don't need can be either be stored elsewhere or cached.

There are many ways to cache one's surplus armaments, some of which are better than others. One of the best 'low-tech' methods I know of simply involves the use of a sturdy box (preferably watertight), plastic trash bags, silica gel dessicant, and WD-40. First, the weapon(s) must be unloaded. If required for it to fit into the box, it can be broken down as well. All plastic and wooden parts (stocks, grips, forearms) should be removed and placed in a large ziplock bag — press out all the air and toss in a few silica gel packets (often enclosed with electronics, vitamins, and leather shoes), then place the sealed bag within another bag — this will protect these parts from being damaged by the penetrating oil. Small amounts of ammunition can be treated in a similar manner, as penetrating oil can ruin the primers (large amounts of ammo, however, should be contained in a proper Mil-Spec, gasket-sealed, ammo can with dessicant). The partially disassembled weapon(s) can then be thoroughly drenched with a thick coating of WD-40. This oil will impede corrosion, and is far easier to clean off than either petroleum jelly or rubberized coatings. Immediately, each oiled weapon should be sealed within a large plastic bag — gallon-sized ziplock bags work well for most handguns, but a trash bag (cinched and knotted) will be necessary for carbines. As a single bag cannot be guaranteed to be watertight, it should be sealed within a second bag — and then a third. The bag(s) containing parts and/or ammo (never store a loaded magazine due to spring fatigue) for a specific piece should be stowed within that weapon's second bag. The sealed bag(s) can then be stowed within the storage box(es) you have selected. A watertight metal or plastic box is best, but I have used wooden boxes — and even guitar cases — without experiencing any problems. Dessicant is dropped into the case (either a single Mil-Spec pouch or a handful of commercial packets), the case is latched, and then the case is taped shut (with duct or electrical tape); after which the case itself is stowed within a large plastic bag (if not a plastic tarp or pool liner) and taped secure. One time, all I had access to was a box of 33-gallon trash bags, which, unfortunately, were not quite large enough to fit over the box in question, so I simply taped it in place, inverted it, then pulled another bag over the other end, taping it in place as well! After the initial weatherproofing has been applied, at least two more layers should be added to ensure it will be adequately protected from the elements. Once it is secure, it can be safely cached anywhere it will not be flooded and immersed (as if it were to be stowed in a drainage pipe or buried below the waterline of a known flood-plain). I strongly recommend that you cache a couple bottles of spring water, a few tins of sardines, a pair of dry socks, and a half-pint of Jim Beam along with your weapons and ammunition.

Don't be lazy and bury your gear in the backyard — or anywhere near your house. That is the first place inspectors will look (after they've ransacked your abode), and they'll have metal detectors as well as sensors to detect 'disturbed ground.' If you want to bury your gear, do it far away — preferably miles away from your property. Underneath the soil of an abandoned dump would be ideal, due to the abundance of rusted scrap metal. Contrary to popular belief, it is not necessary to bury it over three feet deep — 18" should be more than sufficient. Be sure to use several permanent landmarks to pinpoint its position (DON'T use a fucking G.P.S!), then memorize it — do not write the location on a map! If burial is impractical (perhaps due to inhospitable rocky soil), your cache could be stowed in a small cave, crevasse, hollow tree, under a large fallen tree, under a large brush pile, under a number of rocks (then covered with soil and leaves), or even within a large cluster of brambles (like wild blackberry bushes). A weapon stowed in such a manner can be protected from several years worth of rain and snow — just as long as it doesn't end up totally immersed in floodwaters. When the time comes that you need it, your weapon can be unearthed, unwrapped, wiped down, reassembled, loaded, and ready to fire in under ten minutes."

— Jake Bishop (RWT)

THE DOG WILL EAT YOU!!!

"After detecting an intruder, the dog will operate on command of the handler or on situation stimulus. . . . In either case the dog will retain its grip on its quarry until ordered to leave. In the case of highly aggressive dogs, strict compulsion may be necessary. It is this courage and ability of the dog that makes it vulnerable to the intruder. Pad yourself as described below, encourage the dog to attack, biting in a place that you dictate. Present a target to the dog, thereby placing it in a situation where it can be immobilized or destroyed. Adequate protection can be had from wrapping around the arm any of the following: webbing belt, leggings, rifle sling, ponchos, wrapping from equipment, scarves, headgear. . . . The dog is far less dangerous if it makes firm contact on the first run in. . . . Throughout its training the dog has always been allowed to succeed. . . . Give it the opportunity to succeed and then destroy. It is most vulnerable when gripping target. Remember: a dog deterred will bark or growl, drawing the attention of the guards. . . . The destruction of a trained dog is by no means a simple matter. . . . It is often easier to take the dog and immobilize, either by tying to a secure fitting, or binding the front legs. Always muzzle, and if possible render it inoperable, example, breaking a leg."

— excerpted from the S.A.S. Combat Survival course notes

DITCH MEDICINE

"What can you do about dysentery? You will lose water which you must replace. If possible, replace it with boiled water, but at any cost drink quantities of fluids. . . . Charcoal can help. Take any partially burned piece of wood, scrape off the charred portions, and swallow them. . . . Bones — any kinds of bones — can help. They are best if burned and ground into ash, but you can grind bones between rocks to a powder, just swallow the powder. . . . A single louse sucks 1 cc of blood a day. . . . lice can bleed you to death unless you pick them off every single day. . . . Regardless of how cold it is, you must inspect your entire body and every seam of every garment at least once a day, picking off every single louse. . . . You will get worms — all kinds, round, hook, and tape worms. They will come from the food you eat and the dirt and filth where you live. . . . Personal hygiene is the best preventive measure against parasitic infestation. . . . Wash your body and your clothes as often and as well as you can. . . . Here I want to make a plea; if you are bleeding, DO NOT put on a tourniquet. . . . A tourniquet destroys tissue, gangrene sets in, and it is often impossible to save the injured member. Just apply heavy, constant pressure — that alone will stop 99% of all bleeding. If blood is spurting out, stick your finger down on the wound and hold it there. . . . There are three treatments for a wound under extreme conditions: Clean it out if possible with hot water; wash it out with urine, and/or pick out all foreign matter. The book says never to stick your fingers in a wound. If you have nothing else and if there are pieces of metal or clothing in the wound, pick or dig them out with your finger. Maggots were an accepted treatment for infected wounds during WWI. Maggots eat only dead tissue and will clean out a wound better than anything else except surgery. How, you ask, do I get hold of maggots? That's easy . . . just expose the wound. The maggots will find it."

— Dr. Gene N. Lam

BETTER LIVING THROUGH CHEMISTRY???:

"Since the beginning of the war-production drive of 1940-1945, which transformed the United States into the greatest industrial machine the earth had yet seen, chemists had been developing new substances at an astonishing pace. Once they learned the basic techniques of hooking and unhooking atoms their imaginations seemed unlimited. They played with shiny colored balls that represented atoms, building them into beautiful, complex new molecules; then, first in laboratories and later in immense plants that resembled oil refineries, they produced the actual compounds.

Many of these new materials had extraordinarily interesting properties. Some of them could kill insects; these were manufactured by the millions of tons, and given names like DDT or 2-4D. Some were useful as drugs, though they had unsuspected side-effects of nausea, headaches, sweating, gastric upsets, circulatory disorders. Some were glue-like and hardened as strong as steel, but could be molded into infinitely varied shapes. Some could be made into thin, almost weightless transparent films. Some could be used in foods as preservatives, flavorizers, tenderizers, or to make foods stiffer or creamier. Some were dyes, widely used in foods, clothing, plastics. Some were capable of foaming up and then hardening into spongy or rigid forms.

They appeared in paints and varnishes, they were made into bottles and pan-coatings and phonograph records. They were eaten and drunk, sprayed and powdered, applied in a thousand ways upon the landscape and all the creatures who inhabited it. By the end of the seventies there was no human activity in the United States, from contraception to the management of terminal disease, carried out free of materials that had not existed on the face of the earth forty years earlier. This, it was widely believed, was a testimonial to humankind's improvements on nature. People clamored for the new wonder products, and could no longer imagine living without them. . . .

About thirty years after the great boon in chemical production began, American public health officials and doctors realized that the nation was experiencing an alarming new rise in the incidence of cancer. Some attempted to explain this by saying that modern sanitation and medicine enabled people to live longer, and that when they lived longer they just naturally fell prey to diseases like cancer. Others noted the rise in certain cancers due to cigarette smoking, or the taking of popular drugs that had been insufficiently tested, or dietary factors. Research was hampered by the fact that there were so many different types of cancers, and many of them took twenty years or so to develop. Increasingly, however, people of all ages were suffering from the disease — with more than one in every four Americans becoming victims. . . .

Researchers hoping to find a viral cause for cancer were reluctantly driven to the conclusion that, though some virus process might be involved, the precipitating causes of cancer were something like 80 percent environmental. People were doing it to themselves. But this was not a message that most Americans were then prepared to hear; it went largely unreported and undiscussed, and the cancer rates continued rising. . . . People went on breathing air that was known to be dangerous to their health, drinking water known to be contaminated, eating pesticide and additive laden foods, and concentrating their attention on making money in order (as they imagined it) to survive."

— Ernest Callenbach, *Ecotopia Emerging* (pp. 15-17)

"CANNED SUGAR WATER IS GOOD FOR YOU!"

"For the purposes of this discussion, a soft drink is a soda made from carbonated water, added sugar, and flavors. . . . By this definition, a soft drink is the quintessential 'junk food' — high in calories but low in nutrients. . . . the Center for Science in the Public Interest rightfully refers to soft drinks as 'liquid candy.' From a nutritional standpoint, water or almost any other beverage is a better option. . . . Consumption of soft drinks is well known to contribute to tooth decay especially when it is sipped throughout the day, and adolescents who consume soft drinks display a risk of bone fractures three- to four-fold higher than those who do not. . . . Carbonated soft drinks are big business in the United States; they generated more than $50 billion in annual sales just in this country in the late 1990s. Sales are dominated by two companies, Coca-Cola and PepsiCo . . . An obvious way to reach (the) younger age group is through schools. . . . the financial advantages to soft drink companies are substantial. For one thing, sugar and water are inexpensive ingredients. For another, the earlier contracts typically called for a charge of $1.00 for a drink purchased from vending machines, or $24 for a case of 12-ounce cans. In 1999, for example, the wholesale cost of a case was $4.99 . . . If just half the students in a district of 10,000 students consumed one soda per day, gross sales should have been more than $25,000 per week. . . . a Coca-Cola official said that his company would 'continue to be very aggressive and proactive in getting our share of the school business.'"

— Marion Nestle, *Food Politics* (pp. 198, 200-203)

INSTANT MACARONI & CHEESE, RAMEN NOODLES, AND POTATO CHIPS???

"In industrialized countries, overt symptoms of dietary deficiencies are less prevalent even in the presence of poor dietary intake. 'Hunger' — as defined by inadequate ability to purchase food — affects 20 million children and adults in the United States and numerous surveys have identified nutrient intakes below RDA levels among groups living in poverty. Such findings, however, are only rarely accompanied by clinical signs of nutrient deficiencies. When clinical signs do occur, they are usually associated with the additional nutritional requirements of pregnancy, infancy, and early childhood; with illness, injury, or hospitalization; with aging; or with the toxic effects of alcohol or drug abuse.

Regardless of its cause, inadequate dietary intake profoundly affects body functions. It induces rapid and severe losses of body weight, decreases blood pressure and metabolic rate, causes abnormalities in heart function and losses in muscle strength and stamina, and induces undesirable changes in gastrointestinal function and behavior. The result is a generalized lack of vitality that reduces productivity and impairs people's ability to escape the consequences of poverty. Of special concern is the loss of immune function that accompanies starvation. Malnourished individuals demonstrate poor resistance to infectious disease. Infections, in turn, increase nutrient losses and requirements and, in the absence of adequate nutrient intake, induce further malnutrition. . . . Survivors display typical effects of starvation: depression, apathy, irritability, and growth retardation."

— Marion Nestle, *Food Politics* (pp. 379-380)

THE "JAPANESE TOMATO PLANT"

"The Japanese Tomato Plant has been proven to have many healthful attributes, yet its cultivation is prohibited due to the Alien Species Act. It is unlawful to ship the seeds of this beneficial plant through the mail, as well. Furthermore, since the fruit of this rare plant can be sold on the black market for roughly five times the price of uncultivated wild panax ginseng, dishonest folk will think nothing of trespassing on private land to uproot your crop prior to harvest.

It is surprisingly easy to grow your own Japanese tomatoes, as they can adapt to North American climes rather well. If you are lucky enough to acquire a sample of top quality Japanese tomato (as opposed to the many similar, though inferior, tomatoes indigenous to China and Taiwan), simply separate the seeds from the fruit and set them aside to dry. Seeds suitable for cultivation will be large and richly colored. Undersized, pale, black, or cracked seeds will not germinate, and should be discarded. To germinate, secure a medium-sized glass plate, scouring it thoroughly with hot water to displace any possible mold spores. Next, take a square of plain white paper towel and fold it twice, forming a smaller square. Dampen this square with room-temperature spring water. Place about eight seeds on this damp square, spacing them far enough apart that their roots will not entwine, then cover them with a similarly folded and moistened paper towel. Finally, cover the entire plate with a layer of Saran Wrap to prevent the moisture from evaporating. If the plate is placed on an insulated heating pad (on its lowest setting) for about a week, the seeds will probably germinate (if they were viable to begin with). When the root is about three inches long, it will be ready to plant.

The seedling is extremely fragile, and should be handled very carefully. A large peat pot should be secured for each viable seedling. Each pot should be filled with a premium quality potting soil (although one without 'moisture crystals,' or other questionable additives), which must be dampened with spring water and have a 1" X 4" hole burrowed therein. The seedling's root can then be gently guided into the hole before the moist soil is gently pushed up against the stem. The peat pots can then be placed on a windowsill to receive sunlight.

Every day, the pots must be rotated 180 degrees and moistened with no more than an ounce of spring water. The soil should neither become saturated or dry. After about a month of sitting on the windowsill, about half of the Japanese Tomato Plants will probably either die or wilt — these are inferior mutations which must be immediately discarded. The remainder will be about 6" tall with thick stems. These will probably survive. After another month, the plants will double in size. At this time, they are probably about ready to be transplanted to their permanent home. Just prior to transplanting, soak the plant's new home with water and punch a fist-sized hole in the wet soil to accommodate the peat pot, then quickly immerse the peat pot in a bucket of water to facilitate careful tearing of the sides (about four tears should do it) before insertion.

If you intend to keep them indoors, a simple 5-gallon plastic bucket (with a few holes punched in the bottom and a couple handfuls of small stones dropped inside to provide for drainage) filled with topsoil should be adequate (although the addition of compost cow manure and wormcastings will provide more nutrients). If you intend to keep them outdoors, it is best advised to dig a hole for each plant (approximately 1 ft. deep X 3 ft. wide) and fill it with a topsoil blend — although simply dumping a 20 lb. bag of topsoil on the ground for each plant will suffice (although access to groundwater would be somewhat restricted). Some people recommend that you pinch off the new growth in the forks between the branches to promote higher yields, but over-pruning will weaken or kill your plants. Be sure to camouflage your plants and continually alter your route to them, so as not to leave an obvious trail. Water frequently, pick off any insects, and urinate nearby to repel deer. Never spray with pesticide or use liquified 'deer repellant,' as the tomatoes will act like a sponge, absorbing and retaining these toxins, and thereby poisoning anyone who eats them!

After another month or two, the Japanese Tomato Plants will start to take on the appearance of a small shrub. If, however, clusters of tiny green flower buds start to appear near the top, that is an unfortunate mutation which will necessitate immediate uprooting of the affected plants so that they will not contaminate the others. After another couple months, the tomatoes should be large and ripe (the average plant will yield about a dozen, of various sizes). Pick them right off the plant and place them in a wooden (or cardboard) box for about a week or two, till properly dried and cured. Unlike domestic tomatoes, they should not be sun-dried. Remember, the foliage is waste and ought to be discarded. The dried tomatoes can then be broken apart, as needed, being sure to reserve the seeds. They are high in vitamins and contain many essential trace nutrients. They also have a truly unique flavor which makes a great addition to spaghetti sauce, pizza sauce, meatloaf, and even some desserts. It is truly a shame that this exotic, yet wholesome, health food product cannot lawfully be imported into, or distributed throughout, the United States."

— Chewbacca (RWT)

Z.P.G.

"Overpopulation is a major problem throughout the world, and many scholars believe that if the world's population continues to grow, there will not be sufficient resources to sustain it and the survival of the human species will be jeopardized. War, famine, and pestilence have always been brutally effective at reducing the surplus population, but such disasters generally do not occur amongst contemporary industrialized nations, whose populations continue to swell. Certain population control measures, like eugenics, have been so wrongfully abused in the past that few people are willing to speak in support of them. Likewise, the subjects of abortion and euthanasia are so emotionally charged that anyone speaking in favor of them is guaranteed to meet with violent opposition. As the proponents of humane population controls are reviled as 'Nazis,' 'murderers,' or 'godless,' the number of those who suffer from poverty, illness, and neglect continues to grow.

It is a fact that certain mandatory sterilization programs implemented in the past have proven to be nothing more than a form of state-sponsored genocide. Certain ethnic groups were targeted by unscrupulous bureaucrats as a means of preventing them from bearing children. Today, nearly everyone acknowledges that 'ethnic cleansing' is an abomination. However, what about individuals who are mentally retarded? Even though it is against the law to have sexual relations with a retarded person, such individuals frequently breed — often with one another. The progeny of these relationships are also retarded, and are usually subject to neglectful parenting — they often become wards of the state. And what about those individuals who are known to suffer from a serious genetic health defect? While it is true that if they interbreed with someone who lacks this defect there is a chance that the mutation may not be passed onto their children, the risk factor is often unacceptably high. I feel that all individuals known to either suffer from mental retardation or severe genetically transmittable birth defects should be subject to mandatory sterilization for the public good.

Many conservatives lament the number of children begat by multiple fathers to unwed welfare recipients. While, indeed, this does present a severe problem for all concerned, it would be ethically reprehensible to force sterilization upon someone simply because they happen to be poor (as well as irresponsible). In cases like these, the solution is simple — cash incentives! In exchange for $5,000 cash — no questions asked — women receiving some form of public assistance (or even many who do not fit into that demographic, due to the fact that most yuppies have no business reproducing) could undergo a simple (as well as reversible) tubal ligation procedure. If five thousand dollars seems like too much money, consider how many tax dollars would be needed to provide aid for a brood of over a half-dozen neglected children until their 18th birthdays! If the procedure is voluntary, as well as reversible, I see no ethical dilemma.

There are over a million fundamentalist mental cases in this country who are militantly opposed to allowing women to terminate unwanted pregnancies. For some bizarre reason, they are also opposed to birth control and sex education! (Although, they are invariably pro-death penalty, and seem to think nothing of bombing 'heathen' countries, or even physically attacking those who disagree with them.) These degenerates even want to deny the option of terminating a pregnancy to victims of rape and incest, as well as women known to have deformed fetuses and women to whom pregnancy would entail a substantial risk of death (such as some diabetics). If a woman does not want to have a child, then it should not be forced upon her! What kind of parent do you think she would make? Probably a resentful, neglectful, and possibly even an abusive one! As the popular pro-choice bumper sticker says: 'A world of wanted children would make a world of difference.' I think that any woman who wants to have an abortion performed should be offered a cash incentive to undergo a tubal ligation as well. Having no children at all is a lot better than having several ill-cared for hellspawn who will later inflict themselves upon society through their anti-social behaviors. Simply squeezing out a baby does not automatically transform a dirtbag (or yuppie scum) into a good parent — and children usually end up emulating their parents. If their parents are selfish, dishonest, and violent, their children will probably mimic these behaviors and victimize others. Mealy mouthed yuppies who refuse to even raise their voice when addressing their own misbehaving children often end up with a brood of well-dressed sociopaths.

Euthanasia is something else the bible-thumpers are rabidly opposed to. If someone is slowly and painfully dying in a hospital bed from cancer, or some other fatal disease, not only do they want to prolong their suffering (even if it means artificially extending their life via mechanical means), but they insist upon depriving them of painkillers as well! 'We don't want you to become addicted to drugs,' they smirk, knowing full well that the patient is not only in agony, but probably won't live more than another few months anyway! 'Offer your suffering up to God — He just loves that shit!' — It kinda makes you wonder exactly which 'god' these freaks think they're worshiping!

Cash incentives for voluntary sterilization, free abortions to those who need them, and the option of a painless death for the terminally ill. These three things would eliminate much suffering in our society, as well as reduce unwanted population growth."

— anonymous (RWT)

MAINSTREAMIN' THE 'TARDS:

According to Federal educational guidelines, all public schools are mandated to include the mentally retarded in their classrooms. Separate 'special education' classrooms are largely a thing of the past. Funds must be allocated from the school budget to provide a number of services to these mentally retarded 'students' until their 21st birthday. These services include (but are by no means limited to): an aide for each retard in order to escort them to their classes, wipe the drool off their chin, and prevent them from assaulting other students; brand new personal computers to become the property of the 'student' and kept at their home; and transportation and tuition to various Summer activity programs. If the retarded student attends classes until they are 21, they will generally be awarded a High School Diploma — something routinely denied non-retarded students with undiagnosed learning disabilities who are unable to learn a foreign language or pass Regents examinations in advanced mathematics! If the retarded individual is not a semi-functional 'moron,' but rather an 'imbecile' or an 'idiot' who requires constant care and supervision even in regards to the simple functions of eating and defecating, the school will be required to bus those individuals to a special facility which purports to instruct them in 'Basic Life Skills.' Tuition for these alleged courses is very expensive, and after their 21st birthday none of the students have yet mastered the arts of ass-wiping and teeth-brushing. Furthermore, a number of unscrupulous dirtbags have discovered that they can quit their minimum-wage jobs and make a far better living from the government benefits and cash grants they're eligible for by taking in a half-dozen retarded foster kids (their income will rise even more if they decide to adopt them) — and then they're entitled to have employees from local agencies come to their homes to care for their charges at taxpayer expense! Yeah, I feel bad for the 'tards, but this is an exorbitant and unnecessary waste of valuable taxpayer funds intend to be used for educational purposes (and, realistically, the 'tards derive no discernable benefit from the services they're provided). Small school districts are required to spend well over a quarter of a million dollars each year taking care of mental incompetents who really ought to be either kept at home or made wards of the state. Meanwhile, government funding for educational programs is being slashed, grants are being withheld, utility costs are skyrocketing, and the other students are seeing cuts in their services! New textbooks — as well as equipment for science, technology, athletics, art, and music — often must be done without, and even a mere hundred dollars to fund a field trip, a school play, or an 'Odyssey of the Mind' program is unavailable, which necessitates fundraisers and donations. Required maintenance and renovations of school buildings often falls by the wayside for lack of funds. In my opinion, this whole federalized 'special education' program is nothing but a big scam, and a few special interests are making a big profit from destabilizing the public school system."

— Jake Bishop (RWT)

"PURELY THEORETICAL":

"As has been the case throughout recorded history, if the Scientific Establishment cannot conclusively 'prove' something's existence by means of reproducible and verifiable experiments, then persons who put forth theories that subtle and insubstantial things might actually exist can reasonably expect to be attacked through ridicule and character assassination (which can result in loss of: credibility, status, respect, funding, and employment). The core premise of this chapter is that just because something cannot be seen does not automatically mean that it doesn't exist. Certain invisible things (radio waves, electrons, microbes, gases, magnetic fields, cosmic rays, trace elements, etc.) can only be detected through the use of specialized equipment — but, due to the fact that they can be detected, any high school science teacher can expound upon their properties. But what about those things which we have not yet developed the means to adequately detect? They shall be relegated to the realm of the 'theoretical' until technology advances to a sufficient degree as to render them readily perceptible.

Many things in the physical world are invisible to the naked eye. Some of these things (like subcellular organelles and viruses) can be directly observed with powerful optical apparatus (i.e., the electron microscope), whereas others can only be observed indirectly, based upon how they react with an isolated test medium (for example, subatomic particles and cosmic rays). These things (or evidence of them) can be observed, so we know that they 'exist' — but what if we lacked the required technology? Then, even though we were pretty damn sure of our hypothesis, our findings would still be regarded as purely theoretical. Being 'theoretical,' they become 'questionable,' hence easily dismissed as 'mere speculation.'"

— Scribe 27, *Arcane Lore* (pp. 45-46)

THE PHENOMENON OF SUPPRESSION:

"If a finding is slightly anomalous, it may win acceptance after a period of controversy. If it is more anomalous, it may be studied for some time by a few scientists, while being rejected by the majority. . . . Finally, there are some observations that so violently contradict accepted theories that they are never accepted by any scientists. These tend to be reported by scientifically uneducated people in popular books, magazines, and newspapers. . . . This process of rejection does not usually involve careful scrutiny of the evidence by the scientists who reject it. Human time and energy are limited, and most scientists prefer to focus on positive research goals, rather than spend time scrutinizing unpopular claims. In the scientific community, the word will go out that certain findings are bogus, and this is enough to induce most scientists to avoid the rejected material. When theories change, and a certain body of ideas and discoveries becomes unacceptable, there is generally a period of time during which prominent scientists will publish systematic attacks against the unwanted findings. If the attacks are successful, then after some last attempts at rebuttal by diehard supporters, scientists will realize it is not in their best interest to defend the unwanted material or be associated with it. A shroud of silence descends over the rejected evidence, and it continues to exist only in fossilized form in the moldering pages of old scientific journals. As time passes, a few dismissive mentions may be made in occasional footnotes, and then a new generation of scientists grows up, largely unaware that the earlier evidence ever existed."

— Michael Cremo and Richard Thompson, *Forbidden Archeology* (pp. 25-26)

"BUT IS THE HYPOTHESIS FASHIONABLE???":

"The idea that the universe began in a single, primordial explosion, or Big Bang, is accepted without question by most scientists. And this is odd because, although there are compelling reasons to believe that this is true, no-one has ever proved that it is true. On the other hand, if a near-death psychologist were to state flatly that the realm of light NDEers travel to during their experiences is an actual other level of reality, the psychologist would be attacked for making a statement that cannot be proved. And this is odd, for there are equally compelling reasons to believe this is true. In other words, science already accepts what is probable about very important matters if those matters fall into the category of 'fashionable things to believe,' but not if they fall into the category of 'unfashionable things to believe.' This double standard must be eliminated before science can make significant inroads into the study of both psychic and spiritual phenomena. . . . In a universe in which the consciousness of a physicist affects the reality of a subatomic particle, the attitude of a doctor affects whether or not a placebo works, the mind of an experimenter affects the way a machine operates, and the imaginal can spill over into physical reality, we can no longer pretend that we are separate from that which we are studying. In a holograpghic and omnijective universe, a universe in which all things are part of a seamless continuum, strict objectivity ceases to be possible."

— Michael Talbot, *The Holographic Universe* (p. 297)

"COWAN BEGONE!!!":

"The etymology of this word is uncertain, but it appears to be a term derived from the Greek word kyon ('a dog'). The use of this word in English originated in Scotland, where it was a term to describe a stone mason who has picked up his trade without serving an apprenticeship or to a mason who built 'drystane dykes' (i.e., walls without mortar). Like a dog these persons were supposed to be inquisitive, sticking their noses into that which did not concern them.

Cowan was adopted by the Freemasons from the Scottish stone masons to describe those who practice Freemasonry without having been properly initiated or to a person who is not of the brotherhood of Freemasonry. First appeared in this context in Anderson's Constitutions in 1769 C.E.

Wiccans borrowed the term from Freemasonry. Wiccans use it nowadays to describe someone who is not a Wiccan. Cowan may have been synonymous with 'Warlock' (oath breaker) at one point, but is now generally a benign term for an outsider or noninitiate."

— Kerr Cuhulain, *Full Contact Magick* (pp. 232-233)

"THE SECRET OF THE 33rd DEGREE IS . . . IT'S ALL BULLSHIT!!!":

"Now, to both the non-mason and to some masons the most curious thing about masonry is that its secrets are no secrets; I do not mean by this that the so-called secrets are available to all who care to spend enough money on books at any masonic bookseller, although this is, of course, true, but that the secret rituals, passwords and steps of the craft are almost meaningless. That if there is a real secret at the heart of masonry (and many whose opinions I respect affirm that there is) it lies not in these things but in something much deeper which is hidden from him who has not reached the core of masonic initiation — after all an unutterable secret is, by definition, unutterable! The English masons of the eighteenth century appear to have remained comparatively unworried by this problem, for while the Jacobites used their Lodges as covers for political conspiracy, the pro-Hanoverians of Grand Lodge were content to use the masonic rites as an excuse for drunkenness and debauch. . . .

Within a few years several occult-masonic organizations had appeared, each claiming a Templar origin for itself. In Scotland there was the Royal Order, alleged to have enjoyed an uninterrupted existence since the fourteenth century when it was founded, so the story went, by two French Templars who had fled for refuge to Scotland. In Germany and France was the Stricte Observance, under the control of mysterious 'Unknown Superiors' and demanding the unconditional submission and obedience of all other masonic groups. In England there were many 'Templar encampments' — independent, quasi-masonic bodies, usually working in close association with Chapters of Rose-

Croix masons. . . . The last of this long line of occult Templar organizations, the Ordo Templi Orientis, usually referred to as the O.T.O., was founded at the beginning of the (twentieth) century . . . Its original members seem to have all come from the ranks of the German Lodge of the Ancient and Primitive Rite of Memphis and Mizraim. . . . by 1900 Memphis and Mizraim had become a fee-snatching racket of the very worst type."

— Francis King, *Sexuality, Magic & Perversion* (pp. 95-96)

ONE VIEW OF THE "STATE SECURITY SERVICE":

"The State Security Service is not bound by firm rules and laws. In contrast to the normal police it has no intention of acting in a preventive capacity by its mere presence or to find culprits, if necessary, but rather it operates on the principle that 'to prevent is better than to heal.' This means: each person who might become a potential enemy is liquidated now as a preventive measure, in many cases even before he has committed himself against the occupying power. For this reason, entire sections of the population or professional groups rather than just specific individuals are systematically eliminated.

The constant distrust even of their own officials is not caused by the profession as such, but is part of the system. By involving many agencies even during small affairs, no official can deviate from the line. Each must attempt to surpass automatically his colleagues in 'cruelty,' 'faithfulness to the system,' and 'hate toward the enemy.' As a result everyone is watching each other. . . .

If you resist political indoctrination and the enemy realizes that he is failing in his attempt to 'convert' you to his ideology, he will attempt to obtain obedience through fear. He will try to create this fear through terror. The enemy has developed terror techniques which are very effective. . . . These terror measures are:

a. Surveillance of telephone and letters;

b. Establishment of an agent and informer net;

c. Arbitrary arrests;

d. No public trials except 'show trials';

e. Arbitrary sentences;

f. Lengthy prison sentences out of proportion to the offense. . . .

Clubs and associations disliked by the enemy will not be prohibited at once, but will be initially subjected to various types of harassment, etc. If he immediately prohibits such organizations, he takes the risk of having membership lists destroyed. . . . When the enemy has obtained the membership lists he will destroy and outlaw the organizations."

— Major H. Von Dach, *Total Resistance* (pp. 94, 96, 102)

STRONGPOINT:

"You will seldom have enough time to prepare buildings for defense — there are so many things you can do to make an attacker's life a misery. So your first priority is to make sure you can cover your arcs of fire from the building, and loophole the walls accordingly. . . . If they are still operating, switch off the gas and electricity. Gas is an obvious hazard and electricity is unnecessary — if the enemy does attack at night, you will know the layout of the building and he won't. So fight in darkness to give yourself another edge. By the time you have barricaded the place properly, the building will be pretty gloomy even by daylight. The lack of light and the wire obstacles you place in windows and doors will buy you valuable time if the enemy manages to get inside. Once the enemy is inside a room, evacuate it, let them all in, then post grenades through interior loopholes or doorways. Remove the drainpipes from the house — the enemy can climb up them — and use them around the building (inside and out) as 'grenade chutes.' . . . Change the layout of the building to further disorient the enemy troops that manage to break in. Block up the stairs with masses of barbed wire and cut holes in the floors of upper-story rooms; use a ladder to get up and down. You can always pull it up if you need to evacuate the lower story. A double layer of sandbags placed on the upper-story floors is essential if you plan to occupy them. Otherwise, once the enemy gets a foothold on the ground floor he can fire machine guns straight through the ceiling and kill you from there. (Nail shut and barricade) all doorways: block them up and knock mouse holes through the walls instead. The attackers will be confused and will waste time trying to get to grips with the maze you have created. . . . Leave the water on and fill every container you can find with water. You will (a) need to drink and (b) put out fires. . . . Mini-pillboxes inside rooms help protect you from bits of ceiling falling on top of you . . . strip the plaster from the ceiling so it doesn't descend on your head during the battle. You can use the bits to help pack out the sandbags. The enemy will direct heavy fire at the building, trying to suppress your fire by sheer weight of bullets. Don't take up fire positions at the windows, where the heaviest fire is likely to be received. Take cover behind something very solid — a rubble-filled chest of drawers for instance . . . . Knock the glass out of the windows to avoid a shower of glass once the battle starts. . . use chicken wire (to) stop grenades from being thrown inside. For a final touch, saw through the floorboards in front of the upper floor windows so that enemy troops breaking in find themselves playing a combat version of snakes and ladders."

— Peter McAleese, *McAleese's Fighting Manual* (pp. 116-120)

"JUST FOLLOWING ORDERS. . ."

"There is a powerful craving in most of us to see ourselves as instruments in the hands of others and thus free ourselves from the responsibility for acts which are prompted by our own questionable inclinations and impulses. Both the strong and the weak grasp at this alibi. The latter hide their malevolence under the virtue of obedience: they acted dishonorably because they had to obey orders. The strong, too, claim absolution by proclaiming themselves the chosen instrument of a higher power — God, history, fate, nation, or humanity."

— Bruce Lee, *Striking Thoughts* (p. 174)

"REHABILITATION" THROUGH ASSEMBLY WORK & BUGGERY???:

"Prison inmates are being utilized by corporate interests as a source of slave labor. It is not unheard of for certain privatized institutions to work inmates 10-14 hours a day, six days a week, usually at mind-numbing tasks involving repetitive motion. The average 'wage' for this work is about .15 cents per hour, which is credited to their 'inmate account' — and inmates are then expected to use their wages to purchase overpriced soap, toothpaste, and various essential items from the prison commissary. Work assignments are mandatory. Refusal to work is considered a punishable disciplinary offense, which can result in: loss of 'good time,' restrictions on commissary and recreational privileges, loss of visitation and phone privileges, and even isolation in solitary confinement. In other words, they've really got you by the balls.

Slave labor in a privatized corporate correctional facility may be bad, but at least these contemporary workhouses tend to be far safer than the average state-run penal institution. In those hellish cesspools of violence and despair, no attempt is even made to pretend that the tortured creatures incarcerated within are being rehabilitated in any way — no, they are simply warehoused, insulted, abused, threatened, and malnourished until such time that they are finally released back into society (usually in a damaged, diseased, weakened, maladapted, and easily recognizable state) for a few months until they either self-destruct or are arrested for committing another crime. In these concrete death camps, it has been discovered that humiliation through repeated anal rape is unexcelled at breaking the spirit of potentially troublesome inmates; hence, little or no attempt is made to prevent it in a number of state-run facilities. Gang rape is often used to put newly arrived inmates 'in their place,' with the full knowledge and tacit approval of staff and corrections officers. Inmates demoralized in such a fashion are far less likely to: organize, protest, litigate, refuse work assignments, or be insubordinate to guards and staff.

— anonymous (RWT)

EXCERPT FROM A DRUNKEN SOLILOQUY:

". . . and most importantly you need to take a long hard look at the laws you're sworn to enforce, and decide which ones might be a bit unethical to prosecute so zealously. I mean, if someone's beating up old ladies or fucking little kids, that's a fuckin' lowlife piece of shit right there who oughta be provoked into resisting arrest, and if there happens to be a knife at the scene with the scumbag's prints on it, then you've just performed a valuable community service, but if some guy wants to smoke a little reefer in the privacy of his own home, or if some law-abiding young lady carries an unlicensed derringer in her purse so she won't be mugged or raped so easily, then who gives a shit? They ain't hurtin' nobody, so why the fuck does the commie government want you to arrest them so bad? I'll tell you why — the scum in power have plans for this country, and for their plans to become reality they need a population of unarmed, apathetic, helpless, docile sheep. They've been working feverishly towards this evil goal for generations, turning rights into 'privileges' which can be revoked at a bureaucrat's whim, and force-feeding our children lies and half-truths in their schools and through their TV stations, so as to condition them to 'behave properly,' which means: trusting those in power, thinking wrong is right, and being good little robots who do what they're told. Conform or be punished! Be subservient to your Masters! That's what children are being taught in school today! All drugs are bad, you can't smoke or drink, if you're promiscuous you'll catch AIDs and die, only crazy people think they should own guns, and if your parents are breaking the law you should tell the nice policeman who only wants to help them — what a sick, perverted, twisted philosophy they want the next generation to embrace! Why punish good people for victimless crimes? Because they are being willful; they refuse to blindly obey; and must be punished for their small act of defiance. And they're so damn smug that they've gotten sloppy — it's easy to see the corruption, the hypocrisy of the politicians' One Way Law, how if you've got money and connections you just get a slap on the wrist, but if you're an average Joe it's off to the dungeons with ye! Shit, we haven't had true freedom in this country for over a century now, and with the advances in computer technology things have gotten a lot worse."

— Hanse Fletcher

"EIGHT IDEAL CONDITIONS FOR THE FLOWERING OF AUTOCRACY":

"1) Eliminate personal knowledge. Make it hard for people to know about themselves, how they function, what a human being is, or how a human fits into wider, natural systems. This will make it impossible for the human to separate natural from artificial, real from unreal. You provide the answers to all questions.

2) Eliminate points of comparison. Comparisons can be found in earlier societies, older language forms and cultural artifacts, including print media. Eliminate or museumize indigenous cultures, wilderness and nonhuman life forms. Re-create internal human experience — instincts, thoughts, and spontaneous, varied feelings — so that it will not evoke the past.

3) Separate people from each other. Reduce interpersonal communication through life-styles that emphasize separateness. When people gather together, be sure it is for a prearranged experience that occupies all their attention at once. Spectator sports are excellent, so are circuses, elections, and any spectacles in which focus is outward and interpersonal exchange is subordinated to mass experience.

4) Unify experience, especially encouraging mental experience at the expense of sensory experience. Separate people's minds from their bodies, as in sense-deprivation experiments, thus clearing the mental channel for implantation. Idealize the mind. Sensory experience cannot be eliminated totally, so it should be driven into narrow areas. An emphasis on sex as opposed to sense may be useful because it is powerful enough to pass for the whole thing and it has a placebo effect.

5) Occupy the mind. Once people are isolated in their minds, fill the brain with prearranged experience and thought. Content is less important than the fact of the mind being filled. Free-roaming thought is to be discouraged at all costs, because it is difficult to control.

6) Encourage drug use. Recognize that total repression is impossible and so expressions of revolt must be contained on the personal level. Drugs will fill in the cracks of dissatisfaction, making people unresponsive to organized expressions of resistance.

7) Centralize knowledge and information. Having isolated people from each other and minds from bodies; eliminated points of comparison; discouraged sensory experience; and invented technologies to unify and control experience, speak. At this point whatever comes from outside will enter directly into all brains at the same time with great power and believability.

8) Redefine happiness and the meaning of life in terms of new and increasingly uprooted philosophy. Once you've established the prior seven conditions, this one is easy. Anything makes sense in a void. All channels are open, receptive and unquestioning. Formal mind structuring is simple. Most important, avoid naturalistic philosophies, they lead to uncontrollable awareness. The least resistible philosophies are the most arbitrary ones, those that make sense only in terms of themselves."

— Jerry Mander, *Four Arguments for the Elimination of Television* (pp. 97-99)

ILLUMINATION:

"Liberate yourself from concepts and see the truth with your own eyes. It exists HERE and NOW; it requires only one thing to see it: openness, freedom — the freedom to be open and not tethered by any ideas, concepts, etc., until we are blue in the face; all this will not be of the slightest avail — it is only when we stop thinking and let go that we can start seeing, discovering. When our mind is tranquil, there will be an occasional pause to its feverish activities, there will be a let-go, and it is only then in the interval between two thoughts that a flash of UNDERSTANDING — understanding, which is not thought — can take place."

— Bruce Lee, *Striking Thoughts* (p. 43)

STATE OF GRACE:

"The most beautiful emotion we can experience is the mystical. It is the power of all true art and science. He to whom this emotion is a stranger, who can no longer wonder and stand rapt in awe, is as good as dead. To know that what is impenetrable to us really exists, manifesting itself as the highest wisdom and the most radiant beauty, which our dull faculties can comprehend only in their most primitive forms — this knowledge, this feeling, is at the center of true religiousness. In this sense, and in this sense only, I belong to the rank of devoutly religious men."

— Albert Einstein

THE "GREEN & WHITE" PHILOSOPHY:

"Green is the color of life, peace, and abundance. Life is precious; life is temporary; life is an illusion. Peace gives one opportunity to enjoy life to its fullest. Abundance is a gift from the gods, something intended to be shared with others. Striving for abundance as an end in itself leads only to greed, envy, and dissatisfaction.

White is the color of death, truth, and purity. Death comes to us all; death is not to be feared; death is simply a transition to something greater. If you have 'cheated death' more than once, you can consider yourself to be living on 'borrowed time' — this can be a very liberating experience. Knowing death can come at any time, live every moment as if it were your last. Truth is what it is — to go against truth is to reject honor and embrace cowardice, deceit, and injustice. Purity is perfection in action and intent — lead by example."

— Scribe 27 (RWT)

"THE WAY"

"You can be whatever you want to be. If you hate yourself/your life, you have the capabilities within yourself to rebuild your image to whatever it is you aspire to be. Everyone has a great deal of energy/power locked within them — they just have to learn how to reach it, identify it, use it, mold it, and channel it. Everything you do in life comes back around to you. If you do evil to another, it will come back, somewhere, sometime, thrice as bad. Your mind is everything. Take nothing too seriously, as taking things too seriously promotes homicidal rage and suicidal depression. You control your mind. Your mind controls your body. Body language is important. No-one can hurt or imprison your mind — that is something you will always possess, and no-one can take it away from you. Blind faith is wrong. Believe nothing & trust no-one by reason of words alone. Beware the salesman!!! Beware the preacher, the politician, the judge, the policeman, and most of all the demon T.V.! Believe in yourself. Keep your dignity and honor always. Help those in need, when possible (and when you are not harming yourself by doing so). Don't permit anyone to take advantage of you or step on your toes — but if it does happen, remember the circumstances always so that it will not happen again. Misfortunes can be good if they are taken as a learning experience. 'That which does not kill one makes one stronger.' Bring malicious discomfort to no-one. When in doubt, keep your mouth shut. Lots of people say things for their own benefit — to make themselves look better, or to gain unearned respect. Everybody lies. Everybody has weaknesses. A lot of peoples' minds work differently from your own. The majority of the masses are ignorant, naive, and easily influenced by others. Always be cautious. Always be prepared. Look out for yourself and your brethren. It is possible to block out pain, self-destructive emotions, addictive behaviors, bad habits, and even disease. Endurance is more important than strength. Always think an important situation through —

look at all the alternatives and consequences. Your world is what you make it. Take advantage of opportunity. Laziness kills. Knowledge is power. Never mix love & hate. You control your life. Be what you want to be."

— Spider 1%er (from prison)

The Protection Dog

Disclaimer:

The author makes no claim of being an expert dog handler, and is not a certified trainer. This information has been made available for research and reference purposes only. Neither the author, nor the publisher, shall be held accountable for injuries resulting from use, or misuse, of the information herein. The author's intent is simply to educate inexperienced owners of protection dogs, who might wrongfully abuse their animals or needlessly have them euthanized.

> *" 'Tis sweet to hear the watch-dog's honest bark*
>
> *Bay deep-mouth'd welcome as we draw near home;*
>
> *'Tis sweet to know there is an eye will mark*
>
> *Our coming, and look brighter when we come."*
>
> — Byron, *Don Juan*, 1

Contents

Introduction

This information has been compiled because I feel it is important to clarify certain points. Too many misconceptions exist regarding the selection, training, and function of protection dogs. I will not delve into the specifics of training, as that could encompass several volumes and is beyond the scope of this project, though several excellent books on the subject will be recommended. This section will be kept as brief as possible.

First, a protection dog is not the same as an attack dog, sentry dog, or guard dog. Attack dogs are trained to attack individual targets on command, or to track individuals by scent and attack them upon discovery — they are highly trained service animals commonly employed by various law enforcement agencies, and often are seen attached to extremely long (50'+) leads. Sentry dogs accompany handlers, both on perimeter and long range patrols. Their superior hearing enables them to alert to hidden threats, such as ambushes. They have a moderate amount of training and are most often employed by the military and private security interests — they are usually seen attached to a lead of average length. Guard dogs regularly patrol the interior of a building, or fenced perimeter, and are highly motivated to maim or kill unauthorized intruders. They are usually motivated through severe abuse and neglect, and are commonly used by drug dealers, gang members, and militant extremists. On the instances that a lead is used, it is usually just a length of heavy chain. The protection dog, however, is simply a pet dog (of a suitable breed) with strong protective instincts which have been safely controlled through proper bonding and obedience training. The protection dog's abilities and reliability will vary according to the extent of his training, as well as more subtle factors.

A protection dog's primary function is to serve as a deterrent. Aside from the dog's presence being intimidating to the typical miscreant, the dog can also be depended upon to sound an alarm in the event of an attempted break-in as well as physically protect you from an unprepared attacker; however, a protection dog is not a panacea. . . if an intruder were armed with a gun or large knife and was not hesitant about using it, a single dog lacking professional level attack training wouldn't realistically stand much of a chance (and if you were being stalked by a highly motivated enemy who had prior knowledge of your dog, you wouldn't even be able to count on the dog to sound an alarm for you). When not performing his duties, the dog can provide comfort as well as entertainment for you and your family. A well trained and socialized dog is a pleasure to have around. Conversely, an untrained dog is unpredictable and is certain to cause you embarrassment and distress. Proper training is necessary for a dog that will be spending much of its time around people. If he (or she) is going to be treated as one of the family, it is reasonable that certain instinctual behaviors should be strongly discouraged.

Many people feel that a dog will provide them with a sense of security, especially if they obtain a large dog of a breed known to have strong protective drives. This is often true, provided the animal is not neglected, abused, or otherwise mistreated. A dog that loves you does so unconditionally, and his loyalty to you will never waver; due to this loyalty (combined with his natural protective drives), your dog will instantly defend you from any perceived physical threat. If a high level of bonding exists, many dogs will heroically sacrifice themselves in order to protect a family member from harm. Even an untrained family pet that is gentle with children and other animals will spring to attack anyone that dares to menace a "pack member" in his presence. Varying on the size and temperament of the animal, such intervention can range from simple growling and snapping, to "grabbing" and holding a limb in the mouth,, to actual mauling. Although this initially seems to be a desirable trait, some dogs will unexpectedly attack in the event of sudden movement, raised voices, or even a sneeze, and will often feel compelled to intervene in family arguments (a trained dog may alert when encountering the aforementioned stimuli, but will exercise restraint). Your dog needs to be taught, in no uncertain terms, what constitutes unacceptable "protective" behavior. Thousands of dogs are put down each year by intimidated owners unable to suppress their pet's instinctual protective drives in inappropriate situations.

The protection breeds have strong "prey" drives, which compel them to pursue and intercept persons rushing past them. The prey drive, combined with the protective instincts for which they have been bred, virtually guarantee that their owners will be "attacked" at least several times in the first year, until these natural behaviors have been effectively suppressed through training and conditioning. When a dog "attacks" a fellow pack member (or owner), there will be a ferocious display of lunging, barking, and snapping teeth — you may even be bitten — but this is more showmanship than combat. It can be somewhat disconcerting to have a 140 pound snarling beast come flying at you with jaws agape, but unless the animal has been neglected, abused, or is suffering from some sort of congenital brain ailment, it probably will not hurt you. The dog might latch onto your arm, but it is highly unlikely that he will even break the skin, although he has the capability to easily pulverize your bones. The dog is not "out of control". . . it is simply testing you to "find his place" in the hierarchy of your "pack." So many dogs are needlessly killed simply due to a mere a failure to communicate. In their ignorance, the owners fail to realize that their dog's respect must be earned through displaying the appropriate dominant behavior. If, however, your dog likes to bite faces or genitals, it may very well need to be destroyed for the greater good. Your dominant behavior must be backed up by the ability to immediately apply the proper level of "correction." The subject of corrections will be addressed later.

Obtaining Your Dog

After you have decided to obtain a dog, you must then decide upon which breed best suits your particular needs. While many excellent "mixed-breed" dogs exist, they more often either prove troublesome, or turn out to be derived from stock other than what had been specified. With purebreds you usually have a good indication of how large your dog will grow and what his temperament will be like. I am reluctant to recommend or disparage various breeds, as peoples' opinions and requirements vary greatly. The only advice I will give about breed selection follows: A person should never select a dog beyond their capabilities to control — either physically or psychologically. For example, even though the Rottweiler is a highly intelligent and friendly breed (they excel as therapy dogs), they are powerful and stubborn, so they would be a poor choice for someone who is frail or weak; conversely, the Doberman Pinscher is a relatively compact and lightweight breed, yet they are too high strung and energetic for someone who is timid or slow. Exotic protection breeds (such as the Fila Brasileiro, Presa Canario, and Timbershepherd) should be left to the experts, as their temperament and strength require a master dog handler to control. Long-haired breeds are often miserable in hot climates, as short-haired breeds tend to be intolerant of frigid weather. If the dog will often be restricted to the confines of a studio apartment, a smaller breed would be best. Always research the characteristics of a breed you are considering . . . what you learn may surprise you.

Often, upon deciding that a dog of one particular breed is desired, such a dog is obtained when the opportunity first presents itself. Usually, little consideration is given to the breeder's reputation or credentials, and often the result is an inferior dog which might be diseased, infested with parasites, or have a genetic defect (either physical or psychological) which may not manifest for months or even years. Many people do not realize that not all dogs of a particular breed are created equal; indeed, there are often great disparities in size, health, and temperament amongst the puppies from any given litter. . . if you do not know what to look for, you might regret your decision as the dog matures.

If you feel the need to obtain a dog, it is imperative that the dog be obtained from a reputable breeder who loves his animals, has given them their shots and found them to be free of worms, can provide you with their medical records and AKC registration forms, and is willing to guarantee them against defects (such as hip dysplasia or serious illness due to a pre-existing condition). The proliferation of "backyard breeders" and "puppy mills" has had a substantial negative impact on many of the more popular breeds, so it is important to be selective. You do not want to get your dog from a shelter, a newspaper ad, or a shopping mall pet store. Optimally, you should get a puppy between 8 and 12 weeks old. Any earlier than 8 weeks, and the dog will lack the stability of being fully socialized with its mother and littermates; any later than 12 weeks, and you will have missed the critical bonding period. During the first few days of the bonding period you should spend at least six hours each day in close contact with the puppy, and should avoid any sort of formal training. If possible, your puppy should spend the first week sleeping in your room, even if he must sleep in a crate. The puppy will probably want to lick your face often (which can be messy, as well as annoying at times), and it is imperative that this instinctive behavior be encouraged during the critical bonding period — if you yell and push him away, he will become confused and alienated — he truly needs to lick your face in order to feel accepted and secure. If you get two or more dogs from the same litter, they may bond more closely with one another than with you (which would be counter-productive to training, as well as your relationship with them). Never buy a dog impulsively — you will need to live with your decision for the next 8 - 15 years (estimated lifespan).

Before bringing a puppy into your home, it must be thoroughly "puppy-proofed." Puppies, especially those of the protection breeds, will chew on anything, and it is likely that, in the beginning (before he learns the error of his ways), footwear and wood furnishings will be damaged due to gnawing — this is to be expected. Protection dogs are very "mouth-orientated," and will tend to "grab" at one's hand often (until taught otherwise), usually without even dimpling the skin. . .this is more an act of communication than of aggression, although it can prove quite disconcerting to some people. Live electrical cords, cleaning products, and small glass bottles (such as perfume and nail polish) must be inaccessible, as they could conceivably kill a puppy if chewed. Wastebaskets must be placed out of reach, and garbage receptacles should be secured, as the various aromas will tempt curious puppies. Certain medications, such as ibuprofen, are deadly to dogs, and things like Tylenol, chocolate, and many common houseplants are toxic, as is spoiled meat and fermenting garbage, and precautions must be taken that the puppy will never have access to them. In addition to keeping your house neat and uncluttered for the safety of your puppy, it will now become necessary to sweep and vacuum on a near-daily basis in order to control the amount of ever-accumulating dog hair and cookie crumbs. Your dog should be brushed several times each week to limit shedding, and, if practical, should be bathed weekly. Odor neutralizer and carpet freshener should be applied regularly if you want your abode to be presentable for company. If you do lack the time or motivation to constantly keep up with the housework, you should not have a dog. Few things can trash the average house quicker than indoor pets.

Hundreds of different sorts of "dog toy" are available from a variety of sources, but many are inappropriate. Many toys intended for smaller dogs are quickly shredded by the powerful protection breeds. Toys must be durable and safe. Rawhide chew toys must be avoided, as they can result in asphyxiation or a blockage of the intestine (and they quickly become slimy and smelly). Bones should also be avoided, as they can break teeth or splinter. The "Nylabones" hold up for a while, but must be discarded once excessive wear is apparent. Edible bones made from foods like carrot and peanut are available, but often last for only a few minutes. The heavy duty "Kong" toys are excellent, as they are virtually indestructible and can be filled with peanut butter to initially attract the dog's interest. Other dog toys should be played with only under close supervision, as the protection breeds can destroy nearly anything, given enough time.

Responsibilities

The decision to get a dog should not be taken lightly. Do not get a dog unless you are willing to spend time every day walking it, feeding it, grooming it, and playing with it. Furthermore, you will need to spend time training it and having it seen regularly by a veterinarian. If you cannot attend to your animal's basic needs, you will be neglecting it, which is tantamount to abuse. Your dog is a social animal, and needs to be fully integrated into your family, which he perceives as his pack. He needs to not only know his place in the hierarchy, but must feel accepted and loved as well. If you isolate your dog from human contact by chaining him outdoors or confining him to a pen or "crate" for the majority of the time, the animal will develop neuroses and may become frustrated, overly aggressive, and uncontrollable. Your dog is your friend and must be treated with respect. Few things make me angrier than people who obtain more dogs than they can properly care for and end up neglecting the lot.

Your dog should be allowed in the house regularly and should not be allowed to roam the neighborhood unattended. Not only is a free running dog a potential menace, but he is at risk of being hit by a car, attacked by another animal, shot, poisoned, or otherwise hurt via a myriad of possibilities. If your dog is confined to your house or yard, he has a reasonable expectancy of safety. Your dog should always be on a leash when outdoors unless you're training in a fenced-in area. "Invisible Fencing" (consisting of an underground wire boundary used in conjunction with a shock collar) is be a good investment, but it may malfunction (due to electrical problems, blackouts, broken connections, or weak batteries) and cannot guarantee that a powerful animal will remain within its borders in the presence of overwhelming temptation (ideally, a dog must be conditioned to being shocked as he approaches a clearly marked border while still an impressionable pup). After he has proven himself able to consistently obey commands in the presence of attractive distractions (squirrels, other dogs, cars, etc.) you can work with him off his leash with a reasonable expectation of safety. Your dog, especially if he is one of the protection breeds, should never be allowed off his leash while in public (both to protect yourself from liability as well as to protect your animal from being shot by a frightened or surly gunowner).

Dogs have certain abilities which enable them to excel as sentries, as well as in other capacities. The dog's olfactory sense is developed to an incredibly high degree which borders on the supernatural. Using their sense of smell, they can track an individual for miles, alert on minuscule traces of a substance that had been sealed up and masked with distracting scents, and retrieve a specific stone that had been briefly handled before being tossed far into a hayfield (I have even heard of cases where stones were retrieved from underwater). Dogs rely primarily upon their sense of smell, and constantly pick up "scent pictures" of their environment. A dog's hearing is far more acute than that of a human, being able to hear noises far beyond our range of capabilities. Dogs can sense emotions, and can easily pick up on deception or malice. Dogs who have a strong bond with their owners have been proven to develop a kind of psionic link, something which scientists acknowledge but cannot fully understand. However, a dog has poor eyesight. Although they have good night vision and can discern subtle movements, they cannot distinguish colors or recognize individuals approaching from a distance. Although it can be done, it is not easy to sneak up on or trick a dog. They are hypervigilant and are not stupid. A trained protection dog is a valuable asset.

Your dog needs to be fed and watered daily. A dog must have access to fresh water at all times. Water dishes should be dumped out and replenished at least twice daily to prevent contamination or buildup of bacteria. Do not allow your dog's water supply to be depleted on hot days. If your dog becomes overheated and dehydrated, his condition will rapidly deteriorate. Automatic water dispensers can attract a variety of molds and bacterium, so they should only be used when absolutely necessary.

The larger protection breeds should be fed twice daily at regular times (feeding a single large meal each day can cause bloat, which can result in life-threatening stomach torsion). Take care not to overfeed, and do not use kibble dispensers that allow the dog to feed whenever he wishes. Experiment with a variety of foods to see which one he favors the best. If the breeder has been feeding him a specific type of food, you can either continue with that diet or slowly add increasing portions of a new type until he has become accustomed to it. Many dogs have sensitive stomachs, and foods which irritate it will cause vomiting and diarrhea. Be aware that some dogs will steadfastly refuse certain types of food, preferring to go without eating for days, if necessary. Find a nutritious food that is agreeable to your dog, and feel free to mix in leftovers and table scraps (taking care to sort out items that could cause illness or indigestion).

One subject that is seldom discussed is the matter of proper nutrition. Most people, including many trainers and breeders, are surprisingly ignorant on this topic. Commercial dog food is usually provided because it is both economical and convenient. The truth is that most commercial dry food is inadequate for the dog's dietary needs, and many canned foods are actually toxic. There are few regulations concerning what may be put in dog food, and these are seldom enforced. As a result, diseased and dying livestock unfit for human consumption are processed along with euthanized dogs and cats. Rancid meat is often used, and the "meat" is usually contaminated with animal feces. Cancerous tumors are included along with the heads, lungs, feathers, and other offal that are ground into processed dog food. A variety of harmful chemicals (pesticides, antibiotics, growth hormones, vaccines, euthanasia depressants, as well as toxic solvents used in the rendering process) are present as well. Instead of feeding your dog garbage that will weaken him and make him ill, you should take the time to prepare a decent meal for your friend.

Ground beef or turkey can be boiled in the tube or fried on a skillet; beef heart can be boiled and cut up; chicken drumsticks can be boiled or roasted, then deboned; or a cheap cut of steak, such as chuck, can be seared on either side and cut into bite sized cubes. Liver and kidneys should be used only occasionally, if at all, and bulk packaged chicken organs (gizzards & liver) should be avoided altogether. Organs which appear jaundiced or unusually fatty were taken from a sick animal. Be sure to inspect meat for discoloration or odor prior to use. If it is too much trouble to cook for your dog every day, several days worth of meat can be cooked at one time and stored in the refrigerator until ready to be used. Boiled pasta, rice, or several cut up slices of whole grain bread, can be added to each serving of meat — along with a tablespoon of flax oil, a half-teaspoon of minced garlic, and a capful of apple cider vinegar. Brewer's yeast, vitamin powder, or Bragg's liquid aminos can also be added, making supplement tablets (and the unpleasant task of forcing the dog to swallow them) unnecessary. Vegetables, shredded cheese, and cooked eggs can be added to the dog's diet for variety. Table scraps will not hurt a dog, as long as he is not given bones, chocolate, or an abundance of dairy products. A quality biscuit afterwards will help to clean his teeth. Meals supplemented with garlic, brewer's yeast, and apple cider vinegar will repel most parasites, internal as well as external (although the dog should still be tested for heartworm each spring). If you choose to utilize an inferior diet, the result will be an inferior animal.

Ground turkey is very inexpensive and can be stored in one's freezer indefinitely. A pair of frozen one pound tubes can be boiled for an hour, then set aside to cool. One pound can be immediately opened and chopped up into small pieces, then mixed with leftovers and supplements before being served as dinner. After your dog has finished, he should be fed a biscuit to help clean his teeth. The second pound can then be prepared in a similar manner before being stored in the refrigerator until morning. It is recommended that you purchase a set of elevated dishes (set into a plastic table-like structure), which are available at any pet store, as they have been proven to significantly improve digestion.

Training

Most people who own dogs do not bother to train them beyond the command "Sit" (which often must be repeated), and some people "train" their dogs improperly, often incorporating frequent severe beatings either to "put the dog in his place," or to "toughen him up." Your dog, especially if you intend for him to be an active participant in home security, must be able to reliably execute any one of a series of commands instantly, even when distractions or other stressors are present. He must also be willing to sacrifice his life in your defense. If you have been beating your dog rather than loving him, he is far more likely to flee upon being confronted with an overwhelming threat. A dog that loves you will die protecting you and your family. Steadfast loyalty combined with intelligence is far superior to mindless fear-induced aggression. A mean dog that you have only limited control over is more of a potential liability than an asset.

At the bare minimum, your dog should be trained to instantly execute the following commands:

No (the dog instantly stops whatever activity he is engaged in),

Off (the dog refrains from jumping up on a person, or vacates a piece of furniture),

Sit (the dog takes the "sit" position),

Down (the dog lies down),

Stay (the dog remains where he is until ordered to do otherwise),

Come (the dog comes to the handler), and, most importantly,

Give (the dog releases anything held in the mouth, whether it be toy, food, or miscreant.)

A dog that can perform all of the aforementioned commands, but none other, is still considered by many experts to be "untrained" (though much more of a pleasure to be around than a "wild" dog who'll snatch food off your plate and piss on the carpet). You may feel free to substitute other words for the aforementioned commands (shutzhund commands are given in German), unless restricted by the rules of standardized competition, but they must not vary in order to avoid confusing the dog. Additionally, there are over a half-dozen other commands that are commonly taught to show and working dogs, which you may choose to utilize (i.e.: retrieval commands, tricks, etc.).

You may note that I did not include "Heel," which is generally considered to be one of the most basic of all obedience commands (and is usually taught right after the dog has learned "Sit."). That is because, in my opinion, I do not feel it is terribly important that the dog always walk in step with the handler on his lefthand side whenever he is on the leash. Realistically, many owners who taught "heel" to their dogs as puppies stop using the command after a year or two, and most owners (who generally do not retain professional instruction) never had it taught at all. In fact, many owners prefer that their dog walk in front of them! Based on my own observations of hundreds of protection breed dogs, I estimate that more than half of all pet dogs (as opposed to show dogs) are unfamiliar with this command. I feel that "Heel" is unnecessary unless you plan to enter your dog in competition, or regularly walk him through large crowds of people. Through light manipulation of the lead, a well-trained dog will move in any direction you wish, as well as slow down, speed up, or sit.

I did not include any "Attack" type commands because a dog must first show utter reliability and obedience by successful completion of an Advanced Obedience program before being trained to bite on command. If you have a large, aggressive, bite-trained dog, you want to be confident that you have 98% control over that animal at all times (100% is an unrealistic figure, as statistics have shown). Advanced Obedience programs include variations on the aforementioned commands, additional commands, hand signals, and extensive leash work (hand signals are actually fairly simple to teach — each time a verbal command is given, simply add a corresponding hand signal, and soon you'll find that the verbal commands are no longer necessary). Shutzhund training (which incorporates obedience, tracking, and protection) is often recommended, but just as many people advise against it due to the enormous amount of time that must be devoted to training. Shutzhund is more like an Olympic event (which must be constantly trained for) than a "class" one takes a dog to in order to train it to bite people. . . for some reason, many people fail to grasp this.

Be advised: A novice handler has no business attempting to attack train a dog! It is a complicated and dangerous process, and if you make a mistake your animal can be psychologically ruined. If, however, you've read a couple of books and are intending to have a go at it anyway, there are three important rules which must always be followed:

1.) Expect to spend about a thousand dollars on equipment, including protective coveralls and a "hard sleeve" with covers. Never attempt bite training without the proper equipment! Homemade protective gear just won't do it.

2.) Your "agitator" must be a stranger to the dog — never use friends or family members, as the dog will always remember him as a "bad guy." Your agitator must be: experienced, trustworthy, sober, and old enough to sign a binding legal contract preventing you from getting sued for any injuries received.

3.) Never slap or roughhouse with your dog, and never play the part of an agitator! Your dog must never be allowed to think that biting you is acceptable!

A few additional commands (and other words) which might prove useful include:

Back (the dog takes several steps back),

Out (the dog leaves the room),

Hup (the dog jumps into a vehicle, or onto a piece of furniture),

Go See. . . (the dog goes to whomever was named),

Get. . . (the dog retrieves whatever was named),

Okay (a "release" word, used to let a dog know he is freed from a previous "Stay"),

Be Nice (a calming phrase which tells the dog not to harass a certain individual),

Kiss (the dog gives you, or someone else, a kiss),

Naughty (a verbal correction, commonly used for minor lapses of decorum),

Bad! (a verbal correction, rarely used for major offenses).

Many dogs are capable of learning a vocabulary well in excess of a hundred words, including names of people, places, objects, toys, and activities (i.e. "Go Upstairs and Get your Ball"). Commands may also be used in combinations (i.e. "Back, Sit, Stay" would effectively prevent your dog from "greeting" you at the door by immediately jumping up and giving kisses).

A command should only be given once, with immediate execution of said command being the expected response. If you need to repeat the command several times, entice the dog with a treat, or threaten the dog with a physical correction before the command is executed, this means that you have a willful animal that knows the command but is deliberately ignoring you. This is very common among poorly trained dogs owned by lackadaisical or overly tolerant masters. The dog is most likely ignoring the commands because of an inflated ego (dominance) combined with the confidence that he will be allowed to misbehave without fear of punishment. It may sound cruel to some people, but a protection dog must not be allowed to blatantly disregard a valid command from his master. A command needs to be given once, and only once. If the immediate execution of a command is delayed or postponed, a correction must be applied. The subject of corrections will be addressed in detail later.

The time you spend training your dog should be thought of as "working;" it is essential that this work be taken seriously, which means there is zero tolerance for nonsense or disobedience. Working is a serious matter, especially with a protection dog, which can prove to be a significant liability if control is not maintained. Working is also an important opportunity for bonding. . . not only is it typically enjoyable for the dog to be praised after correct execution of a series of commands, but such training firmly reinforces your positions in the pack (you command and he obeys). While working your dog, things like dark glasses or cigarette smoke can easily form a distractive barrier between you, and should be avoided for best results. When you are working your animal, he should be functioning with a high level of precision — anything less is to be considered unsatisfactory. However, training is not all-important, especially in the opinion of the dog. . . if an equal amount of time is not allowed for playtime, the dog will become bored, frustrated, and demoralized, which will surely result in poor work performance. Playtime must be kept separate from worktime, and is generally takes place immediately following a session as a reward for work well done. "Downtime" is separate from playtime, and is when the dog is expected to relax in the company of his people without constant demands for attention (although attention may be freely given, if appropriate). A dog should never be worked or played with in the hour following a meal.

Most of the protection breeds (particularly the Rottweiler, German Shepherd, and Doberman Pinscher) are highly intelligent and capable of understanding a vocabulary of well over a hundred words. In addition to an extensive array of command words, the names of various objects and places can also be learned. When you are spending time with your dog outside of training, feel free to speak to him. He may not understand many of the words, but he will understand your tone and will appreciate the attention. Such intimacy is necessary for proper bonding. However well a dog may appear to be trained, it lacks the ability to reason. Its thought processes consist primarily of instinctual drives (which often must be suppressed through training) and conditioned responses to commands. Remember, even a trained dog may react violently to sudden movements or perceived aggression. Although a dog can exhibit the qualities of loyalty and affection, may possess a remarkable memory, is capable of traversing difficult obstacles without guidance, and may show evidence of having vivid dreams, it cannot think as we do.

When leash training your dog, especially if he is of a larger breed, it may be necessary to use a training collar. Never use a "choke collar," as they can easily do irreparable damage to your dog's windpipe. They can also make a dog panic, which is counter-productive to training. A "prong" or "pinch" collar is both much safer and more effective, although it has a misleadingly wicked appearance. If you were to experiment by placing a choke collar around one of your legs, and a pinch collar around the other, then yanking forcefully on both, you would quickly come to appreciate the significant difference between what is a humane training aid and what is little more than a chain garrotte. The pinch collar consists of interlocking segments, which can be removed to achieve the proper fit — a loose fit can cause the collar to be ineffective or even separate. After the dog accepts the leash, the training collar will no longer be as necessary and can be replaced with either a standard collar or a harness. The leash you choose should be cotton, soft leather or braided nylon and no longer than 6'. Avoid chain or flat nylon leads, as they can easily injure your hand if the dog lunges or pulls forcefully.

Be aware that a large protection dog will barely notice the prongs of a training collar pinching his skin if he is determined to go in a certain direction, and he can easily pull you off balance if he unexpectedly lunges (or attempts to take off running). Never slip the leash's loop over your wrist and allow the dog a great deal of slack — that's just asking to have your arm pulled out of its socket. Instead, slip the loop over your thumb before grasping the loop firmly — this will enable you to keep a secure grip on the lead, while still allowing you to release it in an emergency (simply by opening your hand). If the dog is excited about something, you can take up excess slack by doubling the lead over before grasping it — this will enable you to keep the animal under control while also allowing you to let out slack by slightly loosening your grip. If the dog begins pulling hard, simply bend your knees to lower your center of gravity. If you're trying to restrain a monster Rottweiler that weighs more than you do, you may need to bend your knees even deeper, leaning back and digging your heels in while pulling the lead with both hands (even to the point that you're nearly seated on the ground). As long as the lead has been grasped correctly (and one's center of gravity has been lowered sufficiently), a 100 pound woman could utilize this technique to hold back "Cujo."

Corrections

Corrections should only be applied in the event of willful disobedience or open defiance. Contrary to what many trainers recommend, physical corrections (aside from the standard "leash pop") should only rarely be applied, and never with an object (rolled up newspapers are frequently recommended, but in practice many trainers use rubber hoses, flexible truncheons, or even riding crops, often favoring the muzzle as a target — which can take out an eye with an inaccurate blow). Shock collars should never be used as a training aid (they tend to induce neuroses) unless nothing else seems to work (after repeated attempts by yourself as well as a professional trainer) or you are engaged in specialized training (such as "poison-proofing"). Various ultrasonic training aids are available (from dog whistles to electronic devices), but mixed results have been reported. 90% of your corrections should be verbal, employing a displeased tone and possibly a specific gesture. You should take a dominant stance (but don't lean over the dog) and feel free to growl if necessary to get your point across. . . dogs understand growling. However, you should avoid yelling at your dog, as they perceive this as barking and may become defensive. Never yell at a barking dog!

Corrections should never be applied to an animal who is confused or who is trying his best to comply, nor should they be applied to an animal who might be ill or injured. A puppy should never be subject to physical corrections until after he is at least 5 months old. Puppy corrections should entail "startling" to interrupt unwanted behavior. Startling can take the form of clapping one's hands together, a squirt from a water pistol, or for serious infractions, shaking the puppy and growling.

Today, many trainers have written books advocating that any force beyond popping the leash to momentarily tighten the training collar is both unnecessary and horribly abusive. With lapdogs this may be true, but with a powerful and stoic protection dog, a simple snap of the lead often goes unnoticed. Indeed, a Rottweiler or Mastiff is fully capable of completely ignoring repeated hard yanks if they decide they'd rather go in a different direction. The protection breeds typically are stubborn and very pushy, and they will attempt to dominate anyone they perceive as weaker than themselves — including their owner, if permitted to do so. Forceful corrections will prevent this from happening, and will ensure that the dog will respect your commands (which should only be given once).

Excessive corrections must be avoided, as they can result in a fearful submissive animal, which is the opposite of what you want. Physical corrections are only to be used when verbal corrections are insufficient, and only as much force as is necessary to get your point across should be used. If you feel the need to strike your dog, a single swat to the hindquarters with the flat of your hand should be sufficient. The correction is meant to startle, shame, or assert dominance, and is not intended to result in pain and fear (which often proves counter-productive). Never kick your dog, strike it full force, strike it repeatedly, or use an object to strike it with — even a rolled up newspaper. If you are physically capable, immobilizing or "pinning" your dog via grappling has far more psychological impact than a simple smack, and should be the physical correction of choice for serious infractions (be aware that if you challenge an aggressive dog in this manner, and don't know what you're doing, you could easily wind up having your face sewn back on).

To correct certain bad behaviors, such as jumping up or unwanted mouthing, a squirt of "naughty puppy spray" can be used. Naughty puppy spray is a 50/50 mix of water and apple cider vinegar that can be administered with either a spray bottle or a squirt gun, and is an effective correction if applied instantly (a minute or two later, the dog may have forgotten his action and fail to connect it with the correction). Other sprays (such as lemon juice, diluted "Bitter Apple," or Binaca breath spray) have been recommended by some trainers, but may cause undue irritation to the eyes and nose.

If a large dog exhibits aggressive behavior towards you, such as growling or snapping, it may be necessary to give him a snootful of pepperspray. It is only necessary to tap the button for a fraction of a second unless you truly feel you are in imminent danger of being eaten, as most aggressive behavior is primarily for show. Even though a large dog can easily crush your bones with his jaw pressure, this rarely occurs unless the animal is deranged. Some people may feel that such "cruel" treatment of a dog is unwarranted and may even constitute criminal abuse, but they are wrong. Professional trainers have often beaten dogs severely at the slightest hint of aggression, and thousands of dogs are euthanized each year for biting — next to a stomping or a bullet in the head, the temporary indignity of a stinging runny nose doesn't seem so bad anymore, does it? A powerful dog bred for aggression who believes himself to be dominant will eventually hurt someone, most likely resulting in a lawsuit and forcible destruction of the animal.

When working with a large aggressive dog easily capable of causing serious injury or death in the event of a moment's lost control (such as with a dog rescued from an abusive situation, a mentally unstable dog, or in the event a high-strung dog is suddenly stung by a hornet), it is necessary to have a cannister of pepperspray on your person in the event you need to protect yourself. If you intend to have pepperspray handy inside your dwelling, obtain Mace Pepperfoam, which will not atomize and make the room in question temporarily uninhabitable. A dog who is sprayed will immediately cease his actions, begin foaming copiously at the mouth, and may vomit, but the effects are only temporary and it is much more preferable than beating your dog (which may increase his aggression towards you) or putting him down. After being sprayed once, showed the cannister, and taught the word

"Spray," simply holding one's closed hand aloft and saying "Spray" should be enough of a correction to put an immediate stop to any further misbehavior. Pepperspray is invaluable for breaking up dogfights if there isn't a garden hose nearby . . . never attempt to separate fighting dogs manually!

In the event that you are bitten, do not yank your hand (or arm, leg, ect.) away. Although most protection breeds have the ability to easily crush bones, most bites result only in a few puncture wounds that are easily treated. If, however, you choose to suddenly pull away, a relatively minor wound can be turned into a series of lacerations. If a dog does attack you, immobilize its head and pin it until it calms down or help arrives. Never attempt to flee from an attacking dog — you won't get far. In order to avoid being attacked, never beat, injure, choke, or otherwise abuse your dog. The protection breeds are very dignified, and will deeply resent any mistreatment they perceive as unwarranted. Dogs have long memories, and a friend is far more loyal than a slave in a crisis situation.

Final Thoughts

Your dog should neither be thought of as property nor a mere servant to do your bidding. Your dog should be your friend as well as a part of your family. Mutual respect must exist for you to become properly bonded, and for the dog to reach its full potential. As a result of effort exerted and rapport established, each handler will end up with the dog that he or she deserves.

Once a dog has bonded with you, has learned not to engage in objectionable behavior, and has proven capable of being controlled by command words (even in the presence of distractions or while subject to stress); he can then be relied upon to look after your best interests while walking down the street with you, riding in your car, resting inside your home, or patrolling the fenced perimeter of your yard. A well trained dog is a valuable asset, and should be treated as such. Love your puppy, for you are the most important thing in his life.

Recommended Reading

By far, the finest dog training book I've ever seen is *Dog Logic* by Joel McMains, which focuses on rapport based training and is especially relevant to protection dogs. The "Ten Commandments" after the postscript is, in itself, worth the price of the book. . . this book is required reading for everyone, regardless of experience level.

If you are ignorant of the basics of dog care and handling, *The Complete Idiot's Guide to Choosing, Training, and Raising a Dog* by Sarah Hodgson is invaluable.

If you want to learn about attack training, *Manstopper!: Training a Canine Guardian* by Joel McMains is the best book available on the subject. McMains recommends *The Guard Dog* by Jerrold J. Mundis, but I have not yet seen a copy myself. *The Home & Family Protection Dog* by Duet & Duet gives details on responsible protection training methods, including bite training, although I strongly disagree with them on several key points.

Beyond Obedience by April Frost is an interesting book which delves into advanced bonding techniques that are best described as "mystical"— I cannot vouch for her credibility, but it is definitely worth a look if one is open-minded about such things.

When it comes to dog training, there are no experts whose methods will apply to every dog (or owner), so use discretion and apply only those techniques which seem to work best for you.

Important Tips

1.) Be friends with your dog. Make time to spend with him, include him in things (like roadtrips, picnics, and naptime), and look after his needs. A dog that is fearful and neglected will not be nearly as devoted.

2.) Make sure the dog will reliably respond to your commands. If a command is ignored, or is not immediately executed, verbal corrections (and other expressions of your displeasure) must be immediately applied. Never let a dog think that he can choose to disregard your commands without fear of reprisal.

3.) Expect to get bitten at least once — know in advance how you intend to deal with this eventuality. Be aware that running or shouting in the presence of many dogs can result in an attack.

4.) Never yell at a barking dog, and try to eliminate raising your voice altogether — simply alter the tone. Dogs have excellent hearing, but they will ignore you (if they think they can get away with it).

5.) Corrections must be applied immediately after an offense, and the dog needs to be made aware of what he did wrong. Further punishment through temporary isolation is effective at ensuring that the lesson has been learnt. Never correct a dog that is confused, ill, or injured; and ensure that all corrections are delivered fairly and properly. Do not apply (or increase the severity of) a correction simply because you are "having a bad day."

6.) If you feel that it is necessary to "put the dog in his place," do not attempt to do so by increasing the severity or duration of a physical correction! Isolation or withdrawal of affection/attention both work well as punishments for misbehavior, but for cases of willfulness or disobedience, one can simply put the dog through a series of specific commands (i.e.: "Sit — Down — Up — Back — Sit — Come — Down," etc.). Not only is this a constructive training exercise, but it will further assert your authority over the dog without resorting to solely punitive measures (which might prove counter-productive).

7.) Whether training or bonding, avoid wearing sunglasses, wearing strong cologne, or smoking in the presence of your dog — it is distracting. Furthermore be aware that dogs can readily pick up on strong emotions (particularly negative ones) and impaired states of consciousness (such as inebriation), and may react adversely.

8.) If your dog will be allowed on your sofa or bed, you will need to bathe him every other week, brush him twice weekly, and (distasteful as it may seem) wipe his bung after each bowel movement. . . you do not want malodorous "racing stripes" on the upholstery!

9.) Your protection dog should be properly socialized with guests, children, and other dogs — but take care not to oversocialize. If he is taught that everyone is his friend, and if you allow guests to give your dog both commands and tidbits, he will have difficulty adjusting to a crisis situation and could easily be compromised.

10.) Your beloved companion has a relatively short lifespan, and you need to face the eventuality that someday his time will come. You need to know, well in advance, how you intend to deal with the specific details of this. Make sure that his final days are comfortable, spend lots of extra time with him, and do not selfishly choose to extend his life if he is obviously suffering. After the necessary mourning period which follows, put his photographs and favorite toy in a safe place and think of him fondly. He will always be with you.

ADDENDUM:

1.) "PUPPY IN A BOX": Most of the books I've read instruct you to train your puppy to sleep in a plastic carrying case, oft referred to as a "crate." This defeats the purpose of having a protection dog on duty (although he still might be able to sound an alarm in the event of an attempted break-in), and many irresponsible scumbags tend to neglect their animals by keeping them crated most of the day, but under certain circumstances a crate might prove a sound investment. The crate is best utilized as a way to restrict the movements of your puppy, either as a form of punishment through isolation or as a means of preventing malicious damage through separation anxiety. The puppy will not want to go into the crate at first, but you must make it clear that he really has no other choice. Eventually, the puppy will learn that the crate isn't so bad (be sure to include a cookie as well as a chew-resistant toy), and will enter, on command, without argument. Eventually (hopefully) the crate will no longer be necessary, and may be sold or put in storage.

2.) DIET: Many owners balk at the prospect of cooking meat for their dogs or preparing special meals — and the result is typically an inferior animal. If you want your puppy to reach his full potential, he should be fed at least a half pound of rare steak every day (in addition to regular meals) for the first two years. Supplement his diet with table scraps and an occasional treat (like a boiled beef heart or a quart of 10-ingredient Lo Mein). If your schedule and/or living arrangements necessitate more convenience, and you really need to feed your pup a diet which primarily consists of cereal, you cannot cheap out and buy some corn-based junk-food off the supermarket shelf. No, you'll have to go to the veterinarian or a feed store and buy a big sack of premium dog food. There are a couple of decent formulas, but the one I've used is the Pro-Plan Lamb & Rice from Purina. My

Rottweiler typically gets a half-pound of ground turkey mixed with scraps, a coffee-mug of cereal, and a capful of Bragg's Liquid Aminos twice daily; and my Doberman typically gets two coffee-mugs full of cereal, a smaller portion of scraps, and half a capful of Bragg's twice daily. These meals are supplemented with cookies and treats throughout the day. Every dog's dietary needs are different. If they are getting too fat or have a sensitive stomach, you'll have to make adjustments (some dogs have low tolerances for fat, dairy, or spices).

3.) BITE TRAINING CAN BE FUN!: I do not recommend that you practice versus an "aggressor" (properly equipped with coveralls and a hard sleeve) unless you really know what you're doing. Besides which, such specialized training is really unnecessary. All you really need to practice for is: speed, accuracy, and grip strength. Playing "tug" with a quality rope-based tug-toy (a "figure-8" design is best) is a great exercise for both of you — just be sure that the dog learns how important it is to release his hold upon command! Never let him grab the tug-toy without permission, and always store it in a secure place when not being used (some dipshits might advise you to soak the rope with blood, but this is unsanitary, presents a health risk, and ruins the toy — don't be a dipshit). Letting him attack a tire swing is also good exercise. Accuracy and speed is best trained for by catching tidbits (buttered popcorn, diced cheese, hunks of freshly ground burgermeat, slices of Carl Buddig dried beef, or even snack foods like corn chips). Catching a rubber ball (either on the bounce or tossed underhand) is also excellent training. Don't bother wasting your time with a frisbee!

4.) SNIP SNIP: A lot of veterinarians recommend that you spay or neuter your dog. I would typically advise against this procedure, but if you feel that it is important to sterilize your animal do not do so until it is fully grown (between 18 and 24 months, dependant upon the size of the breed) in order to ensure that the lack of hormones does not impede the growth process (physical as well as psychological). Spaying a bitch is often a good idea, as it will prevent her from going into heat. Not only does heat make her act stupid, make her want to run off, and make male dogs in the vicinity go totally batshit, but it smells bad and she'll drip a bloody discharge for the duration. A bitch can go into heat about three times each year, and it can last for over a week. Neutering (castrating) a male dog is sometimes recommended to curb aggression. Although aggression comes naturally to the protection breeds, sometimes a testosterone overload leads to inappropriate acts of defiance (anything from "arguing" to mauling), and castration can curb this without necessarily resulting in laziness or passivity. Furthermore, it can reduce the severity of urinary tract infections by shrinking the prostate as a result of testosterone depletion. For cosmetic purposes, a pair of synthetic implants can replace the testicles, if you don't want people to know your dog's been de-nutted.

5.) DESTRUCTION: Unfortunately, the time may come that your animal needs to be put down. This may be due to illness, being struck by a car, or injuries sustained in the line of duty. BE ADVISED: Many extremely serious injuries can be survived! I have met dogs who were pretty torn up by cars, gunshot wounds, butcher knives, or other dogs — but they received competent emergency medical care and, after a long recuperative process and lots of TLC, are now leading happy and productive lives. Even if the dog has lost an eye, lost a leg, or has suffered internal injuries, he still can be saved. Veterinary painkillers, antibiotics, and the supplements Flax Oil and Glucosamine Hydrochloride can do wonders. However, if your animal has suffered a massive head injury and blood and cerebro-spinal fluid is seeping out of its nose and ears, or if it has a broken back which has resulted in paralyzation, or if its belly has been torn open and the contents are spread across the road, it would be selfish and cruel to attempt to prolong the poor thing's misery. You'll need to put it down immediately. BE ADVISED: Although your first instinct will be to rush to your dog's side to offer comfort, the shock and pain will leave him so disorientated that you will probably be bitten, so be extremely careful! A veterinarian will typically use either gas or an injection to end an animal's suffering, but this probably will not be an option for you at this time. A firearm will probably be your best bet. First, ascertain that the bullet will not ricochet off something (like asphalt, rock, or cement) after passing through your animal's head — you may need to drag him onto the grass by his leash or back legs, if necessary, which will result in screams of pain. Next, ascertain that no-one is standing anywhere near you in case there is a ricochet anyway — and remember, skull fragments can do just as much damage as a bullet. Finally, after making the area a safe as possible, say goodbye as kindly as you can and shoot your dog in the head. Animal Control Officers generally use a scoped lever-action rifle from a distance of about 15 feet, so as to avoid being splattered with blood, and aim for a spot about 2 inches above the point directly between the eyes. I would advise using a .357 magnum revolver and firing a contact shot. If you've only got a 9mm (or something even smaller), I'd advise using a double-tap. Old tyme vets would dispatch animals with a .22 handgun, but with a large protection dog such a weak projectile may not do the job unless you use at least three rounds. If you live in a city, or even if you live in a rural community with a busybody neighbor, you can reasonably expect to be arrested for "animal cruelty" as well as "discharging a firearm within 500 ft. of a residence" and possibly even "reckless endangerment" or "criminal use of a firearm" — there will be even more charges if the firearm happens to be unlicensed (or you're prohibited from owning it). Once your animal is destroyed, the weapon will immediately need to be made safe and stowed away, and your dog will need to be wrapped in a tarp and removed from the area. Be sure to pick up any shell casings and dump a bucketful of hot water on the blood. If you happen to be home alone, immediately call a trusted friend (or two) who can rush to the scene to secure the area in the event that the police decide to take you away in handcuffs. As soon as is convenient, you'll need to either find a suitable grave site (provided you own land) or arrange with a veterinarian to have him suitably cremated. This is a difficult topic, but if you own a dog you really need to have some idea of how you'll handle a "worst case scenario" in the event that shit happens . . . if you've never taken the time to think things through, you may not act appropriately when the time comes.

Martial Arts Mythology

There is a great deal of bullshit regarding hand-to-hand combat that is commonly believed to be true . . . even by a few respected instructors who really ought to know better. The majority of these myths involve "deadly karate moves" which allegedly enable a martial artist to kill a man with a single blow, and are passed from student to student like a virus being replicated. Due to the fact that the vast majority of martial artists have never been placed in a situation where it is permissible to actually implement such techniques, and also due to the fact that most martial artists have never studied human anatomy at the college level, it is understandable that people who ought to know better are ignorant of such things. Hollywood action films and imported kung-fu flicks perpetuate such legendary falsehoods. In this section, I shall attempt to debunk a few of the cherished fantasies of the dojo ballerinas.

1.) "YOU CAN KILL A MAN BY JAMMING HIS NASAL BONES INTO THE BRAIN!":

Up until the late 1980's most martial artists believed this without question, but then several articles appeared in various martial arts magazines which disproved it. According to legend, a forceful palm heel strike or shuto chop delivered up under the nostrils would force nasal bones into the brain. The nose is constructed primarily of pliable cartilage. There is a bit of bone high on the bridge of the nose, but upon examination of a human skull you can see that there is no way this bone can be forced inside the cranium. Some martial artists say that a properly delivered chop to the bridge of the nose will generate a "shock wave" that causes a "chain reaction" ultimately resulting in bone within the cranium splintering and lacerating the brain (although such an event is highly unlikely). In order to have a reasonable chance of killing someone via this method, it would be necessary to either deliver a forceful horizontal strike to the bridge of the nose with a multi-celled aluminum flashlight, or to repeatedly smash a fallen opponent's face onto the corner of a curb.

2.) "YOU CAN CRACK A MAN'S SKULL BY HITTING HIM IN THE TEMPLE!":

For some reason, many people believe that the temples are the thinnest part of the cranium and easily broken. People tend to believe this without question due to the fact that there is a slight depression at either temple, and they are somewhat sensitive to pressure due to the nerve clusters there. However, upon examination of a bisected human skull, you can clearly see that the temple areas are not significantly thinner than the rest of the skull. Furthermore, live bone tissue is highly impervious to damage, and the rounded shape of the cranium gives it incredible resistance against breakage. The backhand strike is typically recommended for delivering this "lethal" blow, but a backhand strike has virtually no chance of fracturing a skull (unless directed at an invalid with osteoperosis, or a toddler whose cranial plates have not yet fused). In order to kill a man with this strike, it is best to use a ballpeen hammer.

3.) "YOU CAN JAM YOUR FINGERS INTO A MAN'S BRAIN THROUGH THE EYE SOCKET!":

Most martial artists believe this one. Some writers have even gone so far as to describe the bone forming the eye socket as "eggshell thin" and easily broken. Upon examination of a human skull, it is evident that the eye socket has only a small hole at the back to accommodate the optic nerve. Although the eye socket is one of the weakest areas of the cranium, it is still incredibly difficult to break — you are far more likely to break your fingers than to crack through the eye socket. If an incredibly strong man were to use his thumbs to gouge forcefully into the eyes of a smaller opponent (who was held immobile with his head against the floor), it is theoretically possible for this move to actually work. However, you would have a far better chance of executing this technique properly if you were to use a screwdriver.

4.) "A PALM HEEL STRIKE TO THE SOLAR PLEXUS CAN BREAK OFF THE BOTTOM OF THE STERNUM AND DRIVE IT INTO THE HEART!":

In theory, a powerful palm heel strike to the lower chest area can fracture a projection of bone known as the "xiphoid process," possibly detaching it and allowing it to puncture an internal organ (most likely the liver). However, this vestigial projection is only found in approximately one third of the world's population.

5.) "BY FOCUSING YOUR CHI, YOU CAN KILL A MAN BY STRIKING CERTAIN PRESSURE POINTS!":

The legendary "death touch" (also known as "poison finger" or dim mak) supposedly enables a master to shut down various chi meridians by attacking certain accupuncture points at specific times of the day. Chi (bioenergy) has been proven beyond a reasonable doubt to exist, although scientists do not fully understand how it works. Accupuncture has been proven to manipulate chi. Furthermore, martial artists specializing in "combat taijiquan," or pressure point targeting, have given even more credibility to the legend of the death touch. Several authors have written books allegedly explaining how to implement the death touch, and there have even been public demonstrations of masters inducing unconsciousness with a single light touch, or shattering a single brick chosen at random in a stack. However, it takes years to gain even basic proficiency at manipulating the chi of others, and there has never been a credible documented account of a dim mak technique having been executed successfully versus an opponent. Ancient accounts of the "delayed death touch" invariably can be attributed to slow death from ruptured organs or internal hemorrhaging. Don't even consider wasting your time training at something that will not work.

6.) "A MASTER CAN ACTUALLY RIP A MAN'S HEART OUT!":

This is highly unlikely. Theoretically, after spending years conditioning one's hands by thrusting them into kettles of hot sand, a master can use a "spearhand" or "shovelhand" attack to actually penetrate an opponent's abdomen (flesh, muscle, viscera, ect.) and grasp his heart muscle, tearing it free. References to this legendary attack are generally considered little more than fables, but it is possible that a royal executioner of the ancient Orient was able to successfully use this technique versus frail individuals (who would've first been properly immobilized) as a public demonstration. In order for this technique to work, the executioner's hands would have to be so heavily conditioned that he would lose much of his manual dexterity, resulting in his being so crippled that he would be unable to perform many simple tasks without assistance. Martial artists rarely condition their hands to such a level today, and there has never been a credible account of this technique ever actually having been used (outside of countless martial arts films).

7.) "YOU CAN TEAR A MAN'S THROAT OUT WITH YOUR BARE HANDS!":

This, too, is highly unlikely, although more probable than ripping out a heart. The windpipe (more properly, the larnyx and upper portion of the trachea) is protected by cartilage in the front and tendons on either side. While the windpipe is far more accessible than the heart, it would be nearly impossible to extract it from an opponent with a snatch of one's hand. Indeed, it would even be extraordinarily difficult to implement this technique on a cadaver, regardless of how powerful one's hands were. It would be far more effective to simply execute a standard hand attack (such as a chop) to this area.

8.) "ONCE YOU HIT A MAN IN THE THROAT, THE FIGHT IS OVER!":

There are no guarantees in a streetfight. True, a crushing blow to the throat is a killing blow, but it must be delivered with great force to be truly effective. A light blow may cause choking and retching, or it may have no discernable result at all. If you hit a man in the throat with an inadequate blow, you can reasonably expect him to feel justified in killing you through whatever means necessary. Never hit someone in the throat unless you intend to kill them, and if that is your intent you need to strike as hard as possible — and preferably with a weapon.

9.) "YOU CAN DEFEAT ANY OPPONENT BY STICKING YOUR FINGER IN THEIR EYE!":

If you succeed in rupturing the eye globe of your opponent, that will stop over 90% of all fights — in the remaining percentile, your opponent will suddenly go batshit and attempt to chew your face off. Generally, the eyes are an excellent target; however, it is difficult to actually rupture the eye unless you are using your thumbs and have long nails. The eye is flexible and resilient, and will resist being burst. Raking and jabbing attacks to the eyes generally result in irritation, abrasion, or minor lacerations to the outer surface of the eye (or the eyelid), which can be distracting and painful, but seldom result in permanent blindness (unless infection sets in). The fact that your opponent will momentarily be disconcerted (and have blurred vision) will not instantly stop a fight, but may give you opportunity to either escape or land several more blows.

10.) "IF YOU SLAP BOTH OF YOUR OPPONENT'S EARS, THE AIR PRESSURE WILL KILL HIM!":

Supposedly, if you were to cup both hands and slam them over someone's ears, the trapped air would burst both eardrums and rupture the cerebral cortex, resulting in massive hemorrhaging and death. This will not happen. It is possible that one (or both) of the eardrums will indeed burst in the event this strike were delivered properly, which would result in partial (or total) deafness, some minor bleeding, and a great deal of pain. In some instances unconsciousness could result, but death would be highly unlikely. This strike is difficult to implement due to the fact that both ears must be struck simultaneously and accurately — such a move would be simple to block and would leave one wide open for a counter-attack. It would be far more practical to attack a single ear if the opportunity presented itself. This move is best implemented in a grappling situation.

11.) "THE VULCAN NERVE PINCH REALLY WORKS!":

If you were to tightly squeeze a weak person's trapezius muscle near where the shoulder connects with the neck, they would likely wince in pain and beg for you to stop. If you have strong hands and were able to dig your fingertips into the brachial nerve, the arm on that side might even go numb. If, however, you were to try such a move on a man with above average muscular development, he would probably laugh in your face before slapping you upside the head. This move will not work on persons with firm muscles or a high pain tolerance — which excludes all potential attackers except grade-school bullies and surly nursing home residents! If you try to use this move in a fight you truly deserve to get your ass kicked.

12.) "IF SOMEONE GRABS YOU FROM BEHIND, JUST STOMP ON THEIR FOOT AND THEY'LL LET YOU GO!":

Many "self-defense manuals" allege that the metatarsals above the arch of the foot are easily crushed by a stomping blow and the pain will make your attacker instantly release you . . . this is nonsense. If you are wearing rubber-soled sneakers or a pair of loafers, the potential impact of any kick will be significantly cushioned. If, however, you were wearing heavy boots with stacked heels, and your attacker was only wearing sandals, this move could prove quite effective. Unless you are wearing proper footwear and really know how to stomp hard, your assailant will probably ignore your struggling.

13.) "JUST KICK 'EM WHERE IT HURTS!":

A kick to the groin can stop a fight when properly applied, but it is very difficult to hit the testicles of a moving target with a standard snap-kick. Furthermore, most men will diligently guard this area, as they'll instinctively expect an attack there — especially when confronting a woman. Not only are the testicles a relatively small target, but kicks (as well as knee strikes) are easily blocked by a simple shifting of the hips. When you strike the testicles, there is usually a delay of several seconds before the pain begins to be felt — and the same amount of pain that might curl one man up on the floor whimpering will throw another man into a murderous rage. The groin is best attacked by knee strikes, shin strikes, and hand attacks (and can be struck from the rear as well).

14.) "IF YOU JAM YOUR THUMBS INTO A MAN'S ARMPITS YOU CAN KNOCK HIM OUT!":

Many years ago, a woman was accosted by a deviate who decided to grab her. As she struggled to free herself, she pushed him away by shoving her hands up under his arms — and for some unknown reason he suddenly passed out. She called the police, who arrested him, and the newspapers reported her account of the incident. Soon afterwards, a few self-defense manuals began advising people to attack the "pressure points" in the armpits for similar results. Although there are blood vessels, lymph nodes, and nerve clusters there, it is unlikely that an attack to this area would be anything more than uncomfortable (unless delivered with a knife). Do not expect someone to pass out just because you poked them in the armpits.

15.) "A SPINNING KICK TO THE HEAD WILL LAY OUT NEARLY ANYONE!":

I agree . . . nearly anyone who attempts a high kick to an adversary's head in a real fight can reasonably expect to get knocked on their ass. High kicks are slower (and weaker) than any other attack and are easily blocked — even by an amateur. Most people would simply grab your ankle and kick you in the groin. Many expert martial artists who are capable of firing off fast, powerful, and accurate kicks to an opponent's head in competition have stated that they would never use high kicks in an actual fight — in the movies, they jump off trampolines and kick at stuntmen who are paid to fall down. Never attempt a kick to your opponent's head unless he's already been knocked to the ground.

16.) "THE DEVASTATING FLYING SIDE KICK WILL DROP ANY OPPONENT!":

A properly executed flying side kick (with a running start) generates an incredible amount of force. It is one of the few attacks that can literally blow a man off his feet, and can easily crack several ribs at once; however, your intent to execute this move will be telegraphed to your opponent quicker than if you chose to use a haymaker with full roundup (a wild punch commonly seen among drunkards lacking formal martial arts training). As you are charging at your opponent and begin your leap, even an untrained fighter will instinctively step out of the way or attempt to defect your attack with some sort of haphazard blocking — and he will have plenty of time to do so. The flying side kick, an impressive technique favored by Hollywood directors (as well as students of savate and tae kwon do), is best implemented versus an inebriated opponent from behind, with your target of choice being the middle of the spine.

17.) "THE HEADBUTT IS ONE OF THE MOST POWERFUL WEAPONS IN YOUR ARSENAL!":

True, the headbutt can do an incredible amount of damage to an opponent due to the fact that the cranium is quite solid and this attack usually is a complete surprise, however, it is often used incorrectly, sometimes resulting in injury to the initiator. An untrained fighter may attempt to charge an opponent head-first, intending to drive the top of his head into his opponent's solar plexus as if he were engaged in a game of rugby — this highly telegraphed move puts one at extreme risk of receiving a boot in the teeth. Other types of improperly executed headbutts can result in concussion, neck injuries, or even a fractured skull, all of which could have serious complications. In order to be most effective, the headbutt must be directed at the face of an opponent, with the intent being to crush the nose and cause momentary disorientation (the neck should be kept stiff, and one should push off with the legs). Headbutts are best delivered with the back of the head versus an attacker grasping one from behind.

18.) "IT IS A SIMPLE MATTER TO SNAP AN OPPONENT'S NECK!":

It is true that there are about a half-dozen different ways to snap a man's neck (with the likely result being paralysis or death), but the majority of these methods require a surprise attack from behind (after first having engaged in plenty of practice). Neck breaking techniques are best implemented by a very strong man versus a much weaker adversary who is struggling helplessly, otherwise they are extremely difficult to perform. Neck snaps are typically a "finishing move" used on a fallen opponent who is either unconscious or too exhausted to defend himself, hence, they have no reasonable application to the study of self-defense. In our society, performing a finishing move on a helpless individual is known as "murder," and carries stiff penalties.

As you can clearly see, there is a grain of truth to most of these myths, but that does not dispel the fact that these moves will not perform as advertised. If a martial arts student is relying upon one of these untested "death strikes" to protect him in a worst case scenario, and is actually placed in circumstances where it is necessary for him to use deadly force to protect himself from harm, what do you think will happen when his "never-fail-ultimate-fight-stopping-blow" doesn't work? If our student strikes an assailant with an attack guaranteed to "drop any man," and he simply shrugs it off, what do you think will happen to his confidence level? Will he become doubtful? Frightened? Maybe even momentarily paralyzed? How will this affect his ability to defend himself?

You need to be aware that there are no guarantees in a streetfight. Moves should be simple and efficient. It is highly unlikely that you will drop your opponent with a single blow, and you will probably sustain injuries yourself. If you are facing multiple opponents and are unarmed, fleeing is probably your best option (if possible). A streetfight, where the risk of being maimed or killed is quite high, is no place to experiment with untested techniques (with the exception of biting, gouging, and joint destruction), nor is it the place to impress onlookers with your mastery of the "jump-spinning-back-kick-to-the-head."

Engaging in a fight can result in serious consequences (medical, legal, social, etc.). When you are forced to defend yourself versus a man intent on inflicting serious injuries upon your person, it is a grave situation not to be taken lightly — someone is going to be hurt, and it could very well be you. Over-confidence in one's abilities is a weakness, and underestimating one's opponent can lead to your downfall. If he is bigger and stronger than you (as most attackers generally tend to select victims they perceive as weaker than themselves), you can reasonably expect to be hurt. If, prior to the event, you had only engaged in "light-contact" sparring with full padding, a broken nose can be quite a shock.

Self-defense is not an "art," nor is it anything like the exciting choreographed fight sequences one watches on television . . . it is a brutal, painful, terrifying, and ultimately degrading experience. After the fight is over, the "hero" will probably need to visit the emergency room, after which he may face the possibility of criminal charges, lawsuits, and character assassination by the media (as well as others). It is possible that your attacker will be portrayed as "misunderstood" and hostile witnesses (who may not even have actually been present) may give false testimony to the police (and later, the court) stating that you were the initial aggressor! Any martial-arts training you may have, or the fact that serious injuries were inflicted upon your opponent, will be used by prosecutors to show that you are a "violent" man who should be incarcerated for the protection of society. Reality can be a bitch. For these reasons, it is best to avoid physical altercations through whatever means necessary. Fighting (especially with strangers) should never be taken lightly.

Ode to a Scattergun

The lowly break-action single-shot,

Oft neglected and belittled,

How can it compare to the fearsome black rifles?

In the back of your closet,

Or the trunk of your car,

Collecting dust,

Pitted by corrosion,

This simple weapon will not fail you.

The one-round shotgun manufactured by Harrington & Richardson (H&R) and New England Arms (NEA) is among the finest firearms ever put into mass production. It is simple to operate — even someone who has never handled a gun before can figure out how it works, mastering it within an hour. It is reliable — it will never jam or freeze up. It is safe — being single action, it is one of the few shotguns you can safely keep a round chambered in, and it will not discharge unless the external hammer is physically cocked back. It is inexpensive — you can buy a new one for under a hundred dollars, and a used one for under thirty. It is everywhere — though seldom seen in display cases or gunracks, everyone seems to have one of these guns in storage; it often being the first gun they've ever owned. The venerable single-shot is one of the most prolific weapons manufactured, easily being the most widely owned civilian firearm in the world.

This firearm is extremely reliable. I have never known one of these guns to fail to operate, even after years of abuse and neglect. You can leave this gun submerged in a puddle for a month, then run an old snotrag on the end of a twig through the rusty bore once to dislodge any debris, before firing it. After soaking it overnight in WD-40, it will become serviceable once again. In the South American rainforests, these shotguns are held in high regard by the aboriginal tribesmen who live in an extremely damp environment and have no access to proper cleaning supplies. Two centuries from now, after most of the firearms in civilian hands have been rendered inoperable due to snapped springs, lost pins, or broken parts, the vast majority of surviving functional guns will be H&R and NEA single-shots.

This scattergun is often a boy's first gun, with which he learns firearms safety, how to hit a target, and how to hunt. It is designed primarily for taking grouse, turkey, and waterfowl. With properly designed slugs, it can take a deer at close range. It is also one of America's deadliest weapons. Next to the autoloading .22 rifle, the single-shot scattergun is used, far more than any other civilian firearm, for committing homicide. It is often modified by cutting it down with a hacksaw, giving it a barrel length of 8"-12" and a knobby pistol grip, making it resemble a flintlock boarding pistol of yore. In this chopped down configuration, it is sometimes referred to as a "whippit," "sawed-off," "blunderbuss," or "hillbilly dueling pistol." It is a nasty weapon, far bulkier than the biggest automatic pistol or magnum revolver, but is favored by gang members, street punks, and barroom brawlers because, due to its prevalence, it is easily available and often untraceable. With its barrel chopped, it becomes a reloadable claymore mine, literally filling the height and breadth of a corridor with projectiles, peppering all within. Outdoors, however, it only has an effective range of about twenty feet. This modification is highly illegal and anyone found in possession of such a weapon can reasonably expect to spend several years in either the state prison or federal penitentiary.

The H&R and NEA shotguns have been around for many years. They are most commonly found chambered for either 20 or 12 gauge, but models also exist chambering .410, 16, and 10 gauges. Older versions have a top mounted lever latch, like those found on double-barreled shotguns, and an extractor which allows the spent shell to be easily removed by hand. Newer models have a button on the left side that, when depressed, allows the barrel to drop open and the spent shell to be popped out by a spring loaded ejector. There is an external hammer which must be cocked back before firing, and can be carefully decocked if one decides not to fire. Because of the efficiency of the single-action, no safety switch is required. Unlike most other shotguns, it is safe to keep a round chambered at all times. Hammerless shotguns, like doubles, pumps, and autoloaders, all are provided with safety switches, but the internal hammers are kept at full cock over live ammunition — not only is this extremely unwise due to the increased risk of accidental discharge, but the tension on the springs will cause them to weaken over time. Also, unlike the three aforementioned shotguns, the single-shot will never jam. Double-barrels can get rounds under the extractor while reloading, pumps (especially single ports, like the Ithicas) can jam if short-stroked, autoloaders can jam for any of several reasons (and often do). The single-shot is safe and reliable, more so than any other type of firearm.

The single-shot used exclusively for home-defense can be modified several different ways. First, the barrel can be cut down to its shortest legal length. If you are keeping the stock in place, it can be reduced to 18"; if you are affixing an aftermarket Zytel pistol grip, the barrel must be at least 21" to comply with federal law stating that the overall length can be no less than 26". It is strongly urged that the barrel be cut at least 1/4" above the minimum required length to allow for filing the rough metal smooth (as well as worn down yardsticks). The muzzle can be filed smooth with both a flat file and rat-tail file before sanding and rebluing. Cold bluing kits work best, but a touch-up marker or flat black model paint can be used for a half-assed job. Cutting down the barrel will make the weapon more compact for indoor use, reduce weight significantly, and expand shot spread. The only disadvantage is that it will decrease accuracy at longer ranges, which shouldn't be a consideration.

Next, it is advisable that a small light be clamped beneath the barrel. Tactical lights are excellent, but far too costly for such a project. Instead, a mini Mag-lite (or similar quality penlight) can be held in place with a clamp. Clamps for laser sights can be used, or one can be fabricated. I have seen a "clamp" made from scrap wood and electrical tape that was ugly, but worked well. A good quality light with a xenon or halogen bulb will illuminate your zone, destroy an assailant's night vision, and aid targeting.

If the stock is kept in place, an elastic "bullet band" holding five rounds can be slipped on. If the Zytel grip is used, an extra round or two can be slipped inside the hollow and held in place by friction, or with a piece of tape. The stock can legally be cut down and sanded smooth, provided the overall length remains over 26", but care must be taken to ascertain that the stock bolt is not sawed through. I have seen this firearm in all three configurations, and feel that leaving the stock in place is best — it gives you the shortest barrel, the lightest recoil, and five extra rounds. The Zytel grip, which costs about $20 and only fits the newer models, looks good, but due to its design does not allow you to cock the weapon with one hand, as can easily be done with either the original or modified stock.

I feel that the H&R and NEA shotguns are an essential part of anyone's firearm collection. This design will outlast all others, and the user has no choice but to maintain proper fire discipline. You will not suddenly find yourself out of ammunition with this weapon, and you are more likely to hit your target with the first shot. With sabot slugs, a shot from this weapon has stopping power exceeding that of a .44 magnum. With buckshot fired from an 18" barrel, you hardly need to aim at close range. With a mounted light, you don't need to aim at all. True, you wouldn't be happy resorting to a single-shot weapon if you were facing multiple attackers armed with autoloading weapons, but do you realistically see that as a possibility?

This weapon is far better than a muzzleloader, a crossbow, or no gun at all, and even where no gun is readily available, the reliable break-action can often be found, forlorn and long forgotten, in the back of a closet with half a box of birdshot. It can be owned in jurisdictions where handguns are prohibited, and can be fired in populated areas where the penetration of a 9mm, magnum revolver, or rifle round would be a significant concern. Unlike an automatic pistol or pump shotgun, it can comfortably be used by unskilled civilians in times of great stress. Although the thought of a magazine packed full of rounds (instantly discharged and reloaded at the twitch of ones finger) is comforting, additional firepower is usually unnecessary. Statistics clearly show that in the vast majority of cases where a firearm was used for protection, only a single shot was fired — and I guarantee that a single shot from this weapon, at close range and to the center of mass, will effectively terminate any threat sans body armor (even with birdshot).

The reliable, powerful, and omni-present single-shot is all the gun you need.

"Gorilla Punch"

Back in the day, when we were all partying pretty hard on an everyday basis (we've grown and matured since — mostly), a buddy of mine who went by the handle of "Chewbacca" found a guide to making various fancy bar drinks in a box of old books. After flipping through it for a few minutes, making all sorts of derogatory comments about the sissified yuppie scum who'd have the audacity to order some of these blended fruity concoctions in a public drinking establishment, he suddenly paused for a moment. "Hey, here's one called gorilla punch!"

It was a weak vodka-based punch that some tropical nightclub was famous for, and was supposed to be served in a punchbowl with a bunch of chopped fruit tossed in. "Check this out! This is great! I'm gonna make a batch of this for our big party tonight!" I looked at the picture of the grinning elitist drones standing around a punchbowl filled with green fruity stuff with great disdain, and told Chewbacca that if he insisted upon serving this travesty I would stir up each and every glassful with my dick, whereupon an intense debate about the merits and faults of gorilla punch ensued.

Eventually, we reached a compromise: he could make the punch for the party on three conditions: It would not be served in a punchbowl. There would be no fruit. Everclear grain alcohol would be substituted for the vodka. Everyone agreed to try the punch, and Chewbacca was happy.

The recipe, as we modified it, is as follows:

The Sacred Recipe for Gorilla Punch

1.) Obtain a clean plastic bucket (5 gallon capacity), a large glass measuring cup, a big wooden salad spoon, a large funnel, and several empty plastic water jugs with screw-on caps.

2.) Purchase a half-gallon bottle of Everclear grain alcohol (190 proof rocket fuel that is meant to be heavily diluted — a favorite punch ingredient at fraternity parties) and a quart of Blue Curacuo (an artificially blue colored, orange-flavored liqueur used in some mixed-drinks) from a well-stocked liquor store.

3.) Purchase 2 half-gallon cartons of premium orange juice, and 2 half-gallon cans of unsweetened pineapple juice from your local supermarket.

4.) Assemble the ingredients on a clean tabletop. Open the cartons, cans, and bottles, then dump everything in the bucket. If you want to measure things out for a smaller batch, the formula is: 1 part Blue Curacuo, 2 parts Everclear, 4 parts orange juice, and 4 parts pineapple juice. Slowly stir with the big wooden salad spoon while chanting "Green Gorilla Punch Really Fucks You Up" — you need to chant this phrase thirteen times while wearing a pair of boxer shorts on your head.

5.) Using the funnel, carefully fill up three plastic jugs with punch (do not overfill — leave about an inch of airspace), then cap securely for transport. Grab a couple sleeves of disposable plastic cups, and you're good to go! Be sure to take the bucket along. After this party was over, we forced Chewbacca to hang a "party bucket" (on a rope) around his neck for a month.

Gorilla punch is a strange and terrible brew. It looks like antifreeze, tastes like Kool-Aid, and has all sorts of disgusting floating things in it (the pulp) . . . it also has the peculiar tendency to make those imbibing it go totally batshit. The girls loved it — they were taking off their shirts, wrestling on the floor, and hanging upside-down from the railing over the stairwell. The guys acted like baboons on acid, doing backflips, swinging from the chandelier (it broke), and spitting fireballs with the little bit of leftover Everclear (they set one of the stereo speakers on fire and singed the dog's ass). In the morning, we found that someone had punched out the bathroom medicine cabinet and left their underwear inside, another idiot had puked in the aquarium, and the lawn was covered with beer cans and empty plastic cups. Everyone apparently had a good time, though (even if they couldn't quite remember it), and no significant damage was done to the house we were using. We vowed to be more careful next time.

After observing the varied effects gorilla punch had on the nervous system of primates, we worked out the following formula, based on the standard 12 oz. plastic cup:

1 GLASS of gorilla punch is roughly equivalent to 4 beers, and will give you a mild buzz.

2 GLASSES will get you drunk, but you'll still be somewhat functional.

3 GLASSES will fuck you up, and you will feel compelled to do all sorts of stupid shit.

4 GLASSES will make you go totally batshit.

5 GLASSES . . . no-one had more than 4 glasses, and we do not wish to speculate on what might've occurred if they had. The scariest thing about this stuff was that nobody passed out from overimbibing — indeed, it seemed to imbue those who partook with an abundance of energy. People would be jumping about, cackling like lunatics, and it was obvious that they'd been possessed by the alcohol demons. We learned to fear and respect this stuff.

We never had another "gorilla punch party" ourselves, but we made several more batches to take along to other people's parties. We'd show up, all grinnin', toting gallon jugs of what looked like antifreeze. Everyone would be scared to try it at first, but then they'd see that we were drinking it, and soon someone would be brave enough to try a glass. "Hey, this is pretty good!" they'd invariably say, and then everyone would be drinking it. After we'd finished our first (and only) glass, we'd crack open some beers and sit back to await the impending mayhem. "Gorilla punch" really makes people act like gorillas (or, more accurately, monkeys in the zoo)! It was pretty funny.

Afterword

Well, there you have it . . . probably the best parts of the old Righteous Warrior Temple website saved for posterity. I hope you can agree that it was a dollar well spent. Thank you for buying the eBook.

C. R. Jahn
Summer, 2012

Made in the USA
Coppell, TX
11 August 2022